I won't
give up.
That's
all there
is to it.

I *will* fly
myself out
of here.

Eureka seven Gravity boys & Lifting girl

Volume 1

CONTENTS

ORIGINAL STORY | Bones

MANGA | Miki KIZUKI

MAIN SCRIPT | Dai Satō

SCRIPT | Megumi Shimizu (01, 02, 06)
Naruki Nagakawa (03, 04)
Yusuke Asayama (05)

ORIGINAL BOOK DESIGN | Tsuyoshi Kusano

ENGLISH PRODUCTION CREDITS

TRANSLATION	Toshifumi Yoshida
ADAPTOR	T. Ledoux
LETTERING	Keiran O'Leary
COVER LAYOUT	Kit Loose
EDITOR	Robert Place Napton
COORDINATOR	Rika Davis
PUBLISHER	Ken Iyadomi

Published in the United States
by Bandai Entertainment, Inc.

© Miki KIZUKI 2005
© 2005 BONES/Project EUREKA • MBS ©BANDAI 2005
Originally published in Japan in 2005 by KADOKAWA SHOTEN PUBLISHING CO., LTD., Tokyo.
English translation rights arrange with KADOKAWA SHOTEN PUBLISHING CO., LTD., Tokyo.

ISBN-13: 978-1-59409-759-1

Printed in Canada
First Bandai Printing: September 2007

10 9 8 7 6 5 4 3 2 1

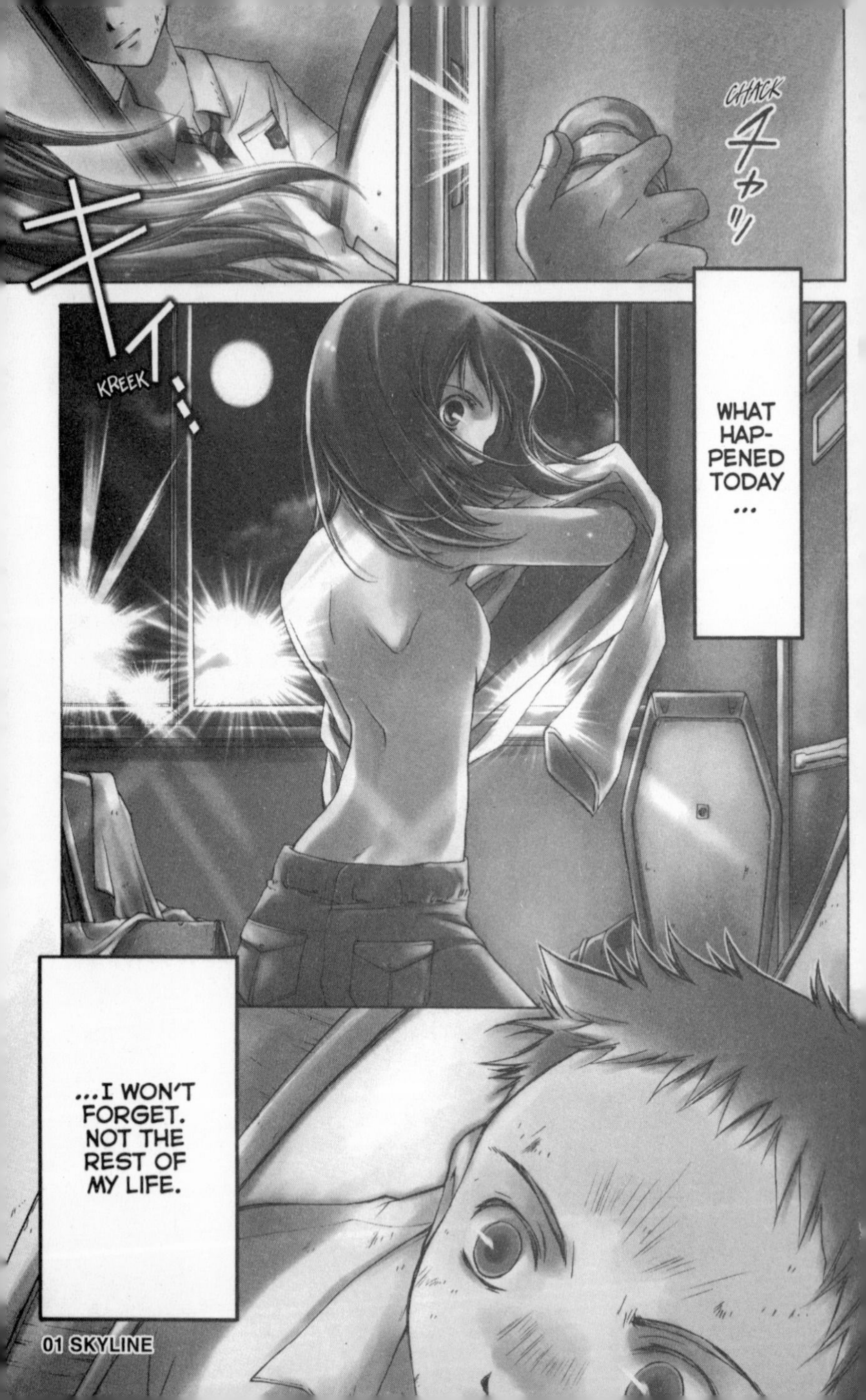
CHACK
チャッ
キイ
KREEK
...
WHAT HAP-PENED TODAY...
...I WON'T FORGET. NOT THE REST OF MY LIFE.

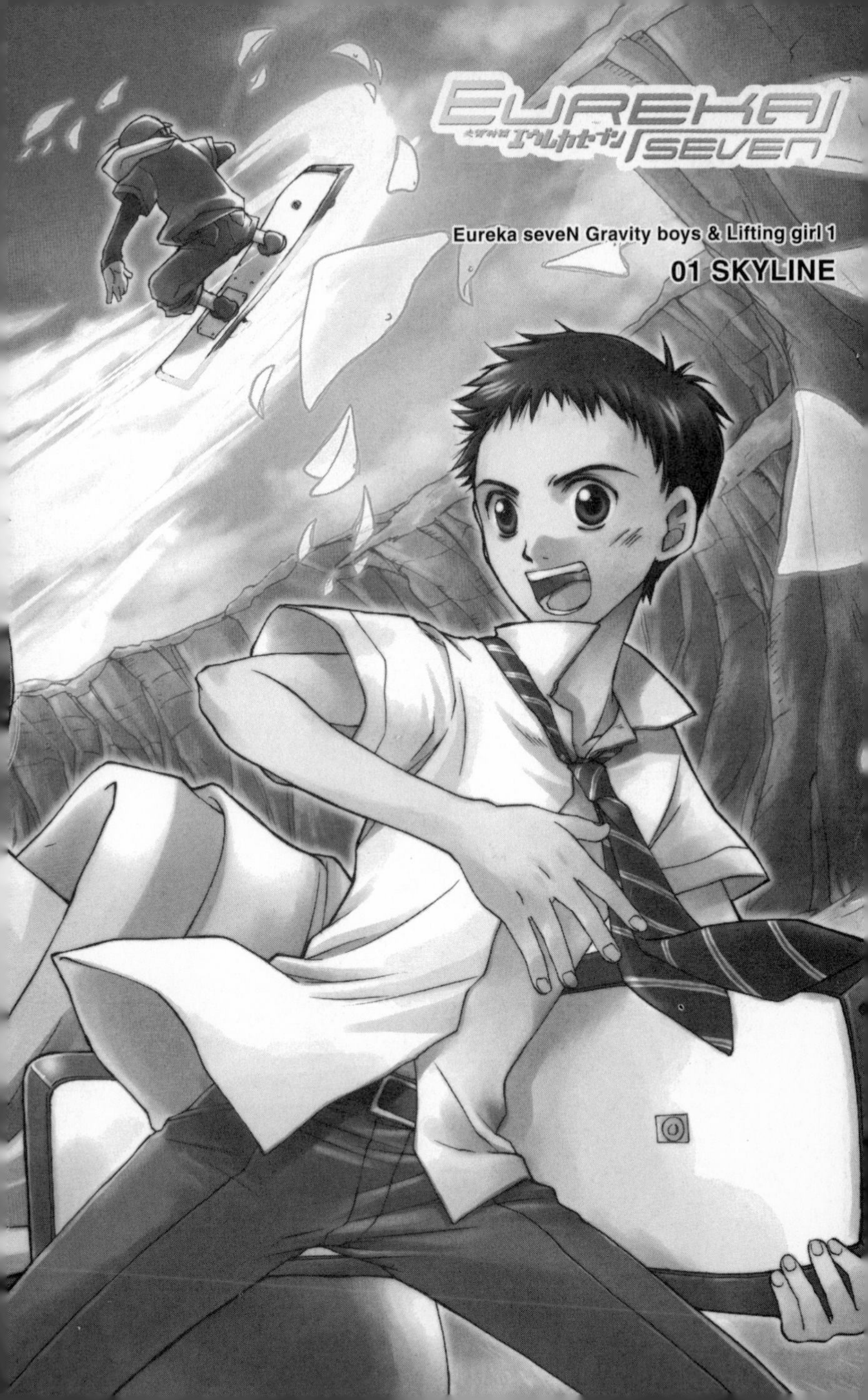
EUREKA SEVEN
Eureka seveN Gravity boys & Lifting girl 1
01 SKYLINE

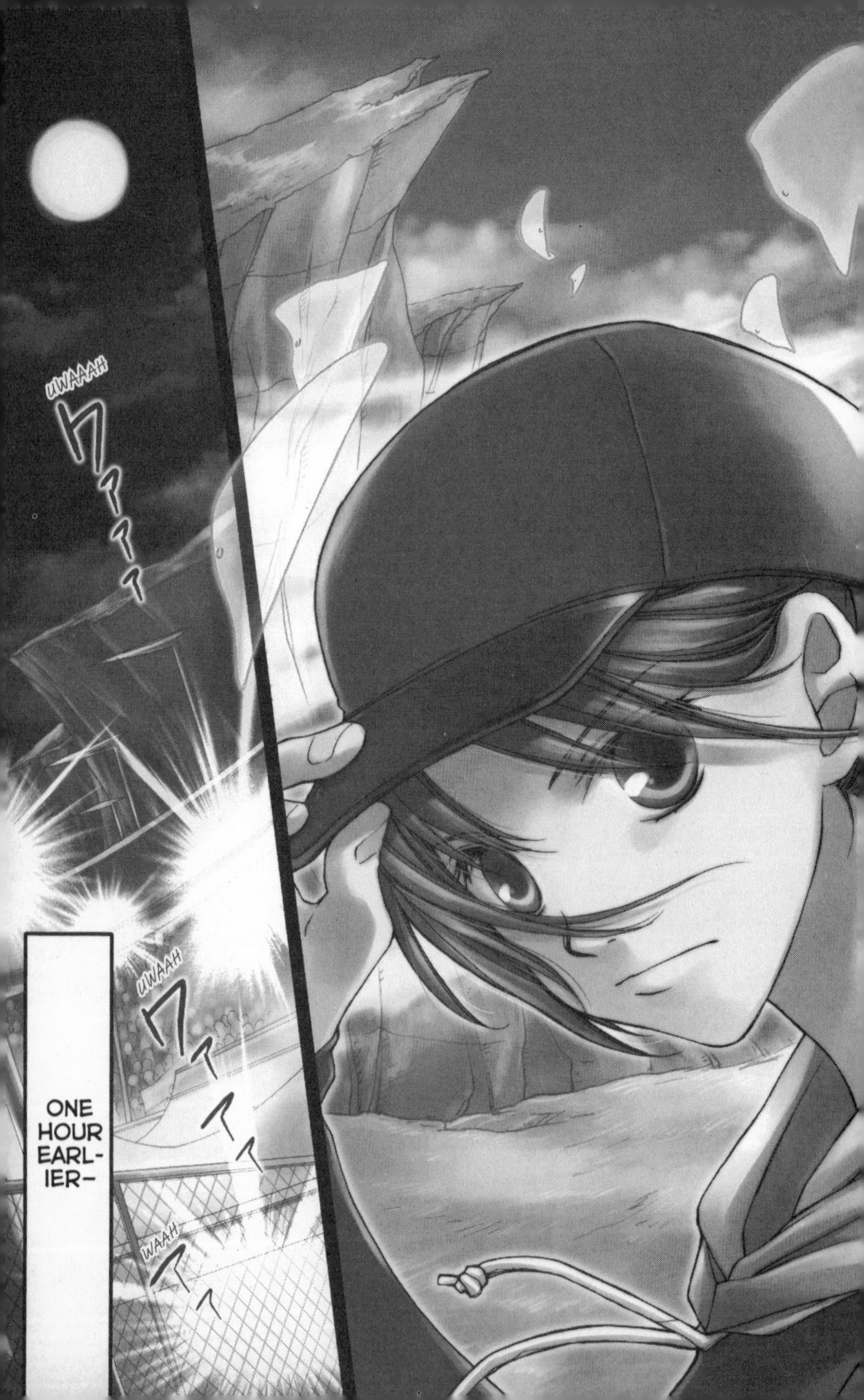
UWAAAH
ONE HOUR EARL-IER–
UWAAH
WAAH

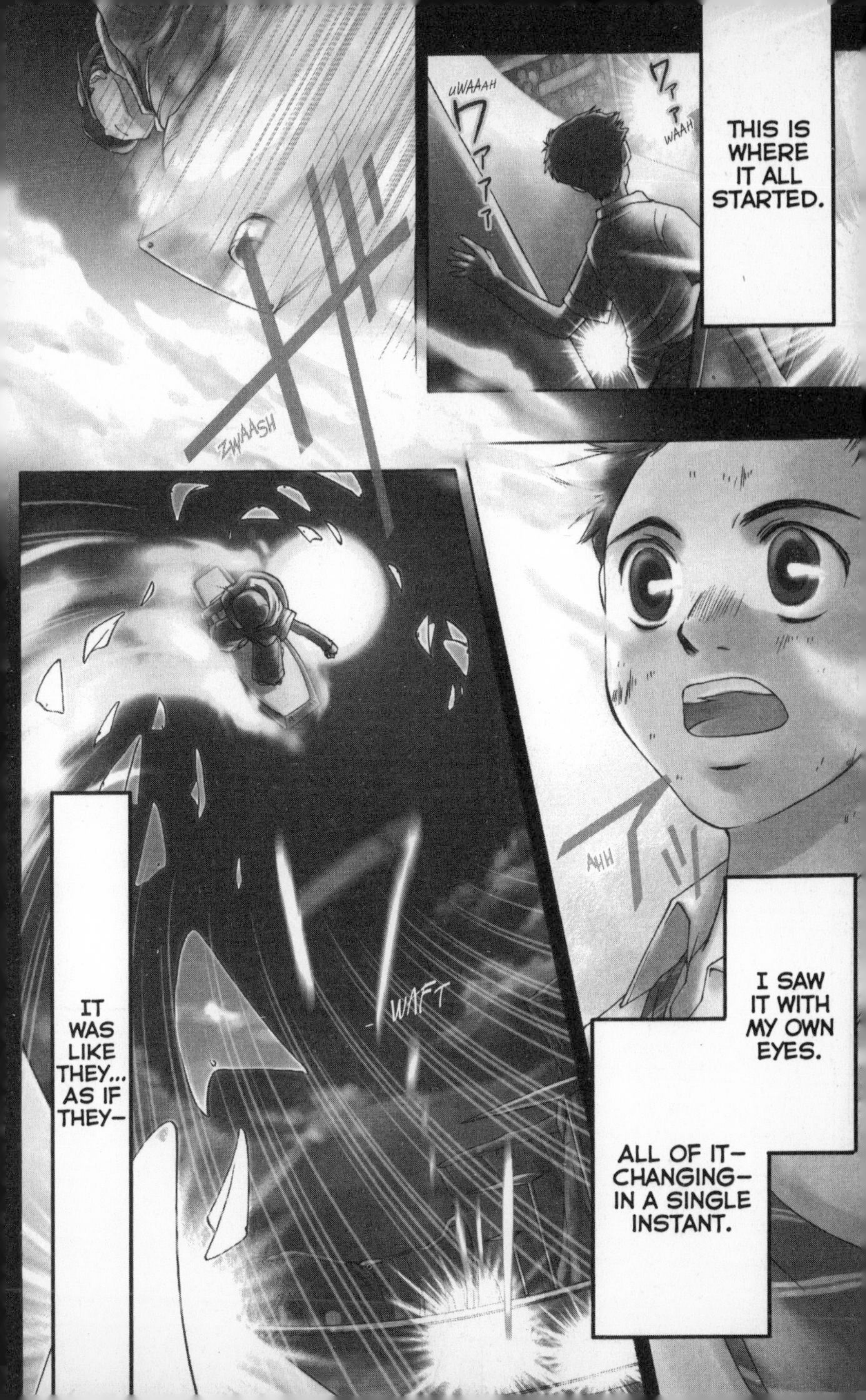
THIS IS WHERE IT ALL STARTED.
ワァァ
WAAH
ワァァァァ
UWAAAH
ZWAASH
AHH
I SAW IT WITH MY OWN EYES.
ALL OF IT— CHANGING— IN A SINGLE INSTANT.
WAFT
IT WAS LIKE THEY... AS IF THEY—

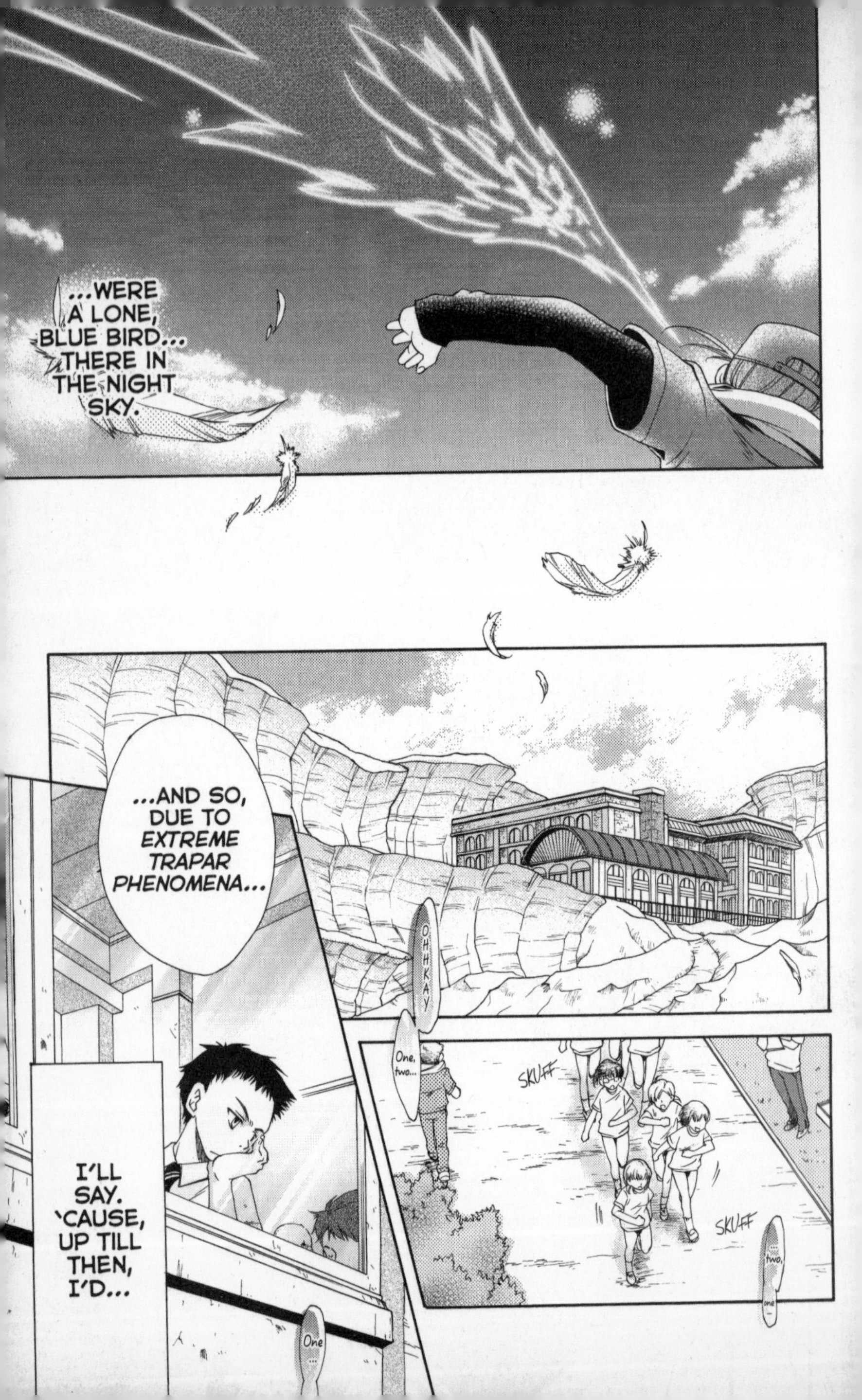
...WERE A LONE, BLUE BIRD... THERE IN THE NIGHT SKY.
...AND SO, DUE TO *EXTREME TRAPAR PHENOMENA*...
OHHKAY
One, two...
SKUFF
SKUFF
...two, one
I'LL SAY. 'CAUSE, UP TILL THEN, I'D...
One ...

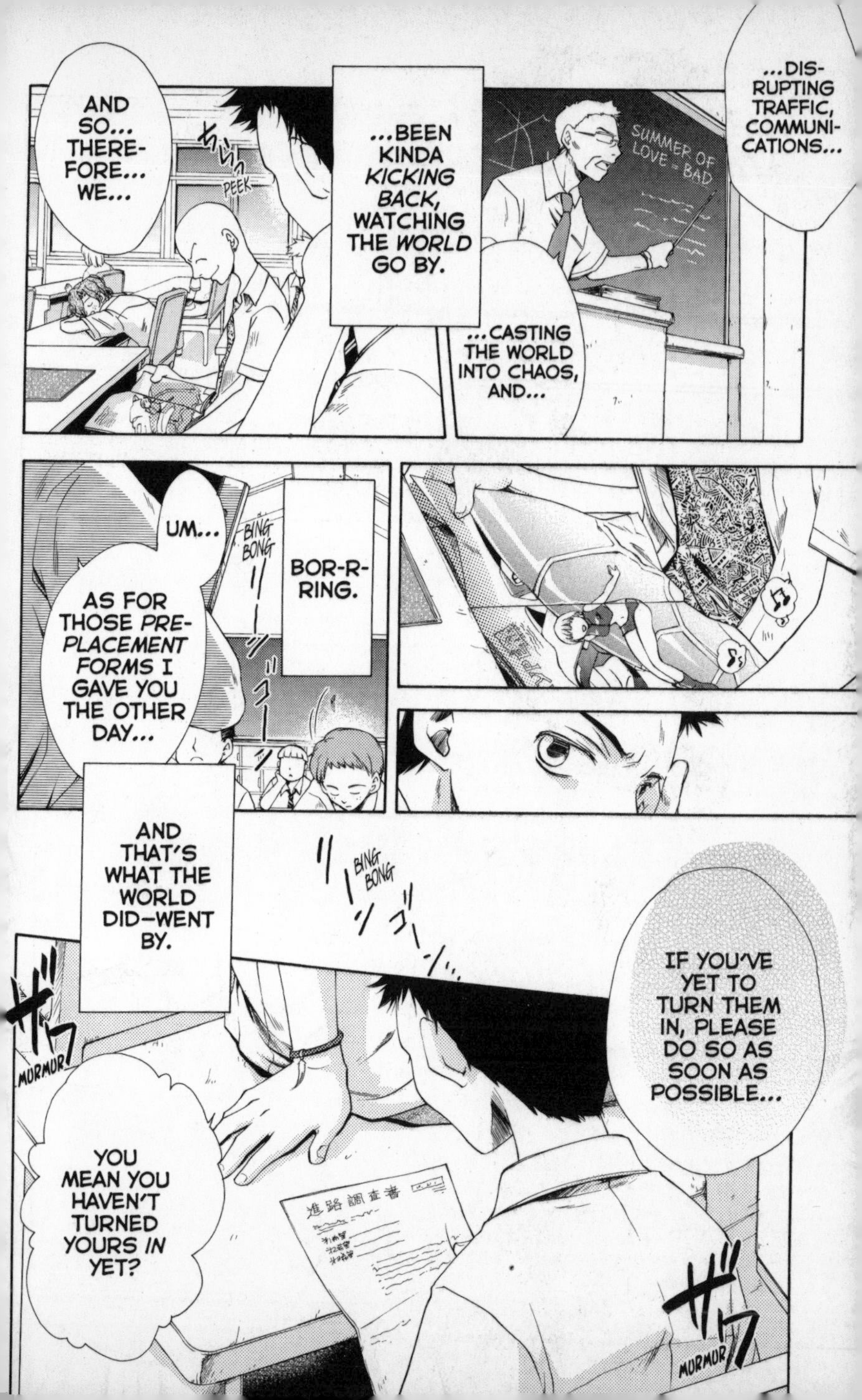
...DIS-RUPTING TRAFFIC, COMMUNICATIONS...
SUMMER OF LOVE = BAD
...CASTING THE WORLD INTO CHAOS, AND...
...BEEN KINDA KICKING BACK, WATCHING THE WORLD GO BY.
AND SO... THEREFORE... WE...
PEEK
BOR-R-RING.
BING BONG
UM...
AS FOR THOSE PRE-PLACEMENT FORMS I GAVE YOU THE OTHER DAY...
AND THAT'S WHAT THE WORLD DID—WENT BY.
BING BONG
IF YOU'VE YET TO TURN THEM IN, PLEASE DO SO AS SOON AS POSSIBLE...
進路調査書
MURMUR
YOU MEAN YOU HAVEN'T TURNED YOURS IN YET?
MURMUR

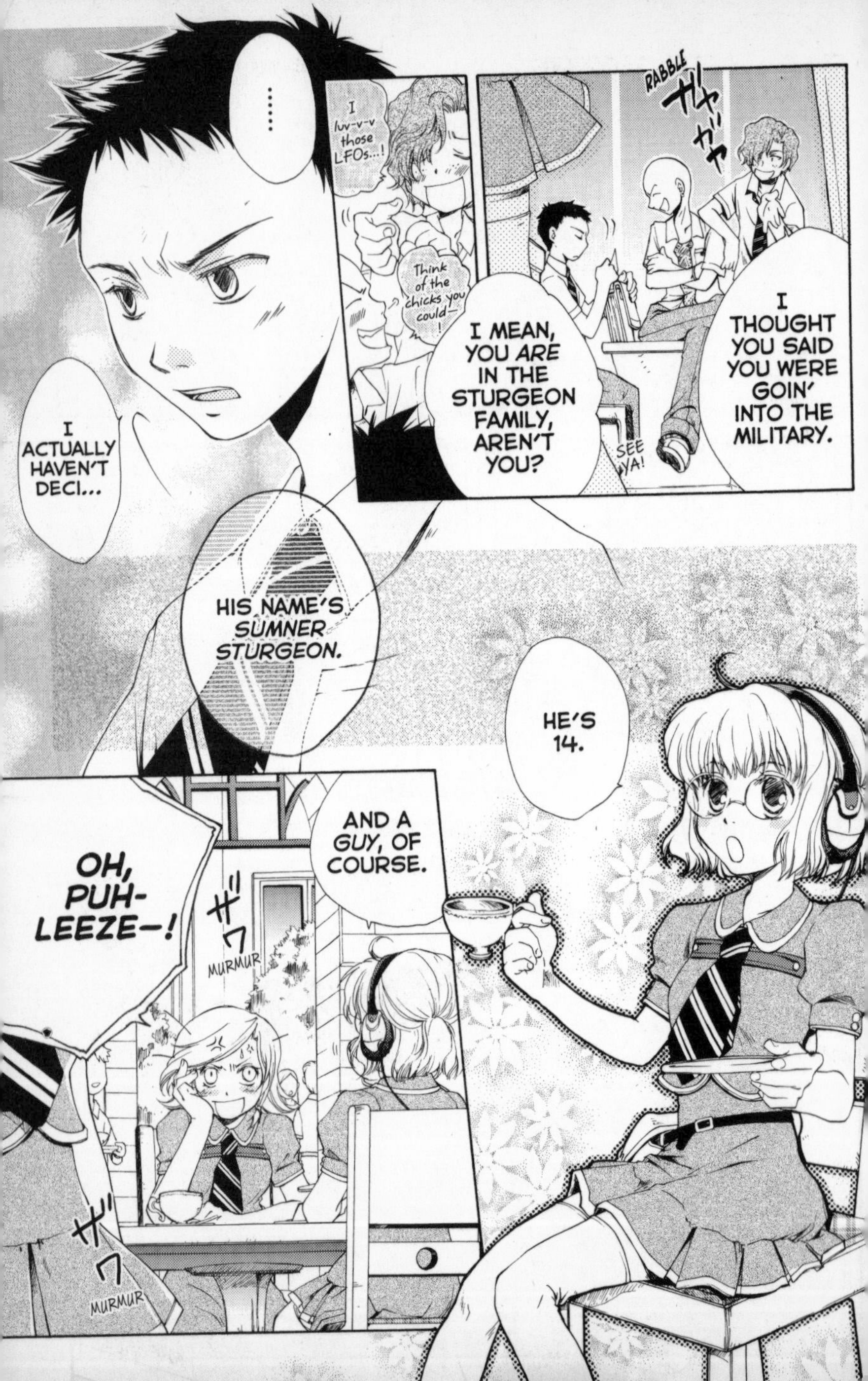

RABBLE
ガヤガヤ
I THOUGHT YOU SAID YOU WERE GOIN' INTO THE MILITARY.
SEE YA!
I MEAN, YOU *ARE* IN THE STURGEON FAMILY, AREN'T YOU?
I luv-v-v those LFOs...!
Think of the chicks you could—!
......
I ACTUALLY HAVEN'T DECI...
HIS NAME'S SUMNER STURGEON.
HE'S 14.
AND A GUY, OF COURSE.
ザワ
MURMUR
OH, PUH-LEEZE—!
ザワ
MURMUR

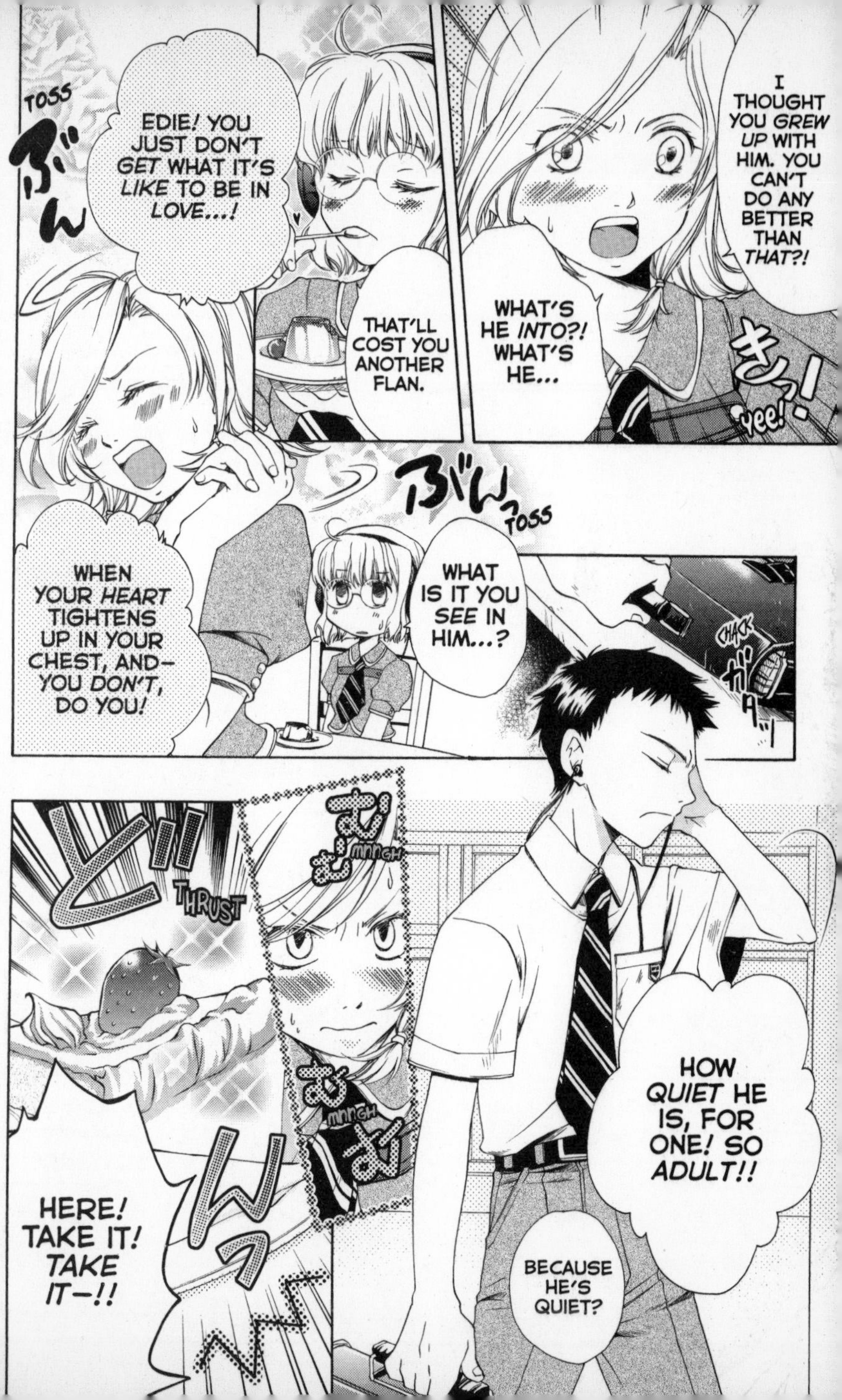
I THOUGHT YOU GREW UP WITH HIM. YOU CAN'T DO ANY BETTER THAN THAT?!
WHAT'S HE INTO?! WHAT'S HE...
きっ! yee!
THAT'LL COST YOU ANOTHER FLAN.
TOSS
ぶん
EDIE! YOU JUST DON'T GET WHAT IT'S LIKE TO BE IN LOVE...!
ぶん TOSS
WHAT IS IT YOU SEE IN HIM...?
WHEN YOUR HEART TIGHTENS UP IN YOUR CHEST, AND— YOU DON'T, DO YOU!
CHACK
ガタッ
HOW QUIET HE IS, FOR ONE! SO ADULT!!
BECAUSE HE'S QUIET?
むむ MNNGH
むむ MNNGH
どッ THRUST
HERE! TAKE IT! TAKE IT—!!
んっ

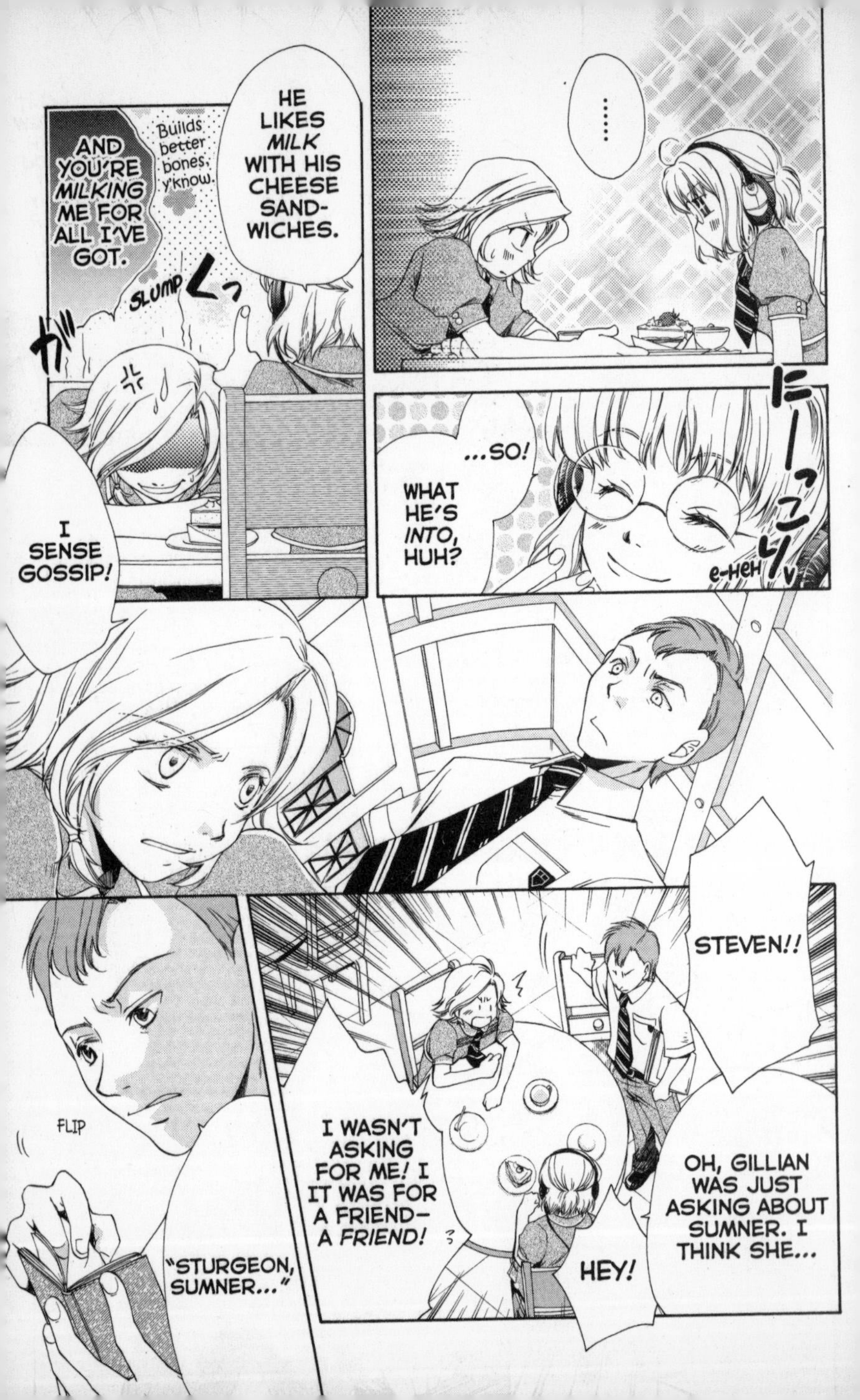
……
HE LIKES MILK WITH HIS CHEESE SANDWICHES.
Builds better bones, y'know.
AND YOU'RE MILKING ME FOR ALL I'VE GOT.
SLUMP
...SO! WHAT HE'S INTO, HUH?
e-HEH
I SENSE GOSSIP!
STEVEN!!
OH, GILLIAN WAS JUST ASKING ABOUT SUMNER. I THINK SHE...
HEY!
I WASN'T ASKING FOR ME! I IT WAS FOR A FRIEND— A FRIEND!
FLIP
"STURGEON, SUMNER..."

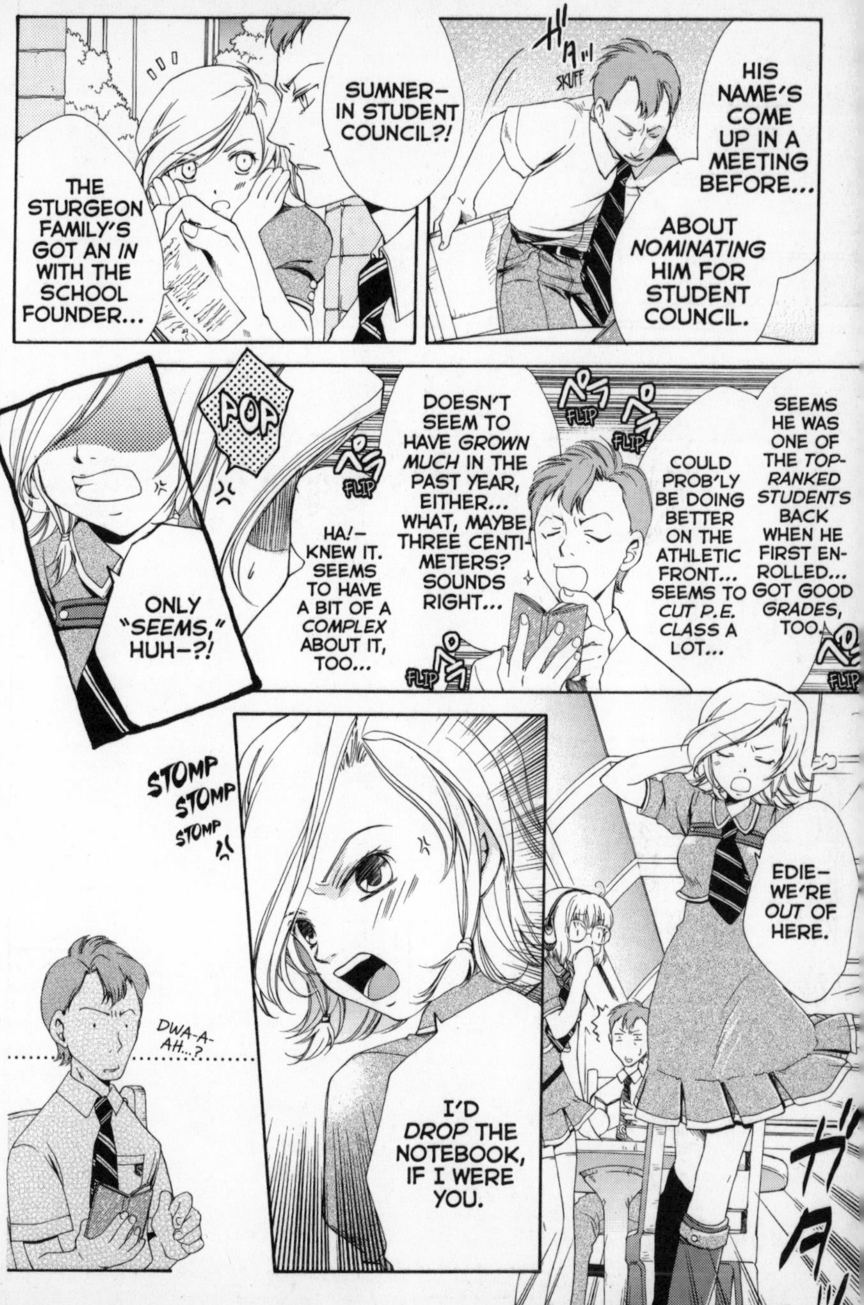
SKUFF
HIS NAME'S COME UP IN A MEETING BEFORE...
ABOUT NOMINATING HIM FOR STUDENT COUNCIL.
SUMNER— IN STUDENT COUNCIL?!
THE STURGEON FAMILY'S GOT AN IN WITH THE SCHOOL FOUNDER...
FLIP
SEEMS HE WAS ONE OF THE TOP-RANKED STUDENTS BACK WHEN HE FIRST EN-ROLLED... GOT GOOD GRADES, TOO.
COULD PROB'LY BE DOING BETTER ON THE ATHLETIC FRONT... SEEMS TO CUT P.E. CLASS A LOT...
FLIP
FLIP
DOESN'T SEEM TO HAVE GROWN MUCH IN THE PAST YEAR, EITHER... WHAT, MAYBE THREE CENTI-METERS? SOUNDS RIGHT...
HA!— KNEW IT. SEEMS TO HAVE A BIT OF A COMPLEX ABOUT IT, TOO...
FLIP
FLIP
POP
ONLY "SEEMS," HUH—?!
KLATTER
EDIE— WE'RE OUT OF HERE.
I'D DROP THE NOTEBOOK, IF I WERE YOU.
STOMP STOMP STOMP
DWA-A-AH...?

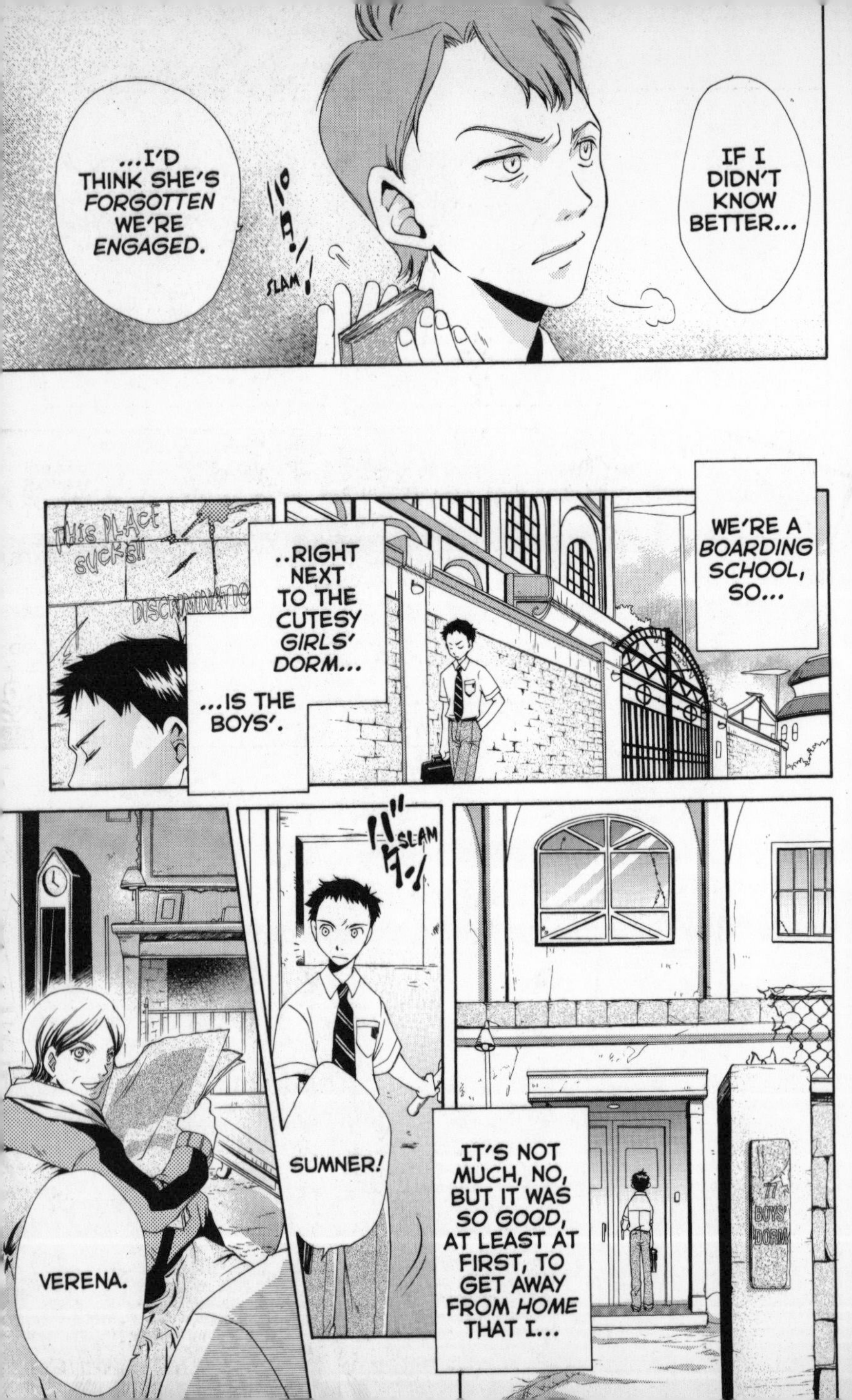
IF I DIDN'T KNOW BETTER...
SLAM!
...I'D THINK SHE'S FORGOTTEN WE'RE ENGAGED.
WE'RE A BOARDING SCHOOL, SO...
..RIGHT NEXT TO THE CUTESY GIRLS' DORM...
...IS THE BOYS'.
THIS PLACE SUCKS!!
DISCRIMINATIO
IT'S NOT MUCH, NO, BUT IT WAS SO GOOD, AT LEAST AT FIRST, TO GET AWAY FROM HOME THAT I...
77 BOYS' DORM
SLAM
SUMNER!
VERENA.

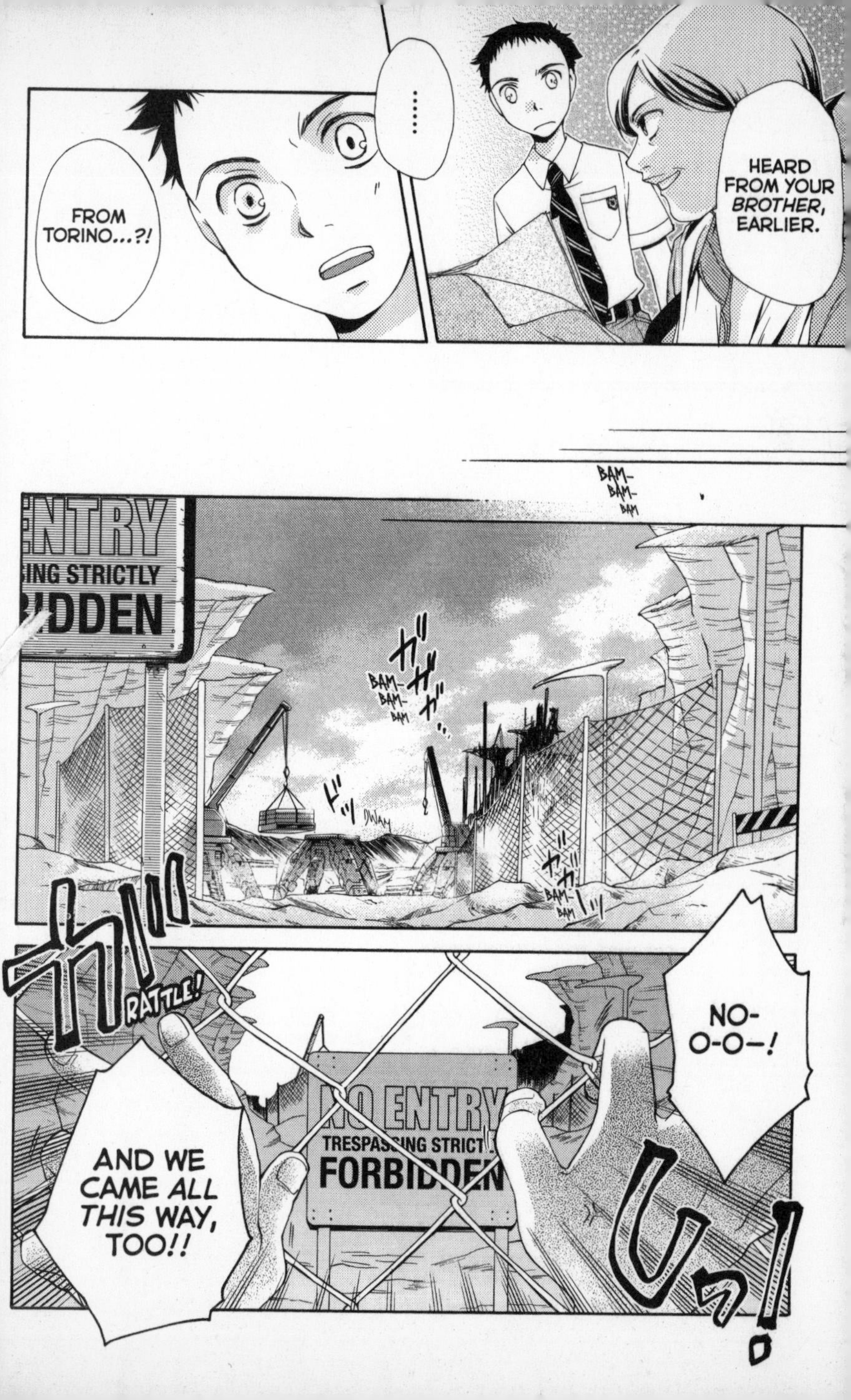
HEARD FROM YOUR *BROTHER*, EARLIER.
......
FROM TORINO...?!
BAM-BAM-BAM
ENTRY
SING STRICTLY
IDDEN
BAM-BAM-BAM
DWAM
BAM-BAM
RATTLE!
NO-O-O-!
NO ENTRY
TRESPASSING STRICT
FORBIDDEN
AND WE CAME *ALL THIS* WAY, TOO!!

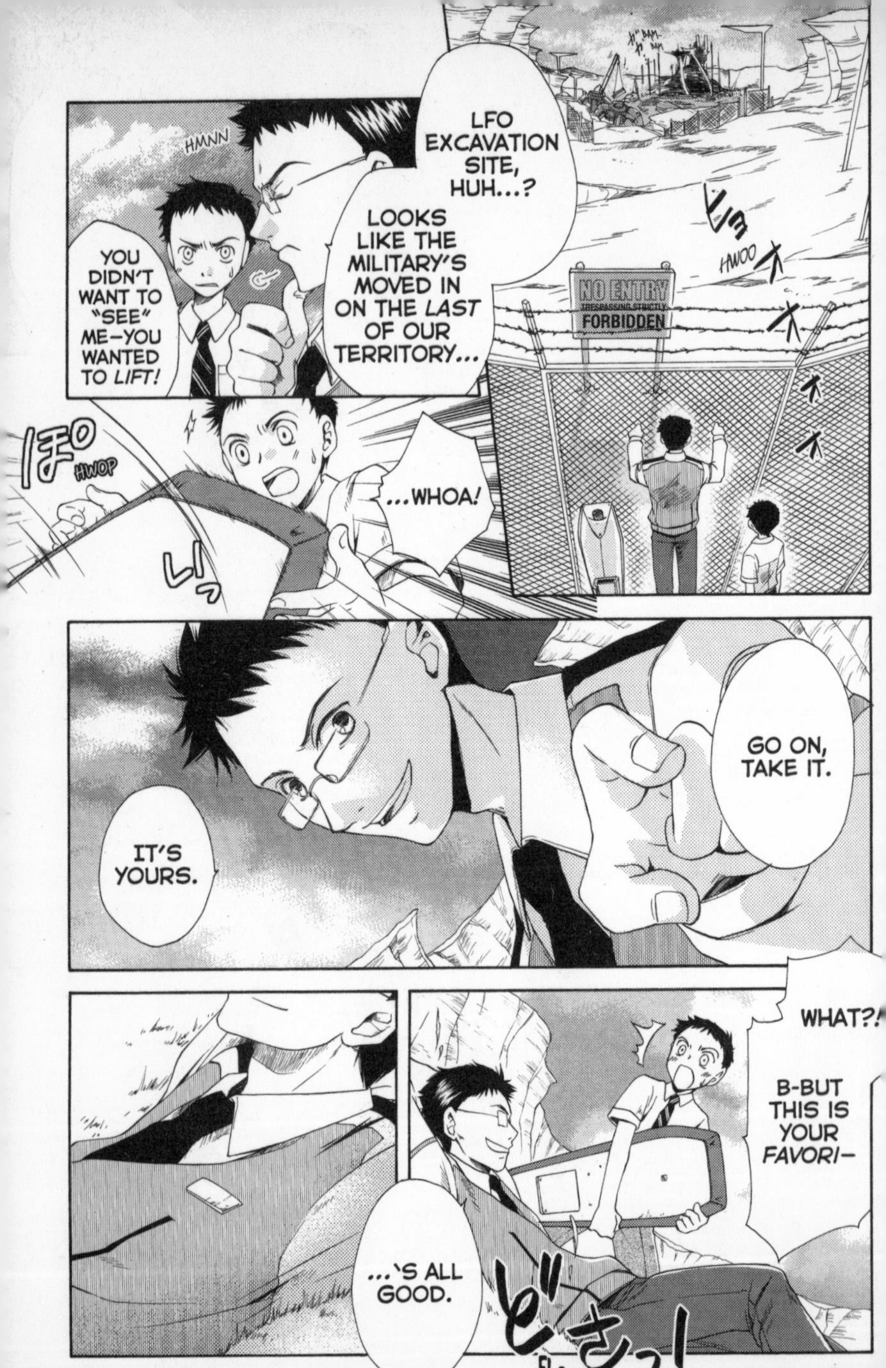
LFO EXCAVATION SITE, HUH...?
LOOKS LIKE THE MILITARY'S MOVED IN ON THE *LAST* OF OUR TERRITORY...
NO ENTRY
TRESPASSING STRICTLY
FORBIDDEN
HWOO
HMNN
YOU DIDN'T WANT TO "SEE" ME—YOU WANTED TO *LIFT*!
HWOP
...WHOA!
GO ON, TAKE IT.
IT'S YOURS.
WHAT?!
B-BUT THIS IS YOUR *FAVORI*—
...'S ALL GOOD.
FLOMP

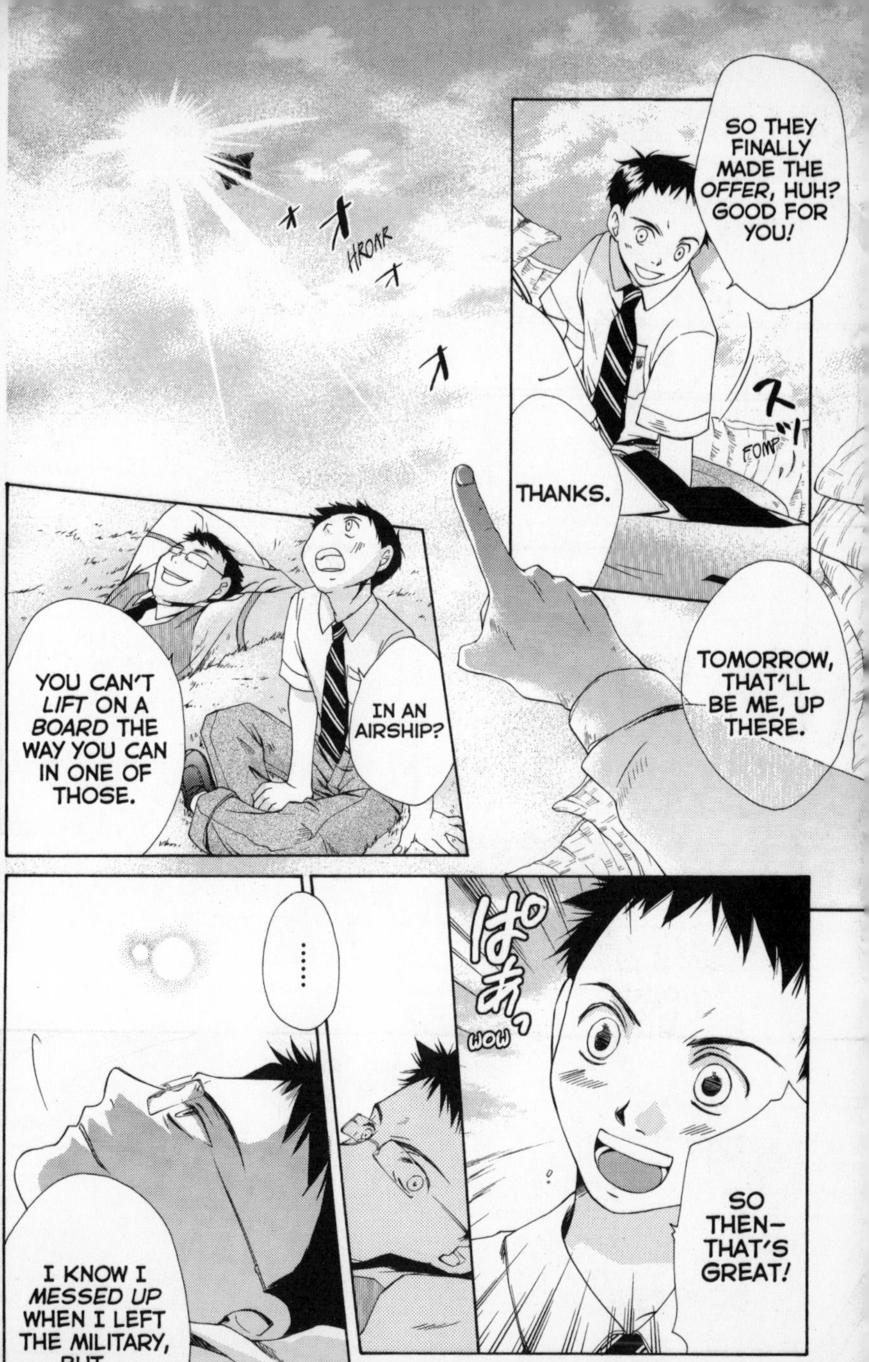
SO THEY FINALLY MADE THE *OFFER*, HUH? GOOD FOR YOU!
FOMP
THANKS.
HROAR
TOMORROW, THAT'LL BE ME, UP THERE.
IN AN AIRSHIP?
YOU CAN'T *LIFT* ON A *BOARD* THE WAY YOU CAN IN ONE OF THOSE.
WOW
SO THEN— THAT'S GREAT!
......
I KNOW I *MESSED UP* WHEN I LEFT THE MILITARY, BUT...

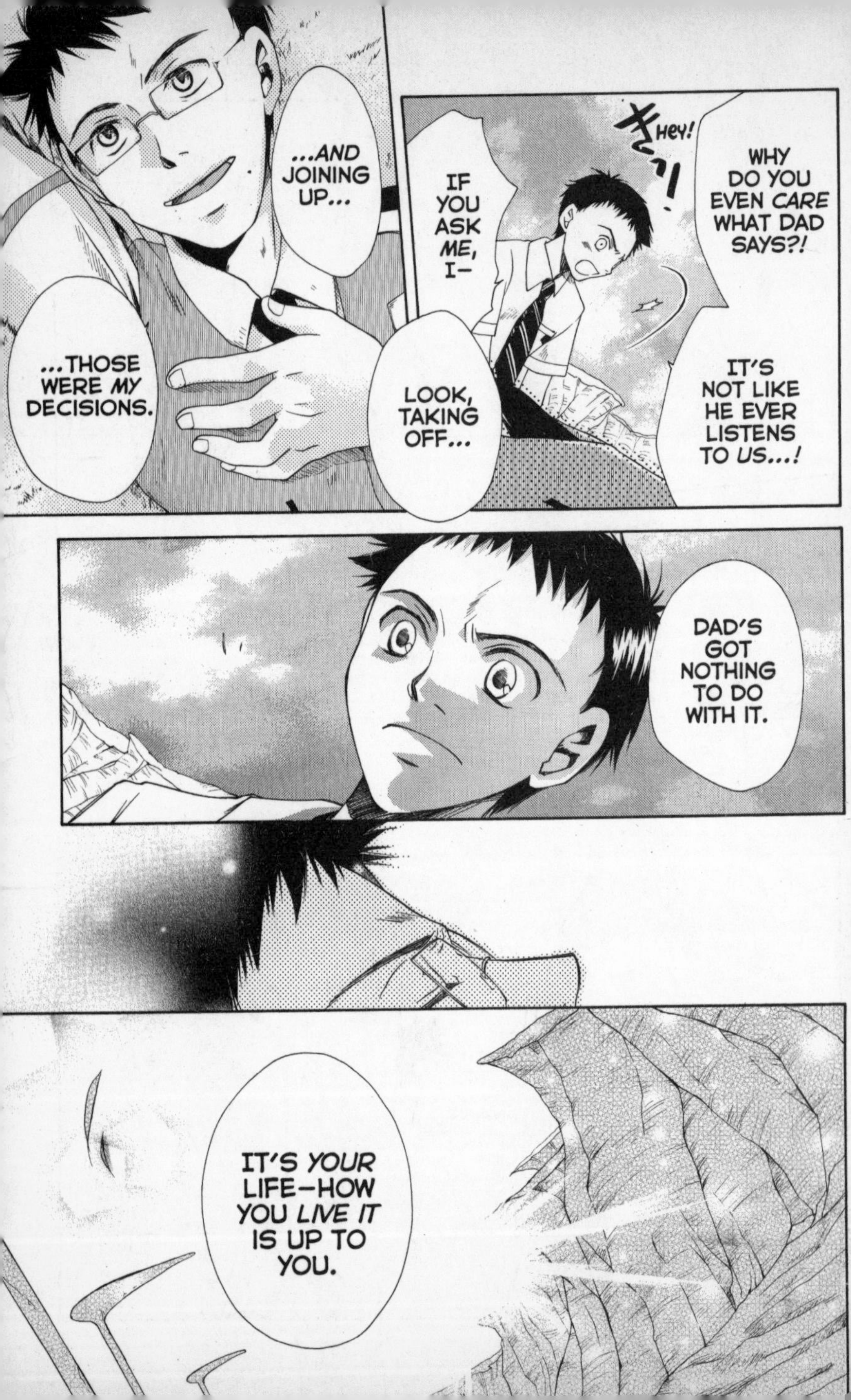
HEY!
WHY DO YOU EVEN *CARE* WHAT DAD SAYS?!
IT'S NOT LIKE HE EVER LISTENS TO *US*...!
IF YOU ASK *ME*, I–
LOOK, TAKING OFF...
...AND JOINING UP...
...THOSE WERE *MY* DECISIONS.
DAD'S GOT NOTHING TO DO WITH IT.
IT'S *YOUR* LIFE—HOW YOU *LIVE IT* IS UP TO YOU.

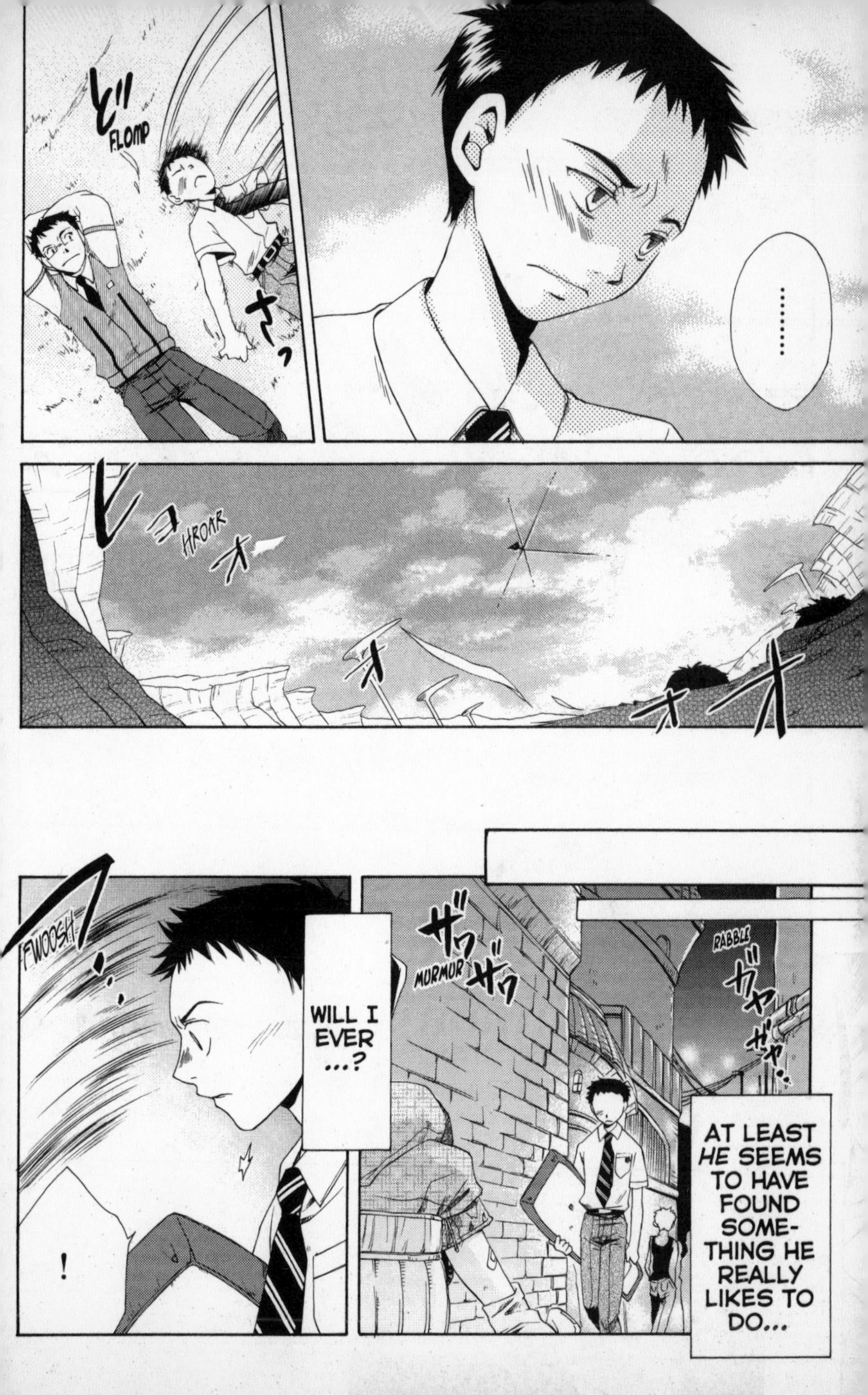

……
FLOMP
HROAR
AT LEAST *HE* SEEMS TO HAVE FOUND SOME-THING HE REALLY LIKES TO DO...
RABBL
ガヤ ガヤ
MURMUR
ザワ ザワ
WILL I EVER ...?
FWOOSH
!

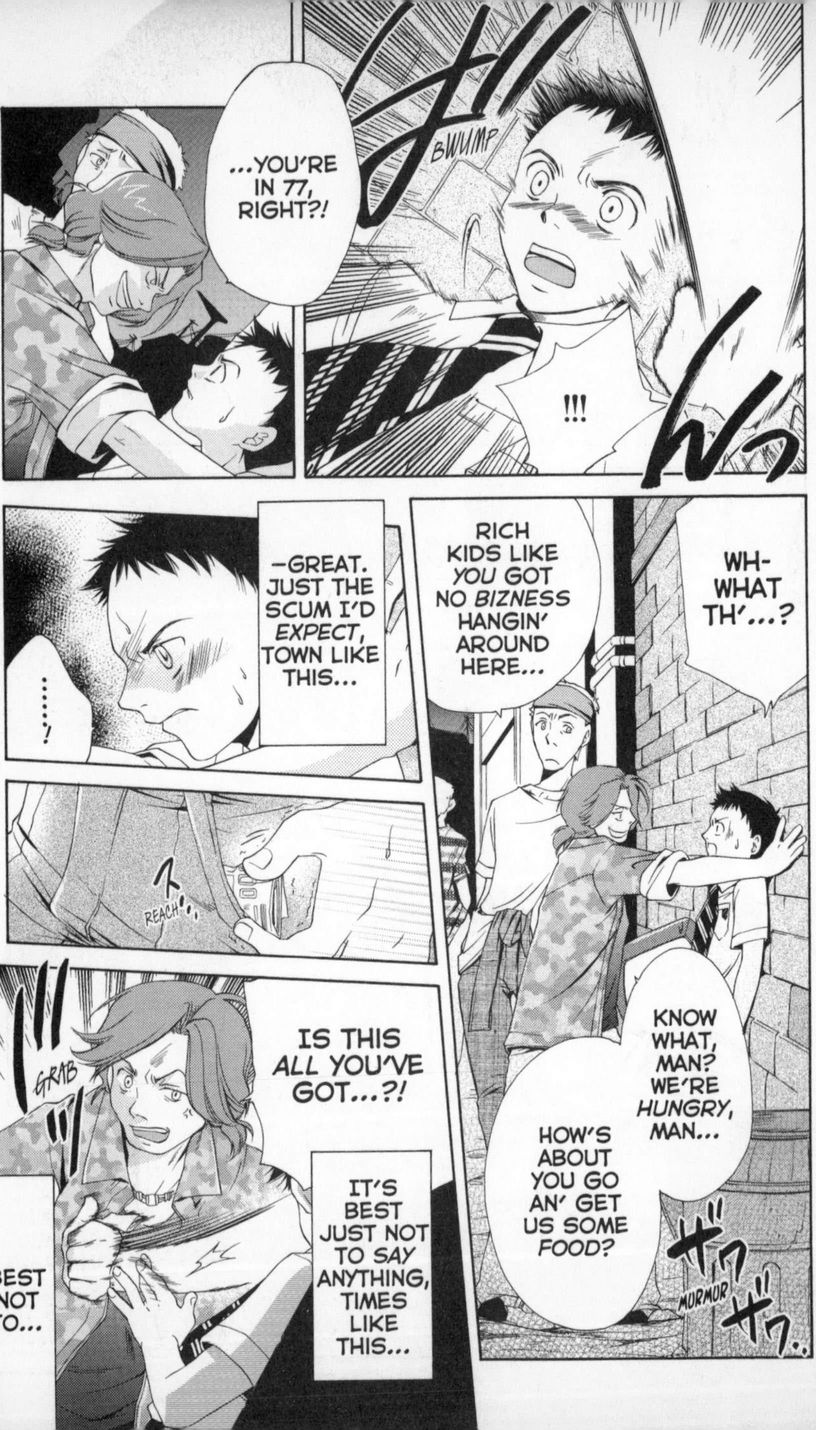
BWUMP
!!!
...YOU'RE IN 77, RIGHT?!
WH-WHAT TH'...?
RICH KIDS LIKE *YOU* GOT NO *BIZNESS* HANGIN' AROUND HERE...
KNOW WHAT, MAN? WE'RE *HUNGRY*, MAN...
HOW'S ABOUT YOU GO AN' GET US SOME *FOOD*?
MURMUR
—GREAT. JUST THE SCUM I'D *EXPECT*, TOWN LIKE THIS...
......!
REACH
IS THIS *ALL* YOU'VE GOT...?!
GRAB
IT'S BEST JUST NOT TO *SAY* ANYTHING, TIMES LIKE THIS...
BEST NOT TO...

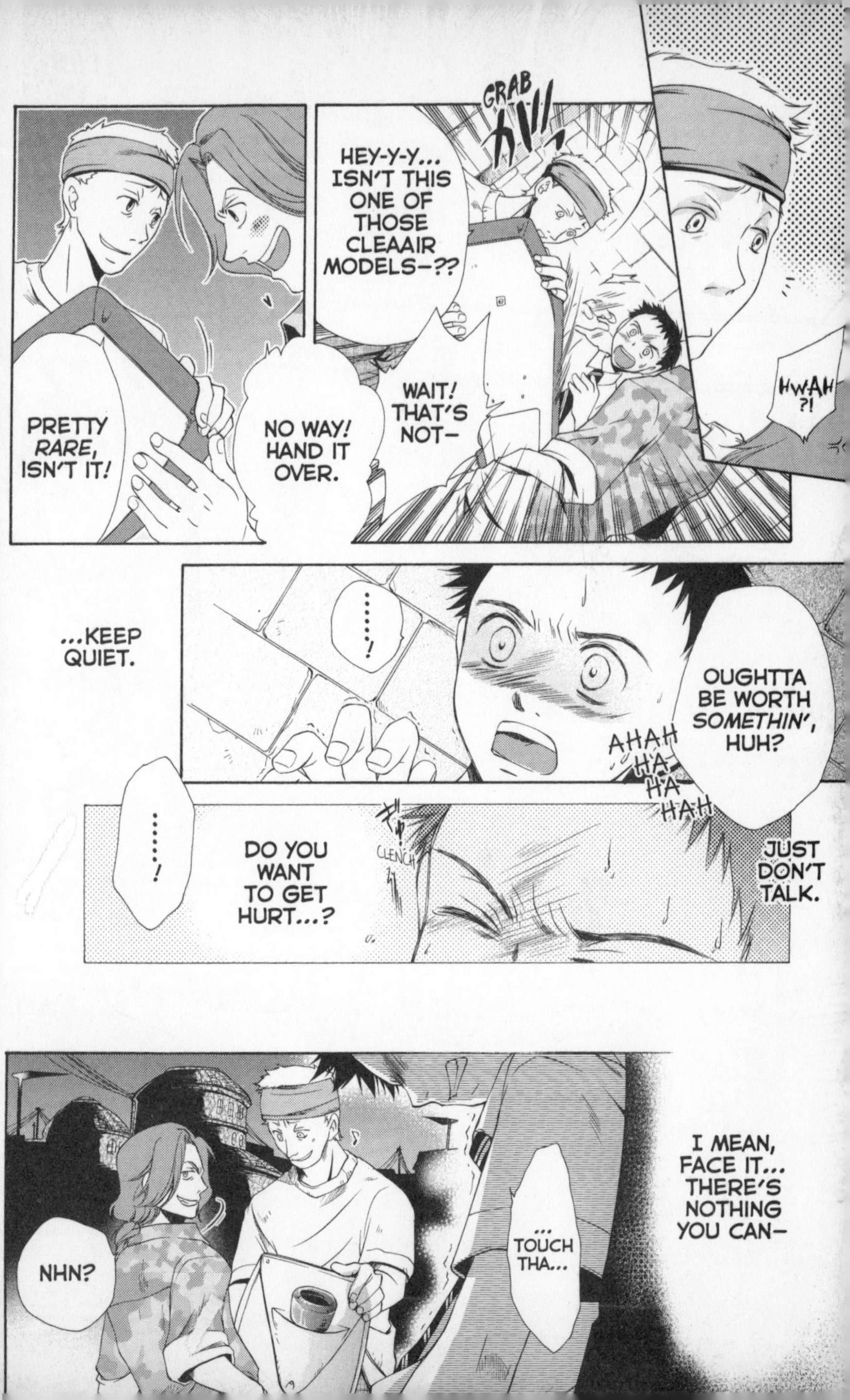
HWAH?!
GRAB
HEY-Y-Y... ISN'T THIS ONE OF THOSE CLEAAIR MODELS-??
WAIT! THAT'S NOT-
NO WAY! HAND IT OVER.
PRETTY *RARE*, ISN'T IT!
OUGHTTA BE WORTH *SOMETHIN'*, HUH?
AHAH HA HA HAH
......!
...KEEP QUIET.
JUST DON'T TALK.
CLENCH
DO YOU WANT TO GET HURT...?
......!
I MEAN, FACE IT... THERE'S NOTHING YOU CAN-
...TOUCH THA...
NHN?

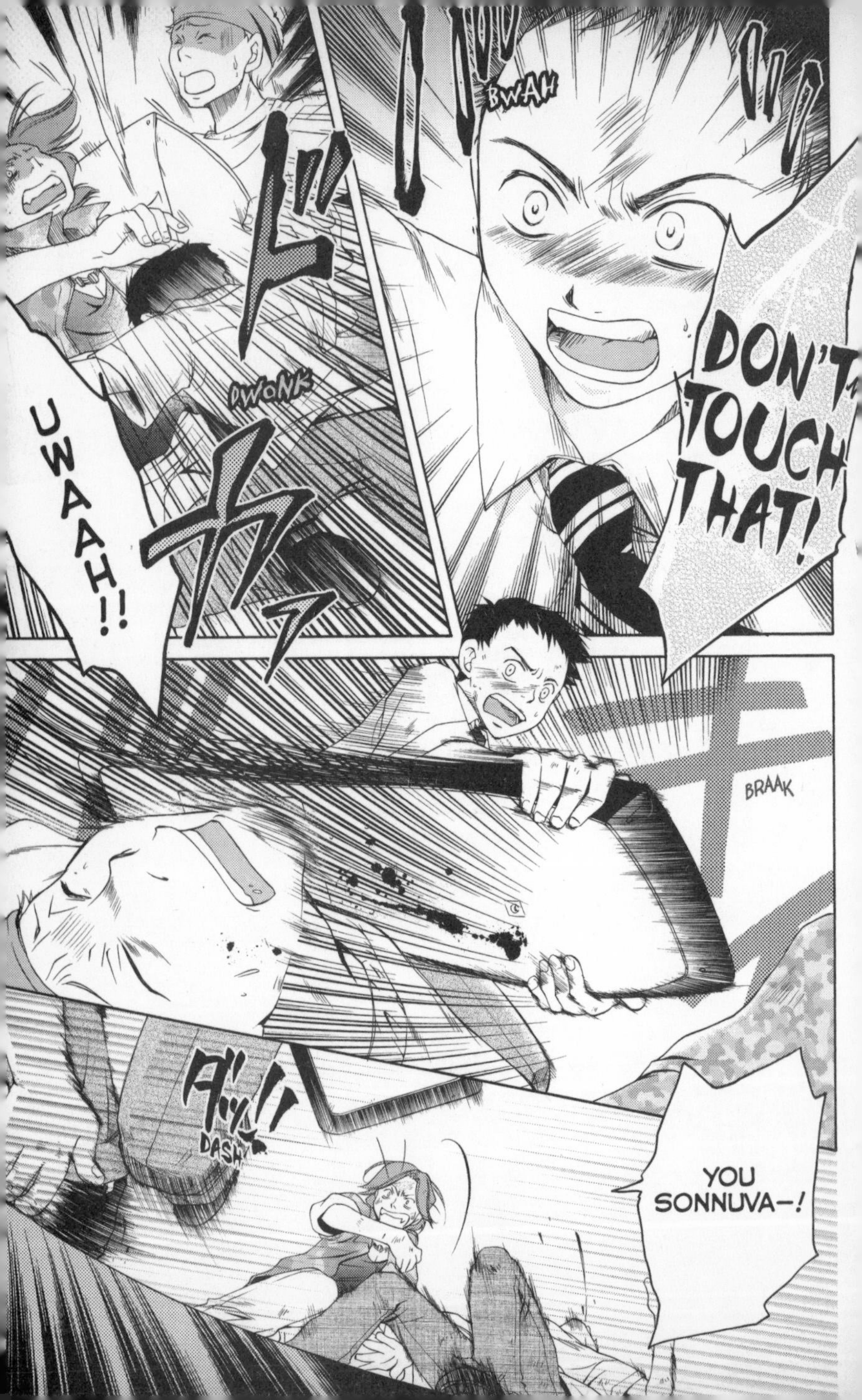

BWAH
DON'T TOUCH THAT!
DWONK
UWAAH!!
BRAAK
ダッ!!
DASH
YOU SONNUVA—!

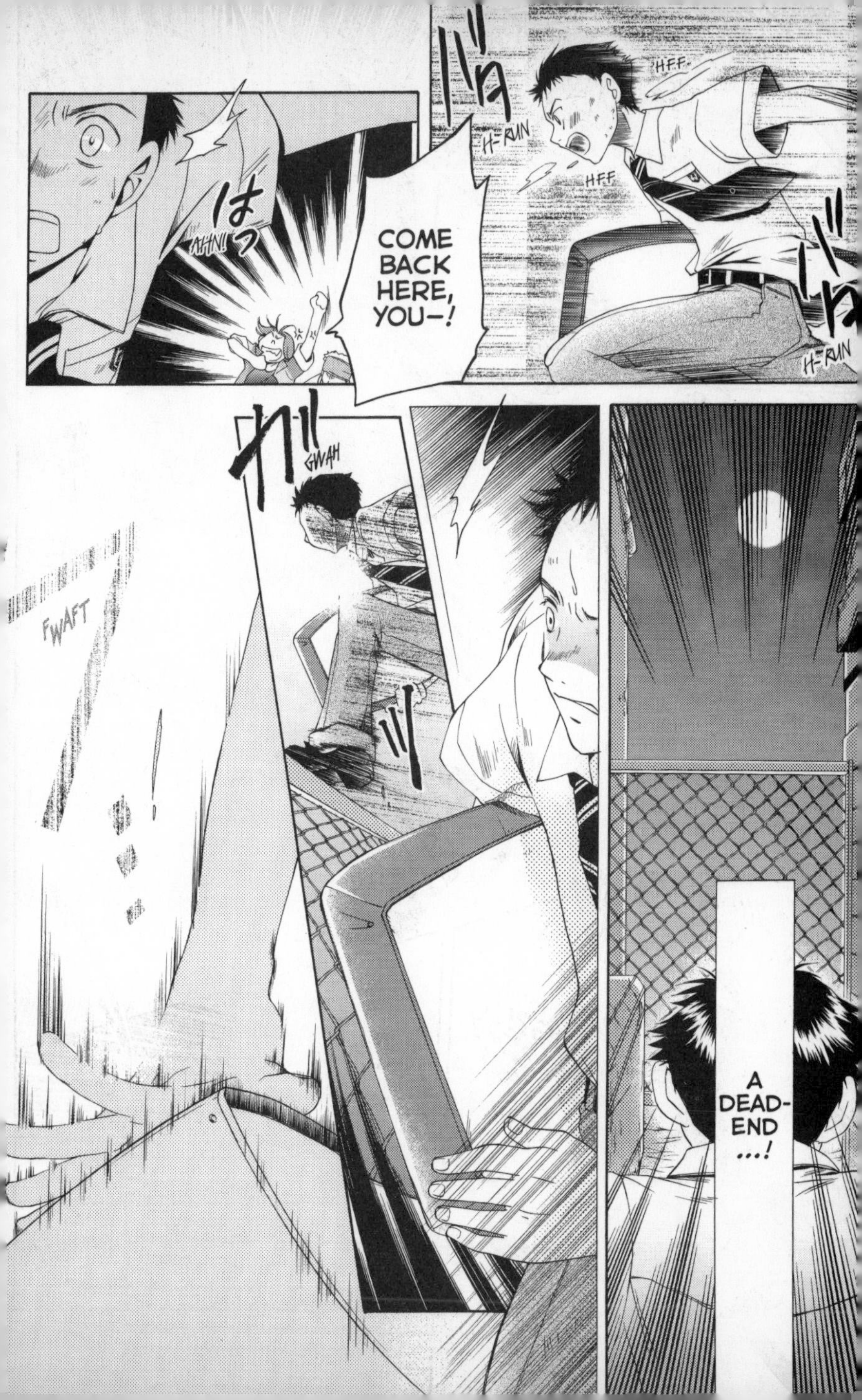
HFF
H-RUN
HFF
H-RUN
COME BACK HERE, YOU—!
はっ
AHN!!
A DEAD-END ...!
GWAH
FWAFT
!

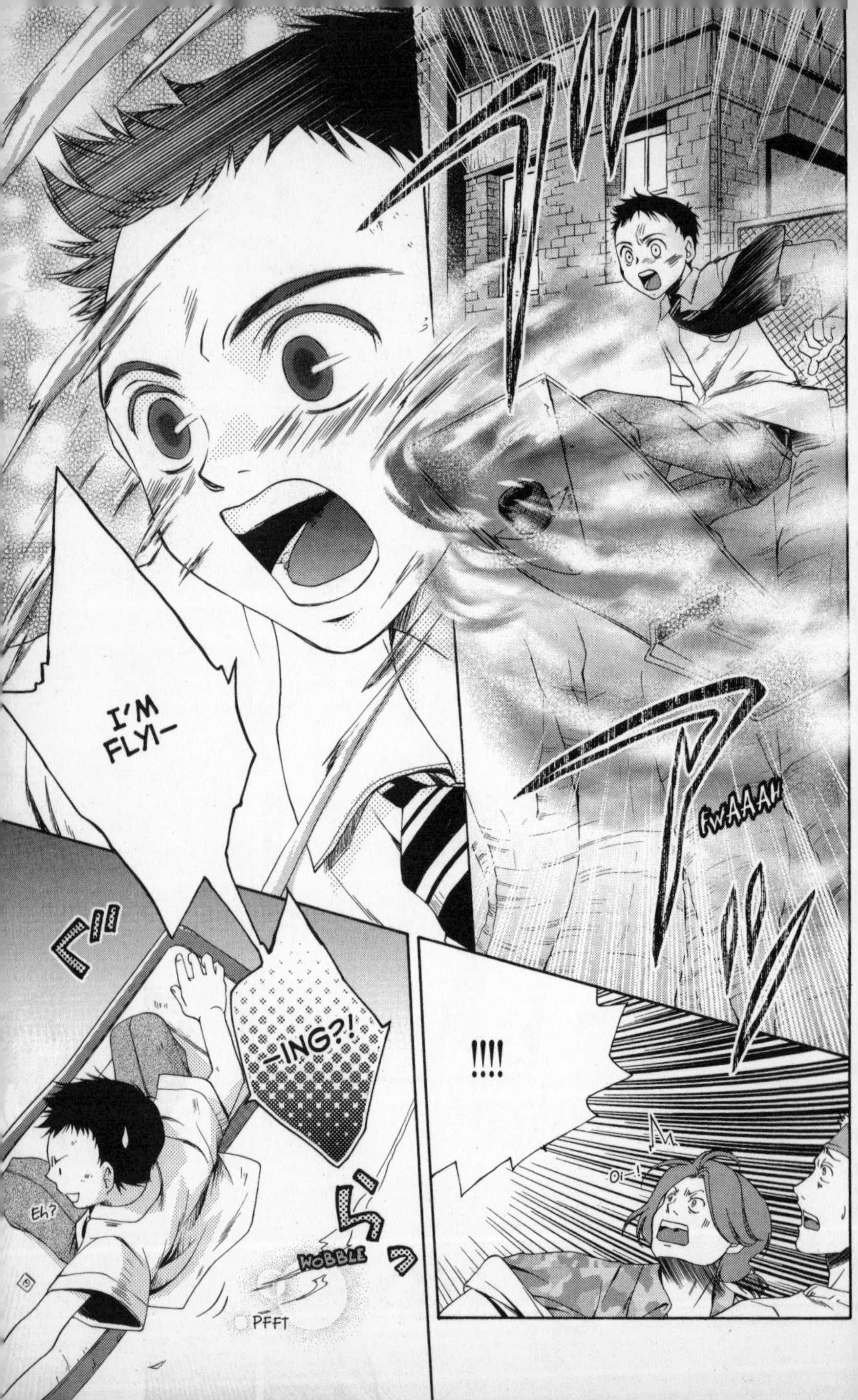
FWAAAH
I'M FLYI-
!!!!
Oi-!
-ING?!
Eh?
WOBBLE
PFFT

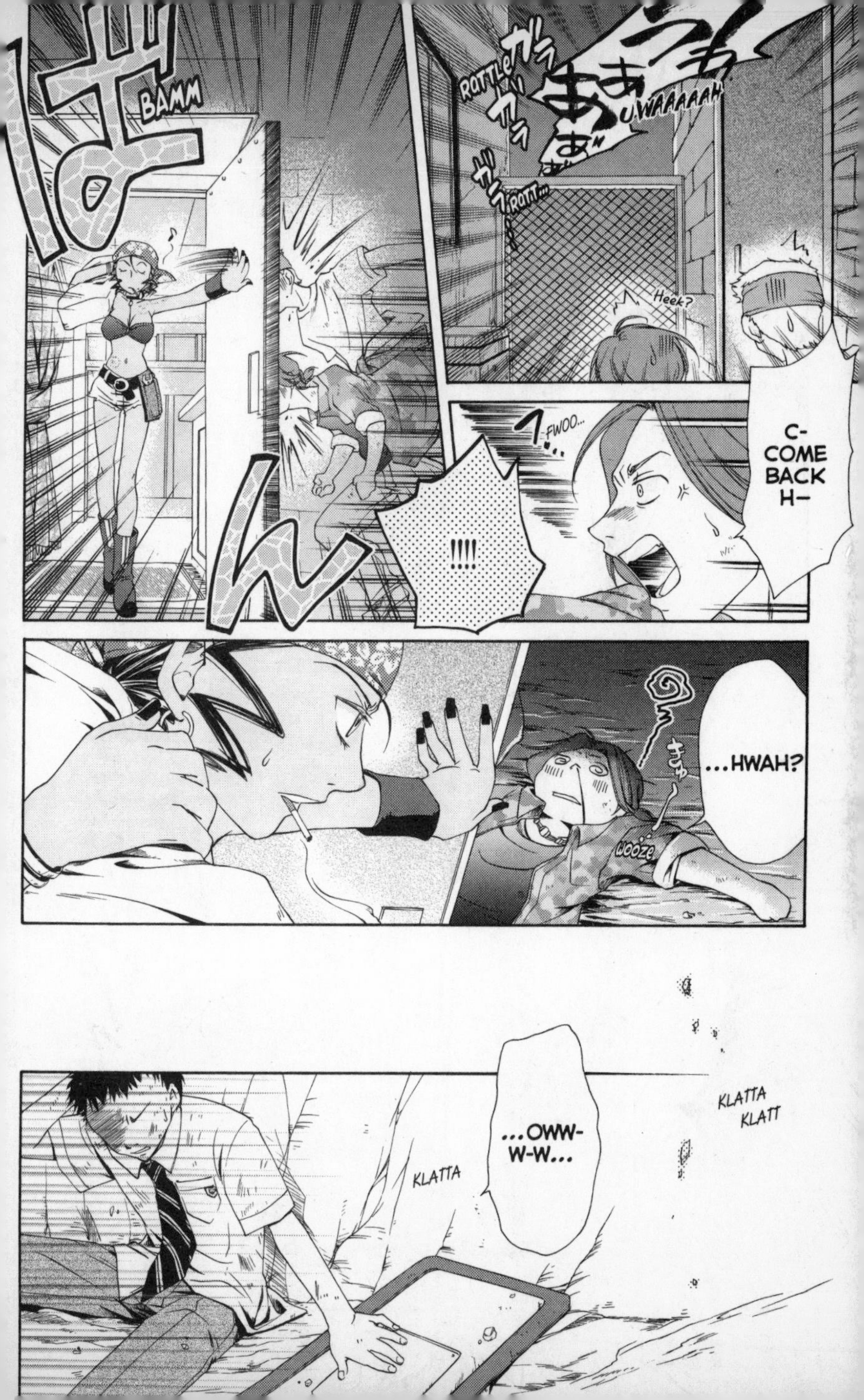
RATTLE
UWAAAAAH
RATT...
Heek?
BAMM
C-COME BACK H–
FWOO...
!!!!
...HWAH?
WOOZE
KLATTA KLATT
...OWW-W-W...
KLATTA

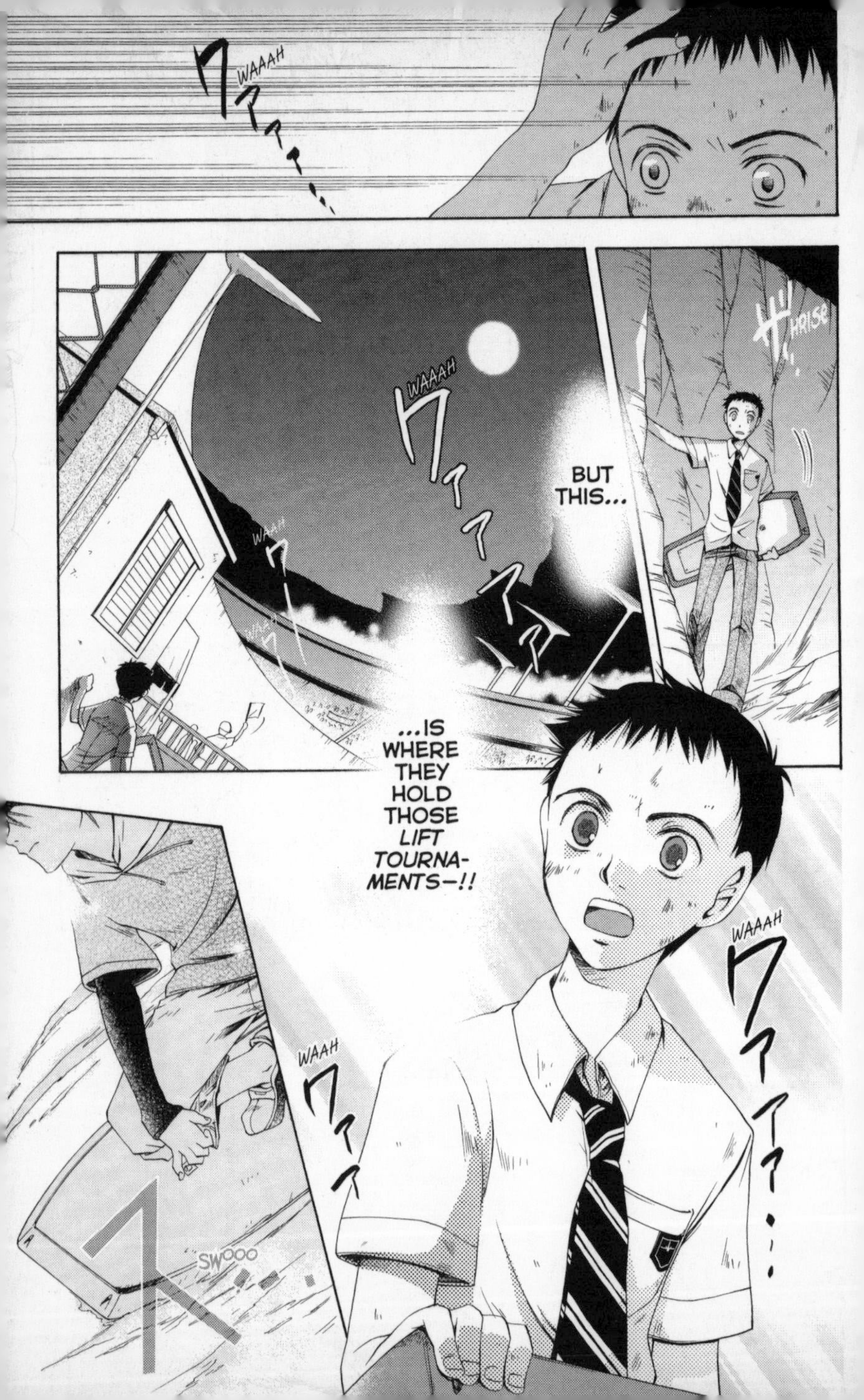

WAAAH
HRISE
BUT THIS...
WAAAH
WAAH
...IS WHERE THEY HOLD THOSE *LIFT* TOURNAMENTS–!!
WAAAH
WAAH
SWOOO

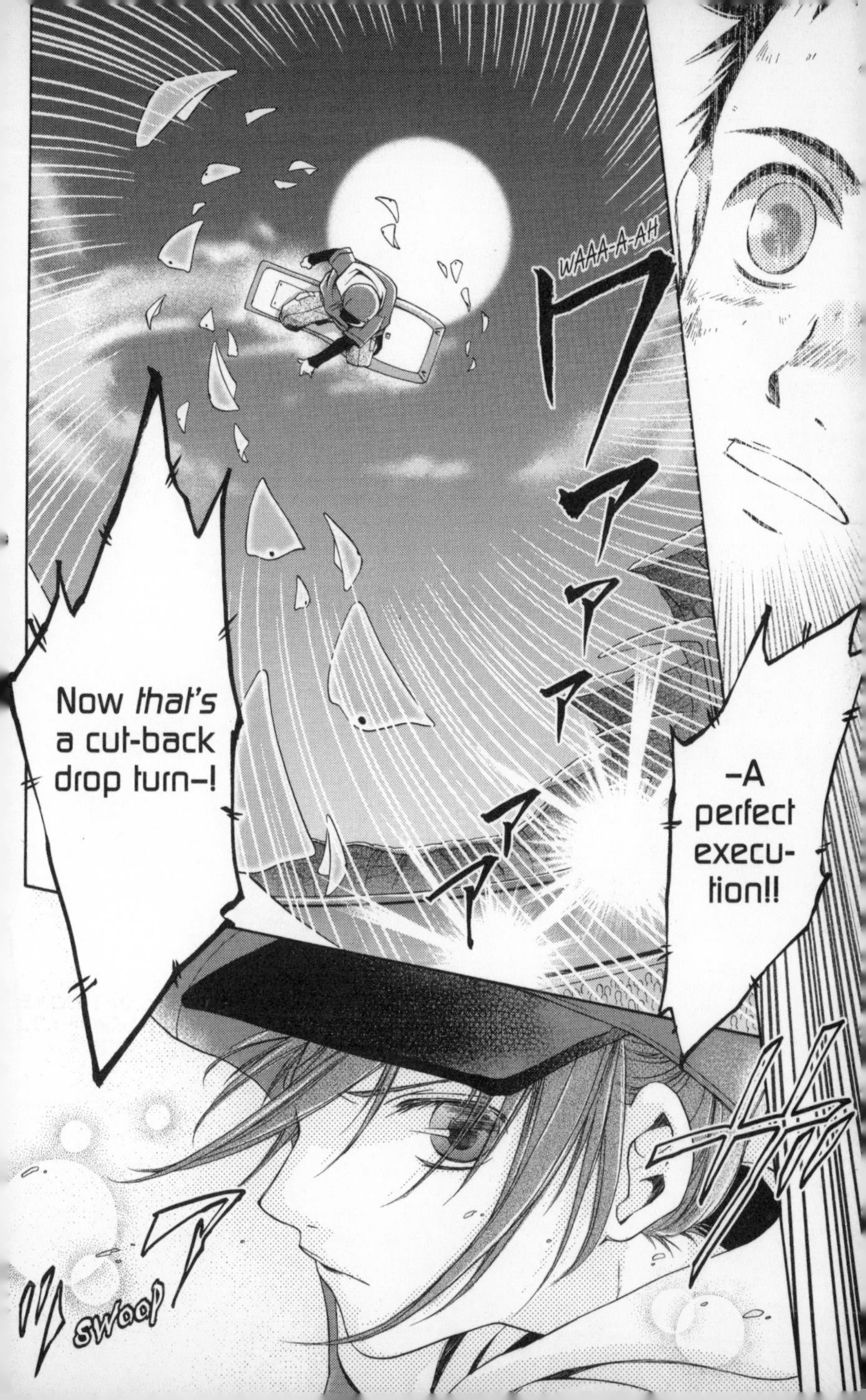
WAAA-A-AH
Now *that's* a cut-back drop turn–!
–A perfect execu-tion!!
SWOOP

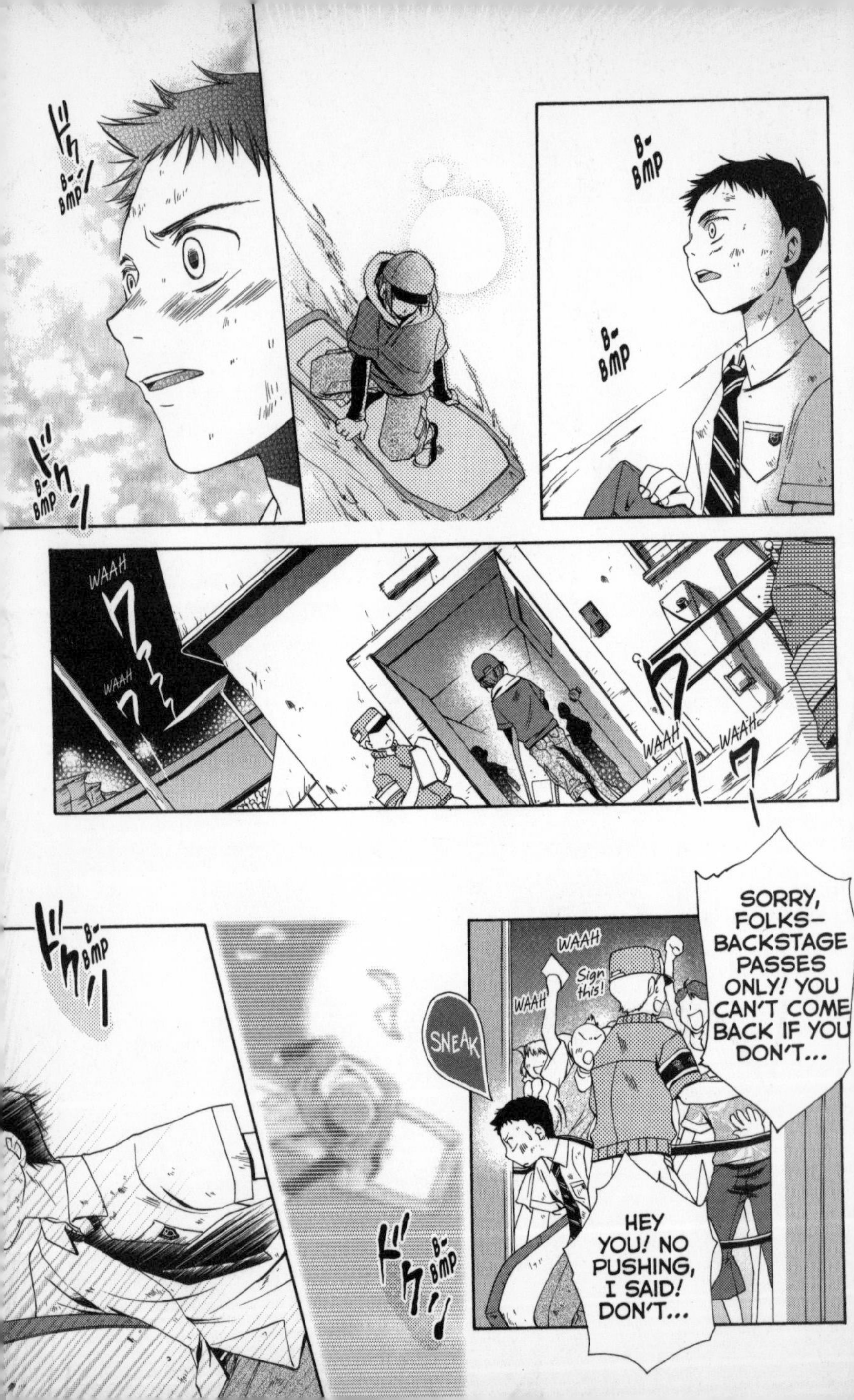
B-BMP
B-BMP
B-BMP!
B-BMP
WAAH
WAAH
WAAH
WAAH
SORRY, FOLKS—BACKSTAGE PASSES ONLY! YOU CAN'T COME BACK IF YOU DON'T...
WAAH
Sign this!
WAAH
SNEAK
HEY YOU! NO PUSHING, I SAID! DON'T...
B-BMP
B-BMP

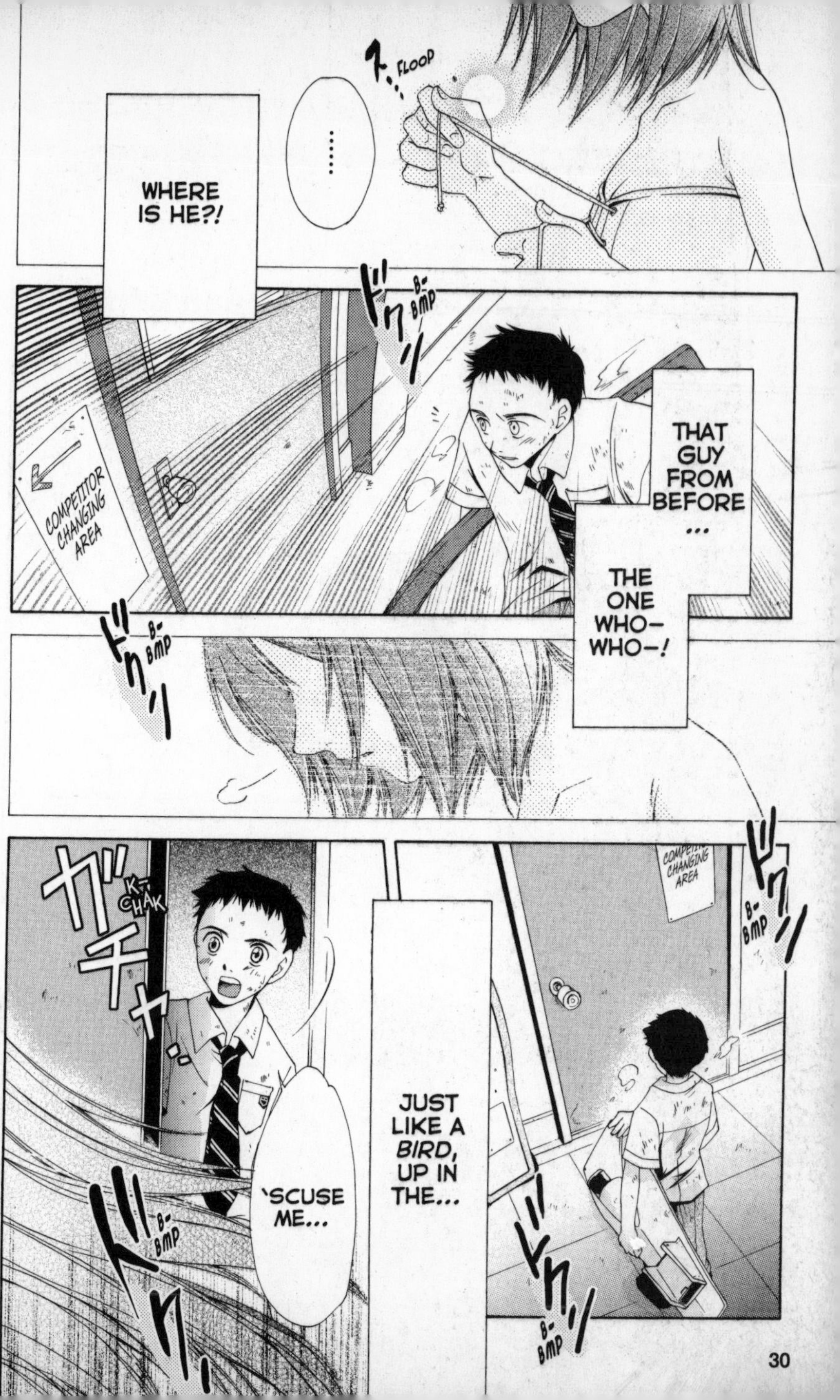
FLOOP
......
WHERE IS HE?!
B-BMP
THAT GUY FROM BEFORE...
THE ONE WHO-WHO-!
COMPETITOR CHANGING AREA
B-BMP
B-BMP
COMPETITOR CHANGING AREA
B-BMP
JUST LIKE A BIRD, UP IN THE...
K-CHAK
'SCUSE ME...
B-BMP

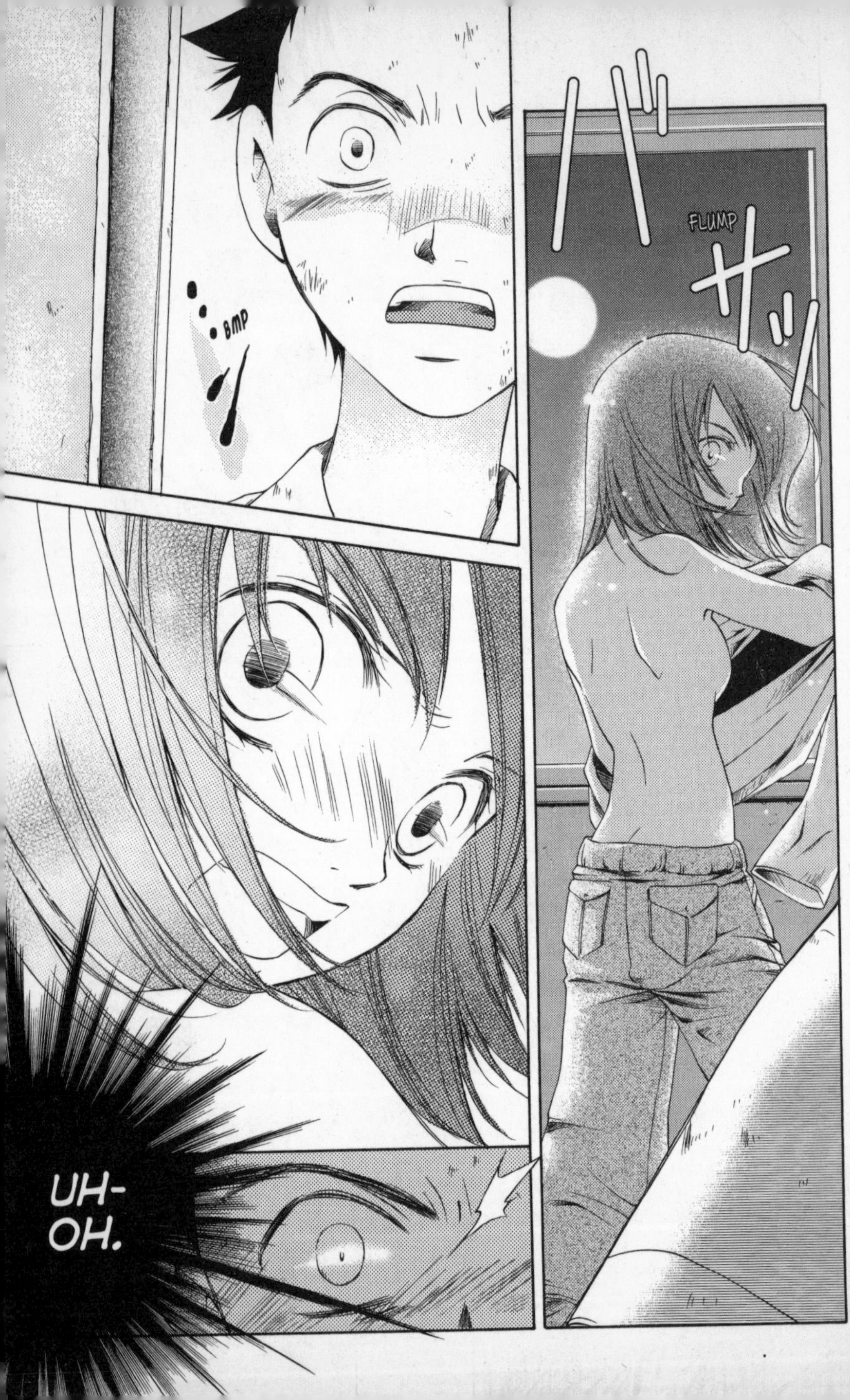
FLUMP
サッ
...BMP
UH-
OH.

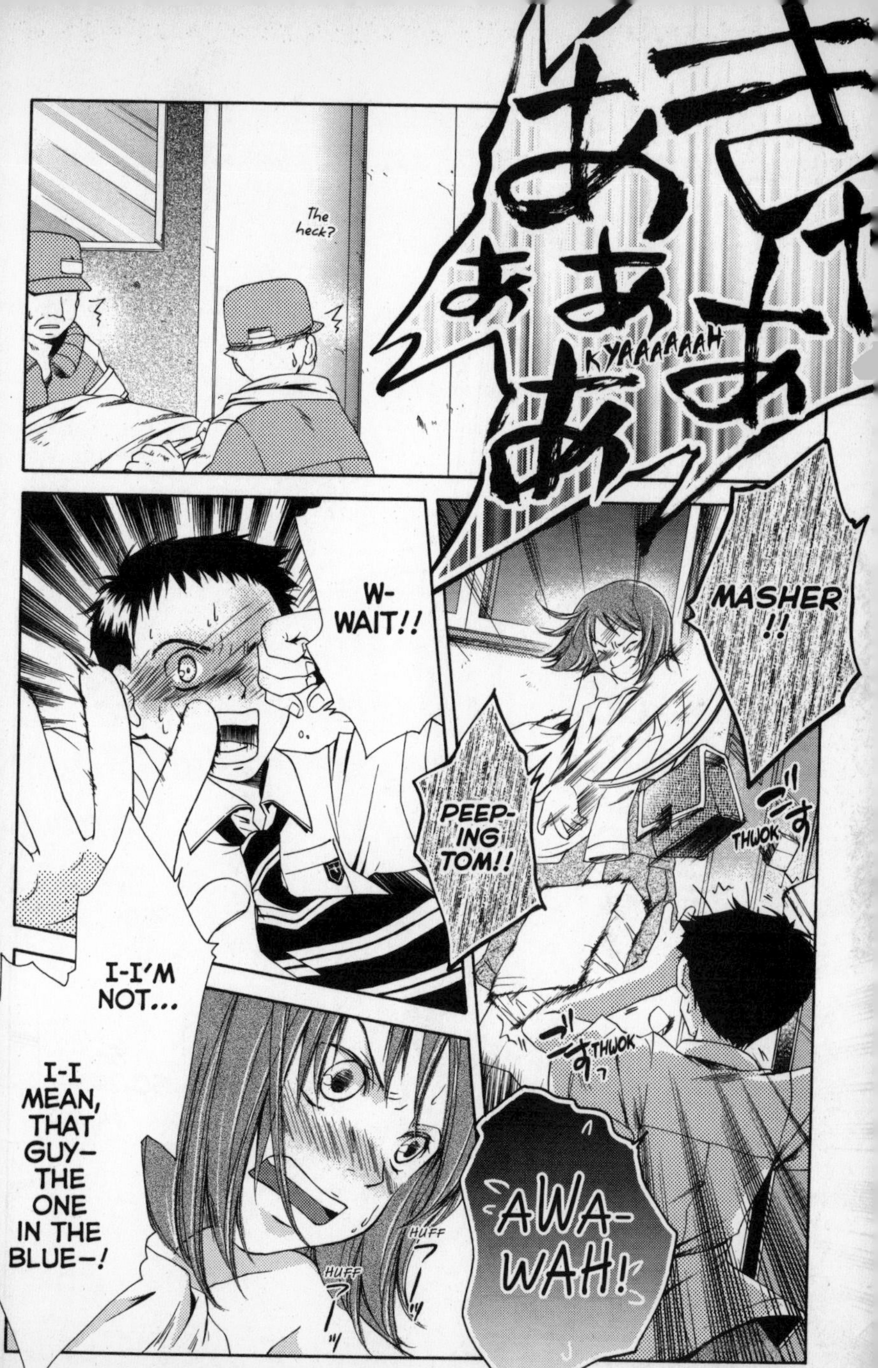

KYAAAAAAH
The heck?
MASHER!!
PEEPING-TOM!!
ごす THWOK
ごす THWOK
AWA-WAH!
W-WAIT!!
I-I'M NOT...
I-I MEAN, THAT GUY— THE ONE IN THE BLUE—!
HUFF
HUFF

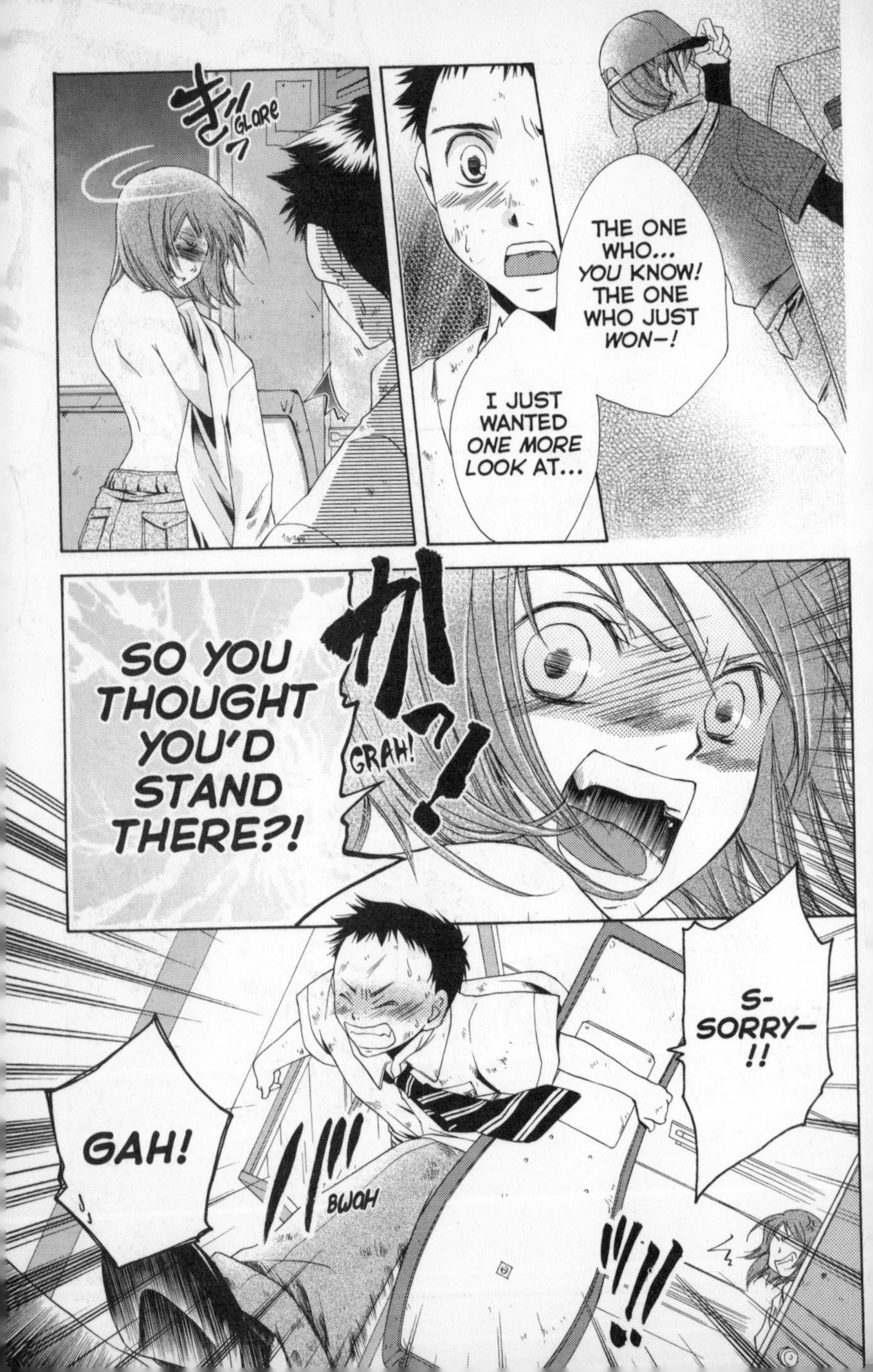
I JUST WANTED ONE MORE LOOK AT...
THE ONE WHO... YOU KNOW! THE ONE WHO JUST WON-!
GLARE
GRAH!
SO YOU THOUGHT YOU'D STAND THERE?!
S-SORRY-!!
BWAH
GAH!

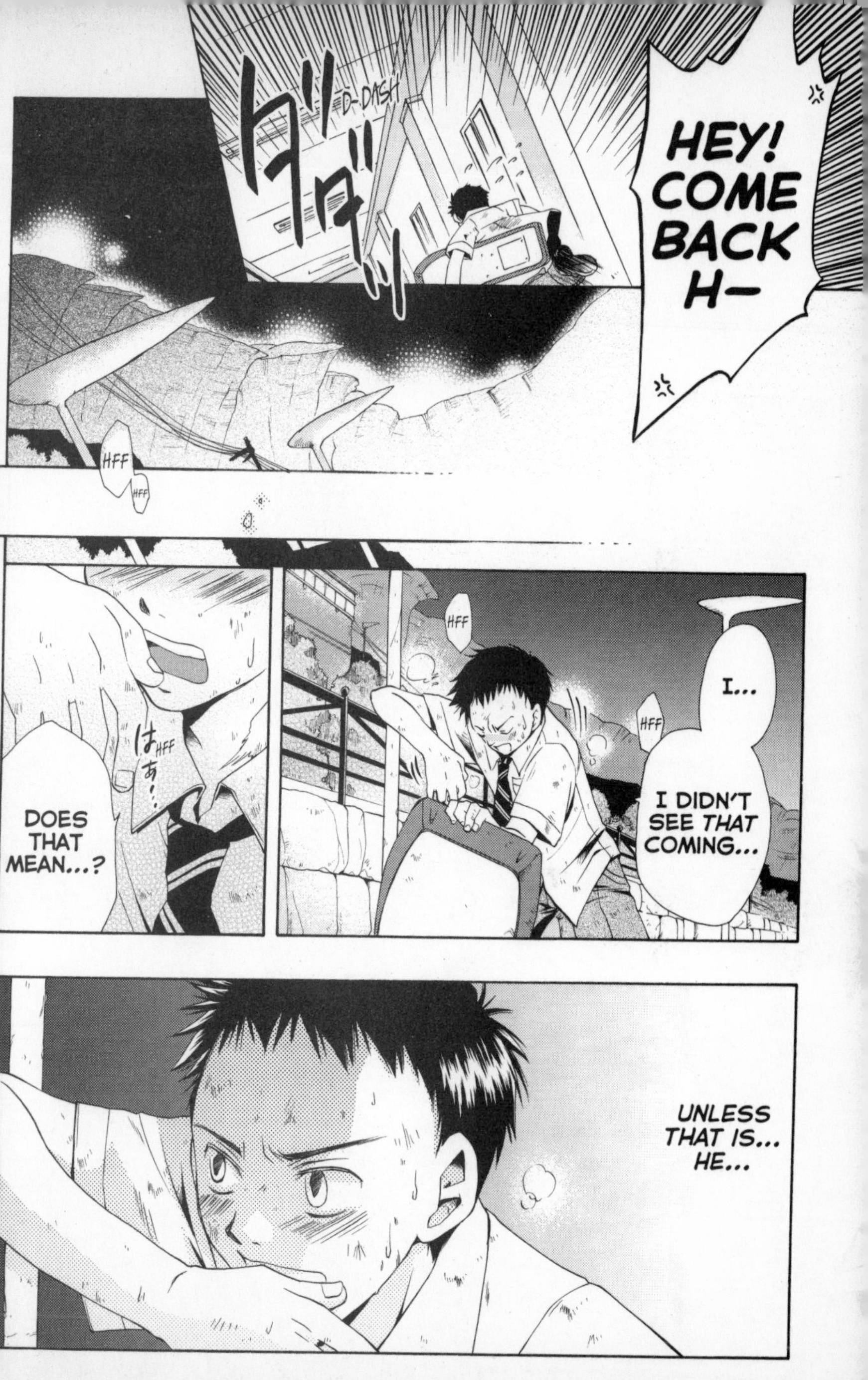
HEY! COME BACK H—
D-DASH
HFF
HFF
I...
HFF
HFF
I DIDN'T SEE *THAT* COMING...
HFF
DOES THAT MEAN...?
UNLESS THAT IS... HE...

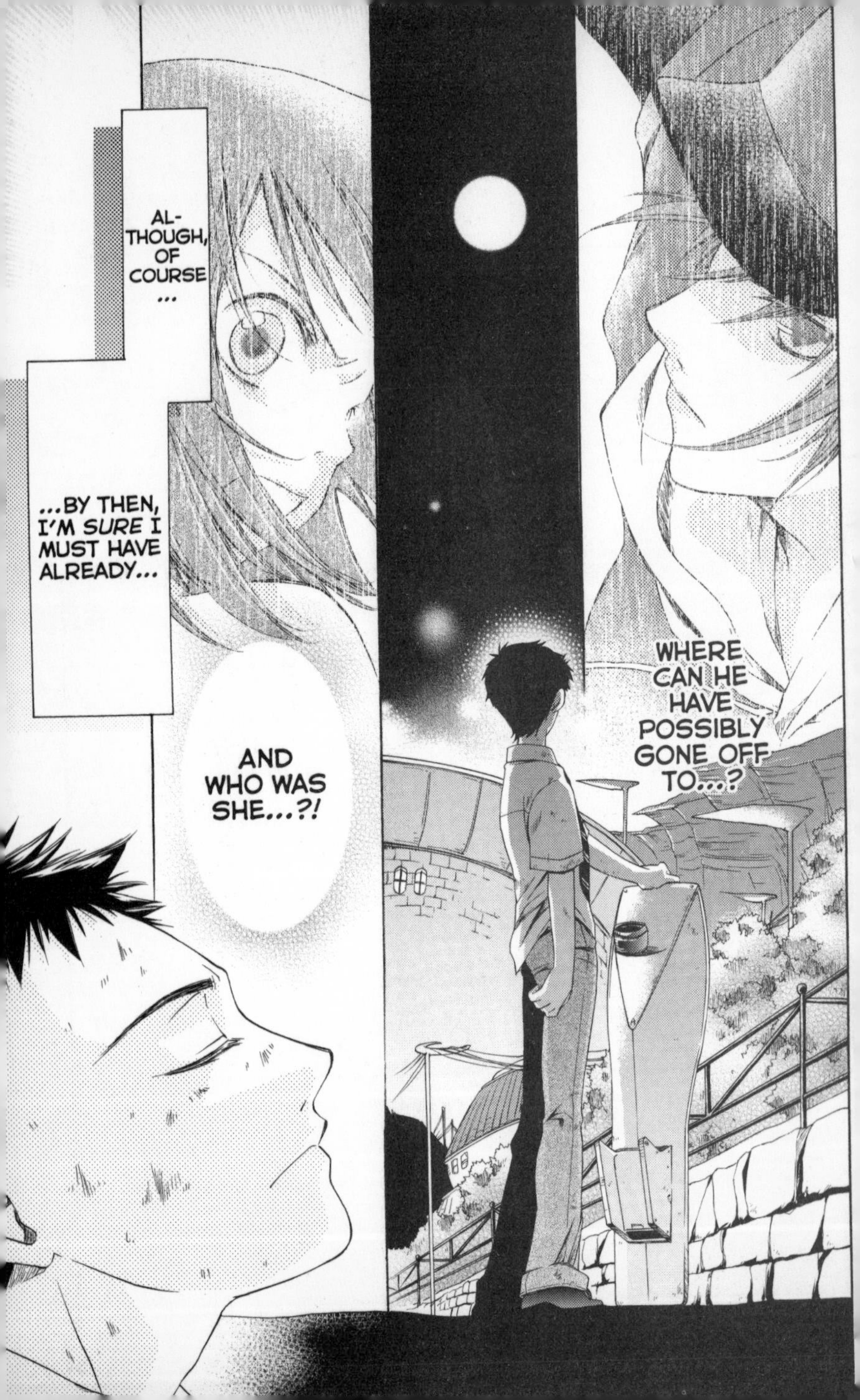
WHERE CAN HE HAVE POSSIBLY GONE OFF TO...?
AL-THOUGH, OF COURSE...
...BY THEN, I'M *SURE* I MUST HAVE ALREADY...
AND WHO WAS SHE...?!

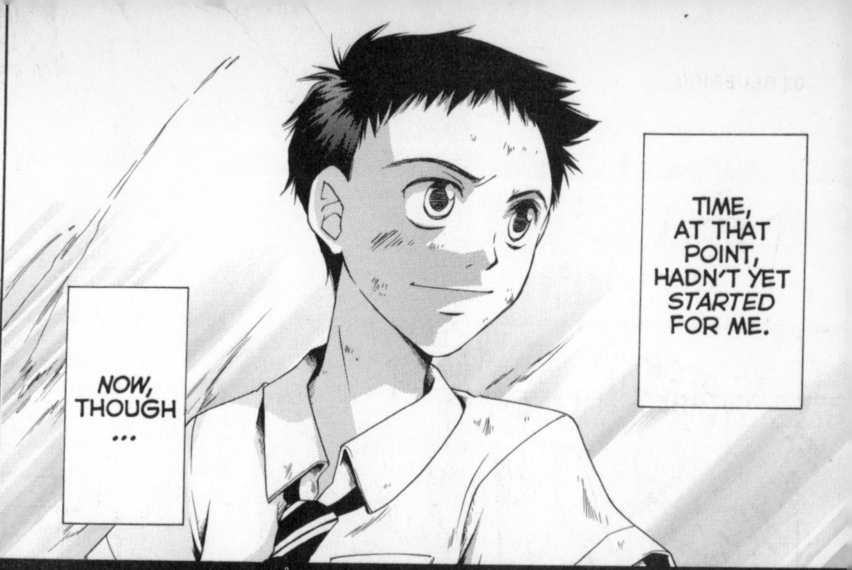
TIME, AT THAT POINT, HADN'T YET *STARTED* FOR ME.
NOW, THOUGH ...

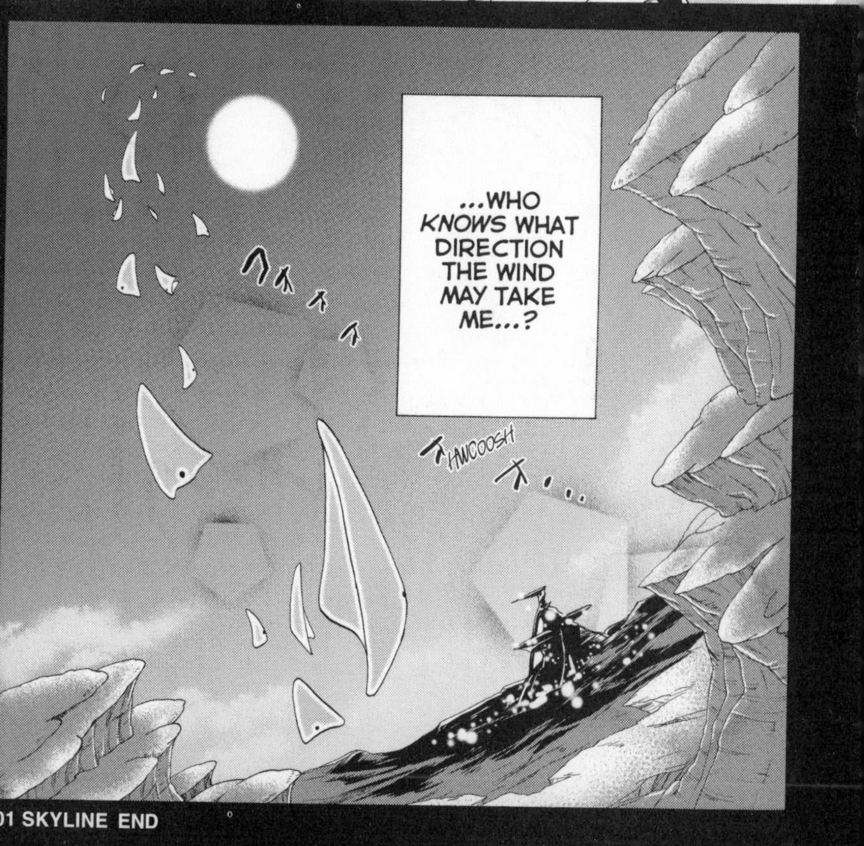
...WHO *KNOWS* WHAT DIRECTION THE WIND MAY TAKE ME...?
HWOOOSH

01 SKYLINE END

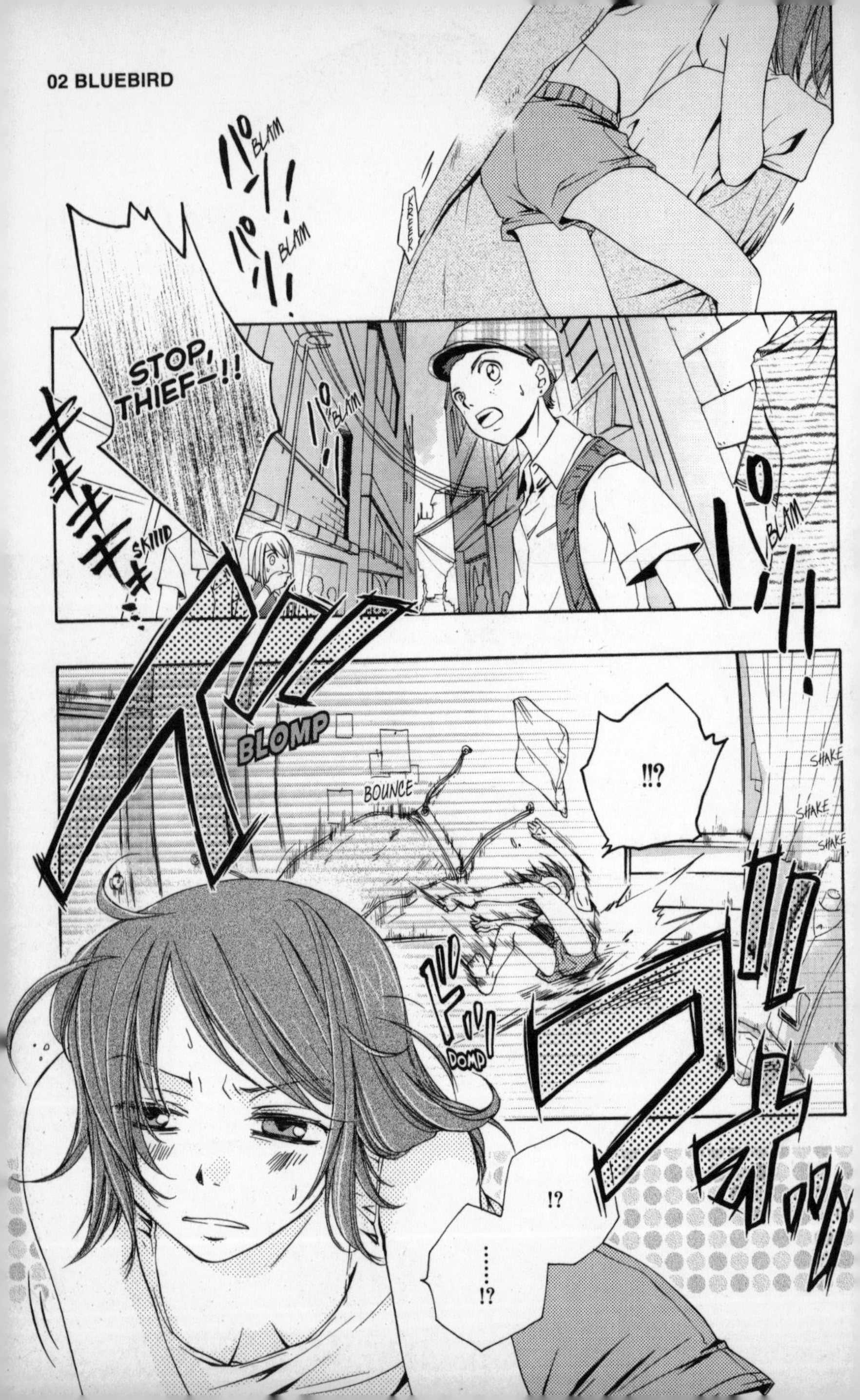
KREEK
BLAM
BLAM
BLAM
BLAM
STOP, THIEF—!!
SKIIID
SHAKE
SHAKE
SHAKE
!!?
BLOMP
BOUNCE
DOMP
!?
……!?

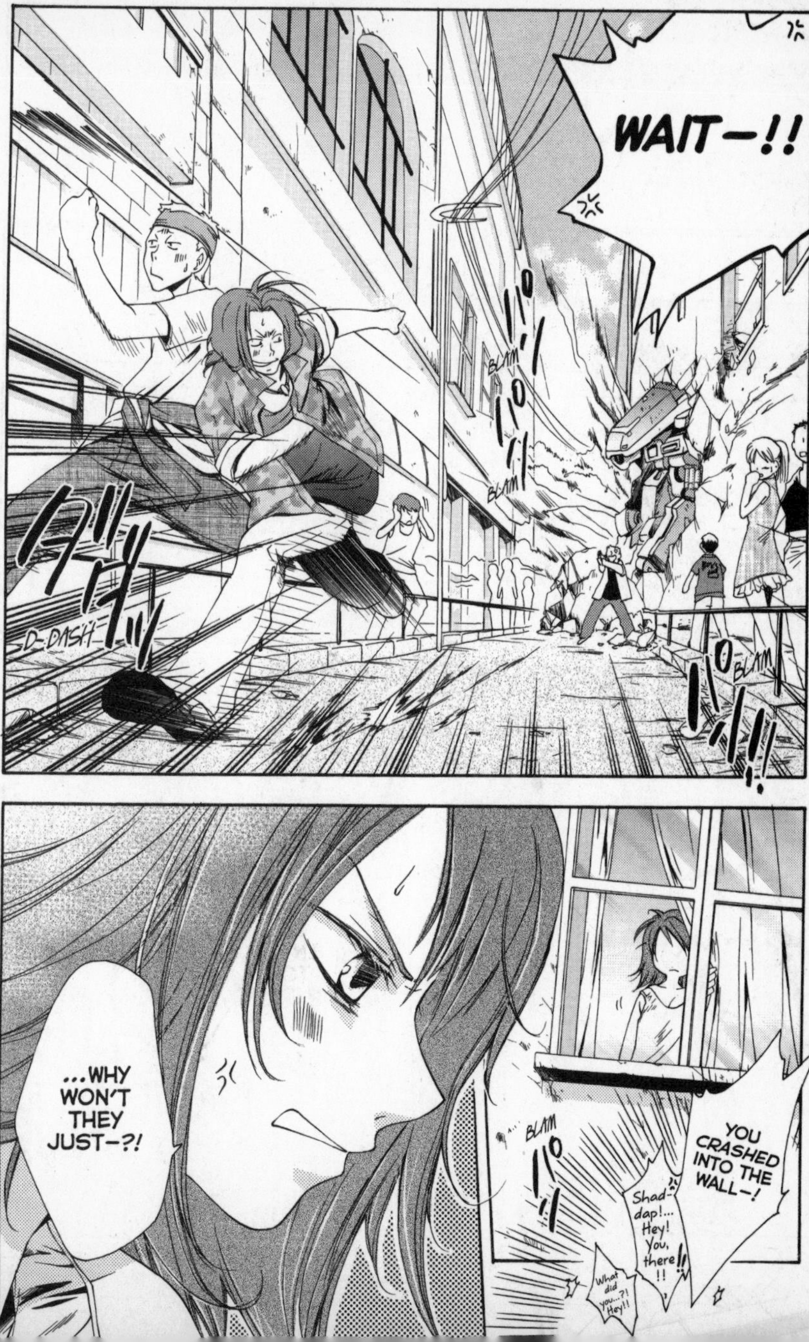

WAIT-!!
BLAM
BLAM
BLAM
D-DASH
YOU CRASHED INTO THE WALL-!
Shaddap!... Hey! You, there!!
What did you...?! Hey!!
BLAM
...WHY WON'T THEY JUST-?!

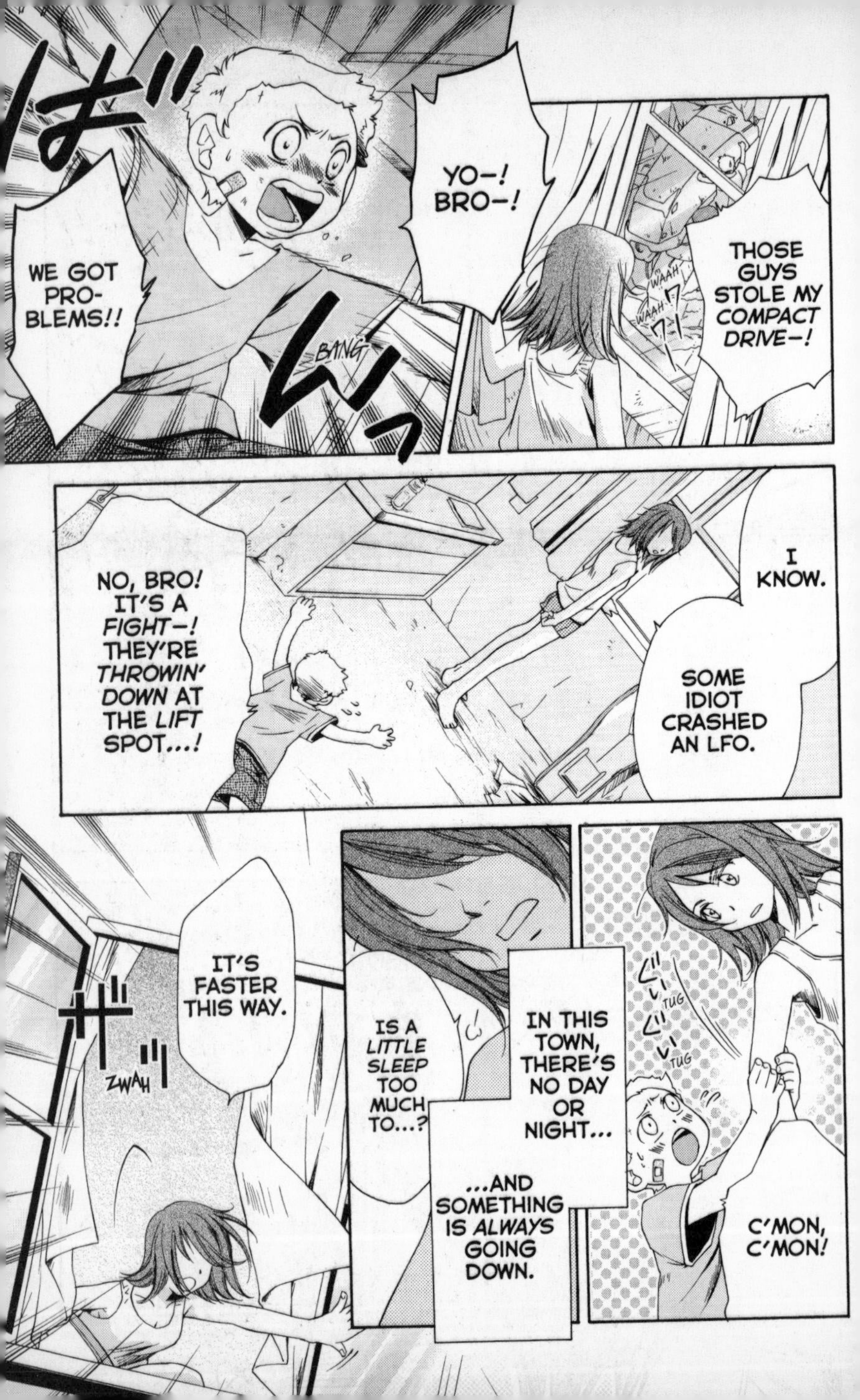
THOSE GUYS STOLE MY COMPACT DRIVE-!
WAAH
WAAH
YO-! BRO-!
WE GOT PRO- BLEMS!!
BANG
I KNOW.
SOME IDIOT CRASHED AN LFO.
NO, BRO! IT'S A FIGHT-! THEY'RE THROWIN' DOWN AT THE LIFT SPOT...!
TUG
TUG
C'MON, C'MON!
IN THIS TOWN, THERE'S NO DAY OR NIGHT...
IS A LITTLE SLEEP TOO MUCH TO...?
...AND SOMETHING IS ALWAYS GOING DOWN.
IT'S FASTER THIS WAY.
ZWAH

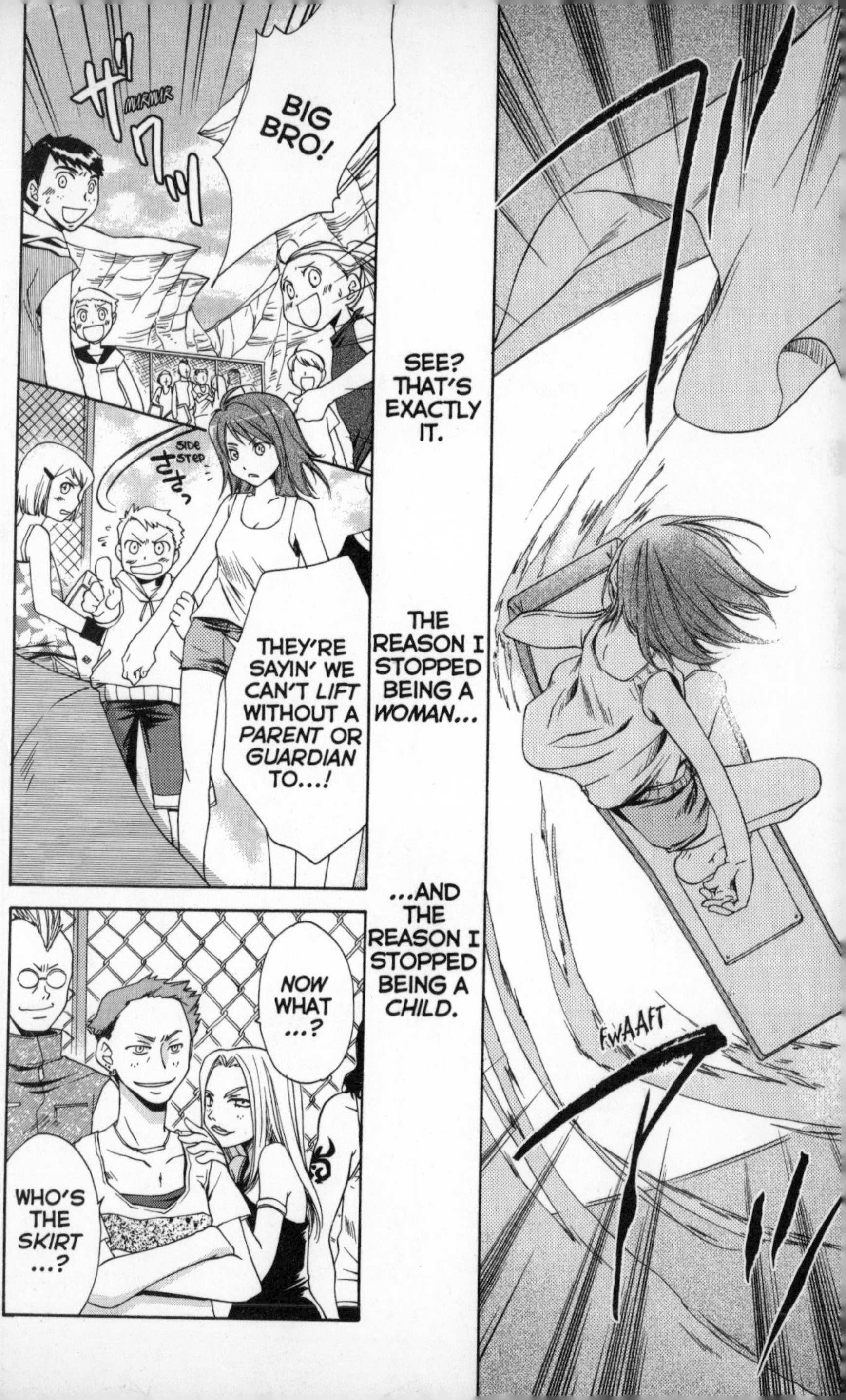
SEE? THAT'S EXACTLY IT.
THE REASON I STOPPED BEING A WOMAN...
...AND THE REASON I STOPPED BEING A CHILD.
FWAAFT
BIG BRO!
MURMUR
SIDE STEP
THEY'RE SAYIN' WE CAN'T LIFT WITHOUT A PARENT OR GUARDIAN TO...!
NOW WHAT ...?
WHO'S THE SKIRT ...?

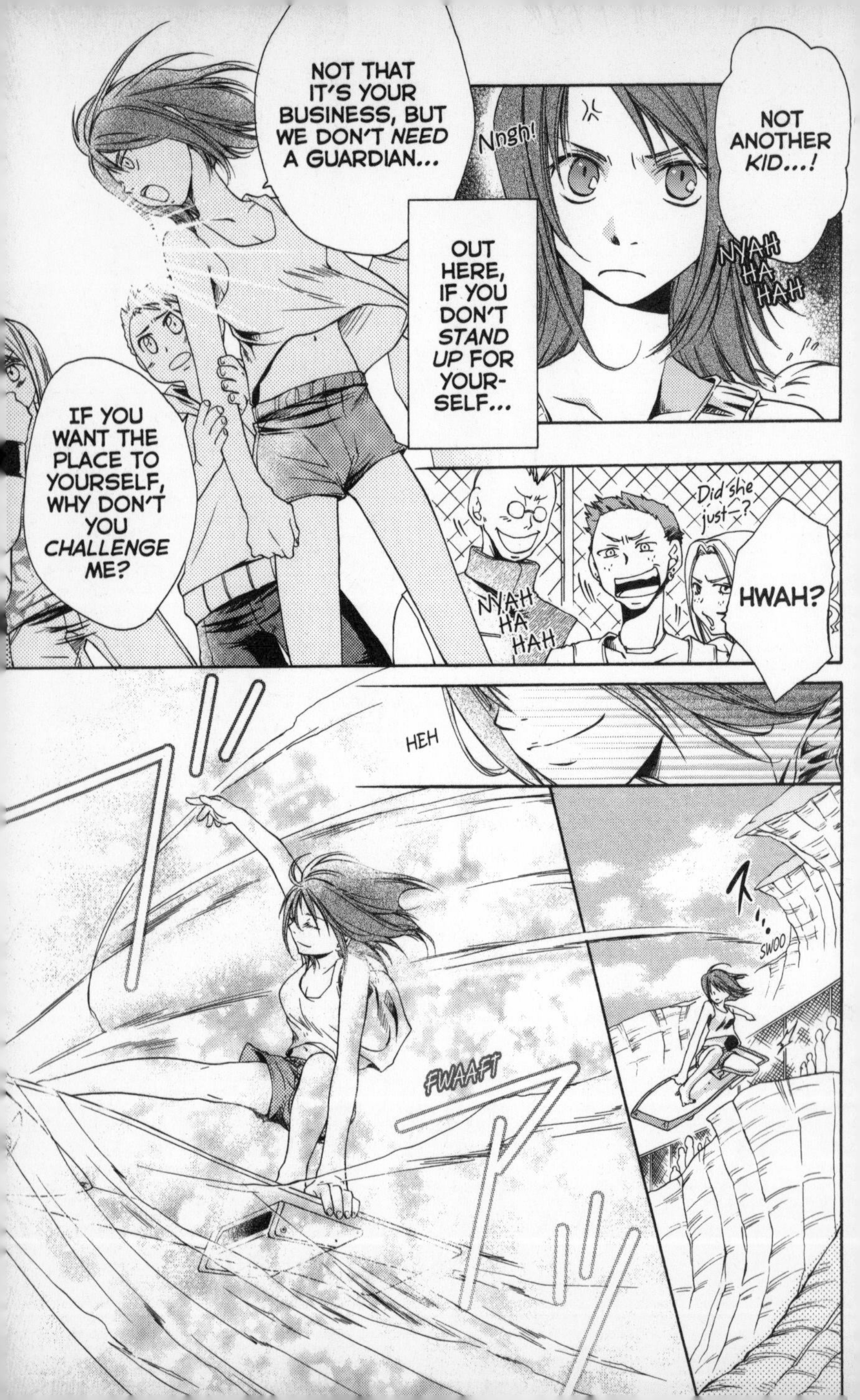

NOT ANOTHER KID...!
Nngh!
NYAH HA HAH
Did she just—?
HWAH?
NYAH HA HAH
NOT THAT IT'S YOUR BUSINESS, BUT WE DON'T NEED A GUARDIAN...
OUT HERE, IF YOU DON'T STAND UP FOR YOURSELF...
IF YOU WANT THE PLACE TO YOURSELF, WHY DON'T YOU CHALLENGE ME?
HEH
SWOO
FWAAFT

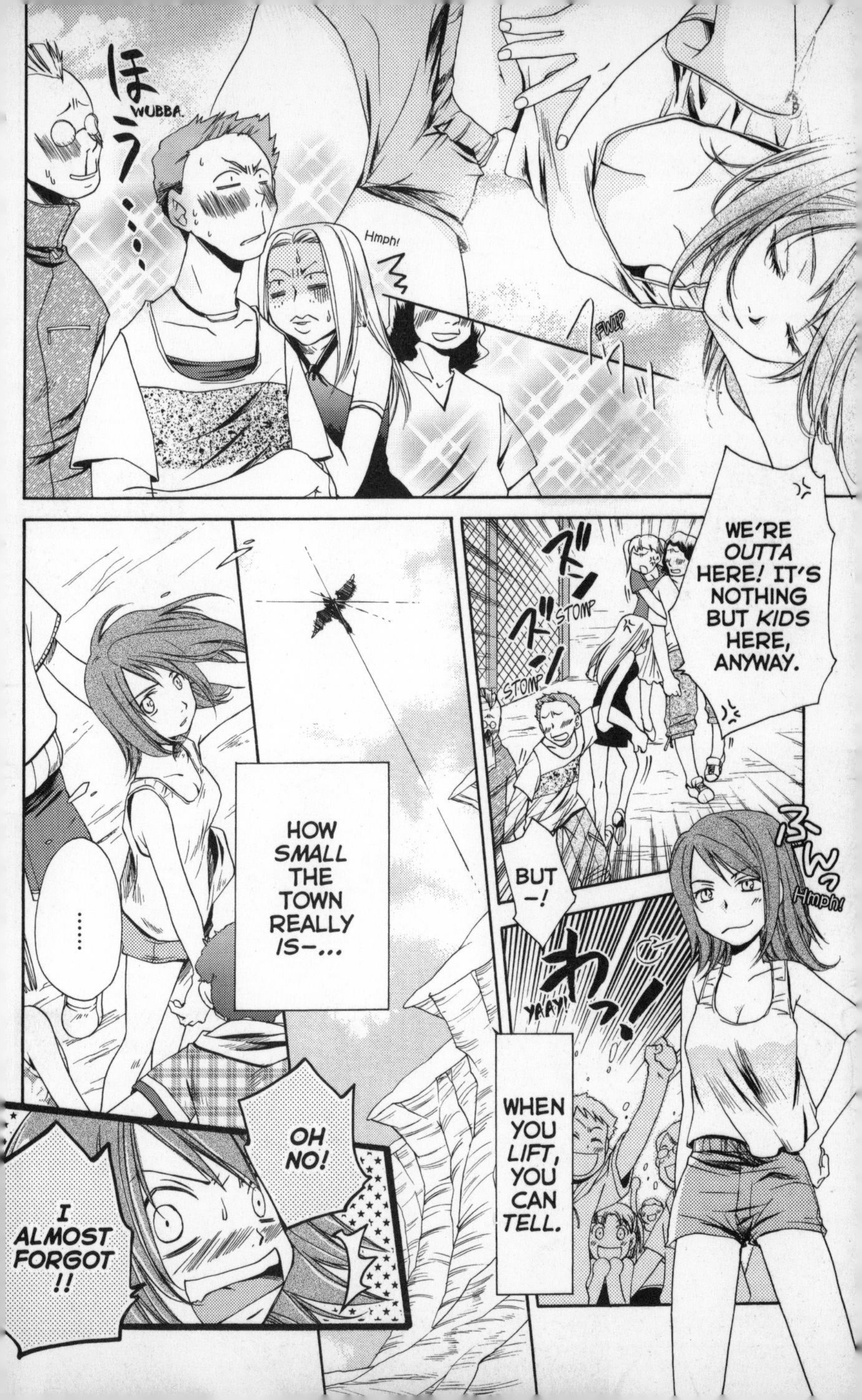
FWIP
Hmph!
ほう……
WUBBA.
WE'RE OUTTA HERE! IT'S NOTHING BUT KIDS HERE, ANYWAY.
ズン STOMP
ズン STOMP
BUT—!
ふーん
Hmph!
わっ!
YAAY!
WHEN YOU LIFT, YOU CAN TELL.
HOW SMALL THE TOWN REALLY IS—...
......
OH NO!
I ALMOST FORGOT!!

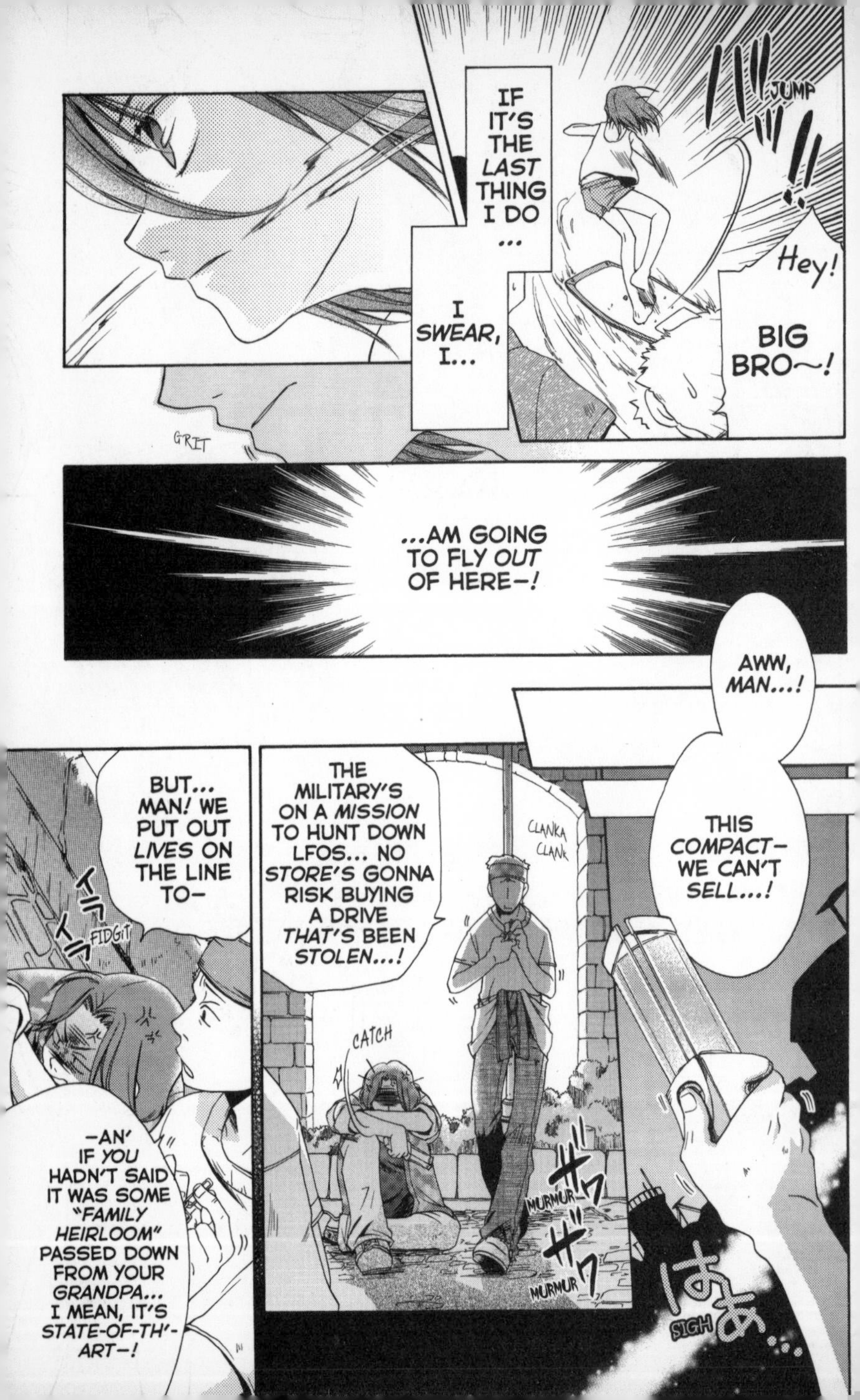
JUMP
Hey!
BIG BRO~!
IF IT'S THE LAST THING I DO...
I SWEAR, I...
GRIT
...AM GOING TO FLY OUT OF HERE—!
AWW, MAN...!
THIS COMPACT— WE CAN'T SELL...!
はぁ...
SIGH
THE MILITARY'S ON A MISSION TO HUNT DOWN LFOS... NO STORE'S GONNA RISK BUYING A DRIVE THAT'S BEEN STOLEN...!
CLANKA CLANK
CATCH
ザワ
MURMUR
ザワ
MURMUR
BUT... MAN! WE PUT OUT LIVES ON THE LINE TO—
イラ イラ
FIDGIT
—AN' IF YOU HADN'T SAID IT WAS SOME "FAMILY HEIRLOOM" PASSED DOWN FROM YOUR GRANDPA... I MEAN, IT'S STATE-OF-TH'-ART—!

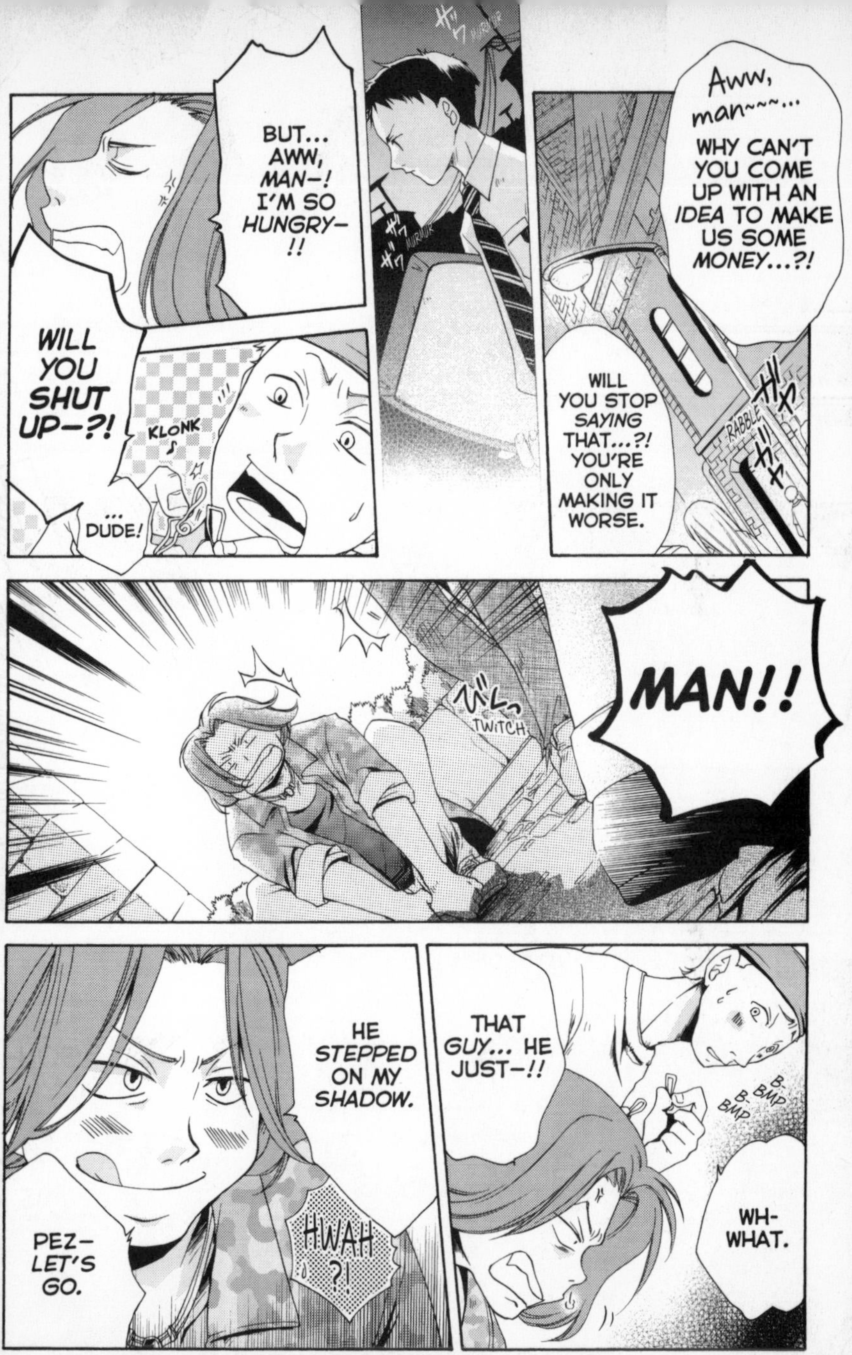
Aww, man~~~... WHY CAN'T YOU COME UP WITH AN IDEA TO MAKE US SOME MONEY...?!
WILL YOU STOP SAYING THAT...?! YOU'RE ONLY MAKING IT WORSE.
RABBLE
MURMUR
MURMUR
BUT... AWW, MAN-! I'M SO HUNGRY-!!
WILL YOU SHUT UP-?!
KLONK
...DUDE!
MAN!!
TWITCH
THAT GUY... HE JUST-!!
B-BMP B-BMP
WH-WHAT.
HE STEPPED ON MY SHADOW.
HWAH ?!
PEZ-LET'S GO.

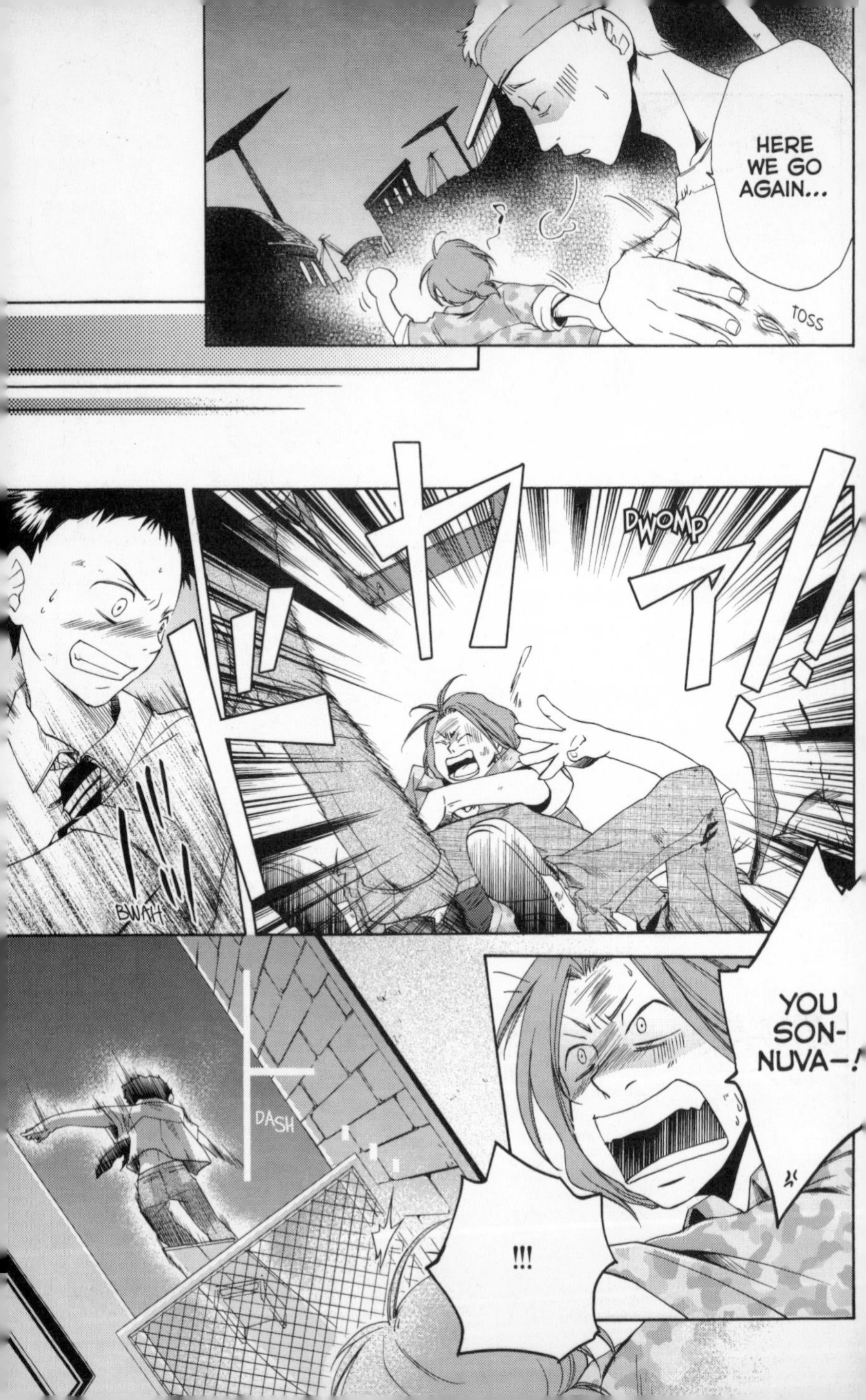

HERE WE GO AGAIN...
TOSS
DWOMP
BWAH
YOU SON-NUVA—!
!!!
DASH

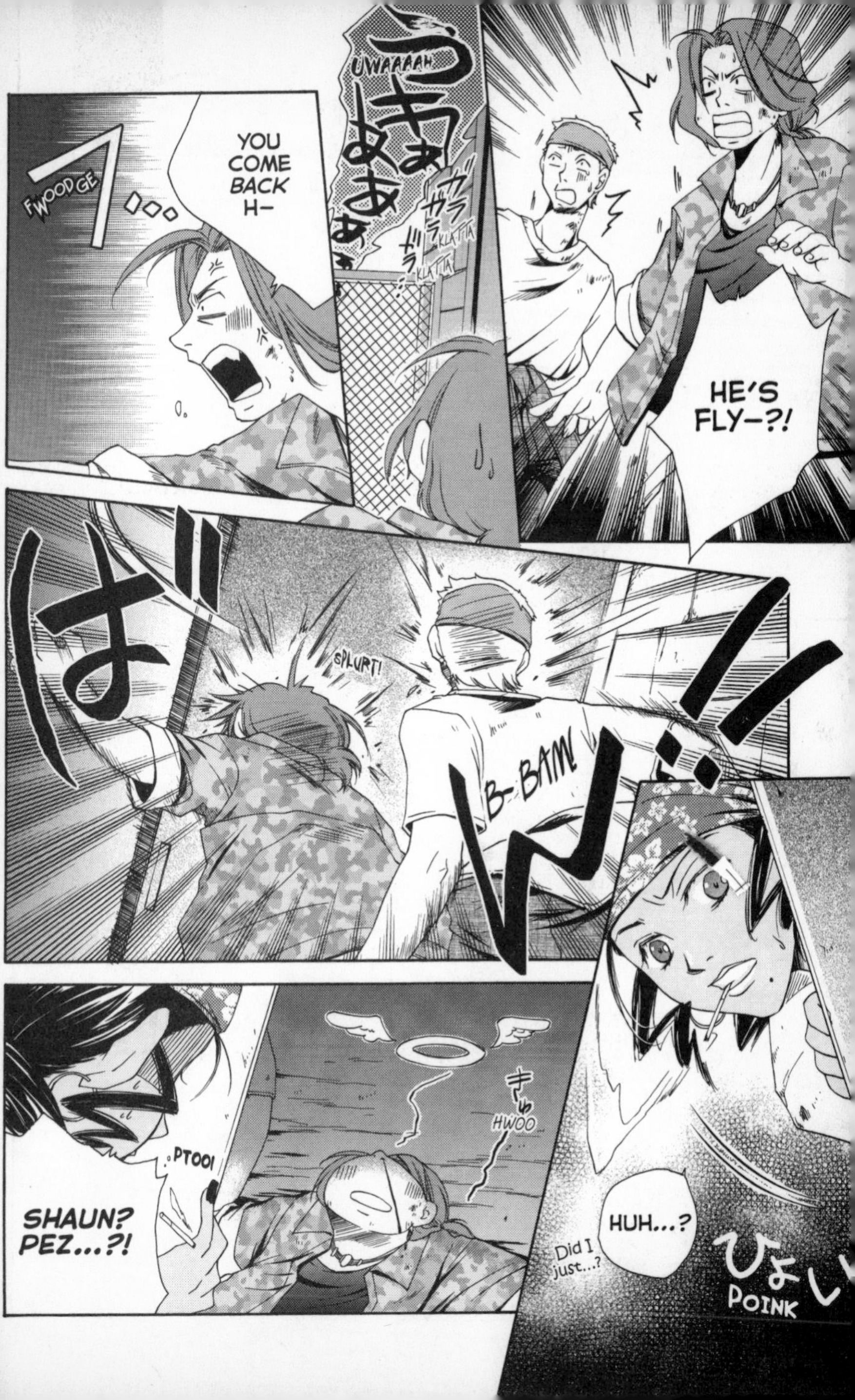
UWAAAAH
KLATTA
KLATTA
HE'S FLY-?!
FWOODGE
YOU COME BACK H-
B-BAM!
SPLURT!
HUH...?
Did I just...?
POINK
HWOO
PTOOI
SHAUN? PEZ...?!

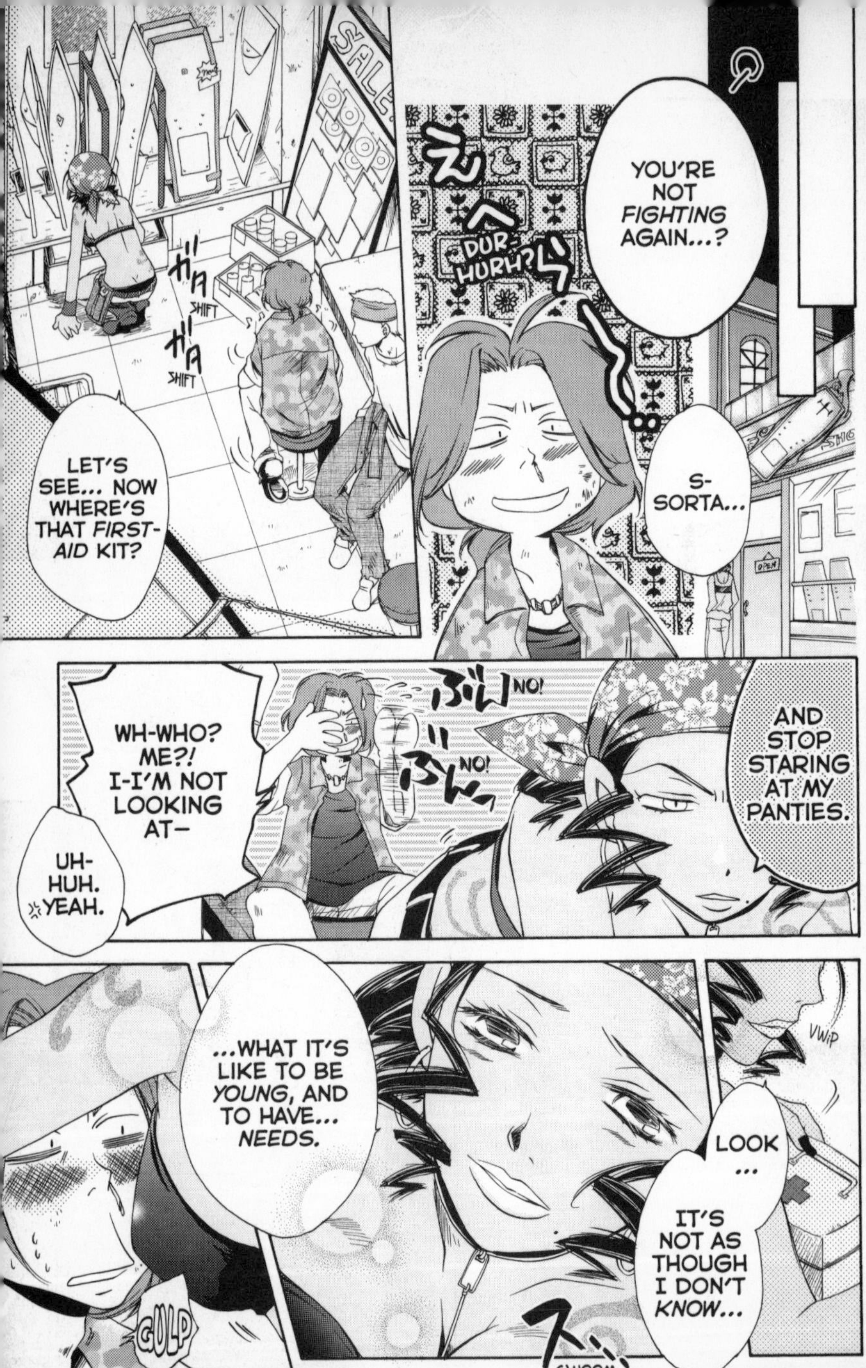
YOU'RE NOT FIGHTING AGAIN...?
DUR-HURH?
S-SORTA...
SHIFT
SHIFT
LET'S SEE... NOW WHERE'S THAT FIRST-AID KIT?
AND STOP STARING AT MY PANTIES.
NO!
NO!
WH-WHO? ME?! I-I'M NOT LOOKING AT—
UH-HUH. YEAH.
VWIP
LOOK...
IT'S NOT AS THOUGH I DON'T KNOW...
...WHAT IT'S LIKE TO BE YOUNG, AND TO HAVE... NEEDS.
SWOOM
GULP

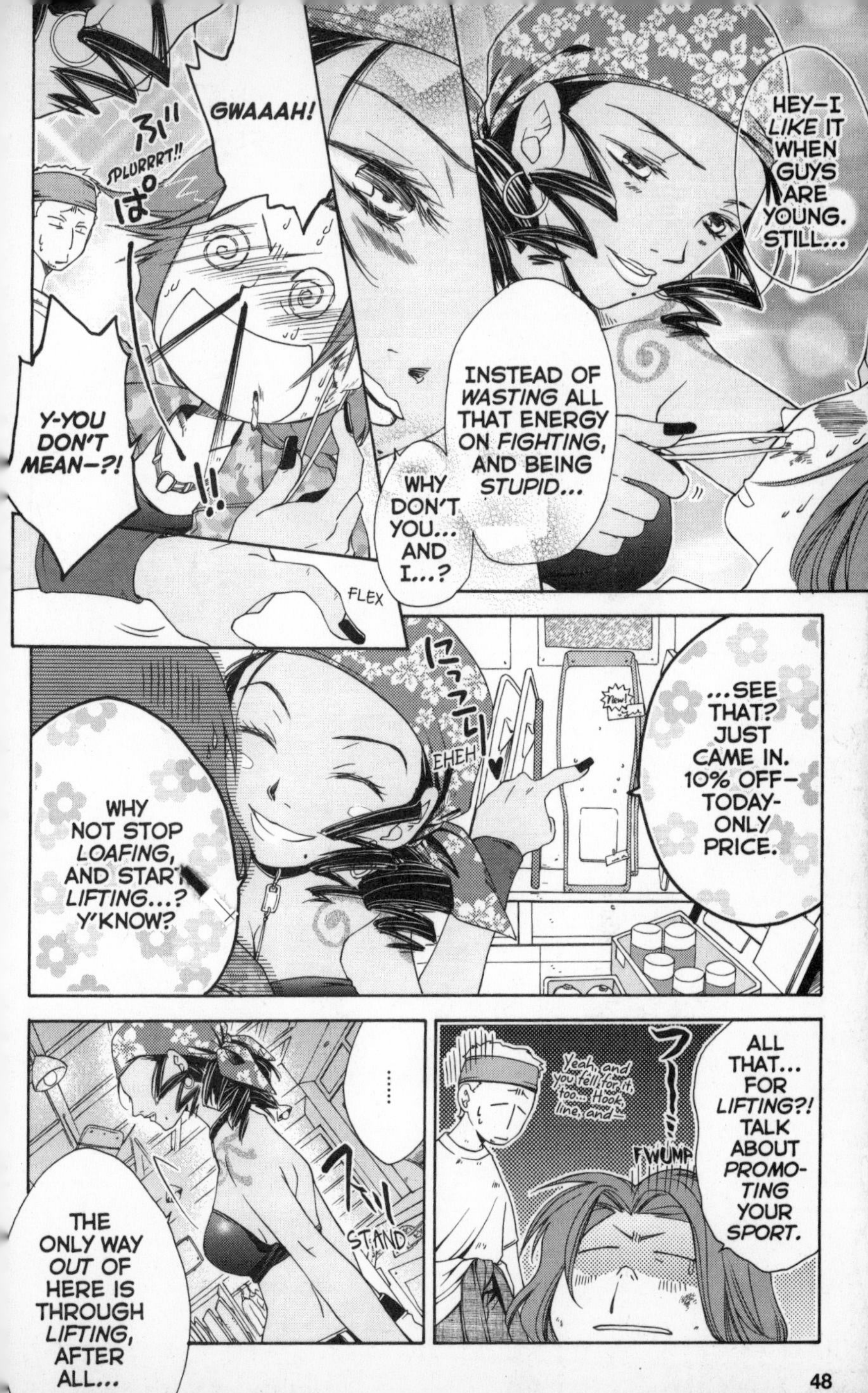
HEY—I LIKE IT WHEN GUYS ARE YOUNG. STILL...
INSTEAD OF WASTING ALL THAT ENERGY ON FIGHTING, AND BEING STUPID...
WHY DON'T YOU... AND I...?
GWAAAH!
ぶ
SPLURRRT!!
ぱ
Y-YOU DON'T MEAN—?!
FLEX
...SEE THAT? JUST CAME IN. 10% OFF—TODAY-ONLY PRICE.
New!
EHEH
WHY NOT STOP LOAFING, AND START LIFTING...? Y'KNOW?
ALL THAT... FOR LIFTING?! TALK ABOUT PROMOTING YOUR SPORT.
Yeah, and you fell for it, too... Hook, line, and—
FWUMP
......
STAND
THE ONLY WAY OUT OF HERE IS THROUGH LIFTING, AFTER ALL...

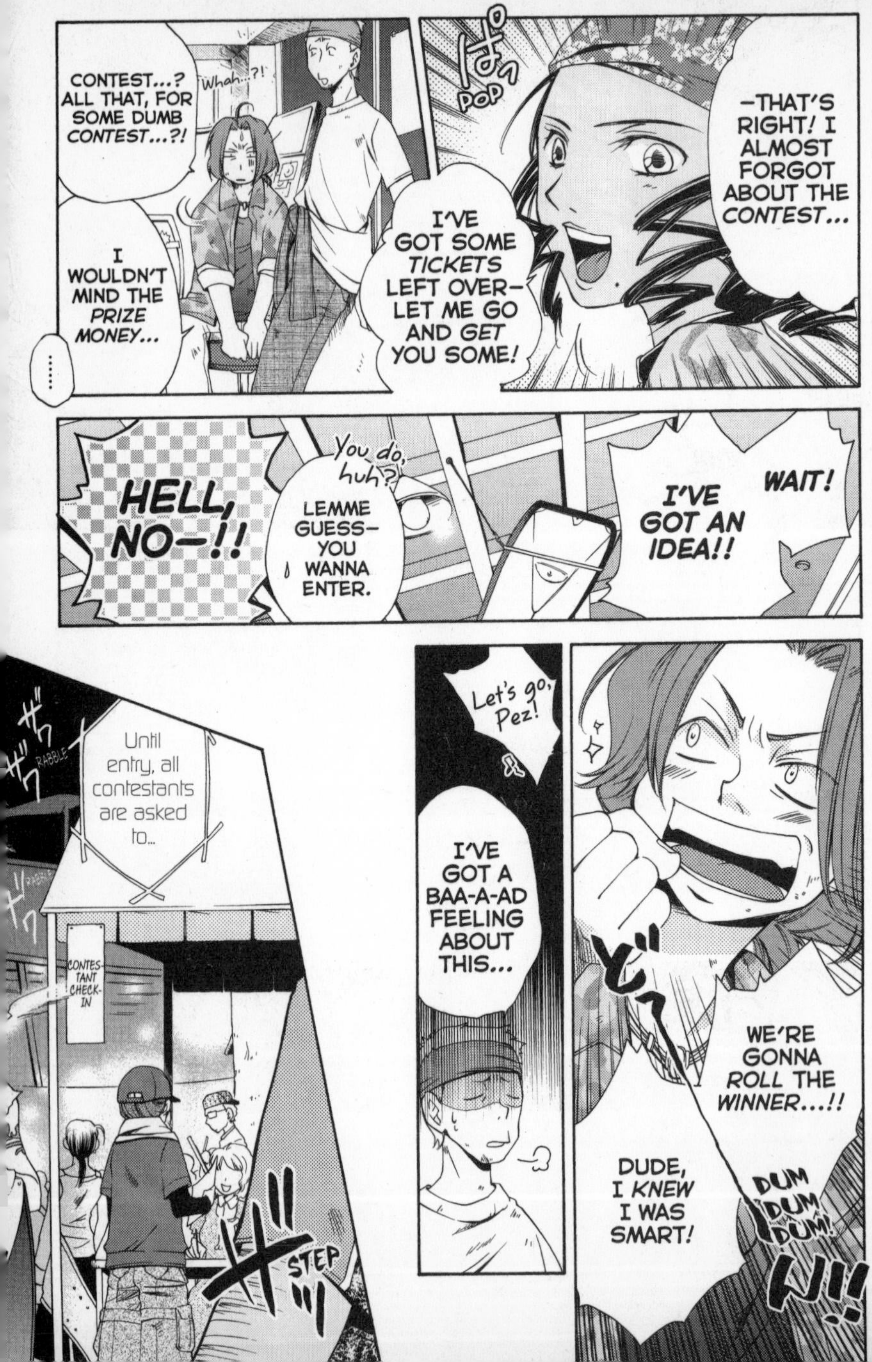
POP
–THAT'S RIGHT! I ALMOST FORGOT ABOUT THE CONTEST...
I'VE GOT SOME TICKETS LEFT OVER– LET ME GO AND GET YOU SOME!
Whah...?!
CONTEST...? ALL THAT, FOR SOME DUMB CONTEST...?!
I WOULDN'T MIND THE PRIZE MONEY...
......
WAIT!
I'VE GOT AN IDEA!!
You do, huh?
LEMME GUESS– YOU WANNA ENTER.
HELL, NO–!!
WE'RE GONNA ROLL THE WINNER...!!
DUDE, I KNEW I WAS SMART!
DUM DUM DUM!
Let's go, Pez!
I'VE GOT A BAA-A-AD FEELING ABOUT THIS...
RABBLE
Until entry, all contestants are asked to...
CONTESTANT CHECK-IN
STEP

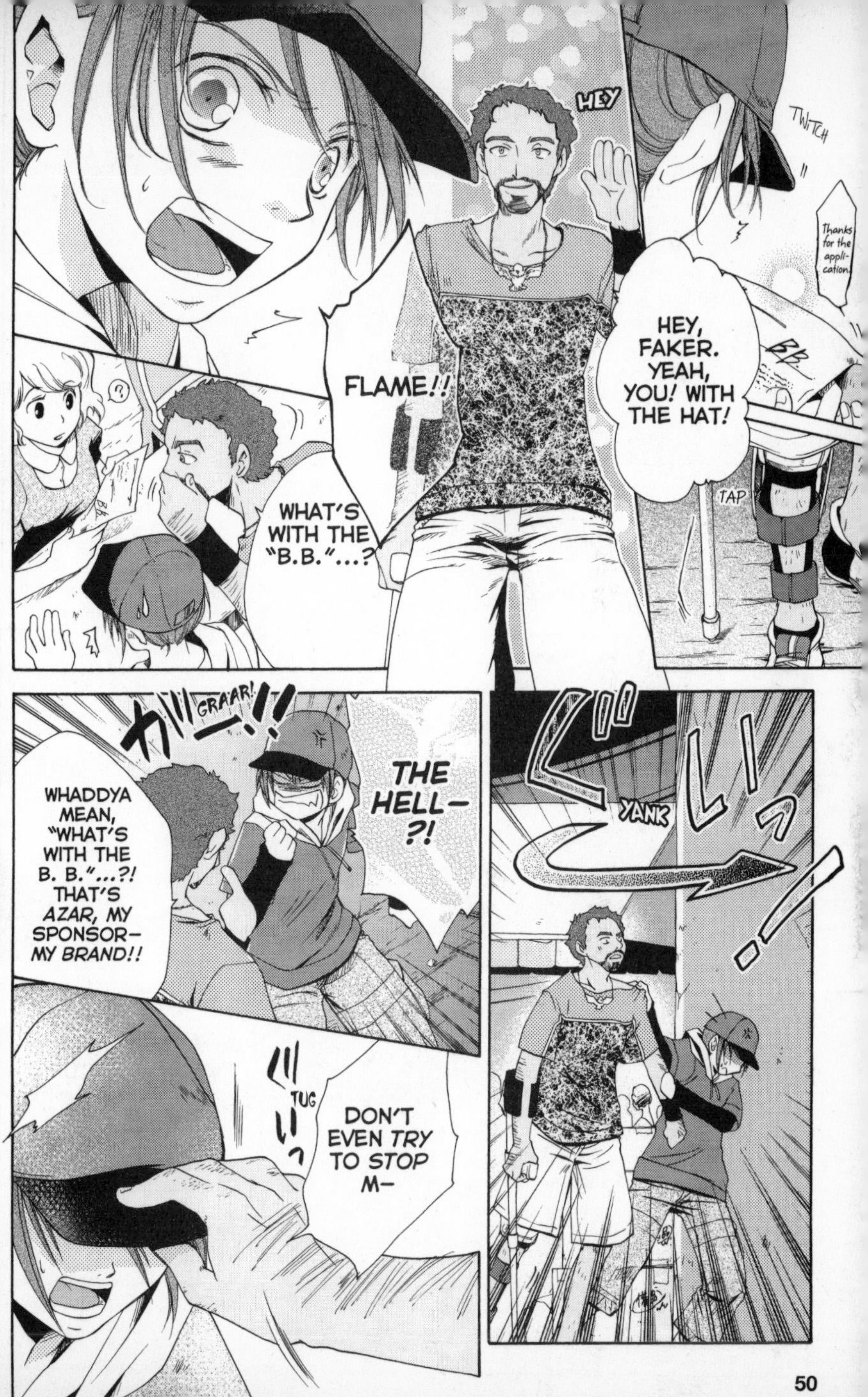
TWITCH
Thanks for the application.
HEY, FAKER. YEAH, YOU! WITH THE HAT!
B.B.
TAP
HEY
FLAME!!
WHAT'S WITH THE "B.B."...?
YANK
GRAAR!
THE HELL-?!
WHADDYA MEAN, "WHAT'S WITH THE B. B."...?! THAT'S *AZAR*, MY SPONSOR-MY *BRAND*!!
TUG
DON'T EVEN *TRY* TO STOP M-

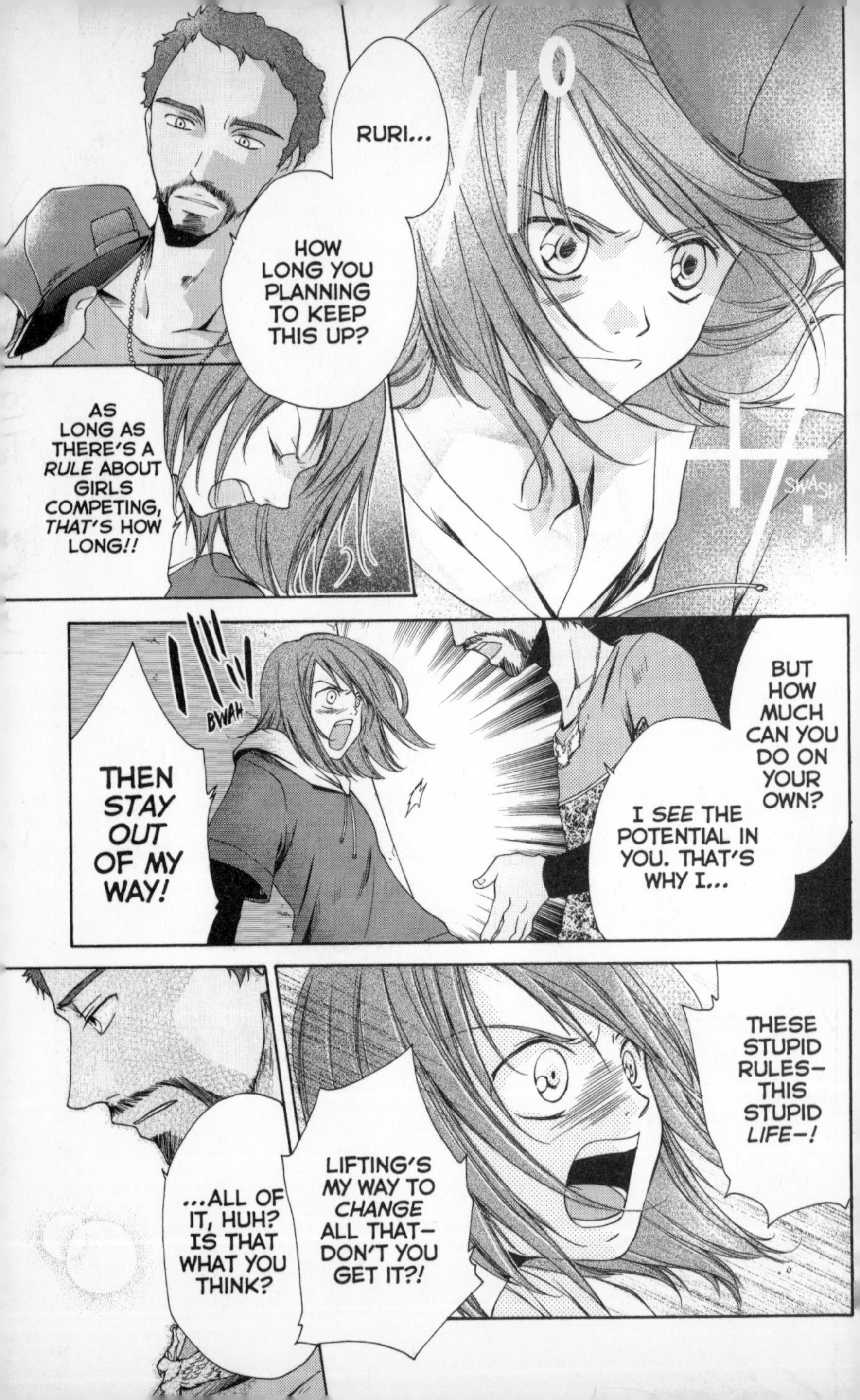
SWASH
RURI...
HOW LONG YOU PLANNING TO KEEP THIS UP?
AS LONG AS THERE'S A *RULE* ABOUT GIRLS COMPETING, *THAT'S* HOW LONG!!
BUT HOW MUCH CAN YOU DO ON YOUR OWN?
I *SEE* THE POTENTIAL IN YOU. THAT'S WHY I...
BWAH
THEN *STAY OUT* OF MY WAY!
THESE STUPID RULES—THIS STUPID *LIFE*—!
LIFTING'S MY WAY TO *CHANGE* ALL THAT—DON'T YOU GET IT?!
...ALL OF IT, HUH? IS THAT WHAT YOU THINK?

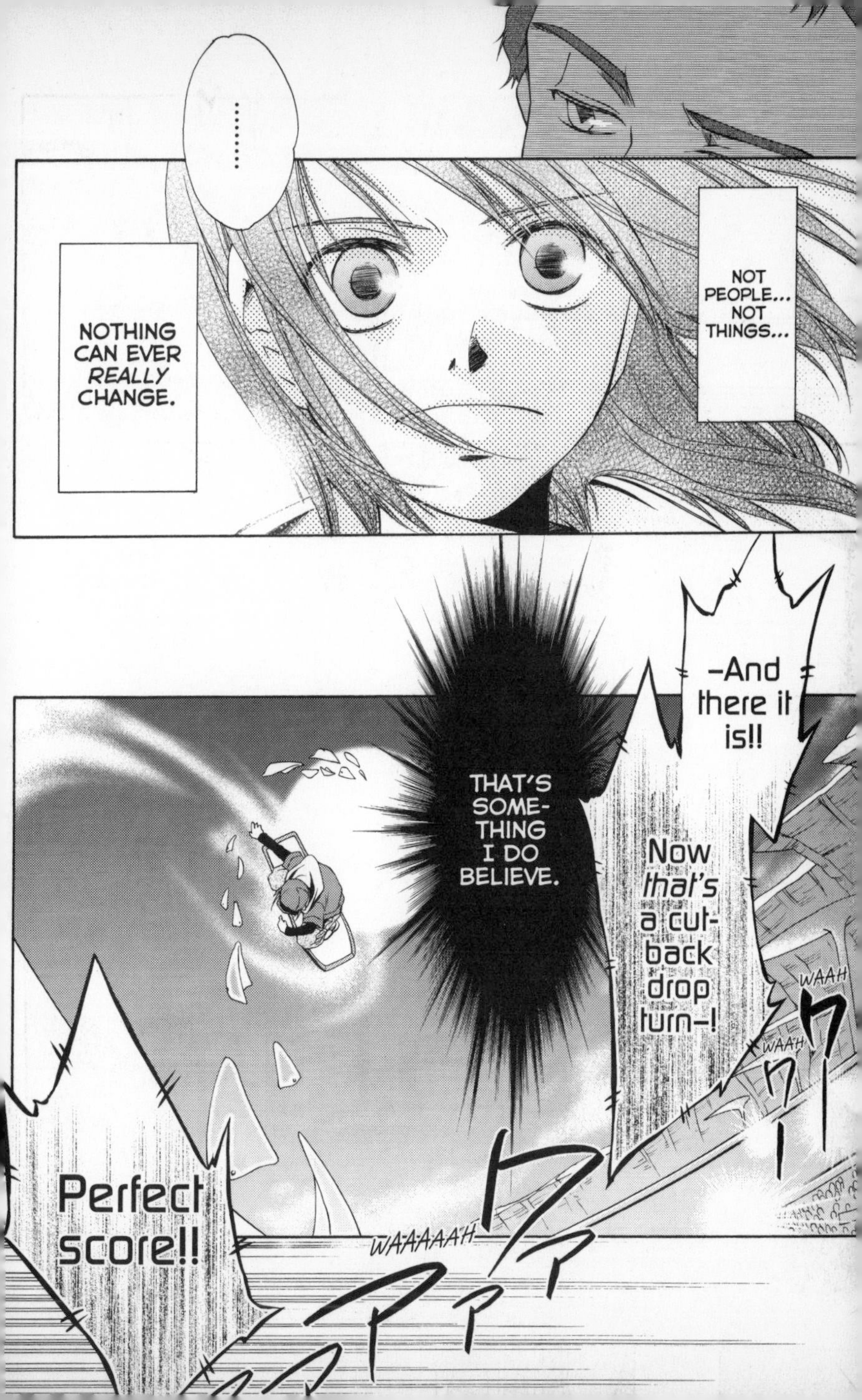
......
NOT PEOPLE... NOT THINGS...
NOTHING CAN EVER *REALLY* CHANGE.
THAT'S SOME-THING I DO BELIEVE.
-And there it is!!
Now *that's* a cut-back drop turn-!
WAAH
WAAH
Perfect score!!
WAAAAAAH

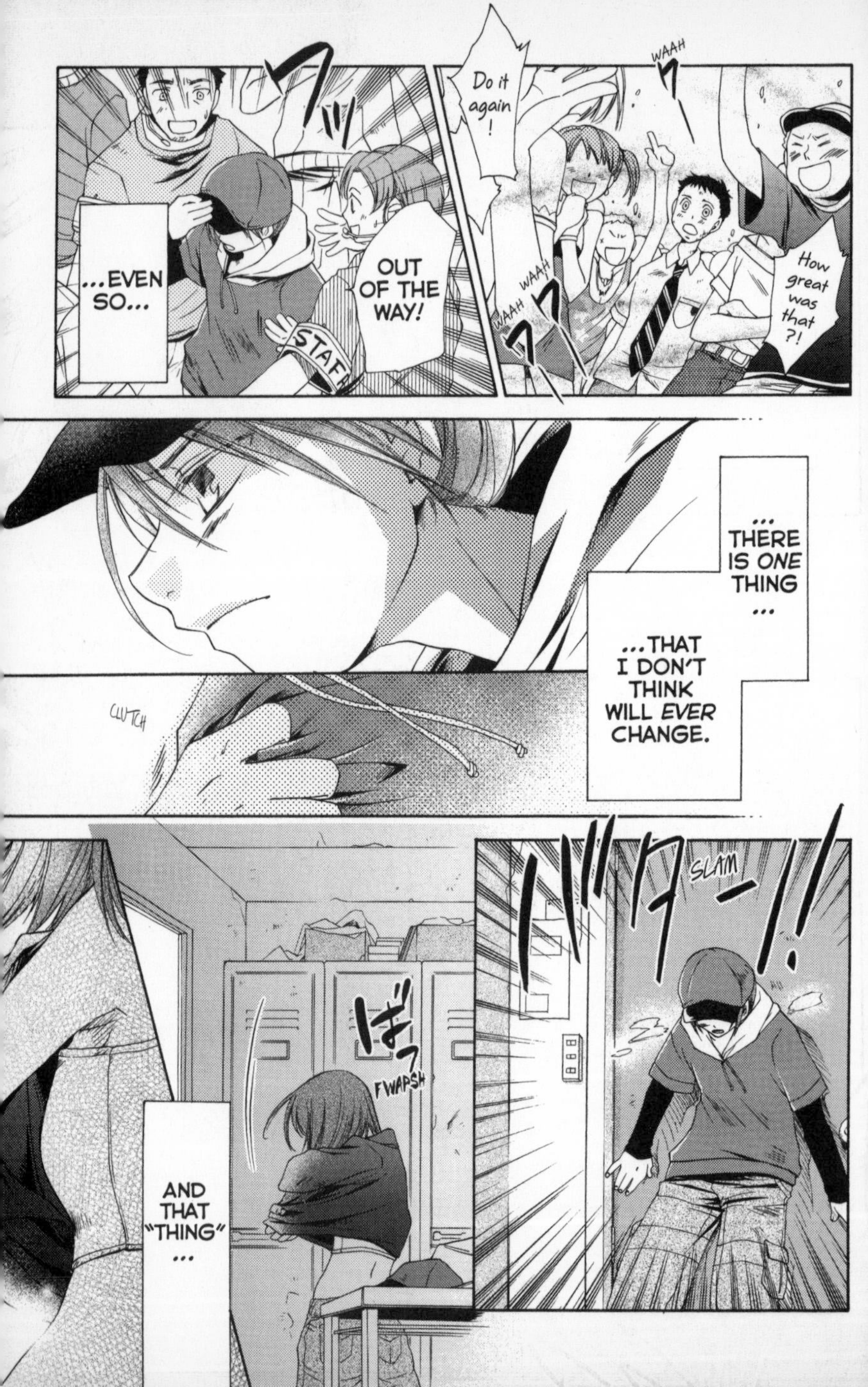
Do it again!
WAAH
How great was that?!
WAAH
WAAH
OUT OF THE WAY!
STAFF
...EVEN SO...
...THERE IS ONE THING...
...THAT I DON'T THINK WILL EVER CHANGE.
CLUTCH
SLAM
FWAPSH
AND THAT "THING"...

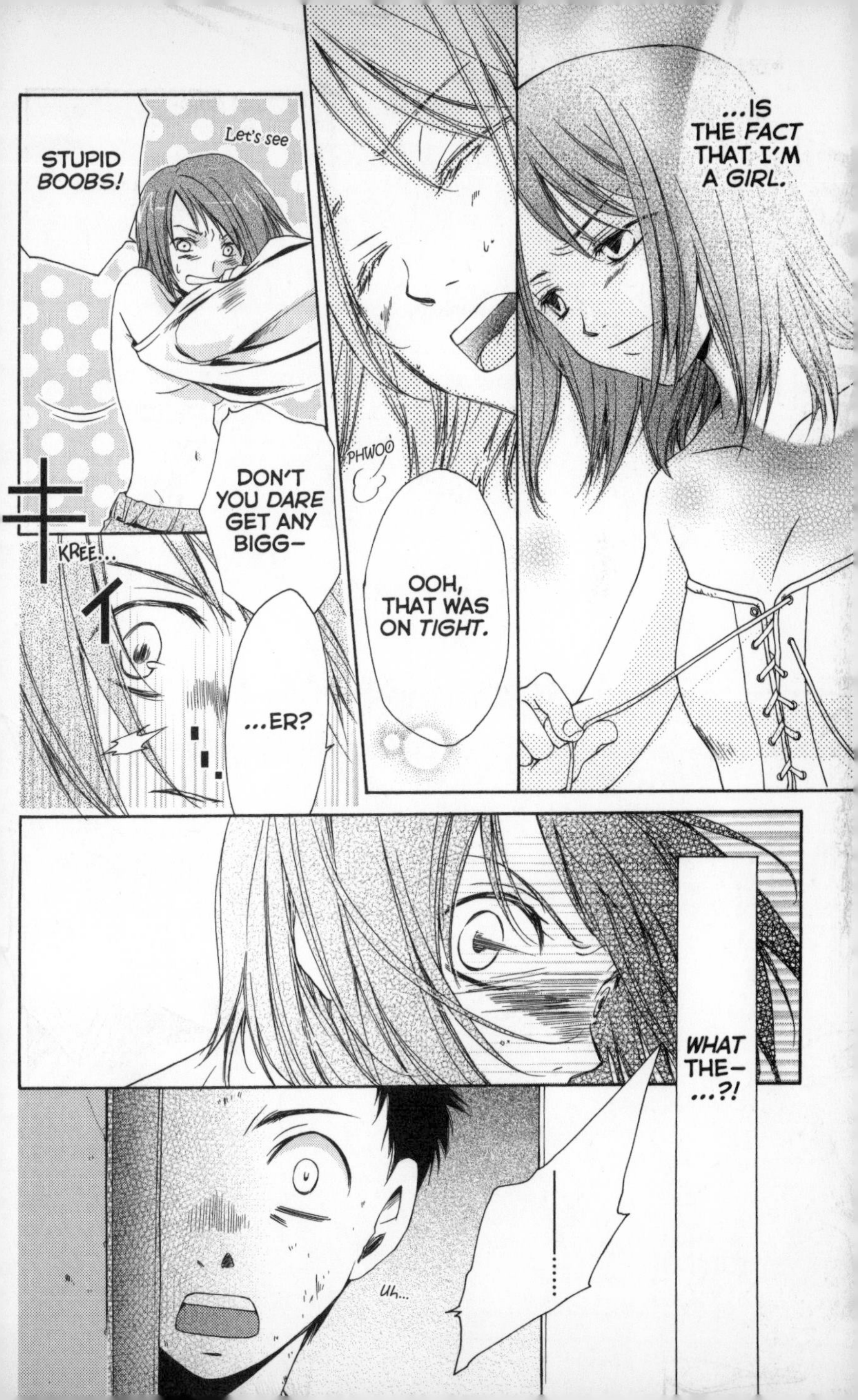
...IS THE FACT THAT I'M A GIRL.
PHWOO
OOH, THAT WAS ON TIGHT.
Let's see
STUPID BOOBS!
DON'T YOU DARE GET ANY BIGG—
KREE...
...ER?
WHAT THE— ...?!
......
uh...

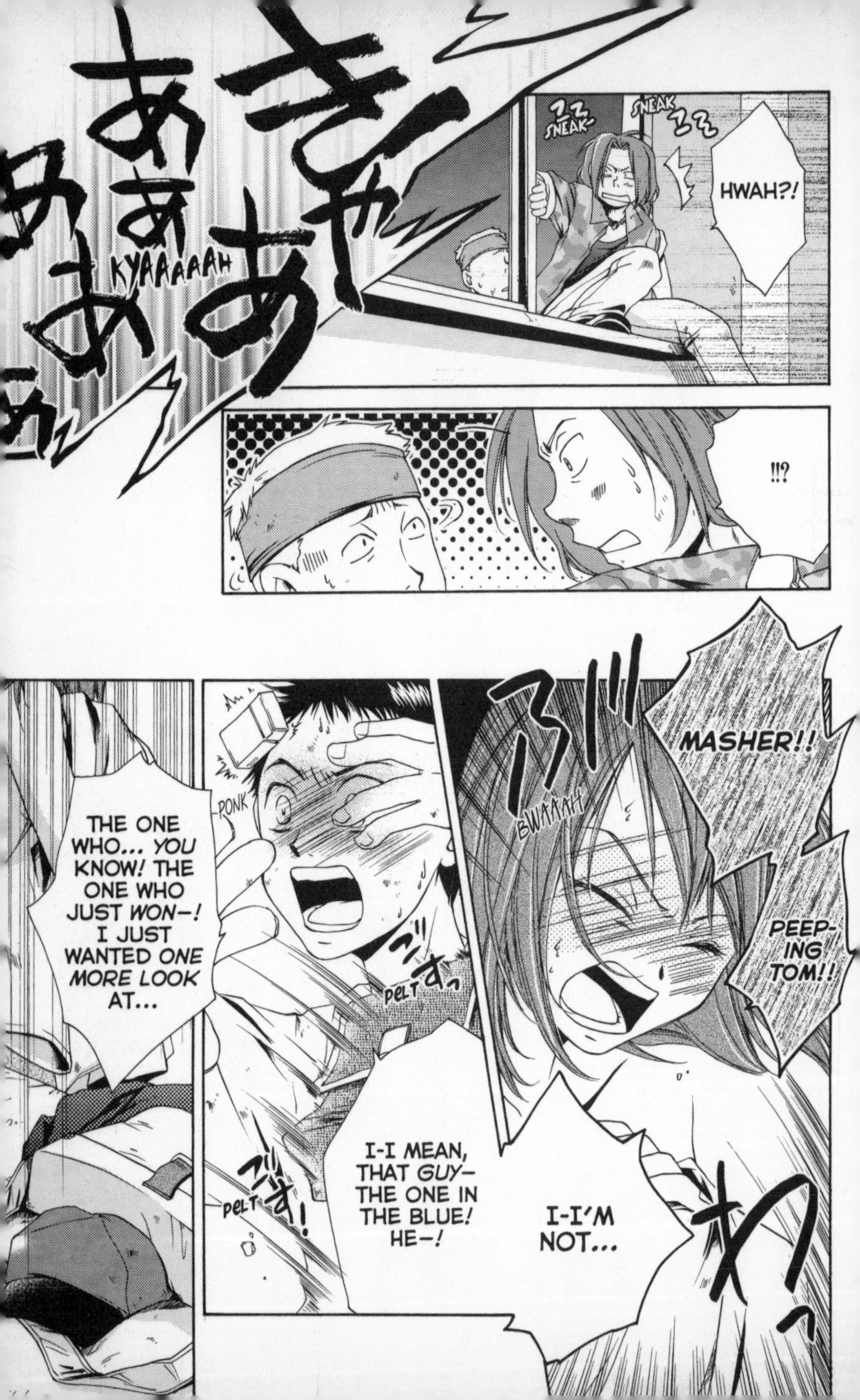
SNEAK
SNEAK
HWAH?!
KYAAAAAH
!!?
MASHER!!
BWAAAAH
PEEP-ING TOM!!
I-I'M NOT...
PONK
PELT
I-I MEAN, THAT GUY– THE ONE IN THE BLUE! HE–!
PELT
THE ONE WHO... YOU KNOW! THE ONE WHO JUST WON–! I JUST WANTED ONE MORE LOOK AT...

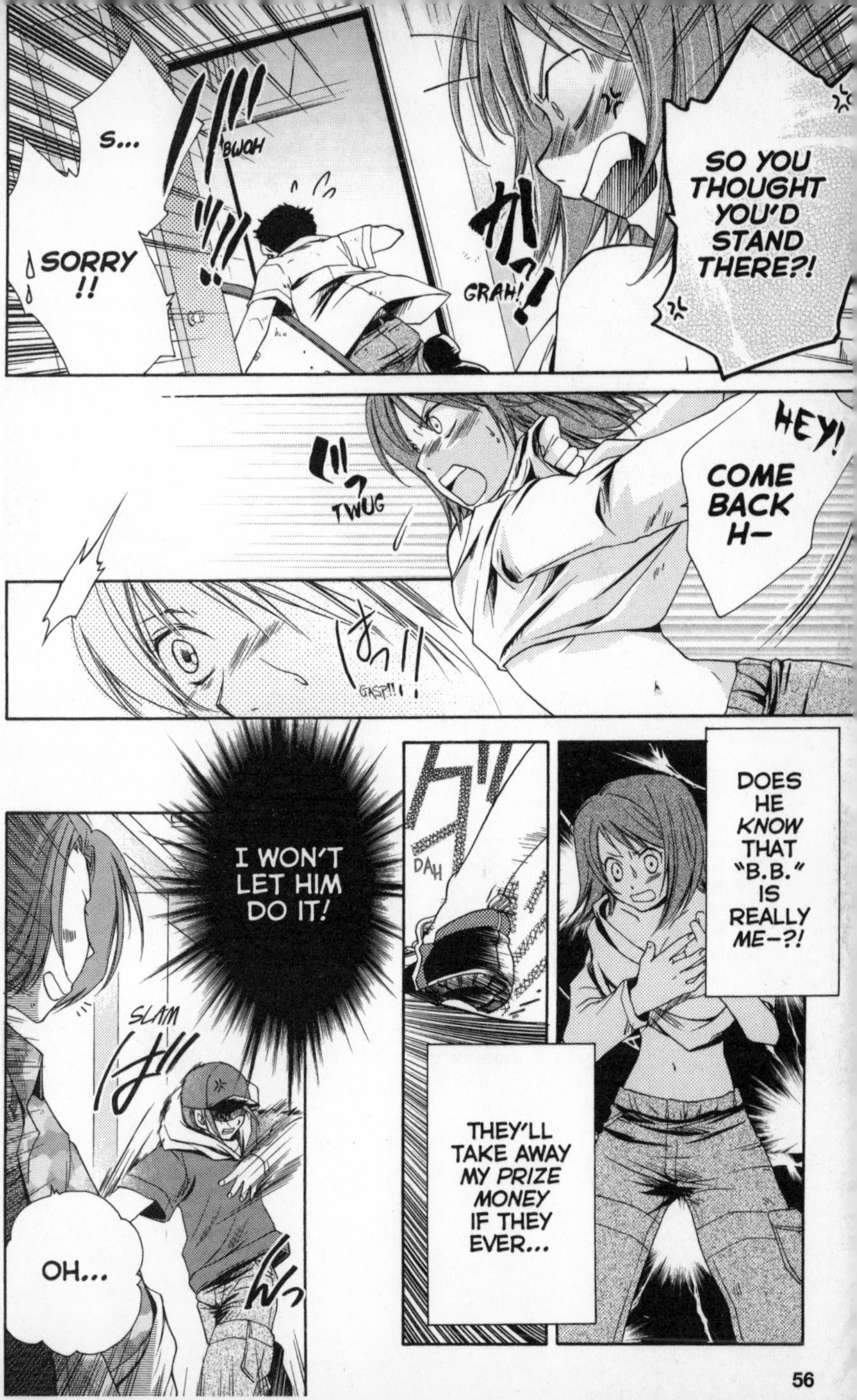
SO YOU THOUGHT YOU'D STAND THERE?!
GRAH!
BWAH
S...
SORRY !!
HEY!
COME BACK H–
TWUG
GASP!!!
DOES HE KNOW THAT "B.B." IS REALLY ME–?!
THEY'LL TAKE AWAY MY PRIZE MONEY IF THEY EVER...
DAH
I WON'T LET HIM DO IT!
SLAM
OH...

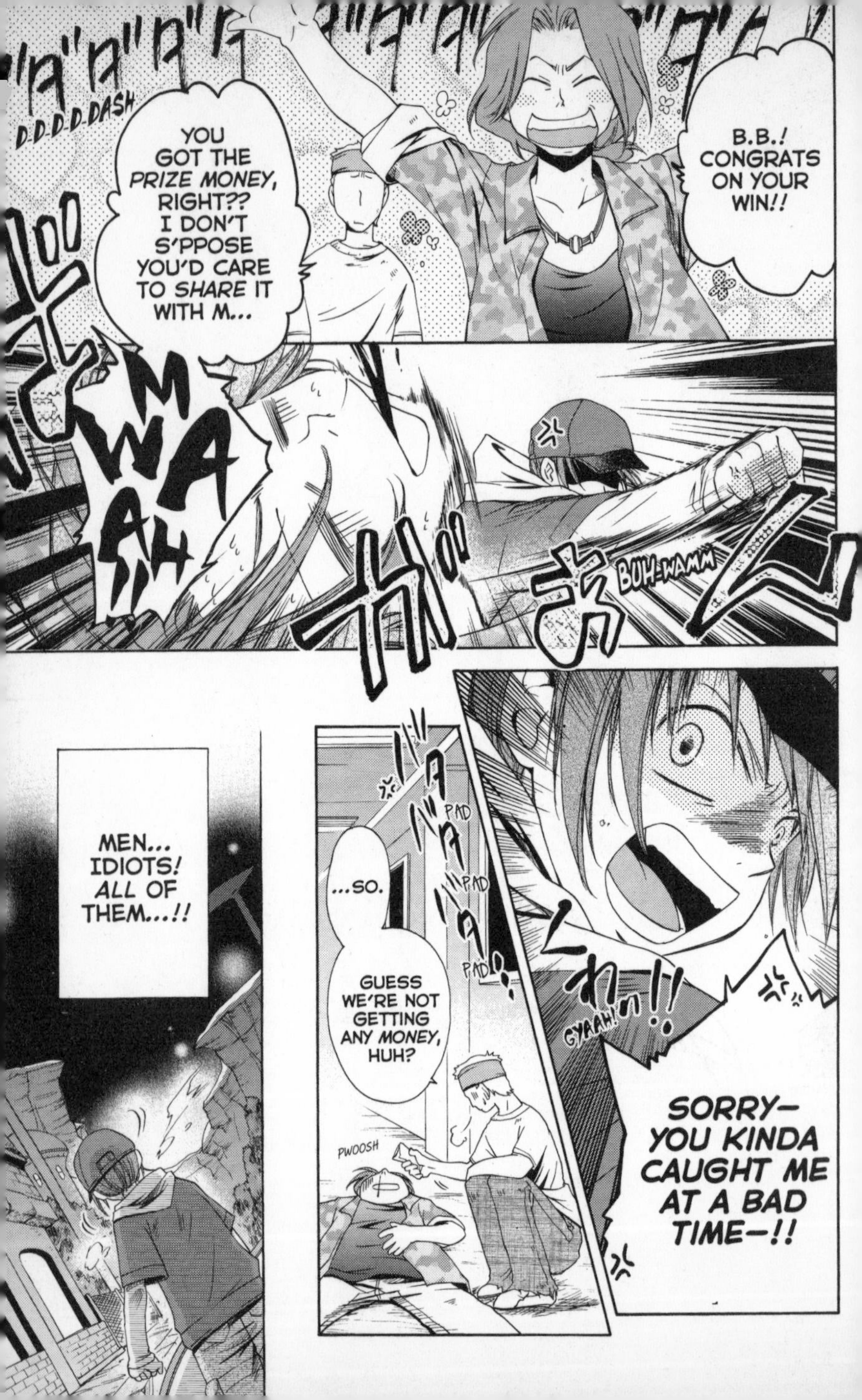
B.B.! CONGRATS ON YOUR WIN!!
D-D-D-D-DASH
YOU GOT THE PRIZE MONEY, RIGHT?? I DON'T S'PPOSE YOU'D CARE TO SHARE IT WITH M...
BUH-WAMM
GYAAH!
SORRY— YOU KINDA CAUGHT ME AT A BAD TIME—!!
PAD
PAD
PAD
...SO.
GUESS WE'RE NOT GETTING ANY MONEY, HUH?
PWOOSH
MEN... IDIOTS! ALL OF THEM...!!

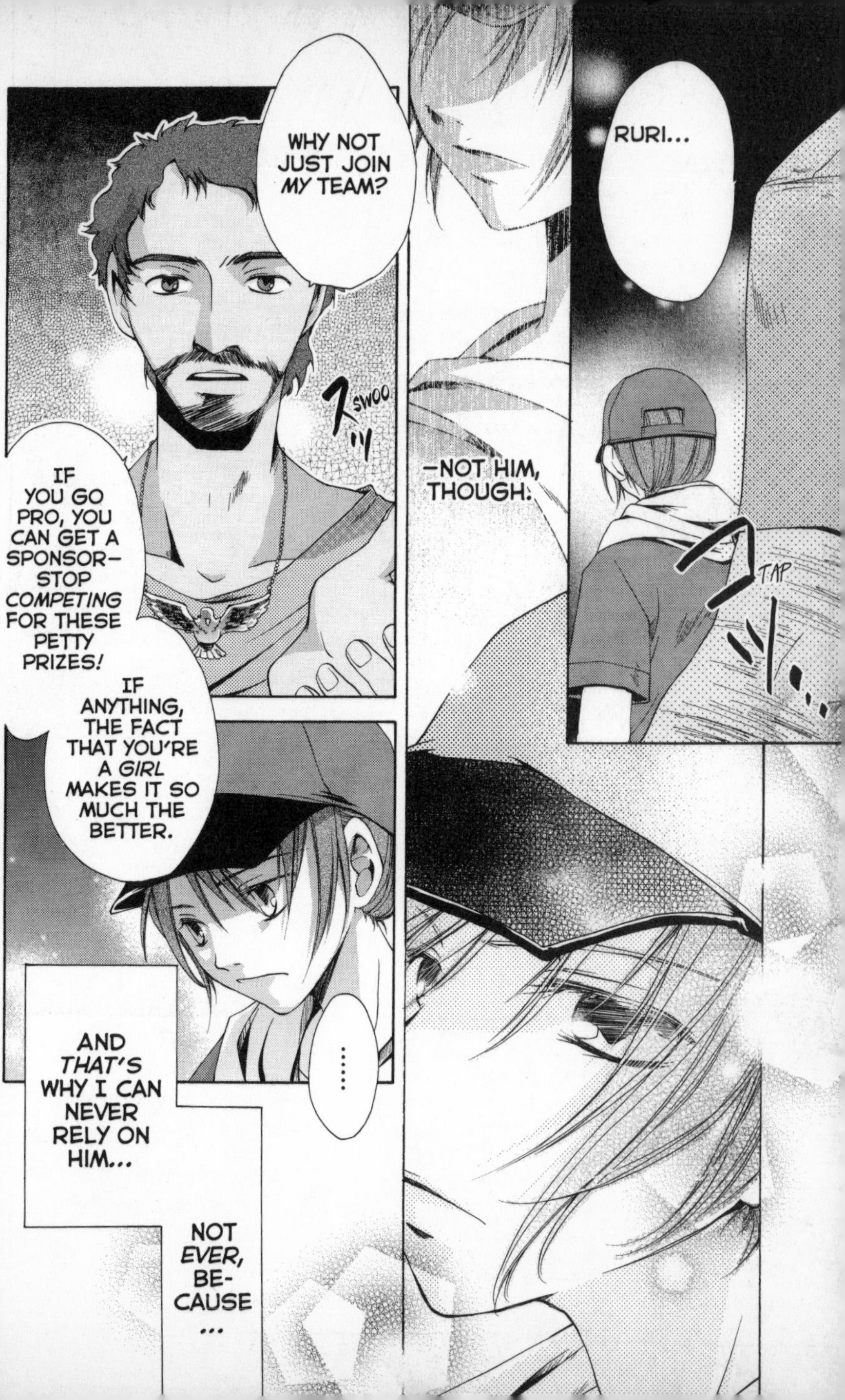
RURI...
TAP
-NOT HIM, THOUGH.
WHY NOT JUST JOIN *MY* TEAM?
SWOO
IF YOU GO PRO, YOU CAN GET A SPONSOR–STOP *COMPETING* FOR THESE PETTY PRIZES!
IF ANYTHING, THE FACT THAT YOU'RE A *GIRL* MAKES IT SO MUCH THE BETTER.
......
AND *THAT'S* WHY I CAN NEVER RELY ON HIM...
NOT *EVER*, BE-CAUSE ...

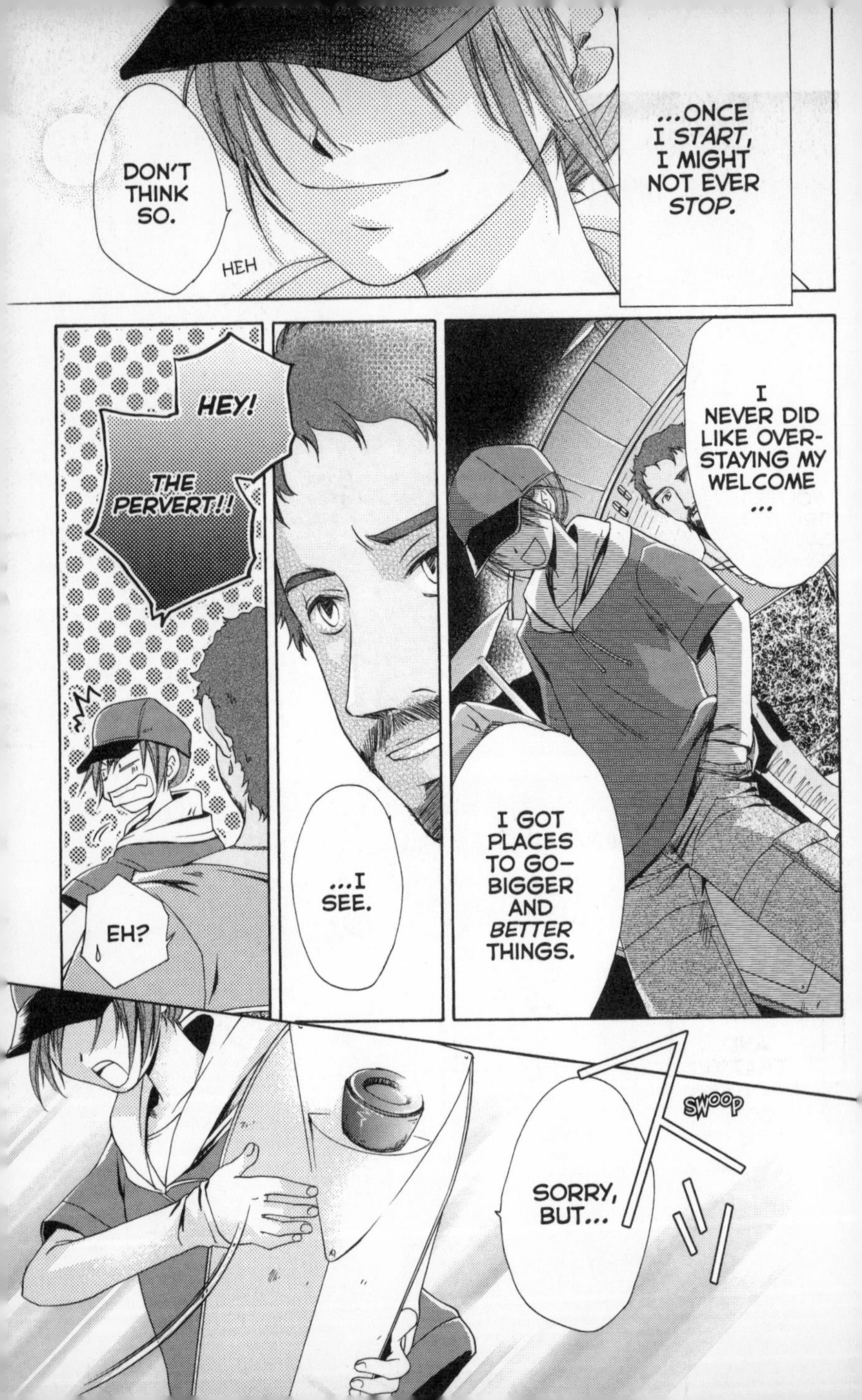
...ONCE I START, I MIGHT NOT EVER STOP.
DON'T THINK SO.
HEH
I NEVER DID LIKE OVER-STAYING MY WELCOME ...
I GOT PLACES TO GO— BIGGER AND BETTER THINGS.
...I SEE.
HEY!
THE PERVERT!!
EH?
SWOOP
SORRY, BUT...

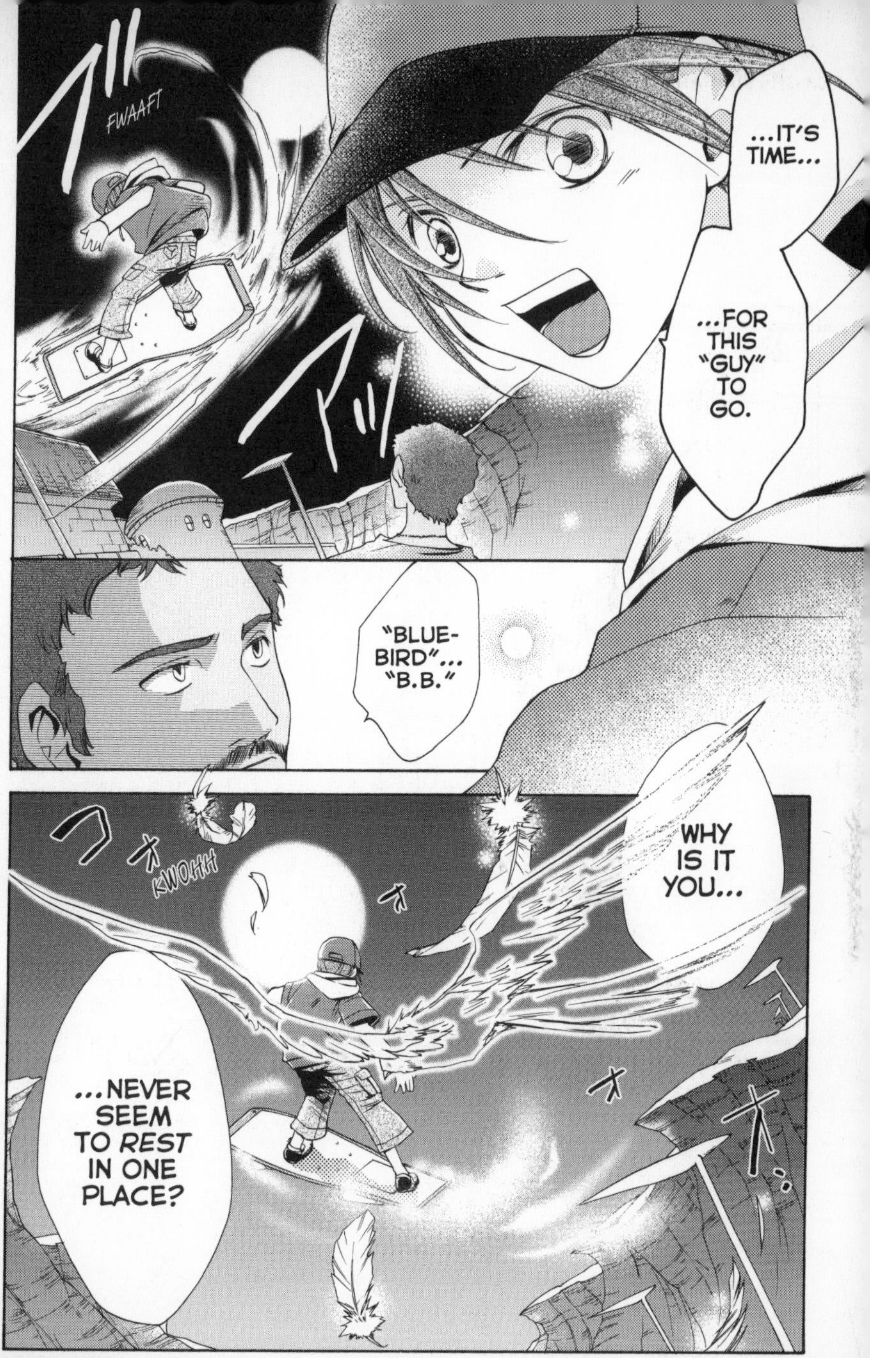
...IT'S TIME...
...FOR THIS "GUY" TO GO.
FWAAFT
"BLUE-BIRD"... "B.B."
WHY IS IT YOU...
KWOHH
...NEVER SEEM TO *REST* IN ONE PLACE?

02 BLUEBIRD END

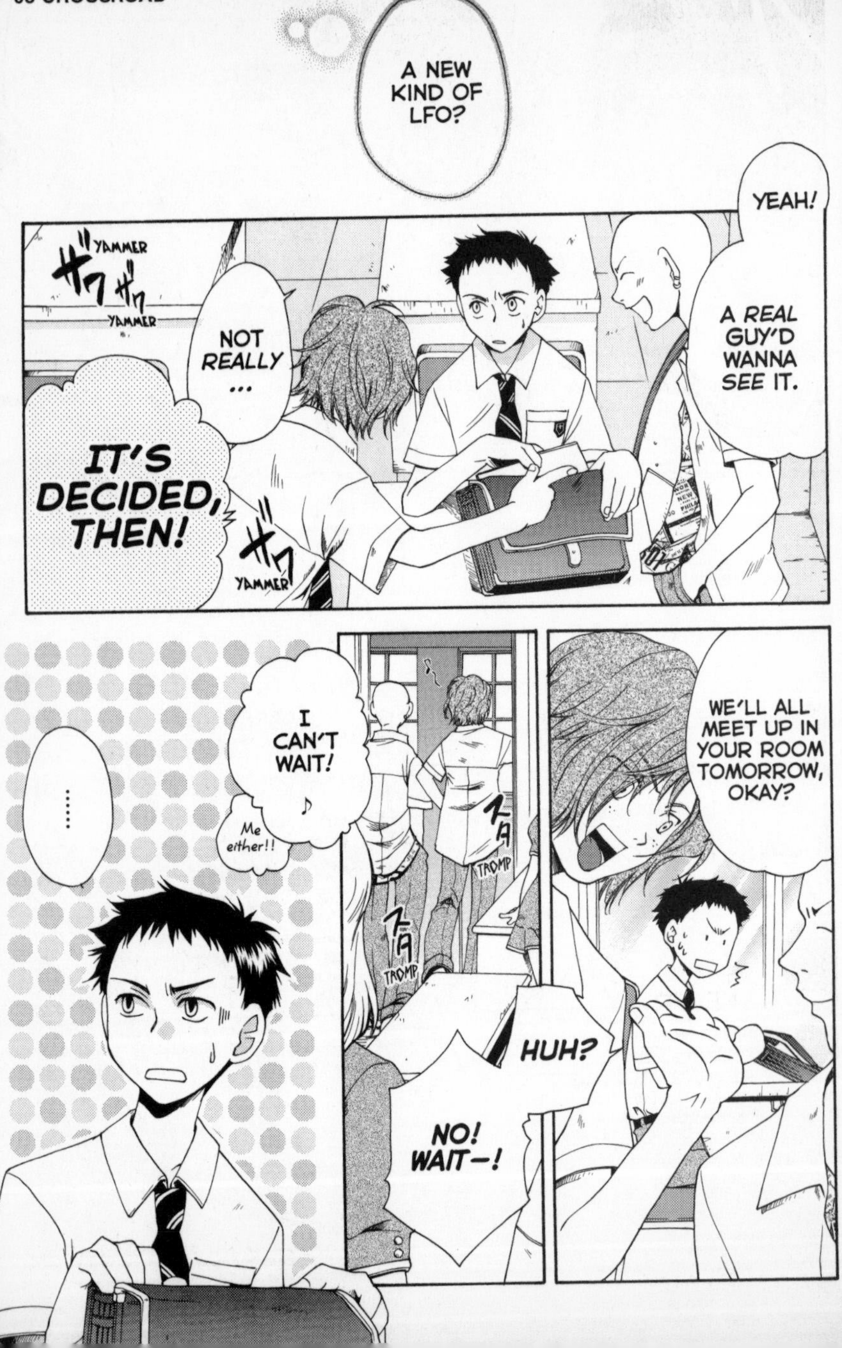
A NEW KIND OF LFO?
YEAH!
A REAL GUY'D WANNA SEE IT.
NOT REALLY ...
YAMMER YAMMER
IT'S DECIDED, THEN!
YAMMER
WE'LL ALL MEET UP IN YOUR ROOM TOMORROW, OKAY?
HUH?
NO! WAIT—!
I CAN'T WAIT! ♪
Me either!!
TROMP
TROMP
......

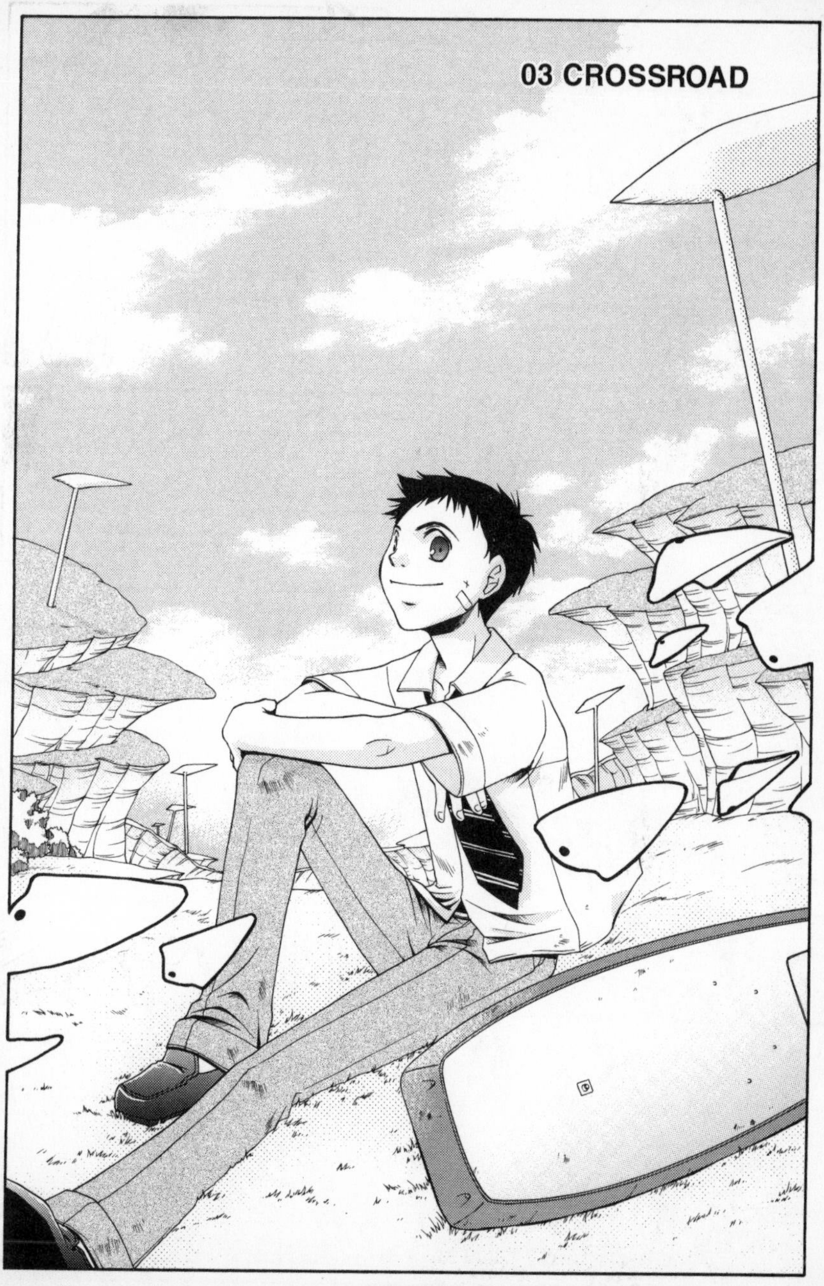
03 CROSSROAD

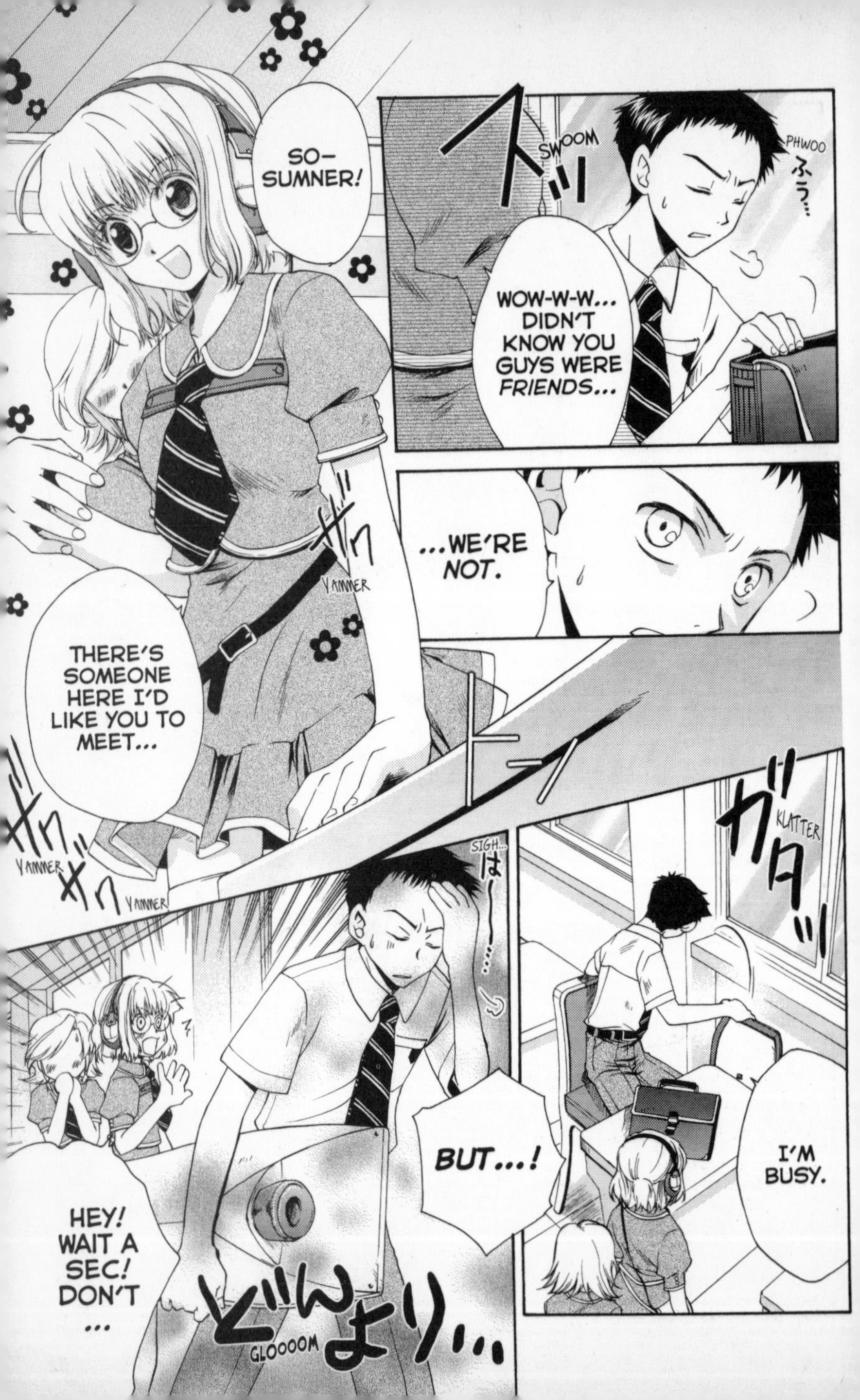
SWOOM
PHWOO
ふぅ…
WOW-W-W... DIDN'T KNOW YOU GUYS WERE FRIENDS...
...WE'RE NOT.
SO-SUMNER!
YAMMER
THERE'S SOMEONE HERE I'D LIKE YOU TO MEET...
YAMMER
YAMMER
ガタッ
KLATTER
I'M BUSY.
BUT...!
SIGH...
はー……
HEY! WAIT A SEC! DON'T ...
どんより…
GLOOOOM

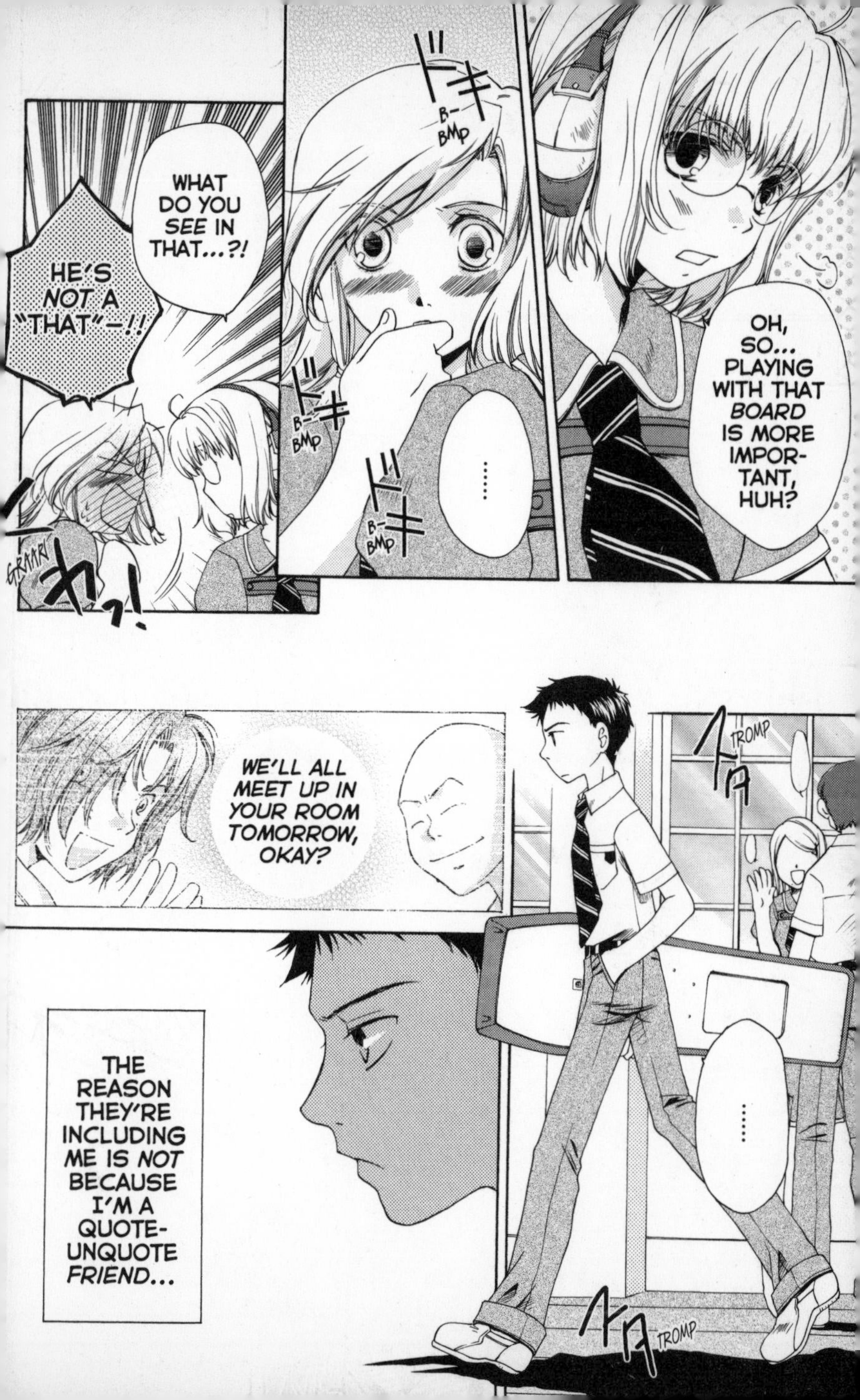
OH, SO... PLAYING WITH THAT BOARD IS MORE IMPORTANT, HUH?
B-BMP
B-BMP
B-BMP
......
WHAT DO YOU SEE IN THAT...?!
HE'S NOT A "THAT"—!!
GRAAR!
TROMP
......
TROMP
WE'LL ALL MEET UP IN YOUR ROOM TOMORROW, OKAY?
THE REASON THEY'RE INCLUDING ME IS NOT BECAUSE I'M A QUOTE-UNQUOTE FRIEND...

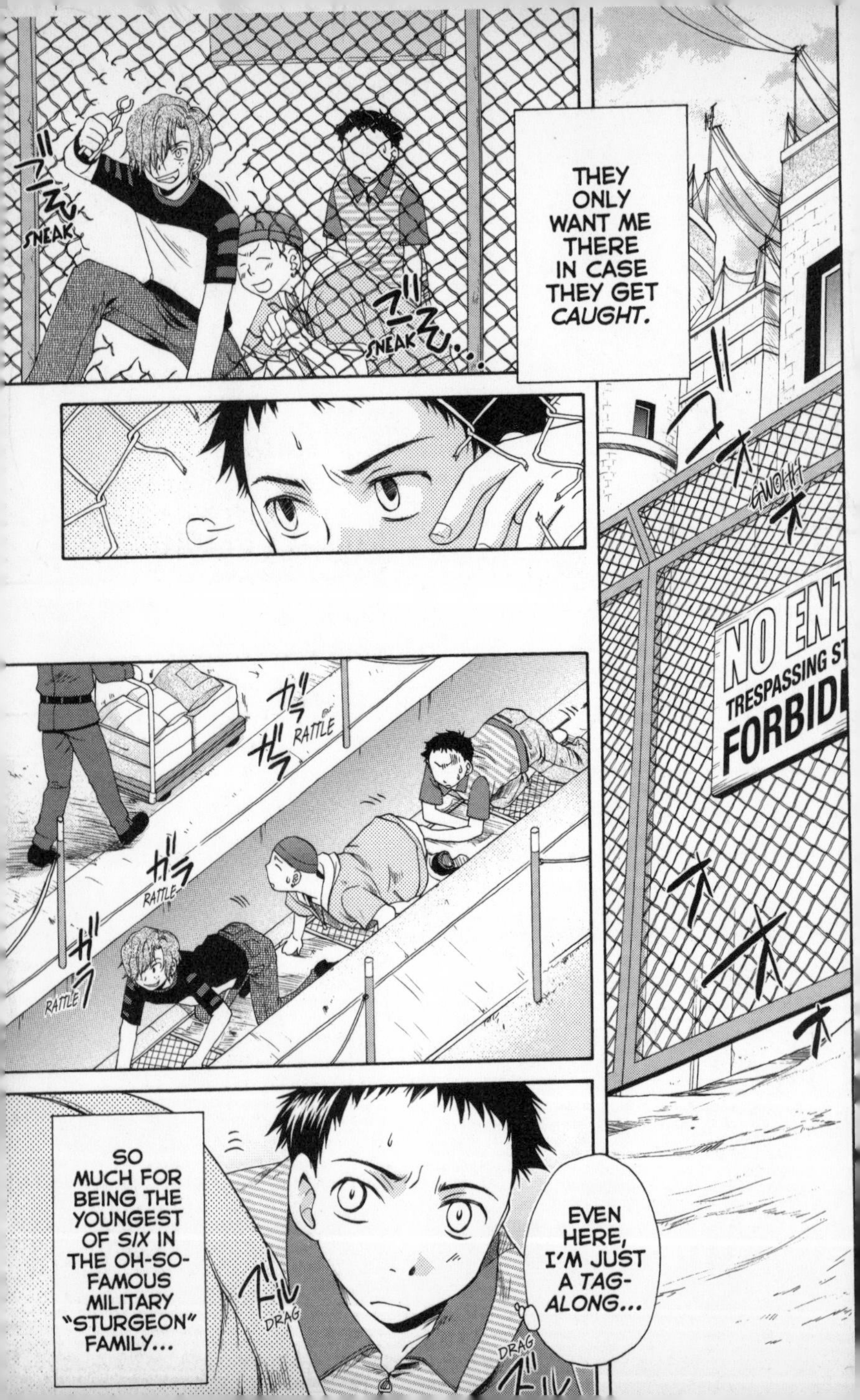
THEY ONLY WANT ME THERE IN CASE THEY GET CAUGHT.
SNEAK
SNEAK...
GWOHH
NO ENT
TRESPASSING ST
FORBID
RATTLE
RATTLE
RATTLE
EVEN HERE, I'M JUST A TAG-ALONG...
SO MUCH FOR BEING THE YOUNGEST OF SIX IN THE OH-SO-FAMOUS MILITARY "STURGEON" FAMILY...
DRAG
DRAG

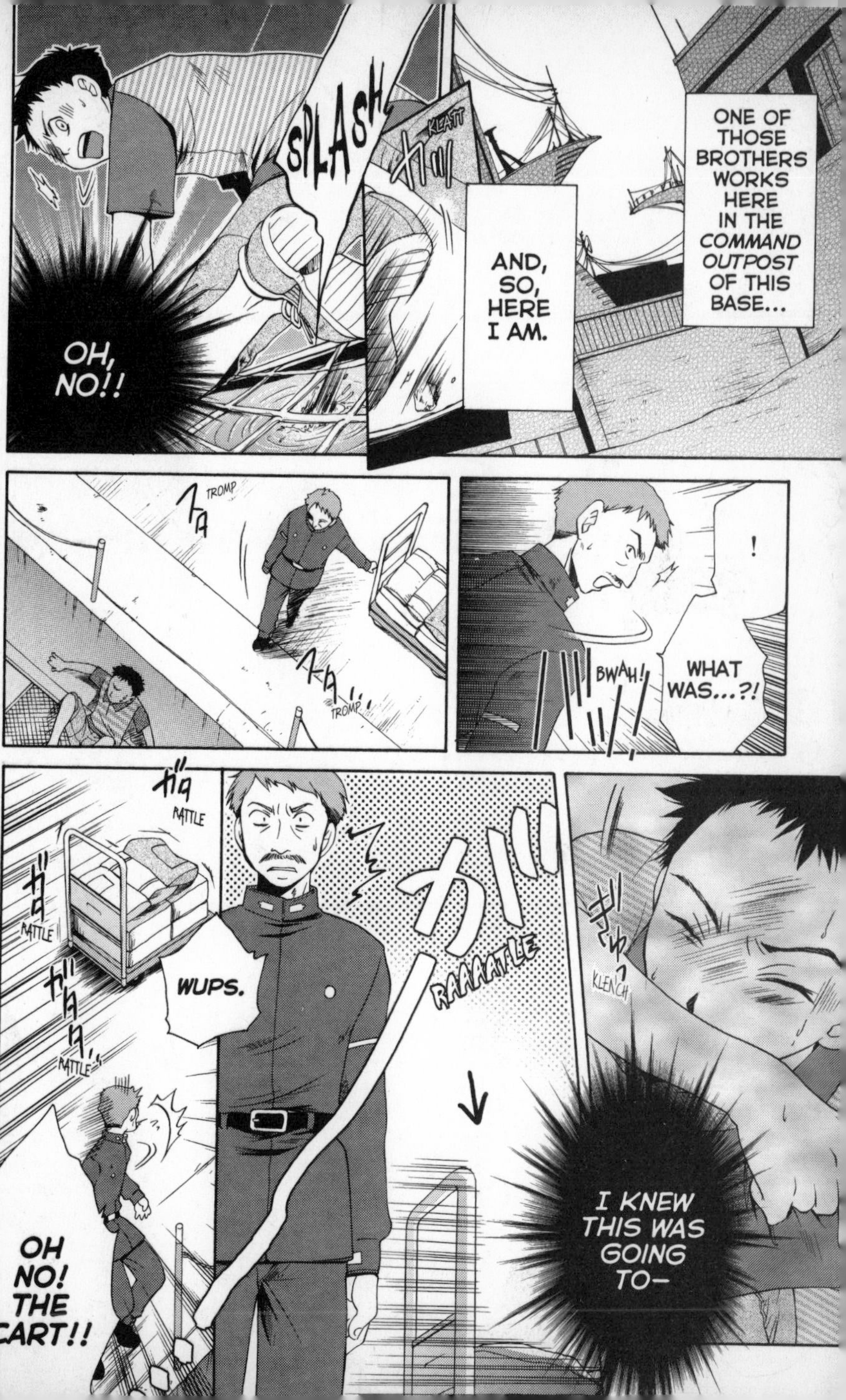
ONE OF THOSE BROTHERS WORKS HERE IN THE *COMMAND OUTPOST* OF THIS BASE...
AND, SO, HERE I AM.
KLATT
SPLASH
OH, NO!!
!
WHAT WAS...?!
BWAH!
TROMP
TROMP
KLENCH
I KNEW THIS WAS GOING TO–
RAAAATTLE
WUPS.
RATTLE
RATTLE
RATTLE
OH NO! THE CART!!

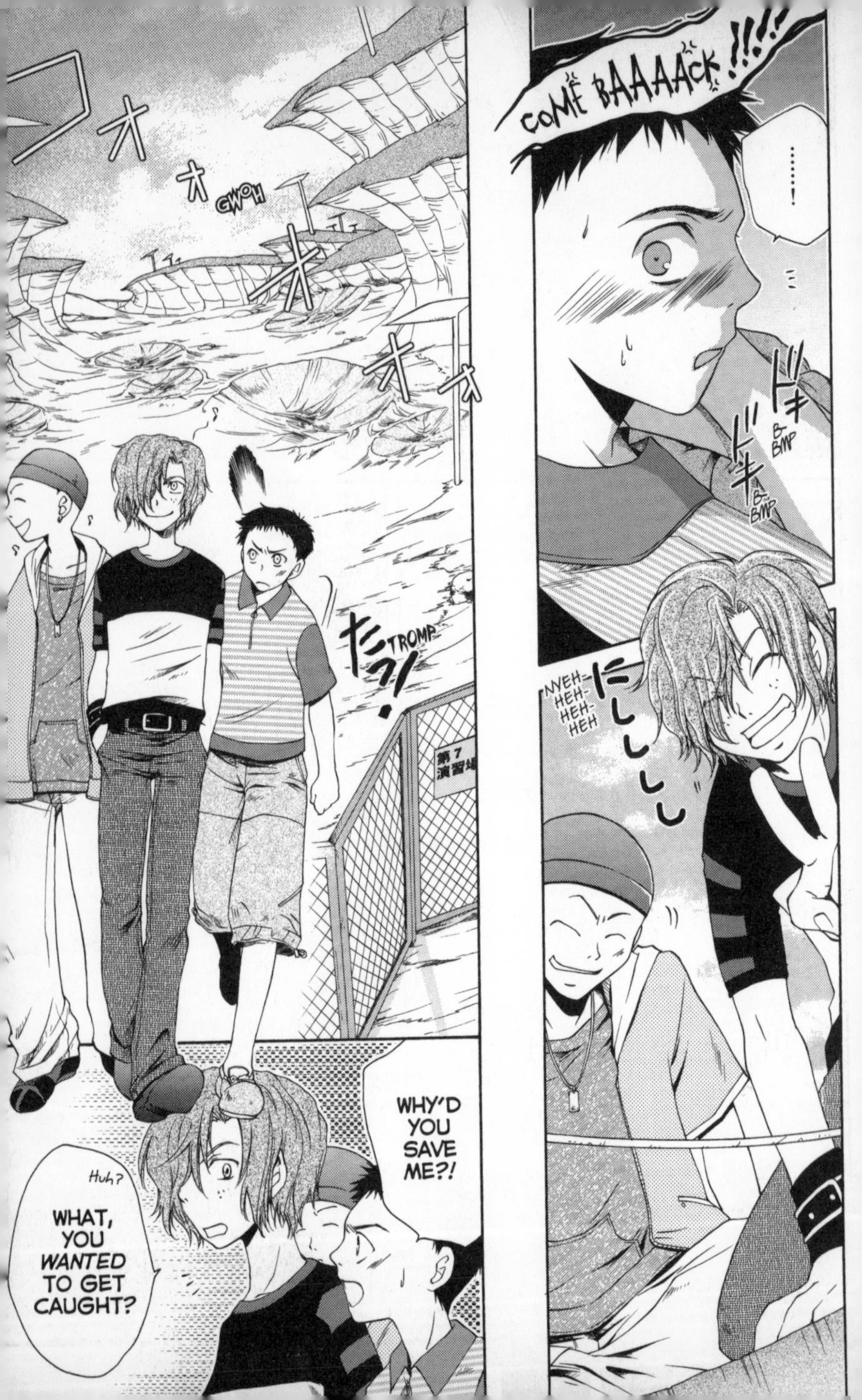
COME BAAAACK!!!!
......!
B-BMP
B-BMP
NYEH-HEH-HEH-HEH
GWOH
TROMP
第7演習場
WHY'D YOU SAVE ME?!
Huh?
WHAT, YOU WANTED TO GET CAUGHT?

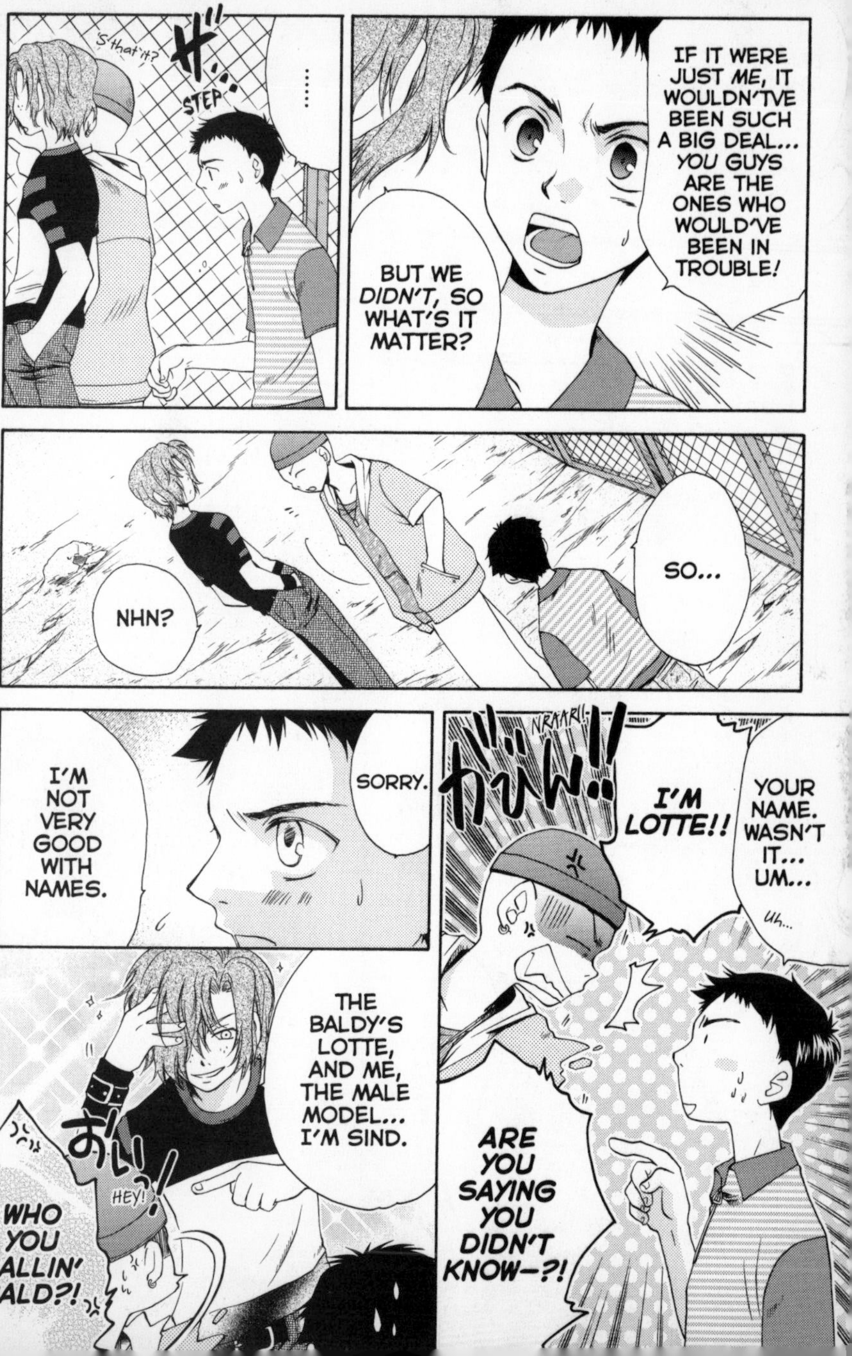
IF IT WERE JUST *ME*, IT WOULDN'T'VE BEEN SUCH A BIG DEAL... *YOU* GUYS ARE THE ONES WHO WOULD'VE BEEN IN TROUBLE!
BUT WE *DIDN'T*, SO WHAT'S IT MATTER?
......
STEP
'S that it?
SO...
NHN?
NRAAR!!
YOUR NAME. WASN'T IT... UM...
uh...
I'M LOTTE!!
ARE YOU SAYING YOU DIDN'T KNOW—?!
SORRY.
I'M NOT VERY GOOD WITH NAMES.
THE BALDY'S LOTTE, AND ME, THE MALE MODEL... I'M SIND.
HEY!
WHO YOU CALLIN' BALD?!

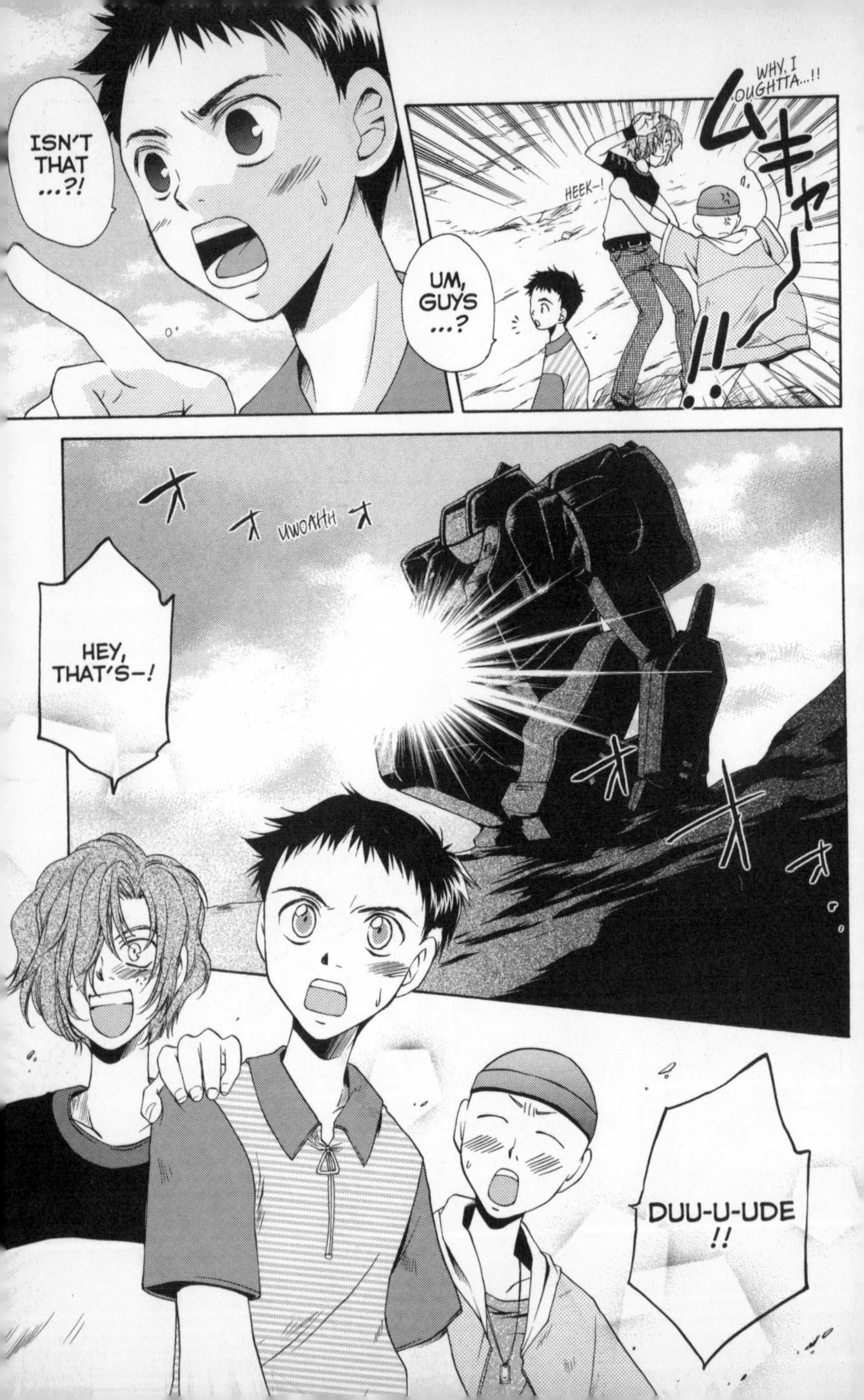

WHY, I OUGHTTA...!!
ムキャ～!!
HEEK-!
UM, GUYS ...?
ISN'T THAT ...?!
UWOAHH
HEY, THAT'S-!
DUU-U-UDE !!

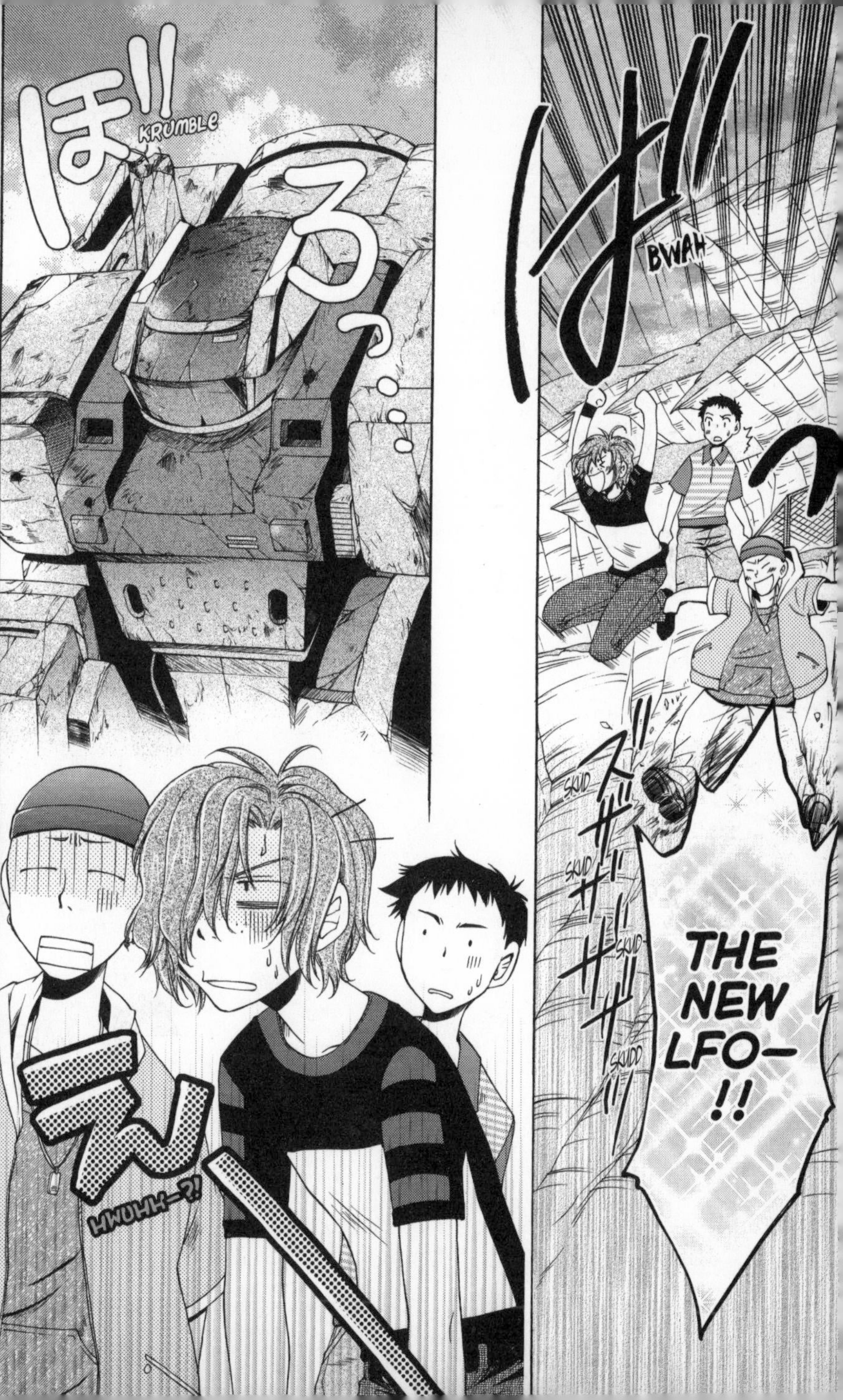
BWAH
SKUD
SKUD
SKUD
SKUDD
THE NEW LFO—!!
KRUMBLE
HWUHH—?!

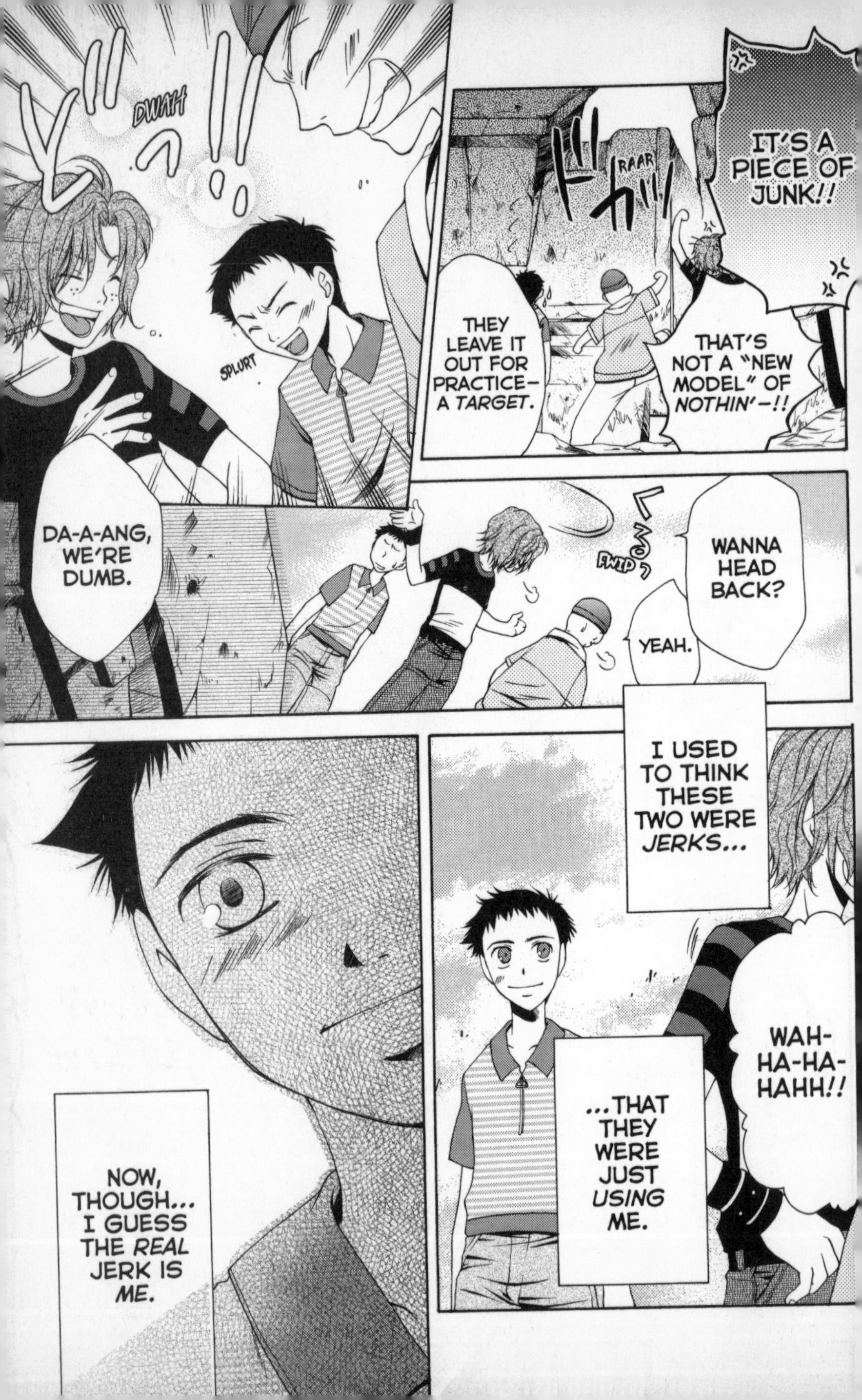
IT'S A PIECE OF JUNK!!
RAAR
THAT'S NOT A "NEW MODEL" OF NOTHIN'—!!
THEY LEAVE IT OUT FOR PRACTICE— A TARGET.
DWAH
SPLURT
DA-A-ANG, WE'RE DUMB.
WANNA HEAD BACK?
FWIP
YEAH.
I USED TO THINK THESE TWO WERE JERKS...
WAH-HA-HA-HAHH!!
...THAT THEY WERE JUST USING ME.
NOW, THOUGH... I GUESS THE REAL JERK IS ME.

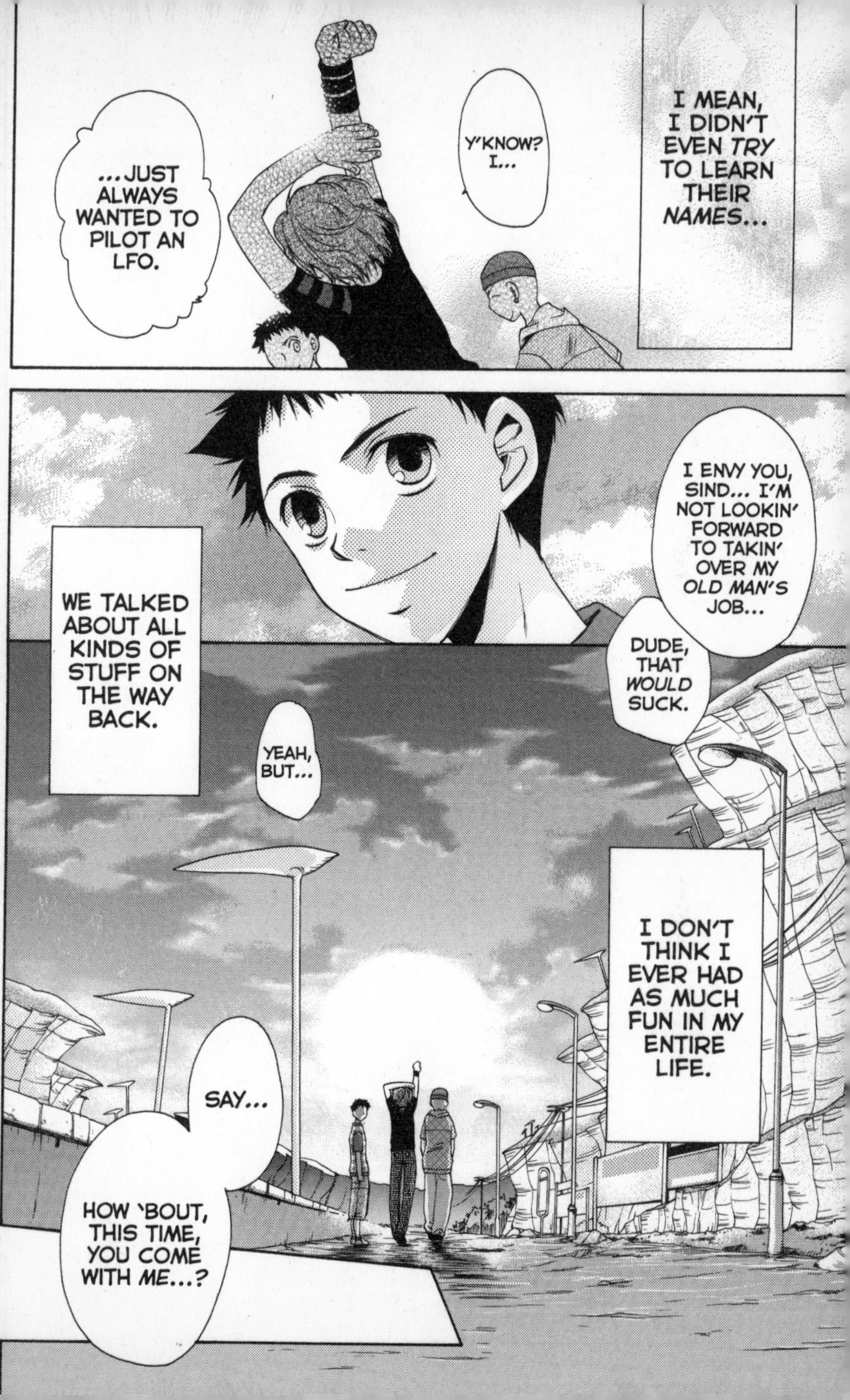
I MEAN, I DIDN'T EVEN *TRY* TO LEARN THEIR *NAMES*...
Y'KNOW? I...
...JUST ALWAYS WANTED TO PILOT AN LFO.
I ENVY YOU, SIND... I'M NOT LOOKIN' FORWARD TO TAKIN' OVER MY *OLD MAN'S* JOB...
WE TALKED ABOUT ALL KINDS OF STUFF ON THE WAY BACK.
DUDE, THAT *WOULD* SUCK.
YEAH, BUT...
I DON'T THINK I EVER HAD AS MUCH FUN IN MY ENTIRE LIFE.
SAY...
HOW 'BOUT, THIS TIME, YOU COME WITH *ME*...?

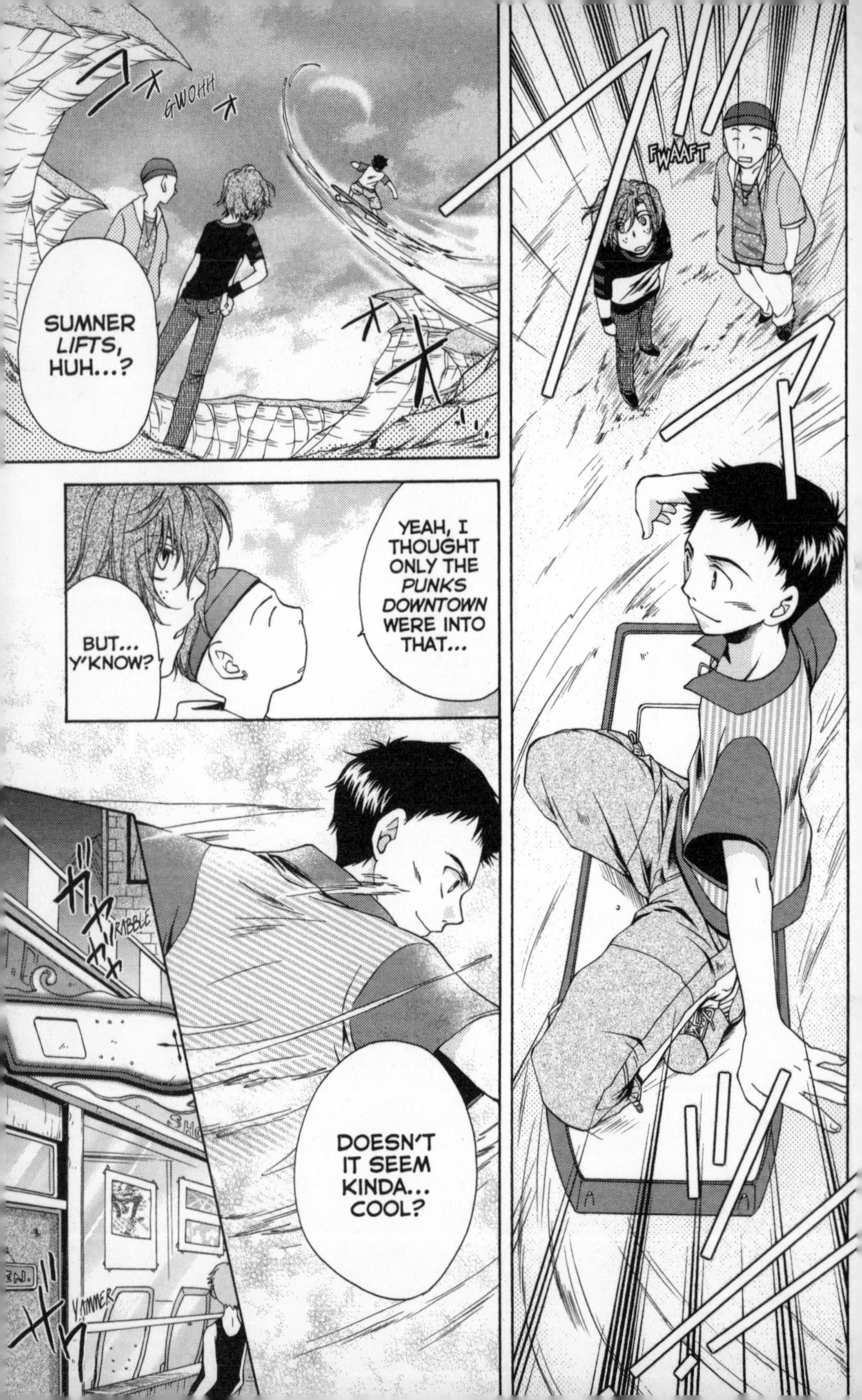
FWAAFT
GWOHH
SUMNER *LIFTS*, HUH...?
YEAH, I THOUGHT ONLY THE *PUNKS DOWNTOWN* WERE INTO THAT...
BUT... Y'KNOW?
RABBLE
DOESN'T IT SEEM KINDA... COOL?
YAMMER

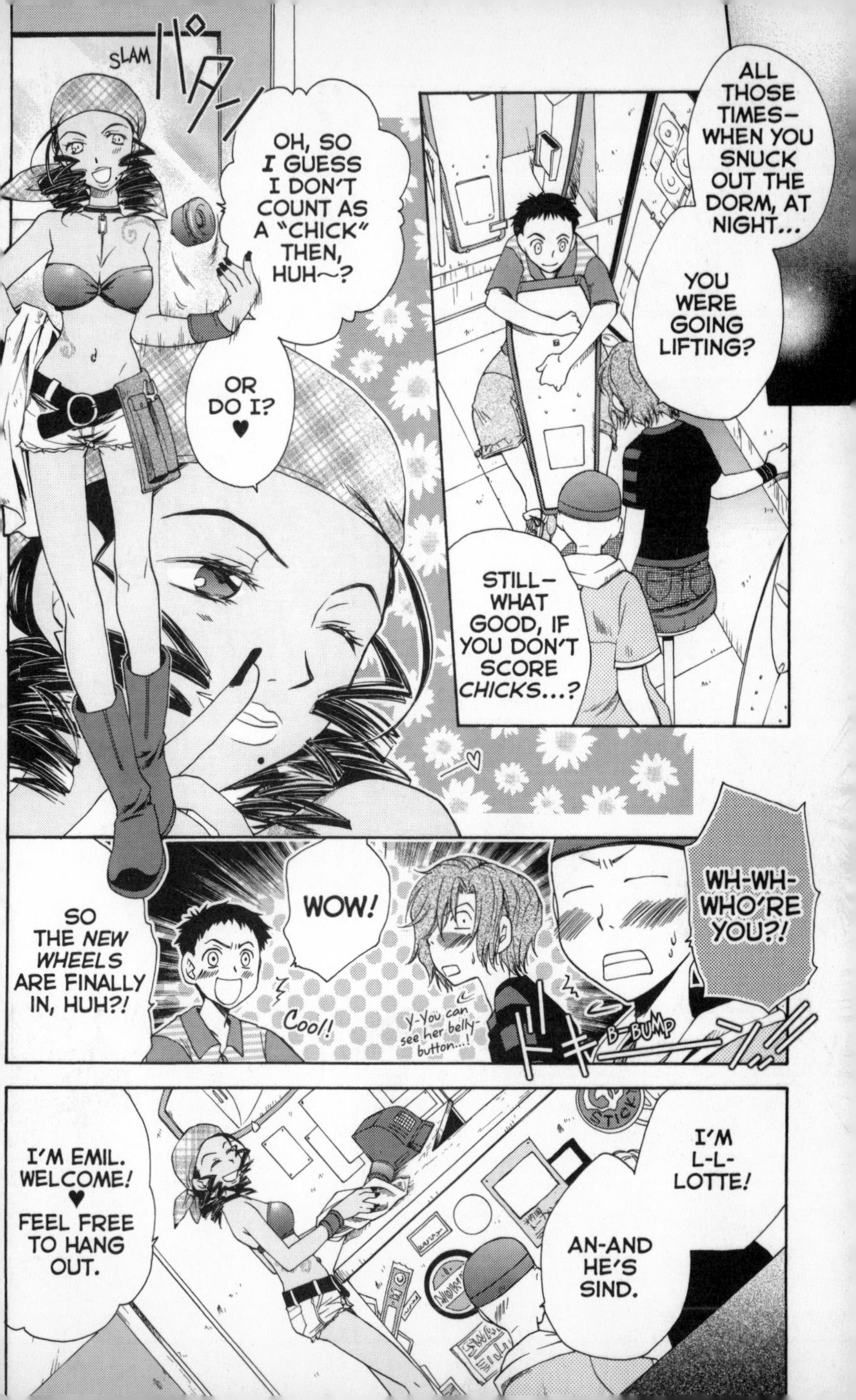
ALL THOSE TIMES—WHEN YOU SNUCK OUT THE DORM, AT NIGHT...
YOU WERE GOING LIFTING?
STILL—WHAT GOOD, IF YOU DON'T SCORE *CHICKS*...?
SLAM
OH, SO *I* GUESS I DON'T COUNT AS A "CHICK" THEN, HUH~?
OR DO I? ♥
WH-WH-WHO'RE YOU?!
B-BUMP
Y-You can see her belly-button...!
WOW!
Cool!
SO THE *NEW WHEELS* ARE FINALLY IN, HUH?!
I'M L-L-LOTTE!
AN-AND HE'S SIND.
I'M EMIL. WELCOME! ♥ FEEL FREE TO HANG OUT.

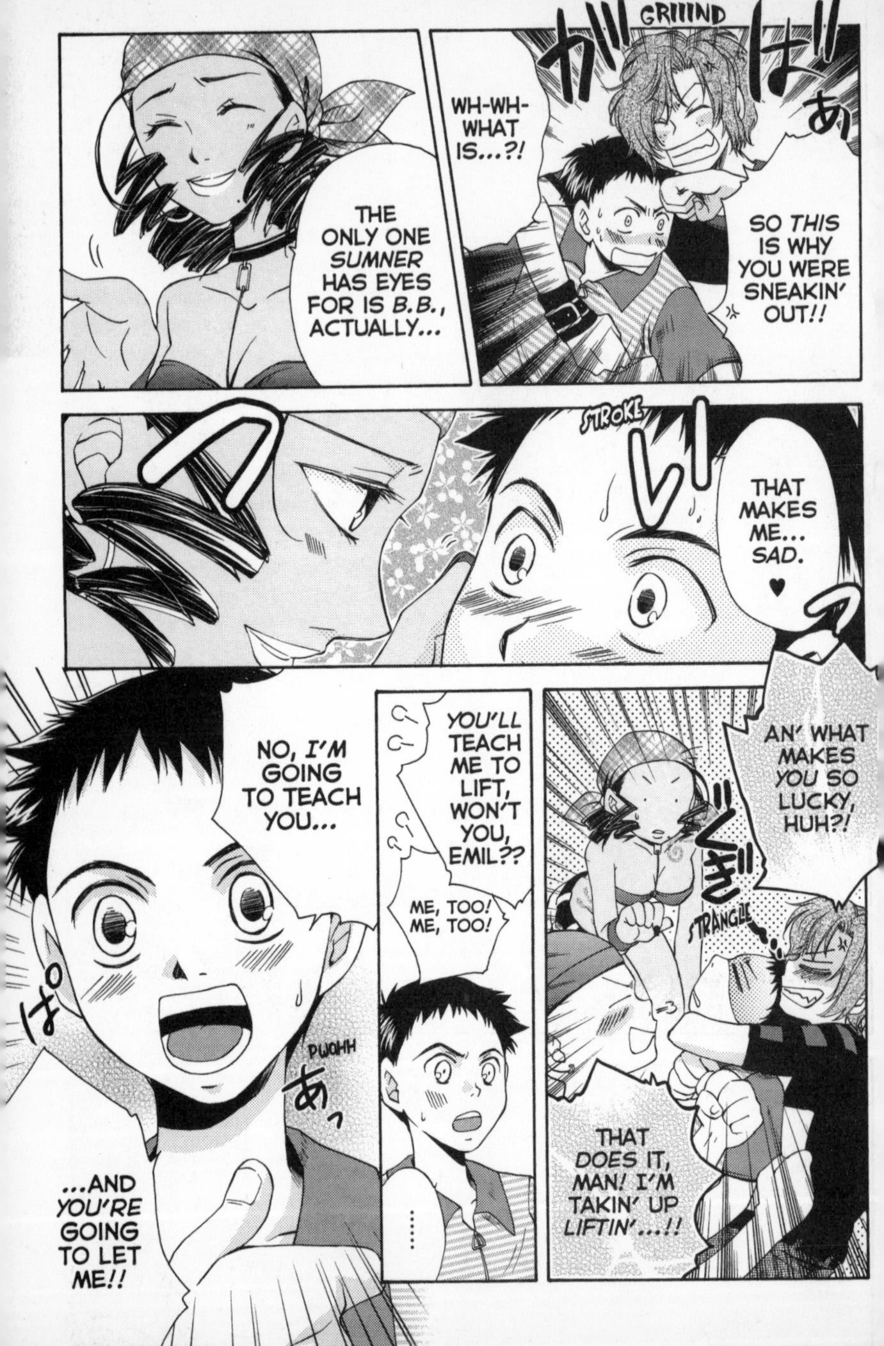
GRIIIND
SO THIS IS WHY YOU WERE SNEAKIN' OUT!!
WH-WH-WHAT IS...?!
THE ONLY ONE SUMNER HAS EYES FOR IS B.B., ACTUALLY...
STROKE
THAT MAKES ME... SAD. ♥
AN' WHAT MAKES YOU SO LUCKY, HUH?!
STRANGLE
THAT DOES IT, MAN! I'M TAKIN' UP LIFTIN'...!!
YOU'LL TEACH ME TO LIFT, WON'T YOU, EMIL??
ME, TOO! ME, TOO!
......
NO, I'M GOING TO TEACH YOU...
PWOHH
...AND YOU'RE GOING TO LET ME!!

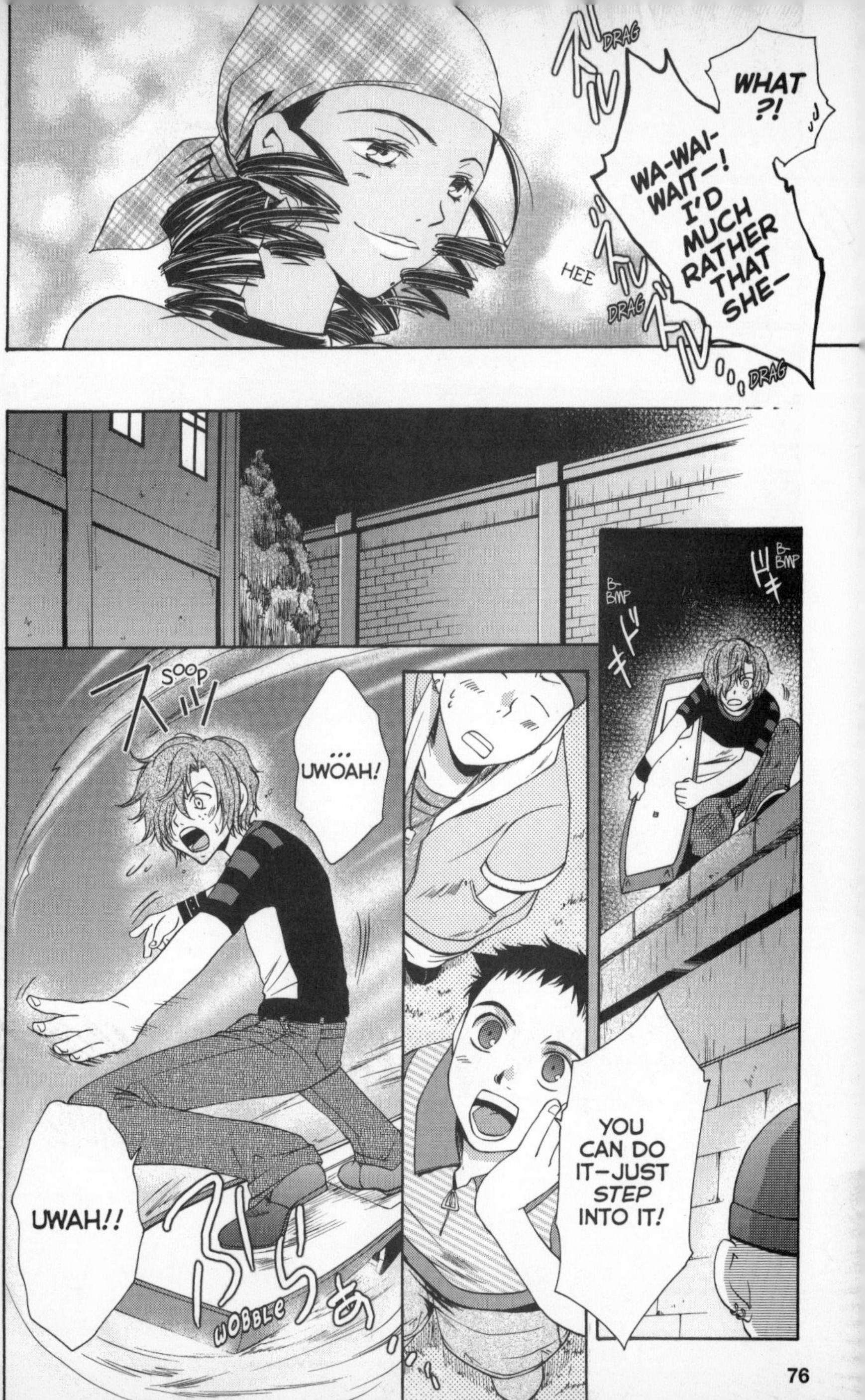
WHAT ?!
WA-WAI-WAIT—! I'D MUCH RATHER THAT SHE—
DRAG
DRAG
DRAG
HEE
B-BMP
B-BMP
YOU CAN DO IT—JUST *STEP* INTO IT!
SOOP
...UWOAH!
UWAH!!
WOBBLE

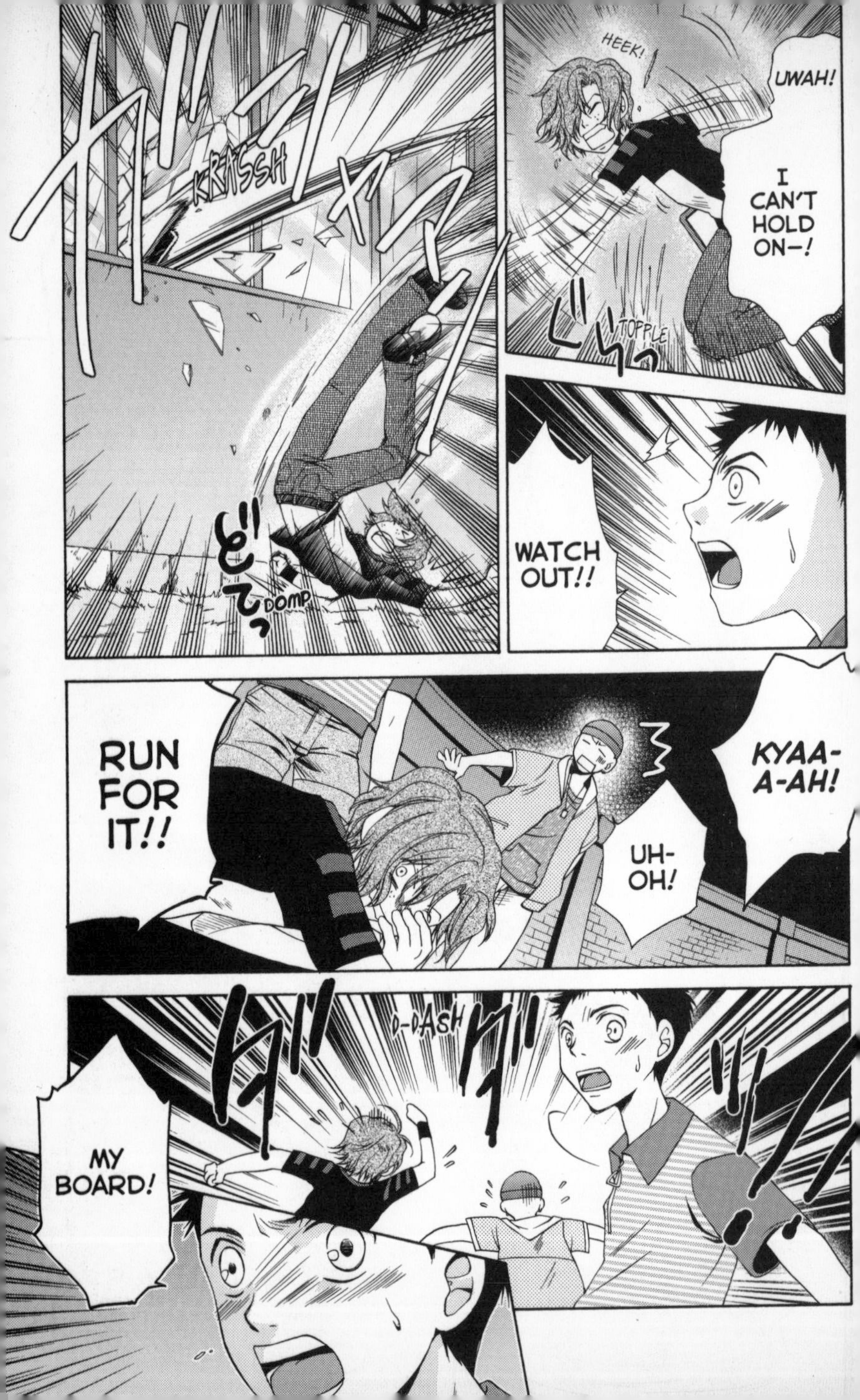
HEEK!
UWAH!
I CAN'T HOLD ON–!
TOPPLE
WATCH OUT!!
KRASSH
DOMP
KYAA-A-AH!
UH-OH!
RUN FOR IT!!
D-DASH
MY BOARD!

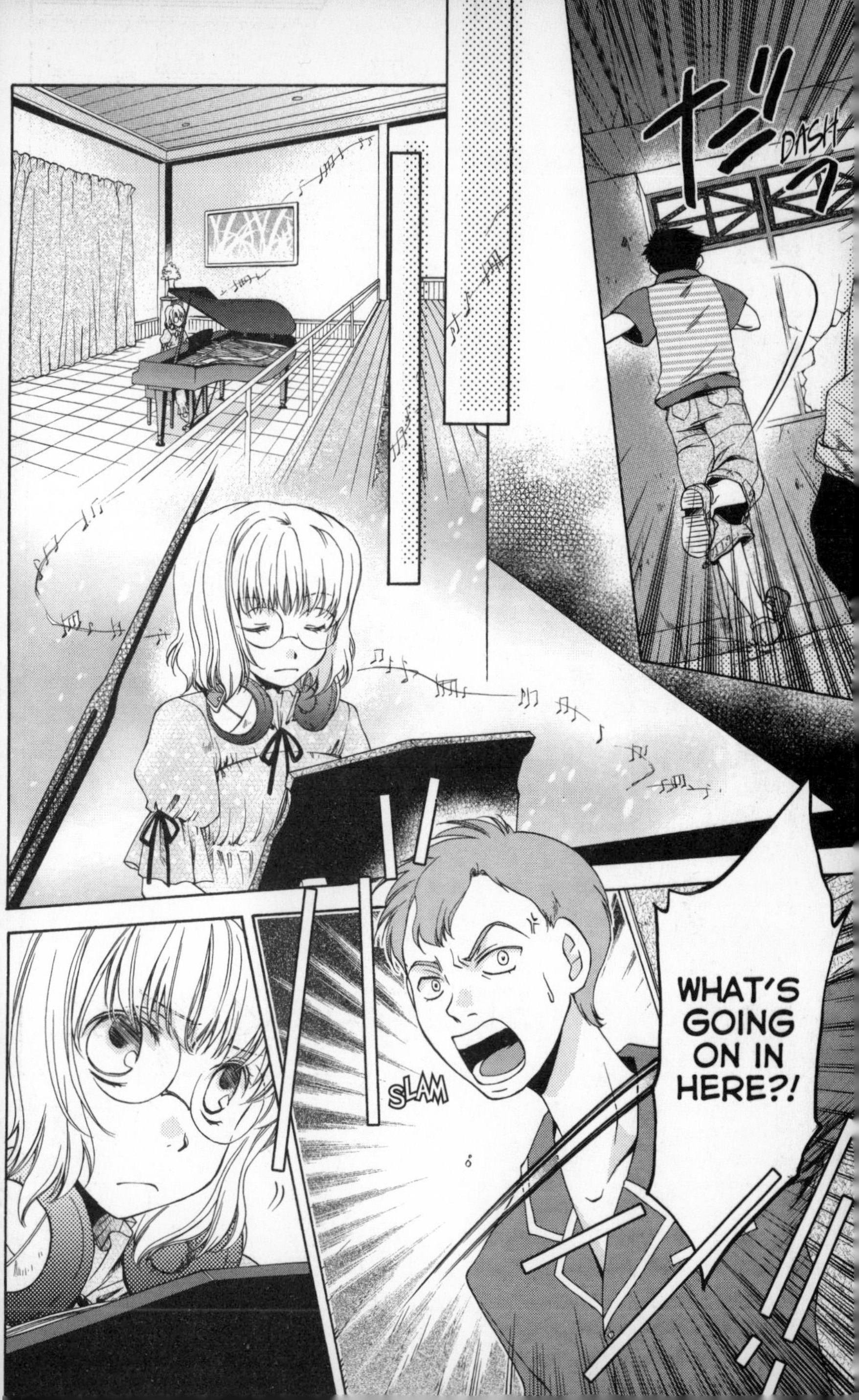
DASH
WHAT'S GOING ON IN HERE?!
SLAM

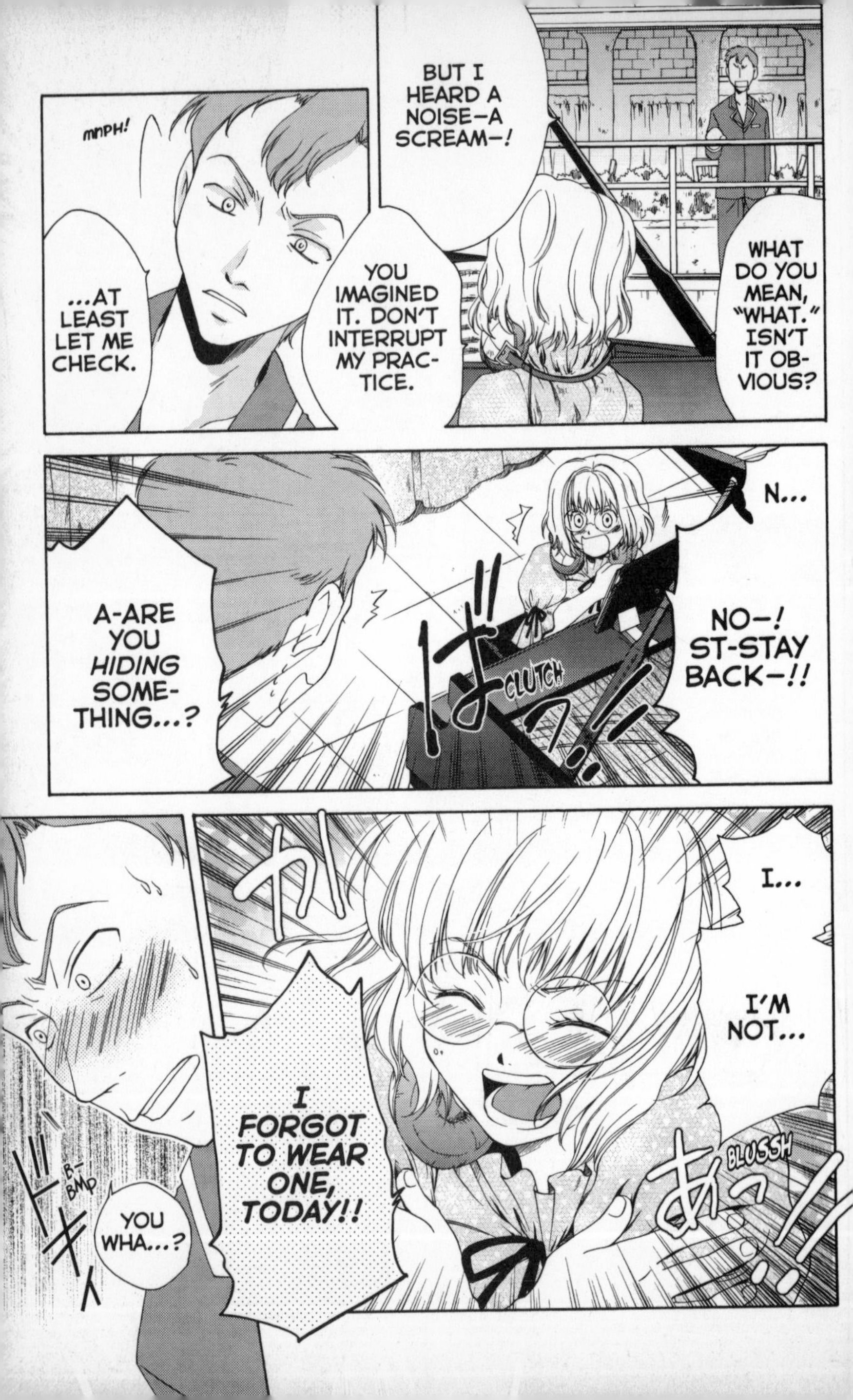
WHAT DO YOU MEAN, "WHAT." ISN'T IT OBVIOUS?
BUT I HEARD A NOISE—A SCREAM—!
YOU IMAGINED IT. DON'T INTERRUPT MY PRAC-TICE.
MNPH!
...AT LEAST LET ME CHECK.
N...
NO—! ST-STAY BACK—!!
CLUTCH
A-ARE YOU *HIDING* SOME-THING...?
I...
I'M NOT...
BLUSSH
I FORGOT TO WEAR ONE, TODAY!!
B-BMP
YOU WHA...?

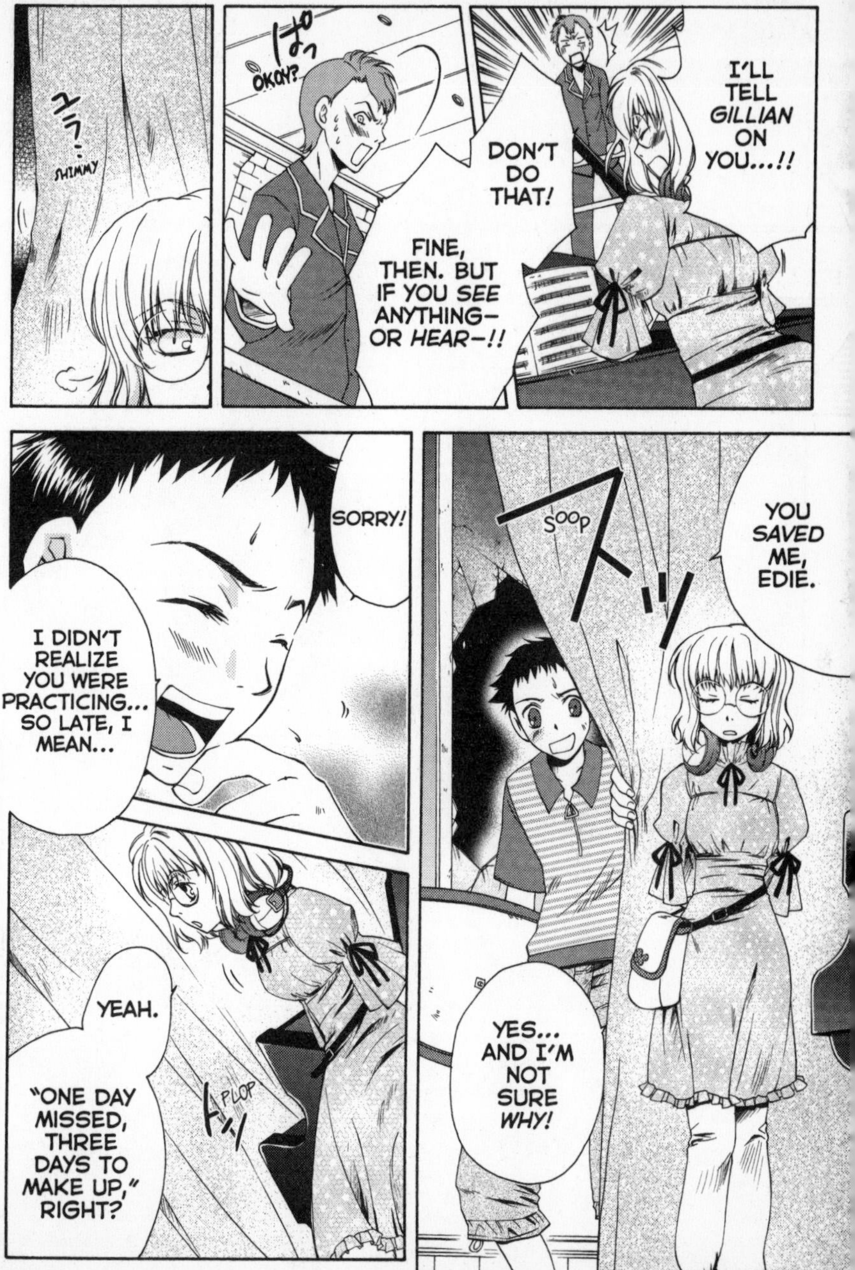
I'LL TELL GILLIAN ON YOU...!!
DON'T DO THAT!
ぱっ
OKAY?
FINE, THEN. BUT IF YOU SEE ANYTHING— OR HEAR—!!
ユラ…
SHIMMY
YOU SAVED ME, EDIE.
スッ
SOOP
YES... AND I'M NOT SURE WHY!
SORRY!
I DIDN'T REALIZE YOU WERE PRACTICING... SO LATE, I MEAN...
YEAH.
PLOP
"ONE DAY MISSED, THREE DAYS TO MAKE UP," RIGHT?

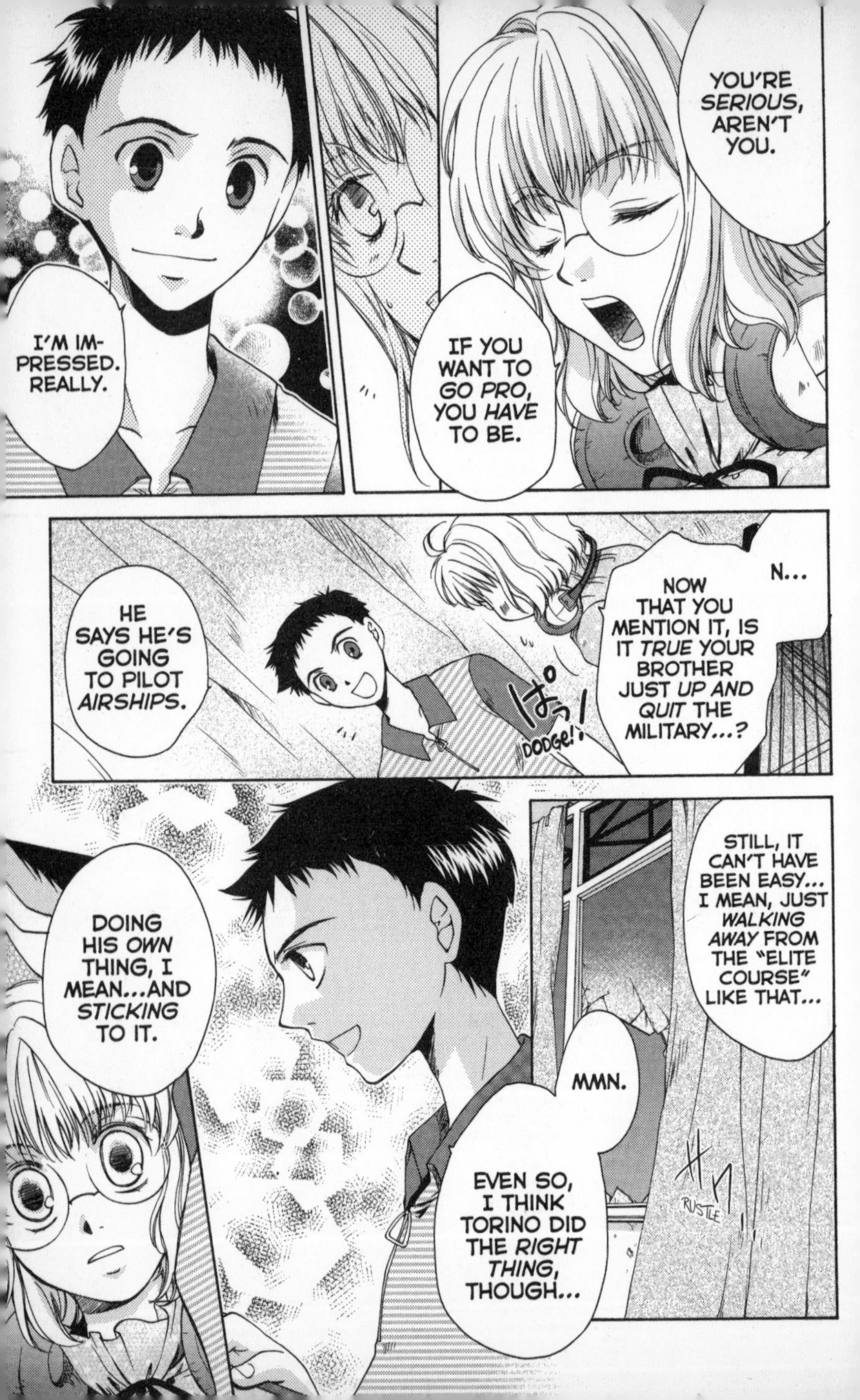
YOU'RE SERIOUS, AREN'T YOU.
IF YOU WANT TO GO PRO, YOU HAVE TO BE.
I'M IM-PRESSED. REALLY.
N...
NOW THAT YOU MENTION IT, IS IT TRUE YOUR BROTHER JUST UP AND QUIT THE MILITARY...?
ぱっ!
DODGE!
HE SAYS HE'S GOING TO PILOT AIRSHIPS.
STILL, IT CAN'T HAVE BEEN EASY... I MEAN, JUST WALKING AWAY FROM THE "ELITE COURSE" LIKE THAT...
RUSTLE
MMN.
EVEN SO, I THINK TORINO DID THE RIGHT THING, THOUGH...
DOING HIS OWN THING, I MEAN...AND STICKING TO IT.

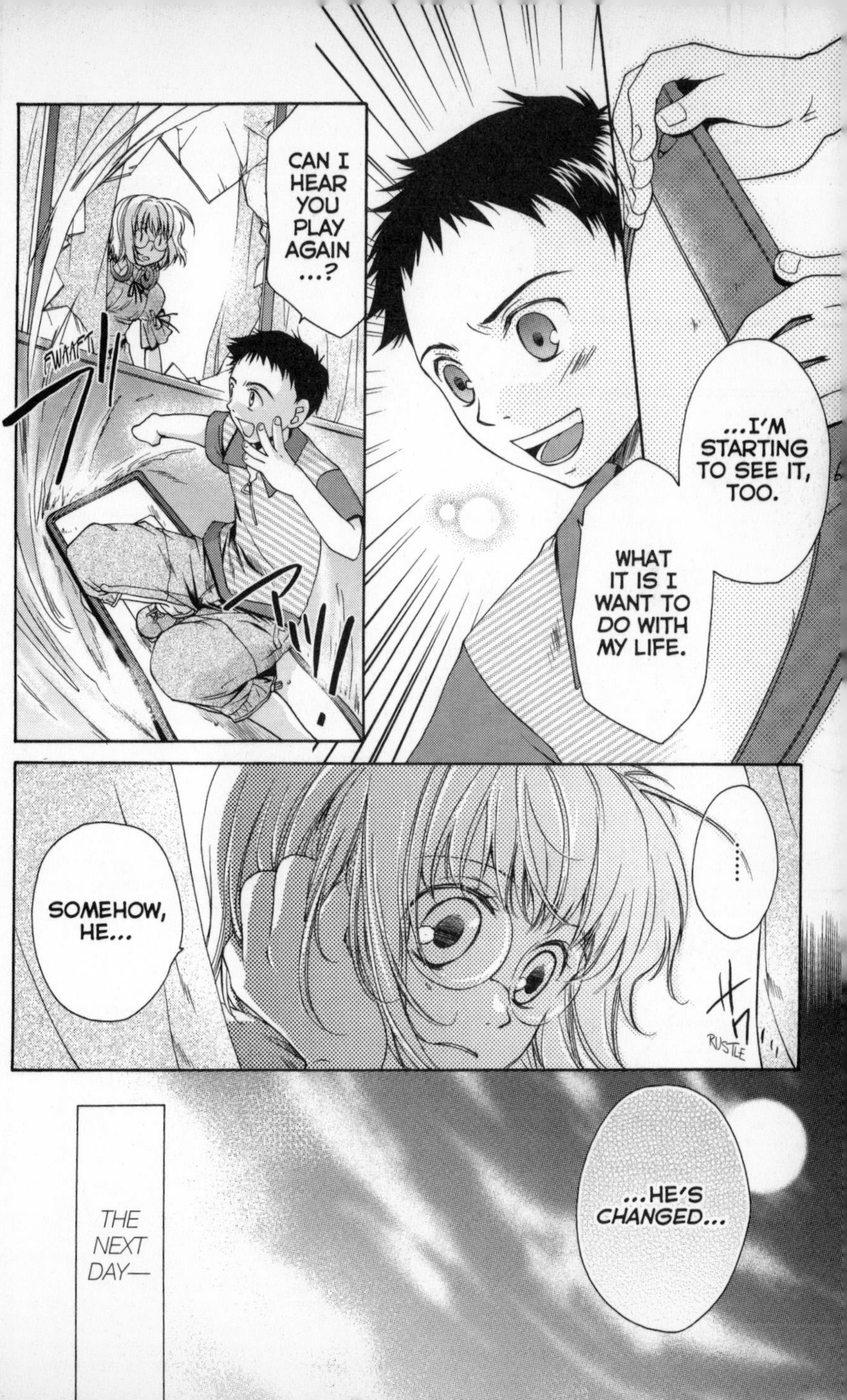
...I'M STARTING TO SEE IT, TOO.
WHAT IT IS I WANT TO DO WITH MY LIFE.
CAN I HEAR YOU PLAY AGAIN ...?
FWAAFT
......
RUSTLE
SOMEHOW, HE...
...HE'S CHANGED...
THE NEXT DAY—

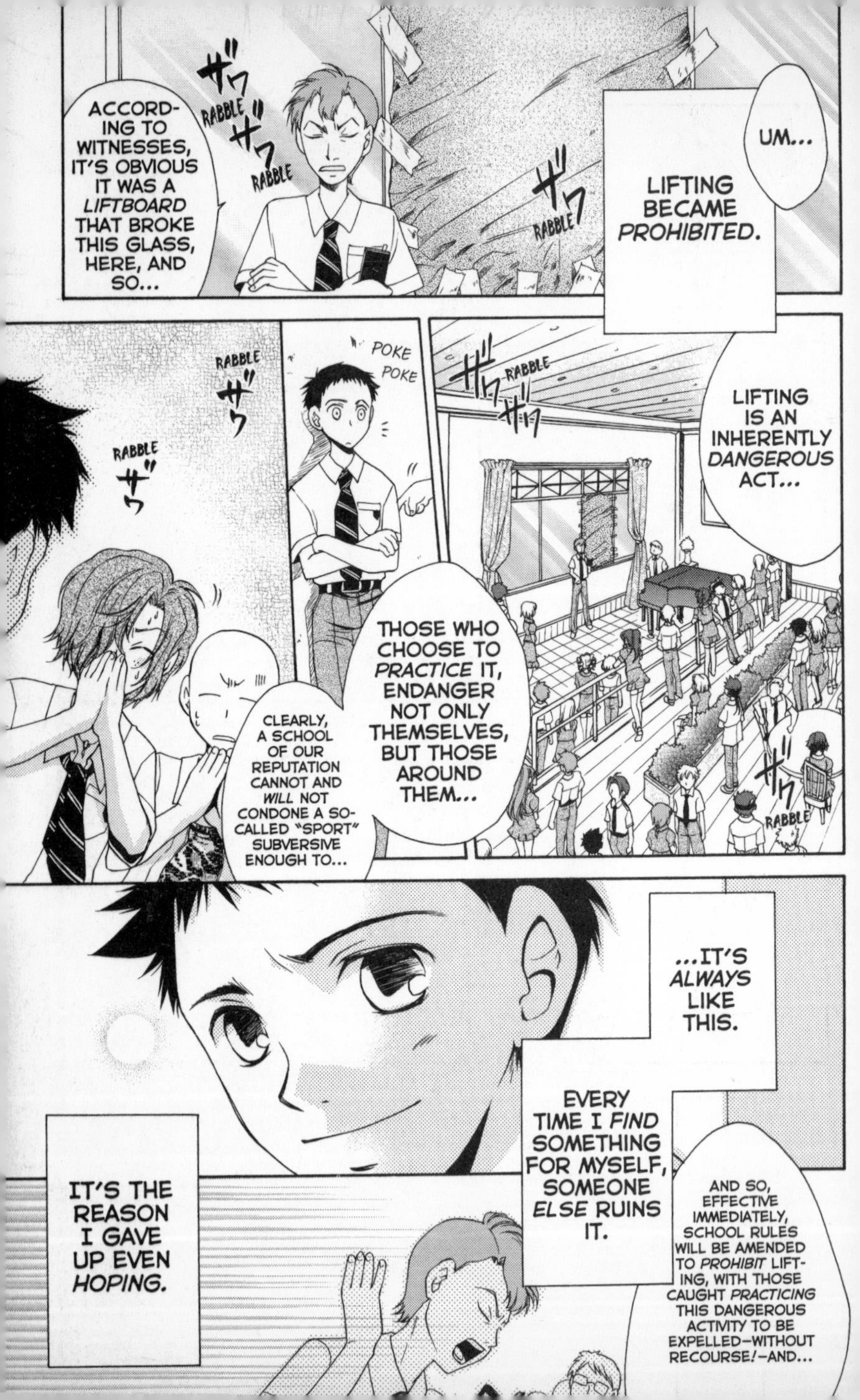
UM...
LIFTING BECAME PROHIBITED.
ACCORDING TO WITNESSES, IT'S OBVIOUS IT WAS A LIFTBOARD THAT BROKE THIS GLASS, HERE, AND SO...
ザワ RABBLE
ザワ RABBLE
ザワ RABBLE
LIFTING IS AN INHERENTLY DANGEROUS ACT...
ザワ RABBLE
ザワ RABBLE
POKE POKE
THOSE WHO CHOOSE TO PRACTICE IT, ENDANGER NOT ONLY THEMSELVES, BUT THOSE AROUND THEM...
RABBLE ザワ
RABBLE ザワ
CLEARLY, A SCHOOL OF OUR REPUTATION CANNOT AND WILL NOT CONDONE A SO-CALLED "SPORT" SUBVERSIVE ENOUGH TO...
...IT'S ALWAYS LIKE THIS.
EVERY TIME I FIND SOMETHING FOR MYSELF, SOMEONE ELSE RUINS IT.
AND SO, EFFECTIVE IMMEDIATELY, SCHOOL RULES WILL BE AMENDED TO PROHIBIT LIFTING, WITH THOSE CAUGHT PRACTICING THIS DANGEROUS ACTIVITY TO BE EXPELLED—WITHOUT RECOURSE!—AND...
IT'S THE REASON I GAVE UP EVEN HOPING.

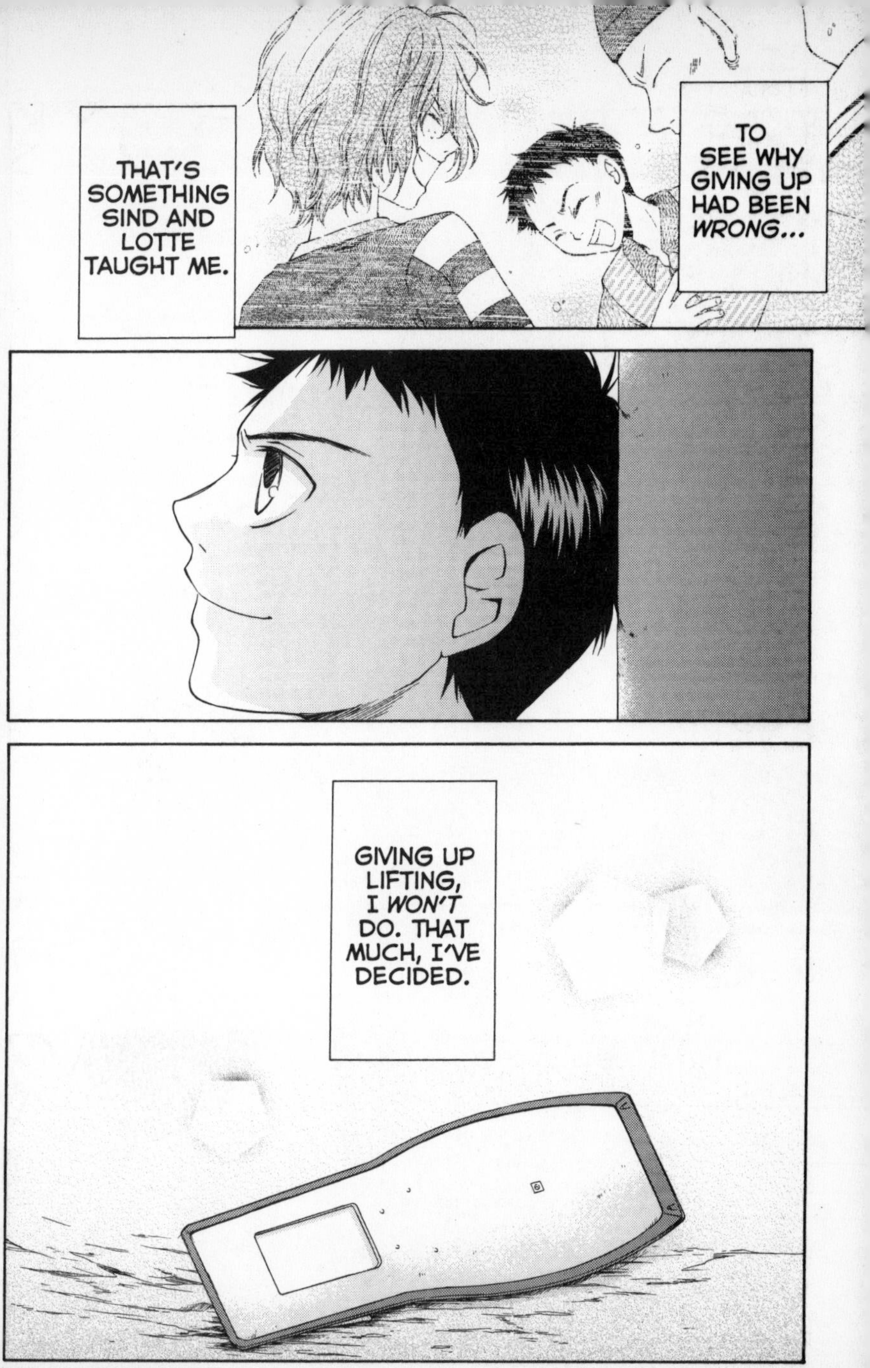
TO SEE WHY GIVING UP HAD BEEN *WRONG*...
THAT'S SOMETHING SIND AND LOTTE TAUGHT ME.
GIVING UP LIFTING, I *WON'T* DO. THAT MUCH, I'VE DECIDED.

03 CROSSROAD END

04 CHALLENGER

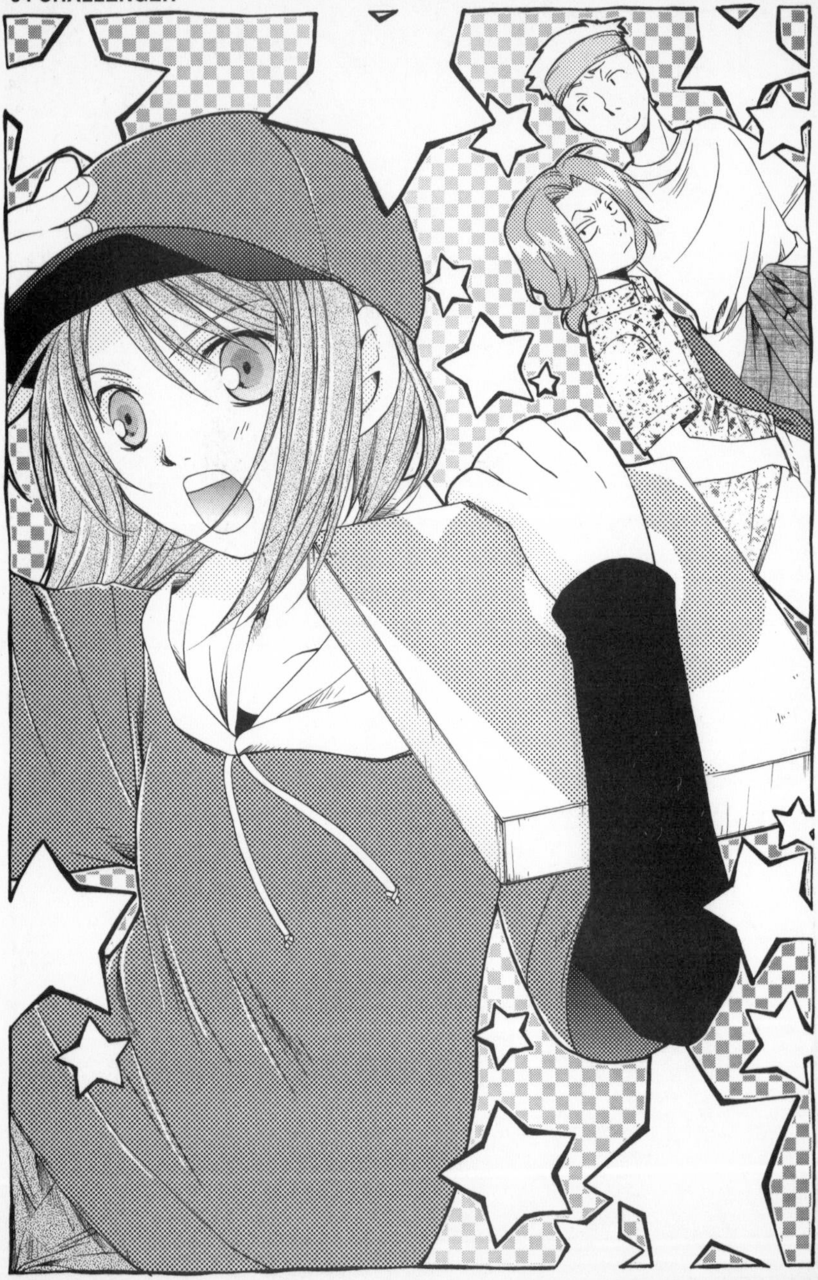

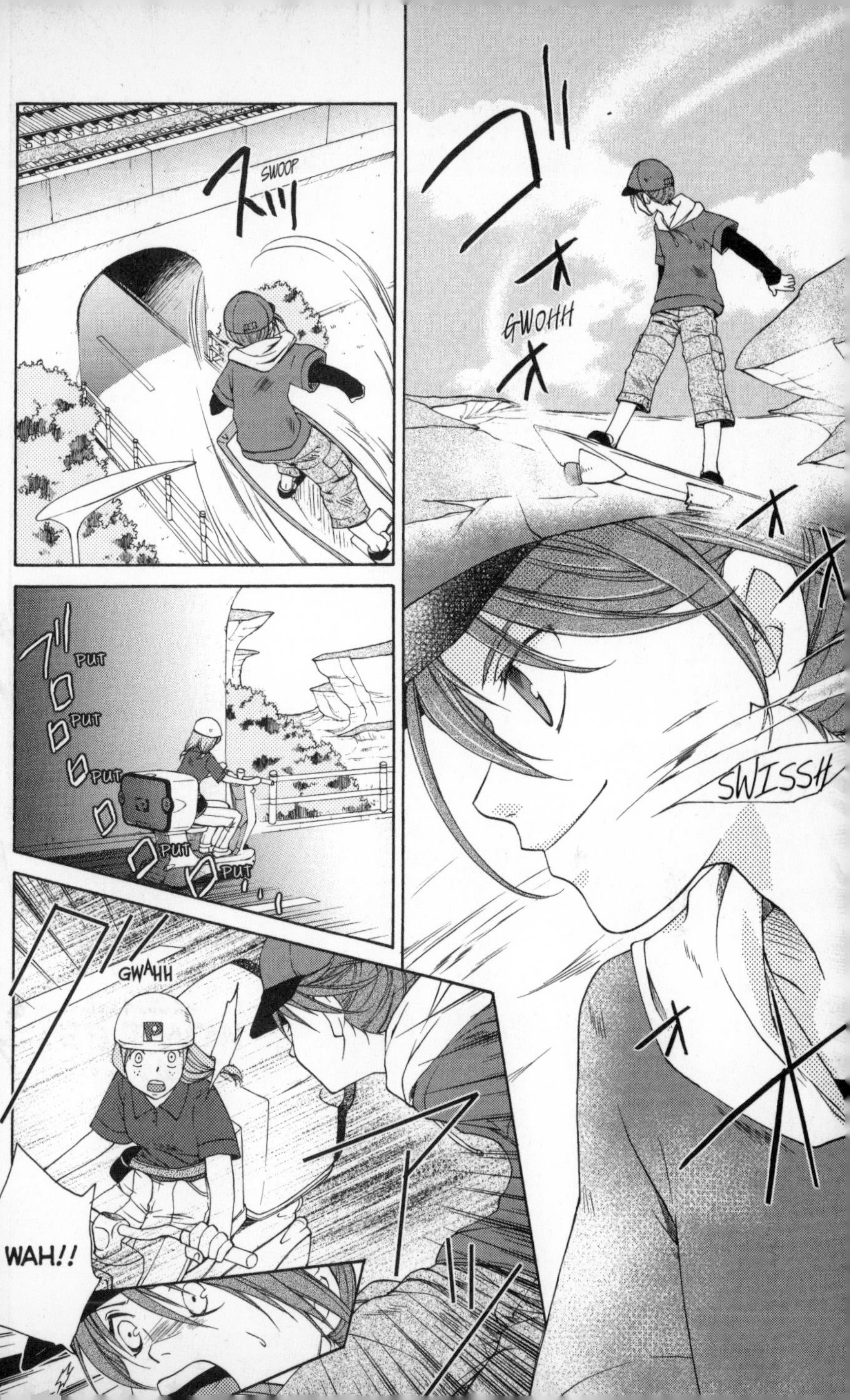
GWOHH
SWISSH
SWOOP
PUT
PUT
PUT
PUT
PUT
GWAHH
WAH!!

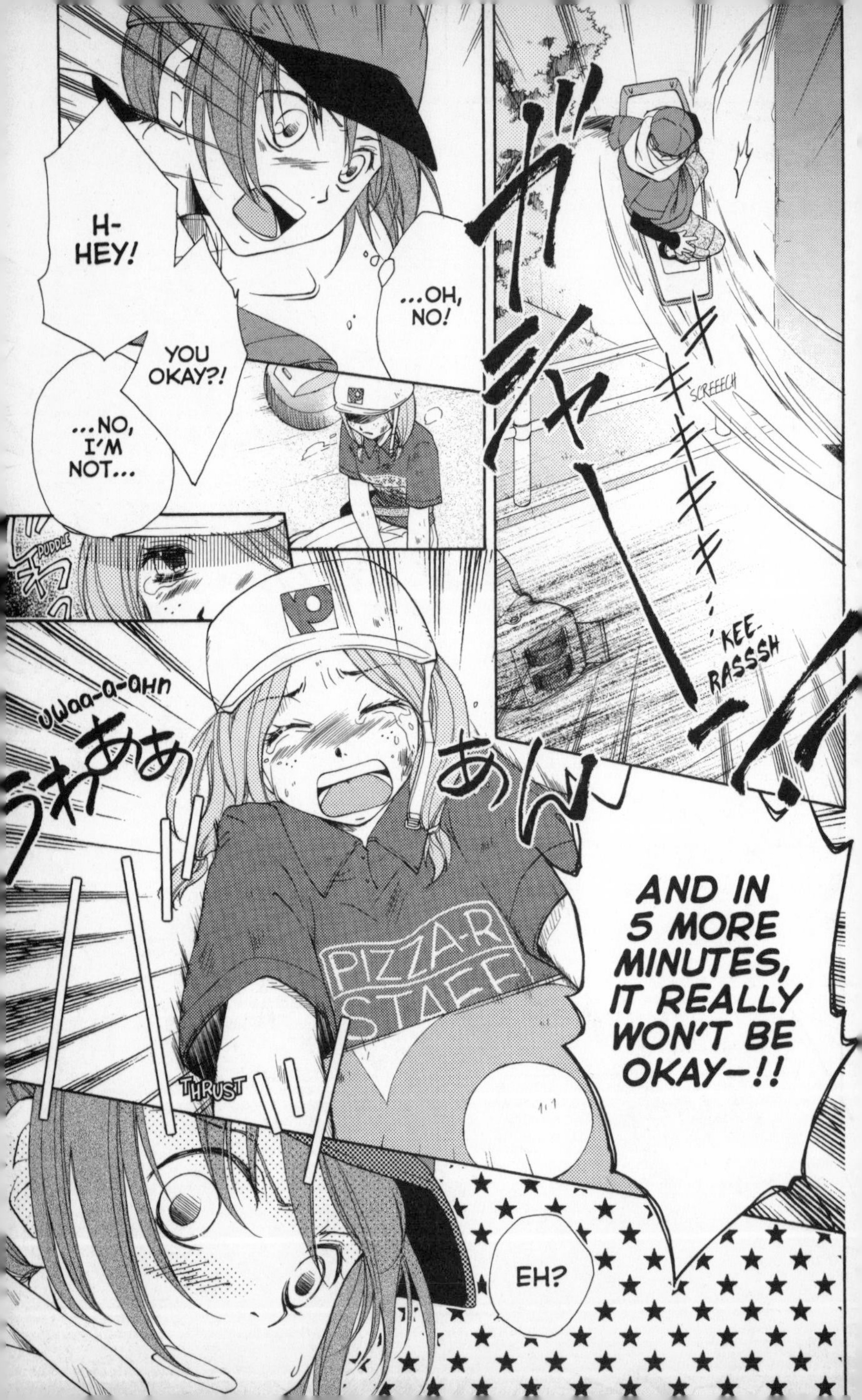

ザシャー
SCREEECH
KEE-RASSSH
H-HEY!
...OH, NO!
YOU OKAY?!
...NO, I'M NOT...
PUDDLE
AND IN 5 MORE MINUTES, IT REALLY WON'T BE OKAY—!!
うわあああん
UWAA-A-AHN
THRUST
EH?

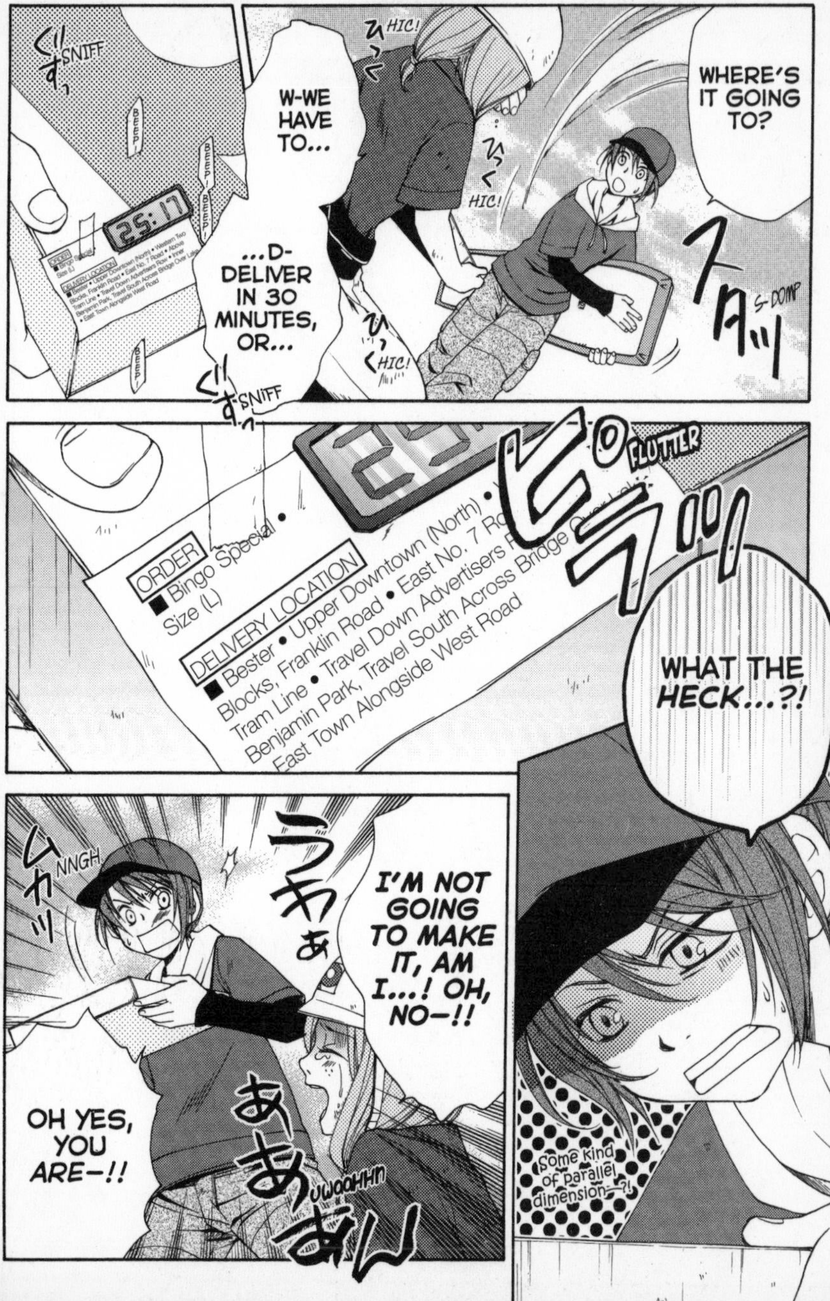
WHERE'S IT GOING TO?
S-DOMP
HIC!
W-WE HAVE TO...
HIC!
...D-DELIVER IN 30 MINUTES, OR...
HIC!
SNIFF
BEEP!
BEEP! BEEP!
25:17
ORDER ■ Bingo Special • Size (L)
DELIVERY LOCATION ■ Bester • Upper Downtown (North) • Western Two Blocks, Franklin Road • East No. 7 Road • Above Tram Line • Travel Down Advertisers Row • Inner Benjamin Park, Travel South Across Bridge Over Lake • East Town Alongside West Road
BEEP!
SNIFF
FLUTTER
ORDER ■ Bingo Special •
Size (L)
DELIVERY LOCATION ■ Bester • Upper Downtown (North) •
Blocks, Franklin Road • East No. 7 Ro
Tram Line • Travel Down Advertisers R
Benjamin Park, Travel South Across Bridge Over Lak
East Town Alongside West Road
WHAT THE HECK...?!
Some kind of parallel dimension—?!
I'M NOT GOING TO MAKE IT, AM I...! OH, NO-!!
NNGH
UWAAHHN
OH YES, YOU ARE-!!

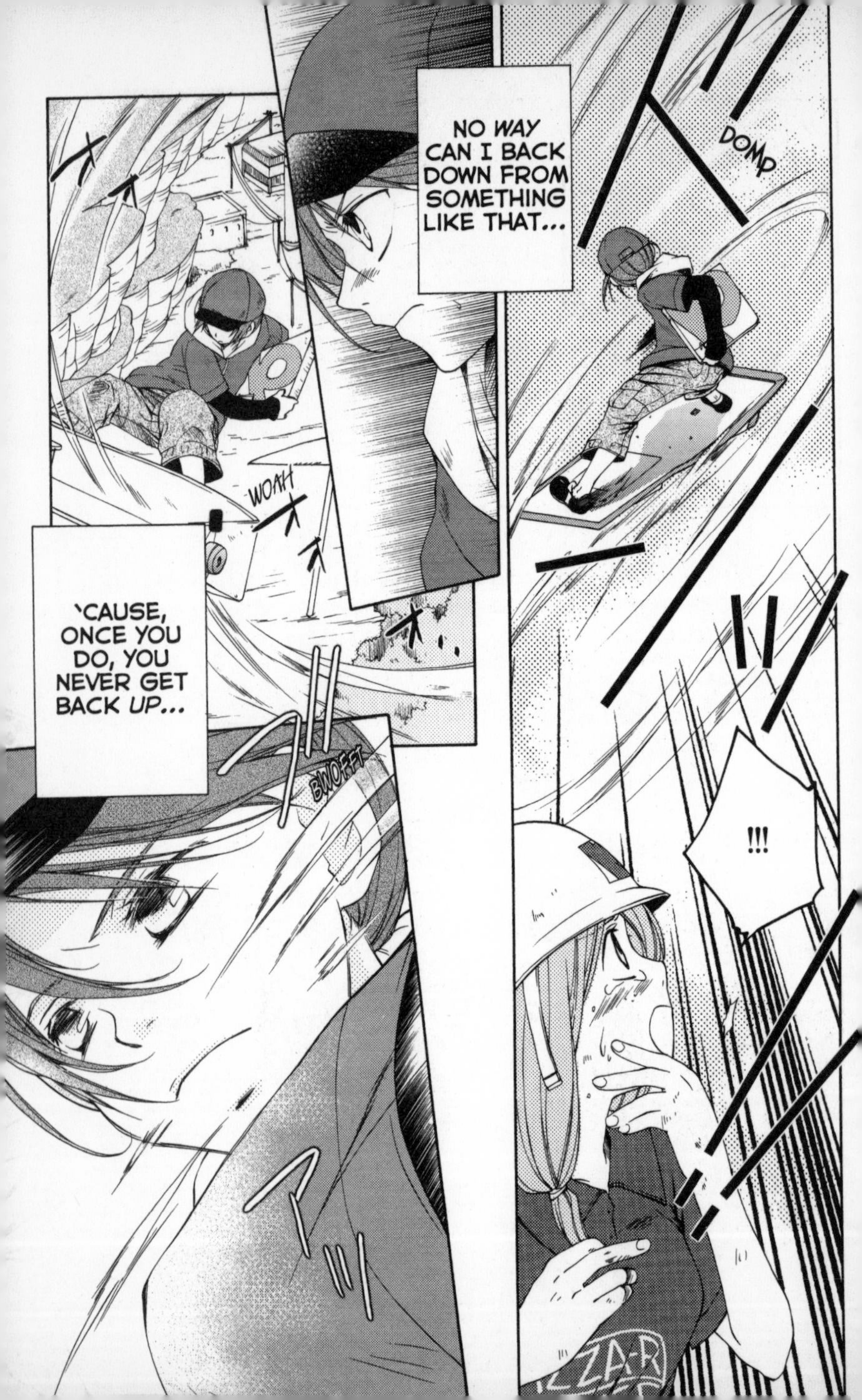
DOMP
!!!
NO WAY CAN I BACK DOWN FROM SOMETHING LIKE THAT...
WOAH
'CAUSE, ONCE YOU DO, YOU NEVER GET BACK UP...
BWOFFT

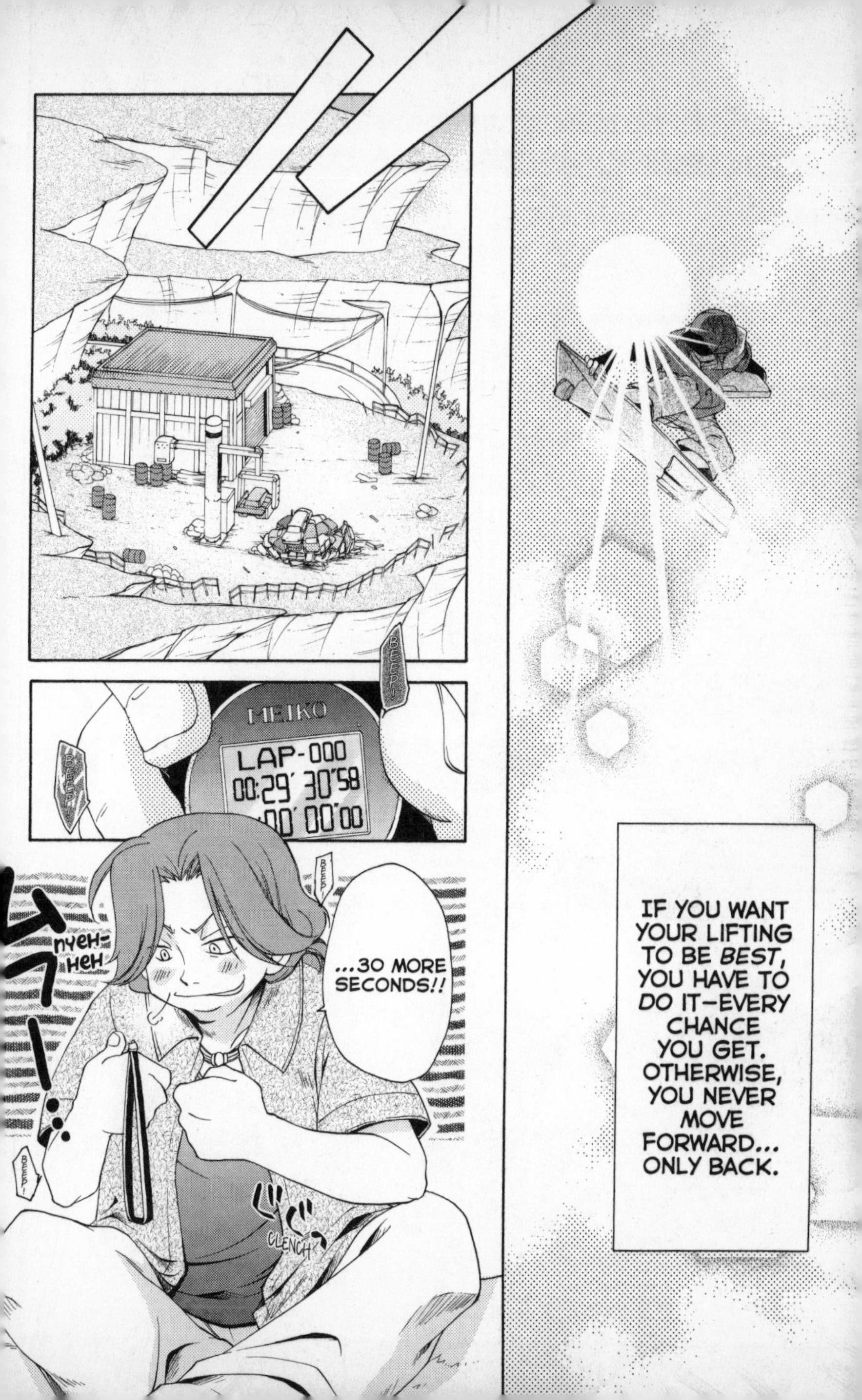
IF YOU WANT YOUR LIFTING TO BE *BEST*, YOU HAVE TO *DO* IT—EVERY CHANCE YOU GET. OTHERWISE, YOU NEVER MOVE FORWARD... ONLY BACK.
BEEP!
BEEP!
MEIKO
LAP-000
00:29′ 30″58
00′ 00″00
BEEP
...30 MORE SECONDS!!
nyeh-heh
BEEP-
CLENCH

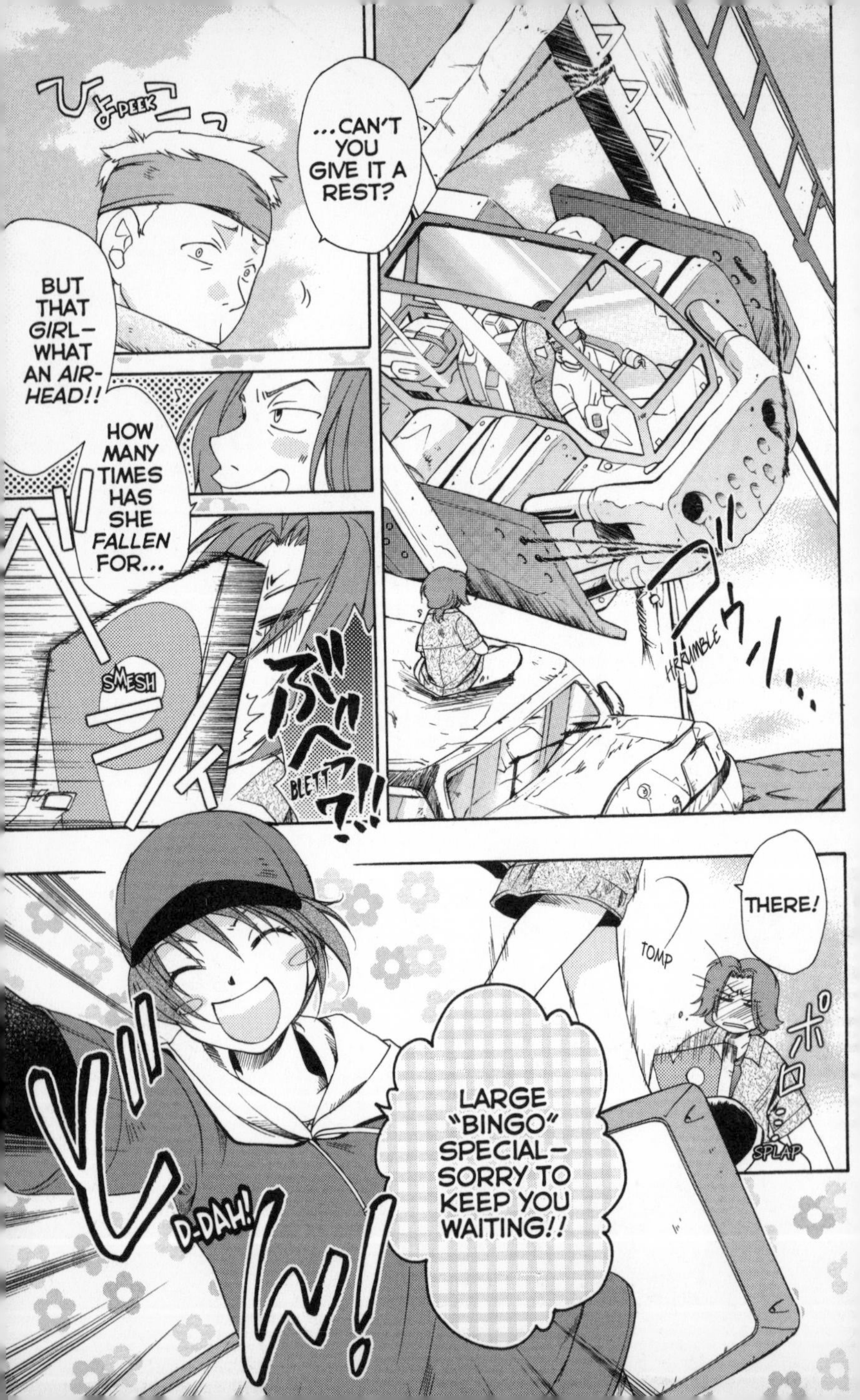

HRRUMBLE
PEEK
...CAN'T YOU GIVE IT A REST?
BUT THAT *GIRL*— WHAT AN *AIR-HEAD!!*
HOW MANY TIMES HAS SHE *FALLEN* FOR...
SMESH
BLETT
THERE!
TOMP
SPLAP
LARGE "BINGO" SPECIAL— SORRY TO KEEP YOU WAITING!!
D-DAH!

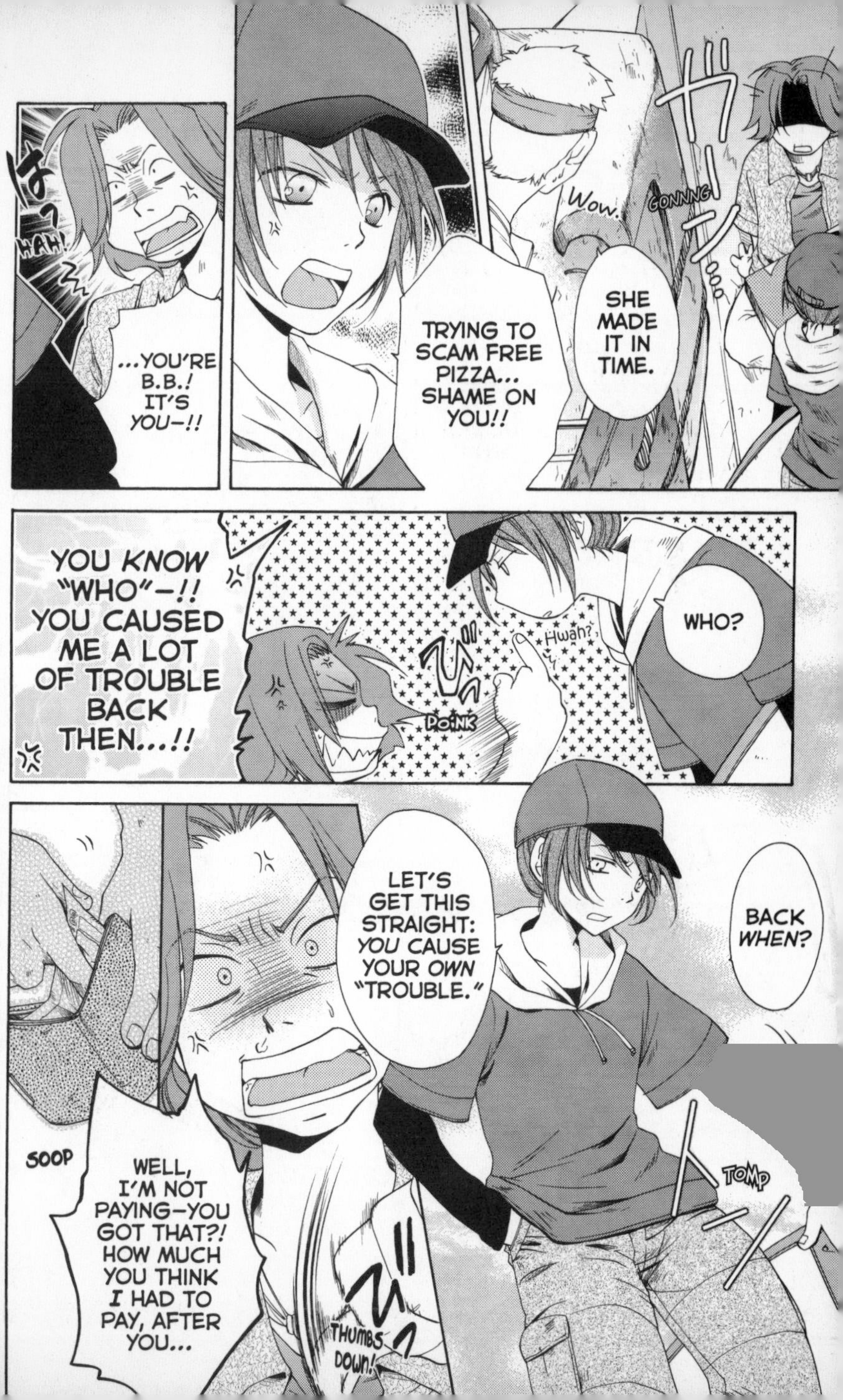
Wow.
GONNNG
SHE MADE IT IN TIME.
TRYING TO SCAM FREE PIZZA... SHAME ON YOU!!
WAH!
...YOU'RE B.B.! IT'S *YOU*—!!
WHO?
Hwah?
DOINK
YOU *KNOW* "WHO"—!! YOU CAUSED ME A LOT OF TROUBLE BACK THEN...!!
BACK *WHEN*?
TOMP
LET'S GET THIS STRAIGHT: *YOU* CAUSE YOUR *OWN* "TROUBLE."
SOOP
WELL, I'M NOT PAYING—YOU GOT THAT?! HOW MUCH YOU THINK *I* HAD TO PAY, AFTER YOU...
THUMBS DOWN!

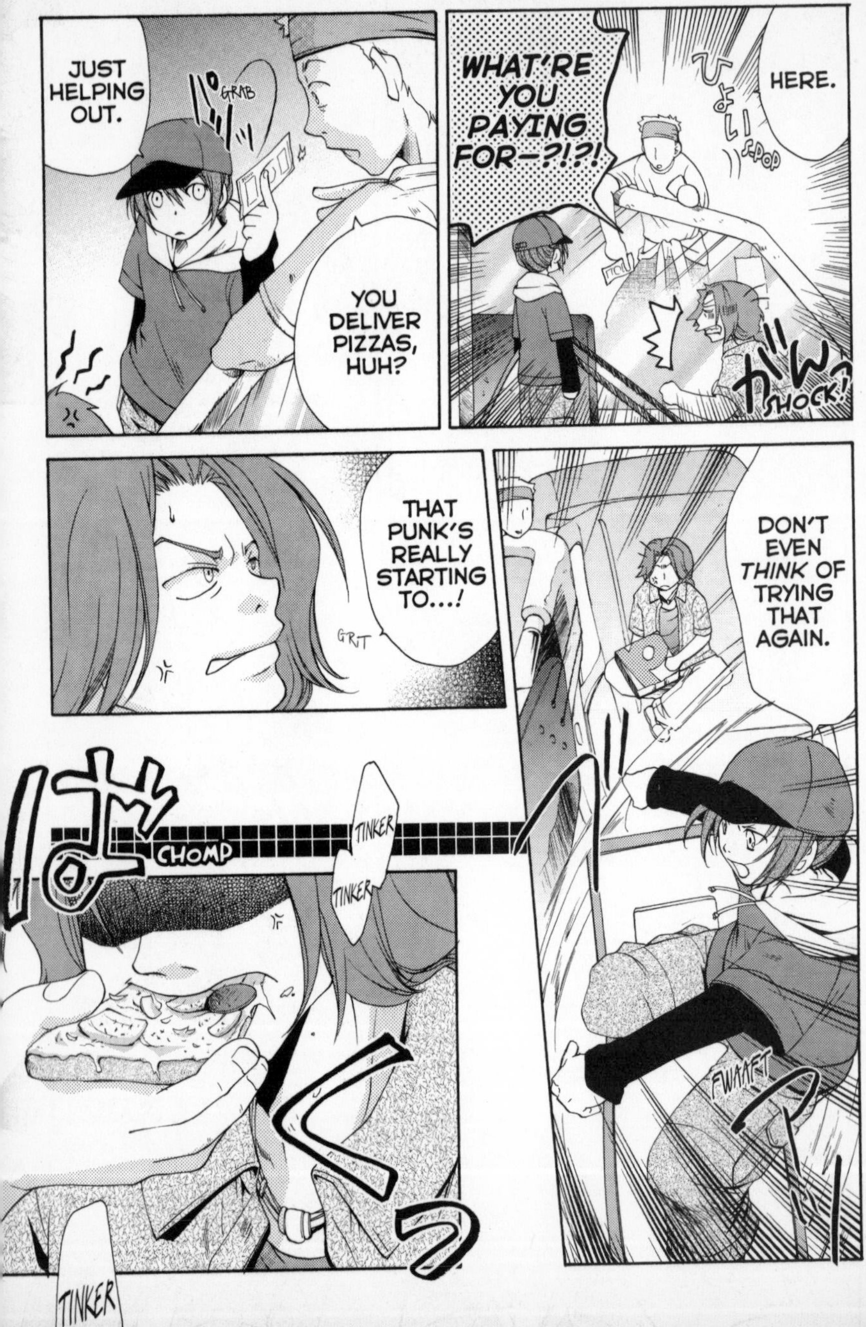
HERE.
ひょい
SPOP
WHAT'RE YOU PAYING FOR-?!?!
SHOCK
YOU DELIVER PIZZAS, HUH?
JUST HELPING OUT.
GRAB
DON'T EVEN *THINK* OF TRYING THAT AGAIN.
FWAAFT
THAT PUNK'S REALLY STARTING TO...!
GRIT
CHOMP
TINKER
TINKER
TINKER

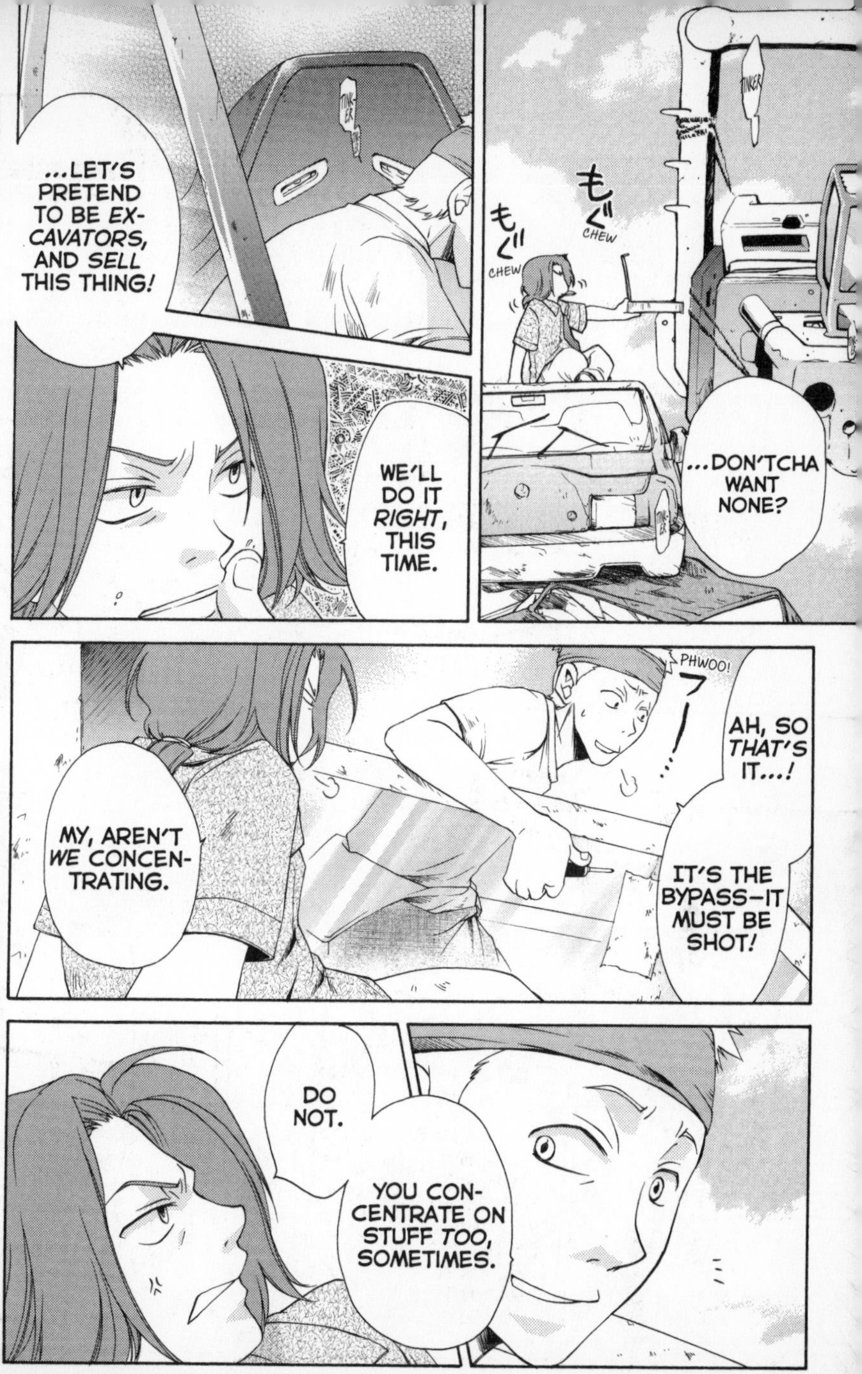
TINKER
もぐ
CHEW
もぐ
CHEW
...DON'TCHA WANT NONE?
...LET'S PRETEND TO BE EX-CAVATORS, AND SELL THIS THING!
WE'LL DO IT RIGHT, THIS TIME.
PHWOO!
AH, SO THAT'S IT...!
IT'S THE BYPASS—IT MUST BE SHOT!
MY, AREN'T WE CONCEN-TRATING.
DO NOT.
YOU CON-CENTRATE ON STUFF TOO, SOMETIMES.

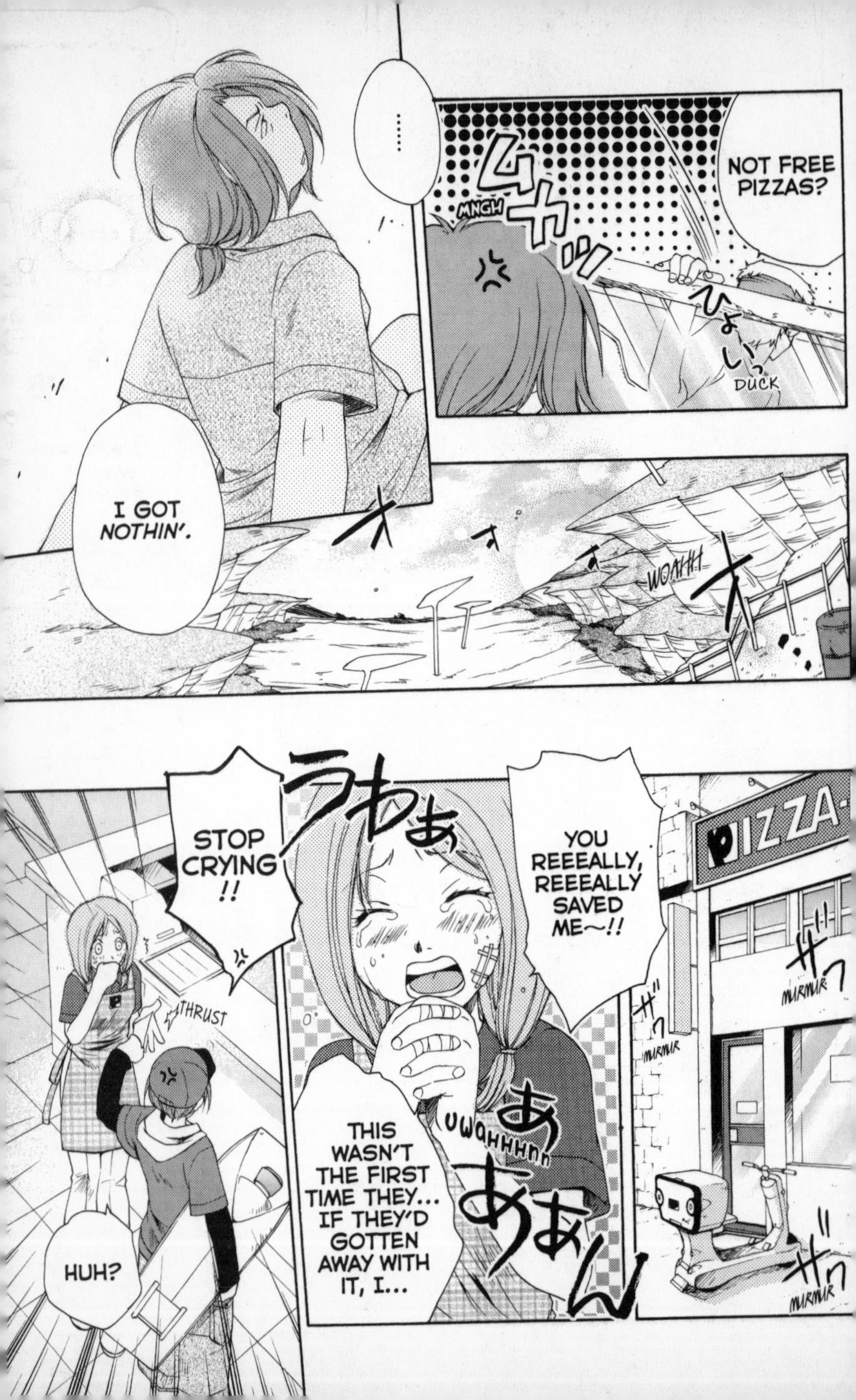
NOT FREE PIZZAS?
MNGH
DUCK
WOAHH
......
I GOT NOTHIN'.
YOU REEEALLY, REEEALLY SAVED ME~!!
MURMUR
MURMUR
MURMUR
UWAHHHnn
THIS WASN'T THE FIRST TIME THEY... IF THEY'D GOTTEN AWAY WITH IT, I...
STOP CRYING!!
THRUST
HUH?

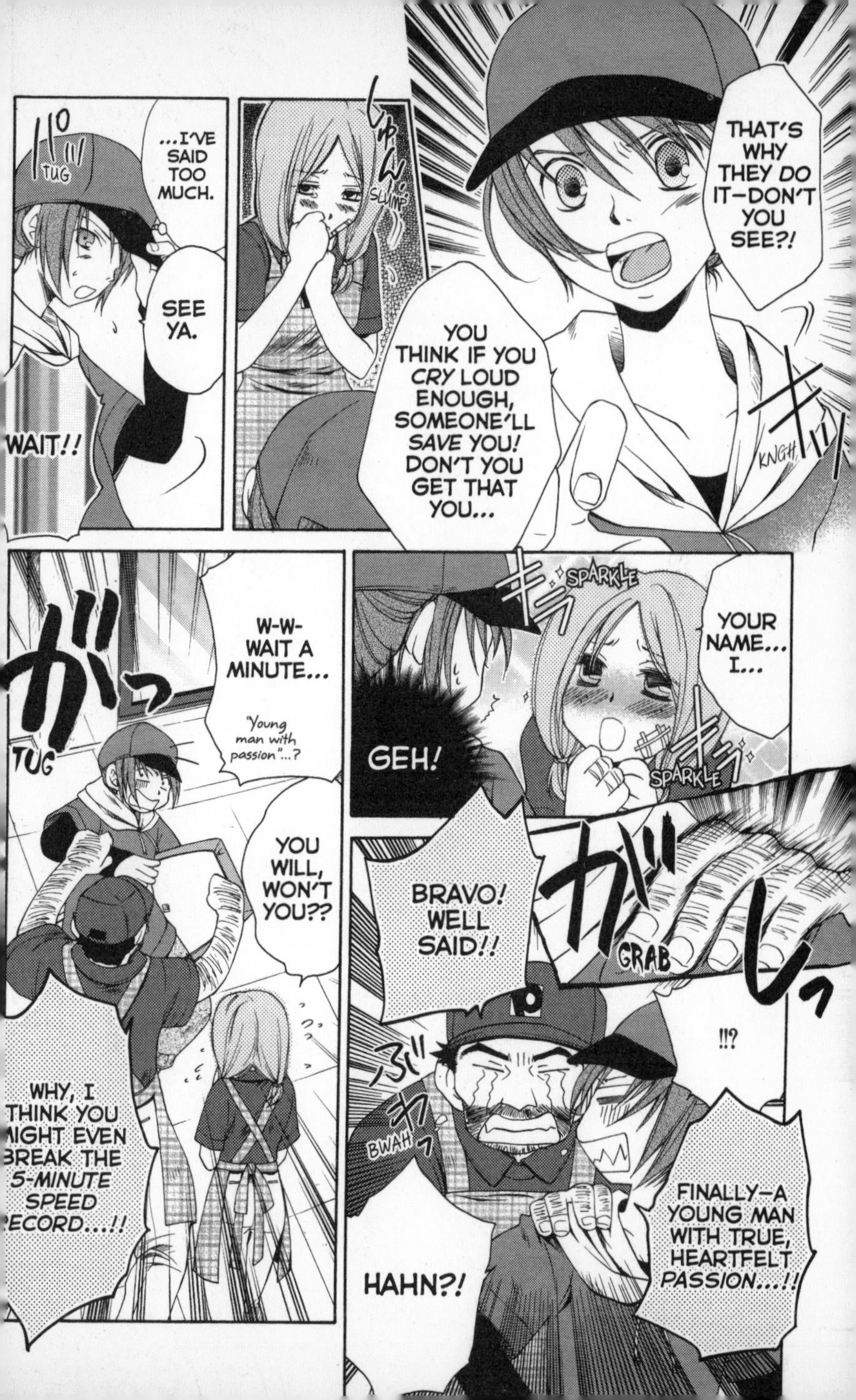
THAT'S WHY THEY *DO* IT—DON'T YOU SEE?!
YOU THINK IF YOU *CRY* LOUD ENOUGH, SOMEONE'LL *SAVE YOU!* DON'T YOU GET THAT YOU...
KNGH
SLUMP
TUG
...I'VE SAID TOO MUCH.
SEE YA.
WAIT!!
YOUR NAME... I...
SPARKLE
GEH!
SPARKLE
GRAB
BRAVO! WELL SAID!!
!!?
BWAH
FINALLY—A YOUNG MAN WITH TRUE, HEARTFELT *PASSION*...!!
HAHN?!
W-W-WAIT A MINUTE...
TUG
"Young man with passion"...?
YOU WILL, WON'T YOU??
WHY, I THINK YOU IGHT EVEN BREAK THE *5-MINUTE* SPEED ECORD...!!

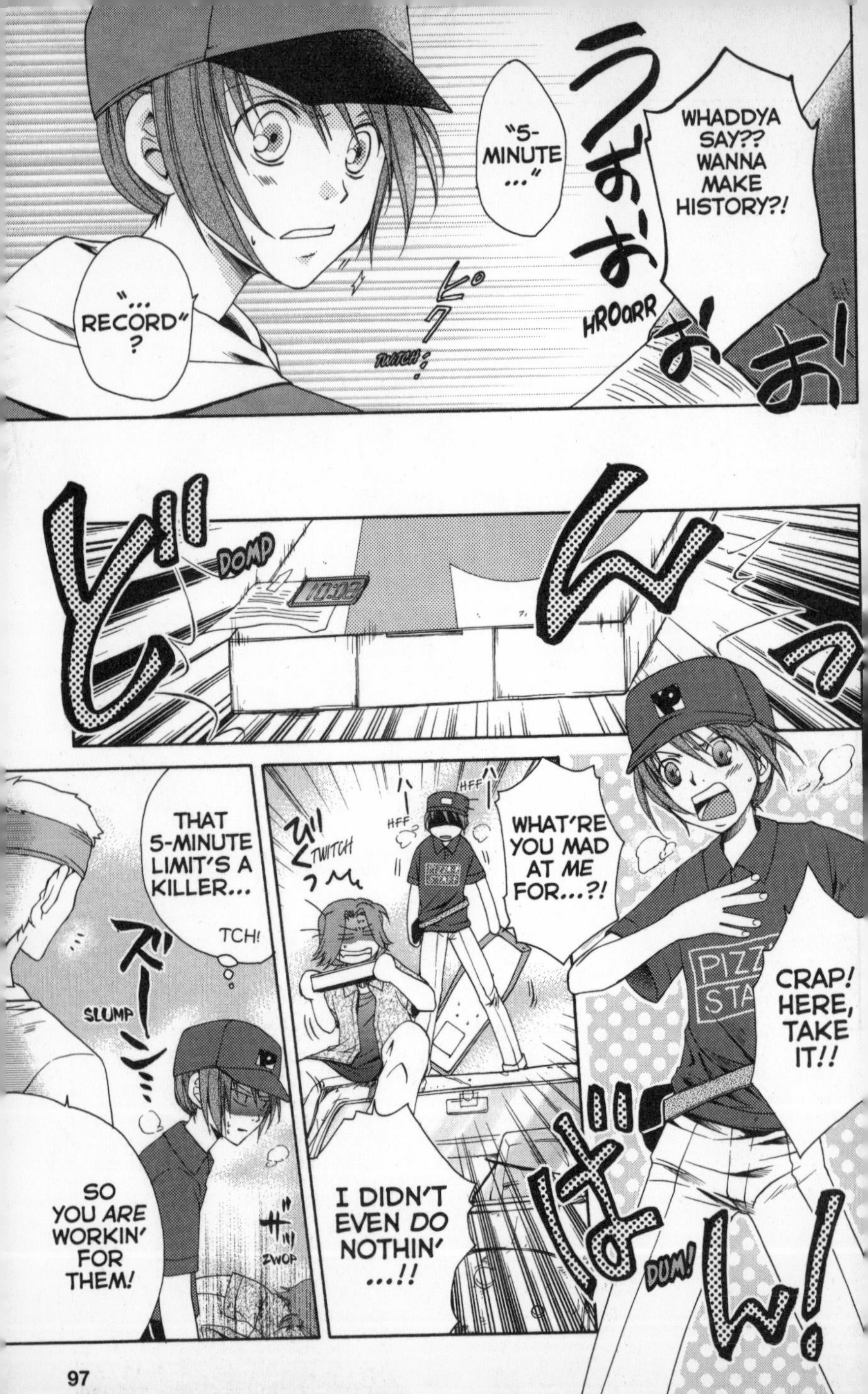
WHADDYA SAY?? WANNA MAKE HISTORY?!
うぉぉぉお!
HROARR
"5-MINUTE..."
"...RECORD"?
ピク
TWITCH
どん
DOMP
CRAP! HERE, TAKE IT!!
ばん!
DUM!
WHAT'RE YOU MAD AT ME FOR...?!
ハー ハー
HFF HFF
びく
TWITCH
I DIDN'T EVEN DO NOTHIN'...!!
THAT 5-MINUTE LIMIT'S A KILLER...
TCH!
ズーン
SLUMP
SO YOU ARE WORKIN' FOR THEM!
ZWOP

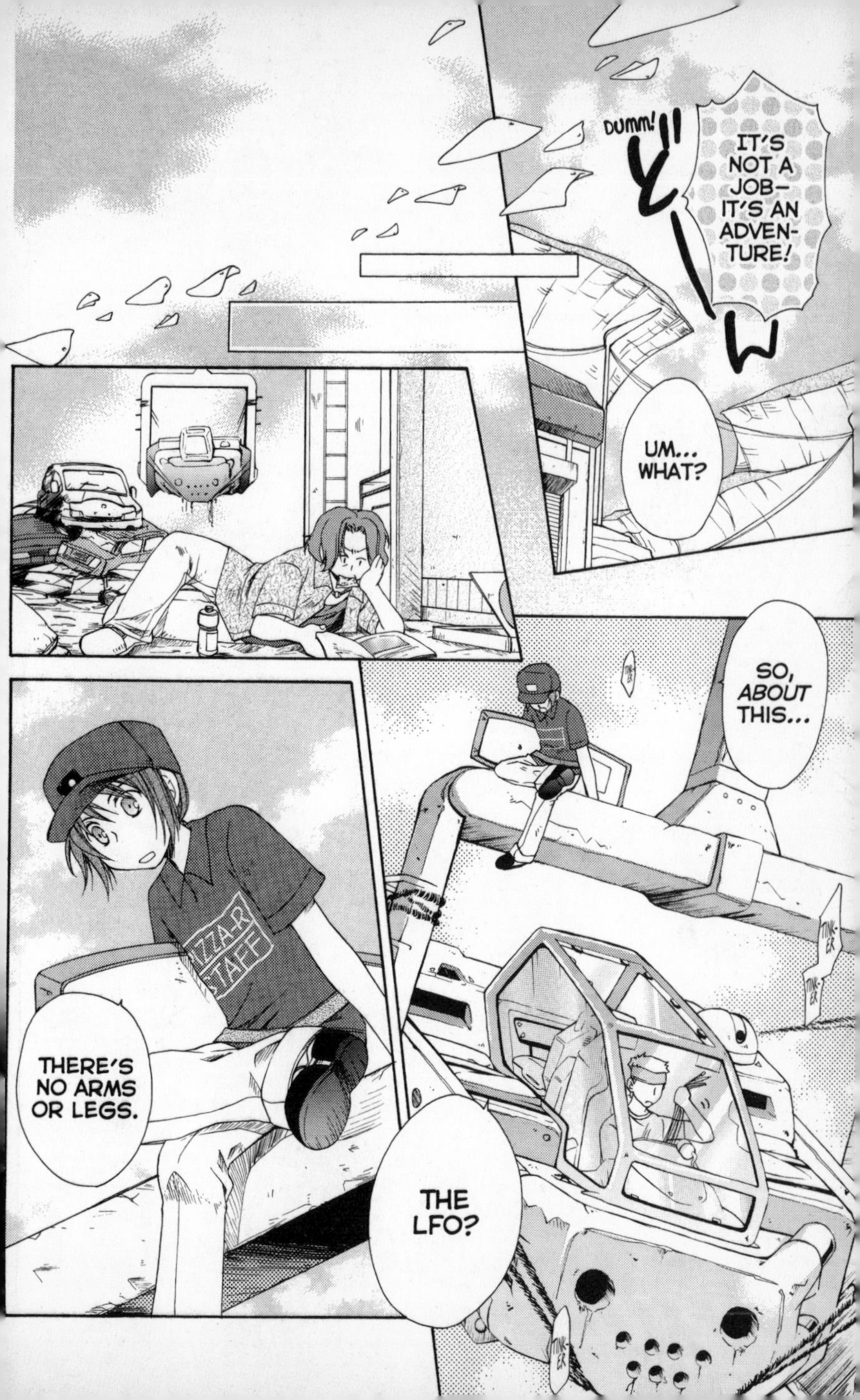
DUMM!
IT'S NOT A JOB— IT'S AN ADVENTURE!
UM... WHAT?
TINK-ER
SO, ABOUT THIS...
TINK-ER
TINK-ER
THE LFO?
TINK-ER
THERE'S NO ARMS OR LEGS.

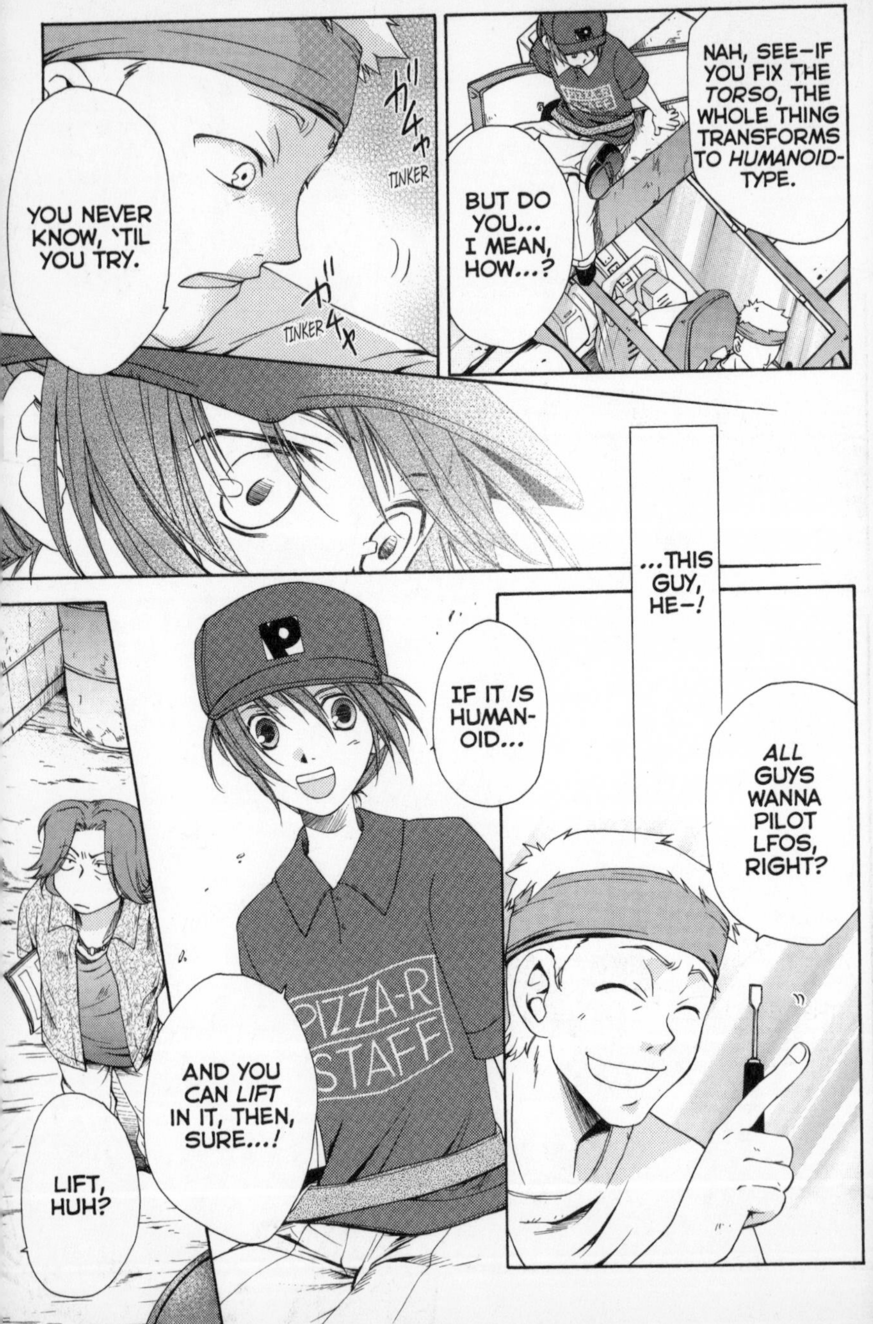
NAH, SEE—IF YOU FIX THE *TORSO*, THE WHOLE THING TRANSFORMS TO *HUMANOID*-TYPE.
BUT DO YOU... I MEAN, HOW...?
ガチャ
TINKER
YOU NEVER KNOW, 'TIL YOU TRY.
ガチャ
TINKER
...THIS GUY, HE—!
ALL GUYS WANNA PILOT LFOS, RIGHT?
IF IT *IS* HUMANOID...
AND YOU CAN *LIFT* IN IT, THEN, SURE...!
LIFT, HUH?

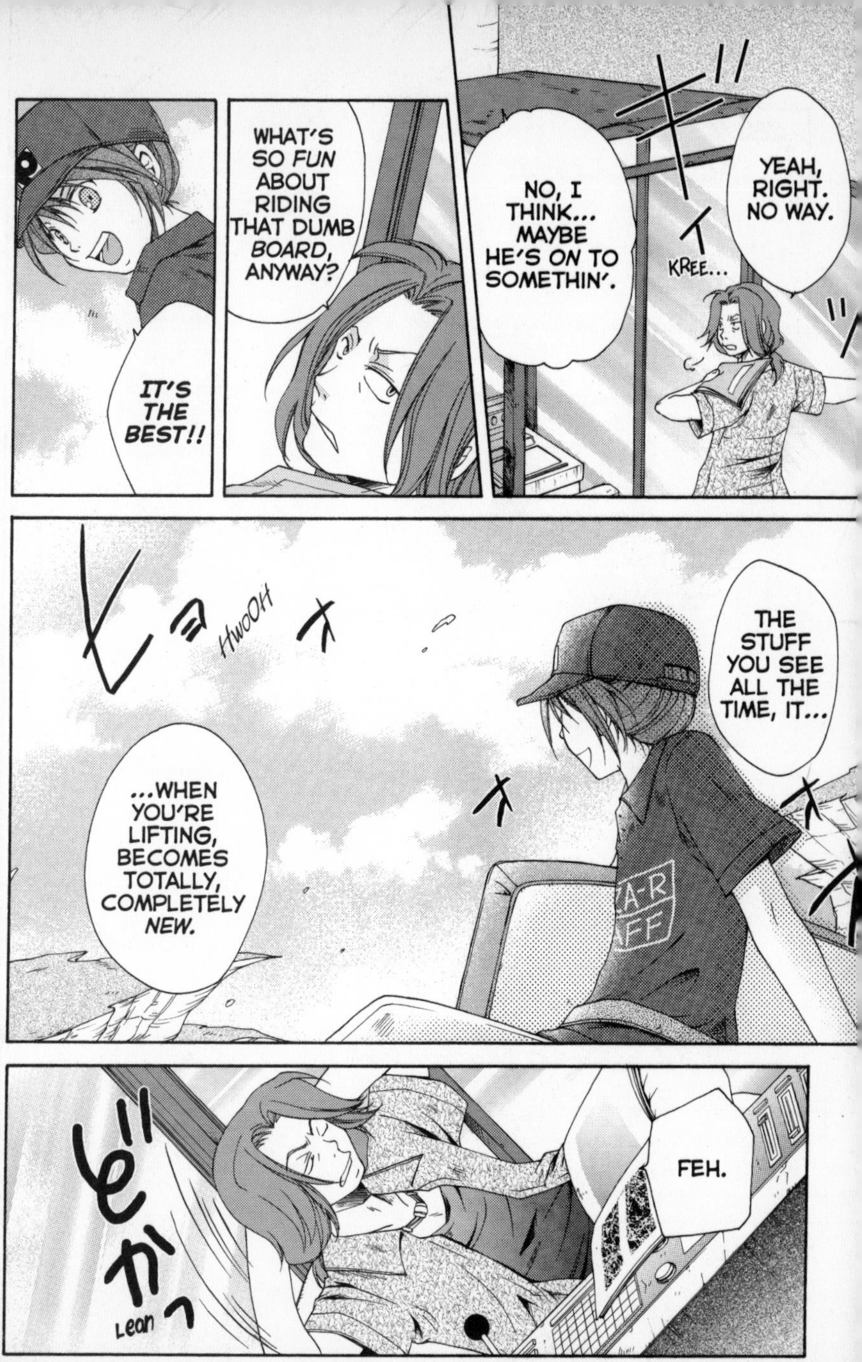
YEAH, RIGHT. NO WAY.
KREE...
NO, I THINK... MAYBE HE'S ON TO SOMETHIN'.
WHAT'S SO *FUN* ABOUT RIDING THAT DUMB *BOARD*, ANYWAY?
IT'S THE BEST!!
HWOOH
THE STUFF YOU SEE ALL THE TIME, IT...
...WHEN YOU'RE LIFTING, BECOMES TOTALLY, COMPLETELY *NEW*.
FEH.
Lean

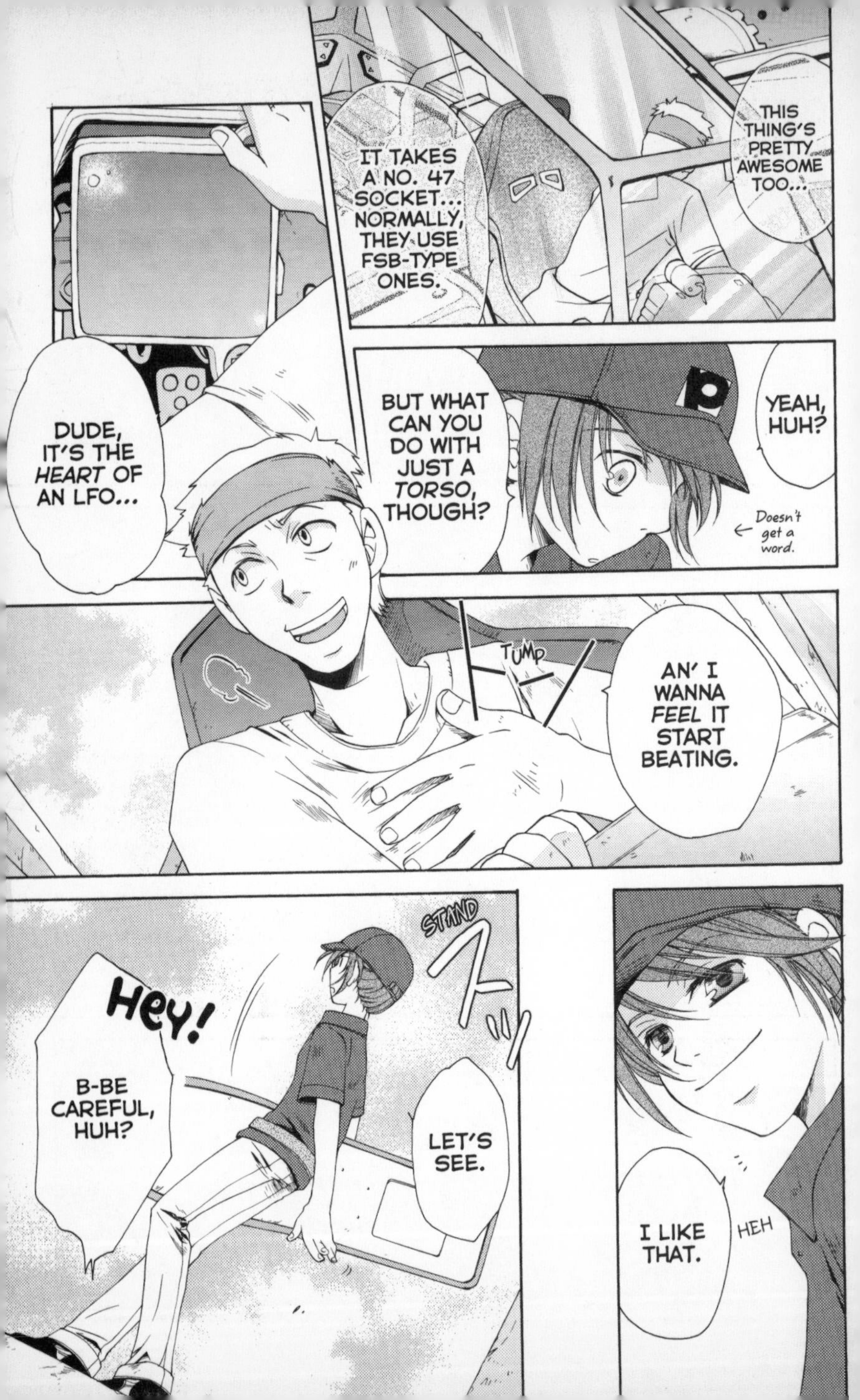
THIS THING'S PRETTY AWESOME TOO...
IT TAKES A NO. 47 SOCKET... NORMALLY, THEY USE FSB-TYPE ONES.
YEAH, HUH?
Doesn't get a word.
BUT WHAT CAN YOU DO WITH JUST A *TORSO*, THOUGH?
DUDE, IT'S THE *HEART* OF AN LFO...
TUMP
AN' I WANNA *FEEL* IT START BEATING.
HEH
I LIKE THAT.
STAND
LET'S SEE.
HEY!
B-BE CAREFUL, HUH?

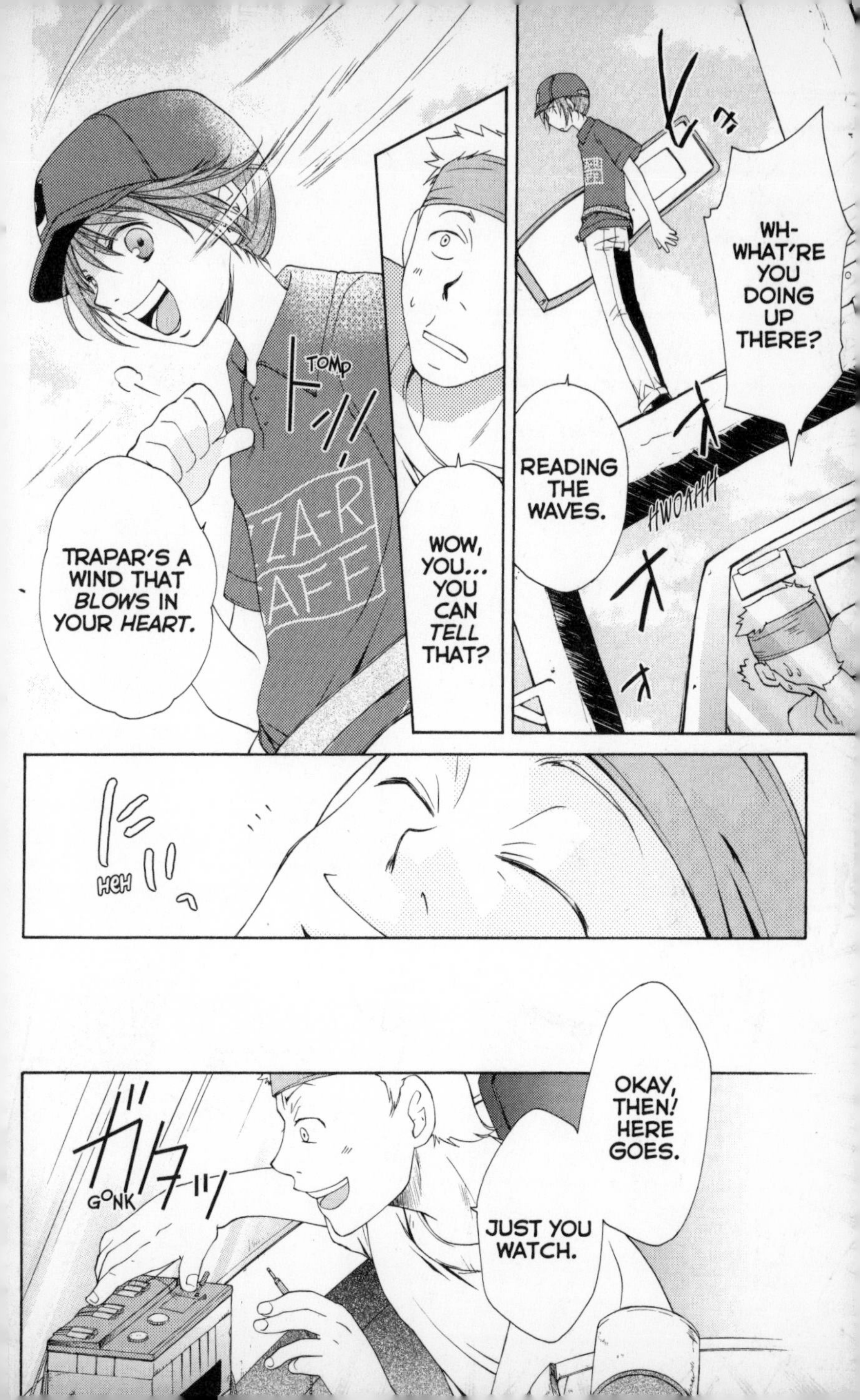
WH-WHAT'RE YOU DOING UP THERE?
READING THE WAVES.
HWOAHH
WOW, YOU... YOU CAN TELL THAT?
TOMP
TRAPAR'S A WIND THAT BLOWS IN YOUR HEART.
HEH
OKAY, THEN! HERE GOES.
JUST YOU WATCH.
GONK

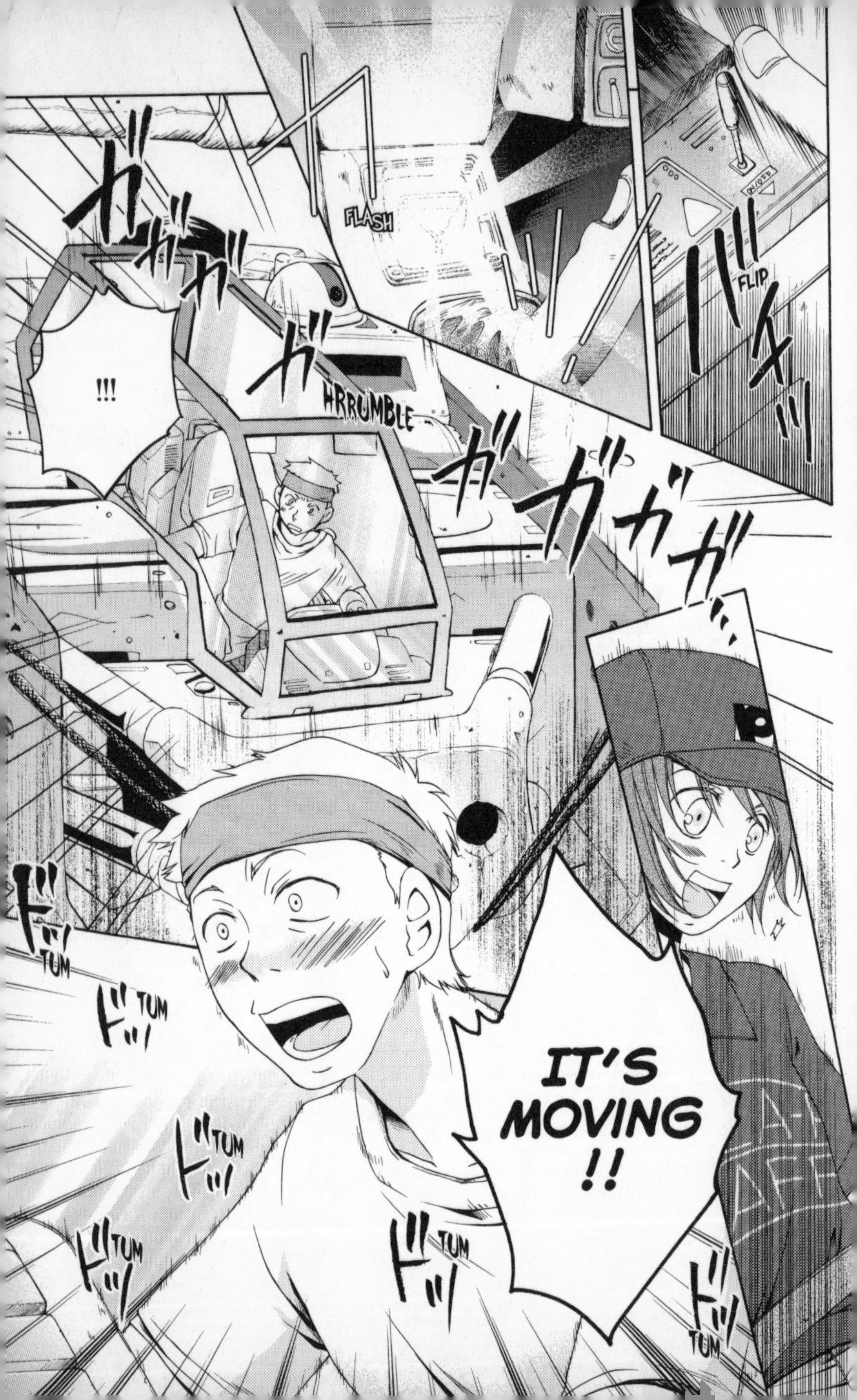

ON/OFF
FLIP
FLASH
HRRUMBLE
!!!
IT'S MOVING !!
TUM
TUM
TUM
TUM
TUM
TUM

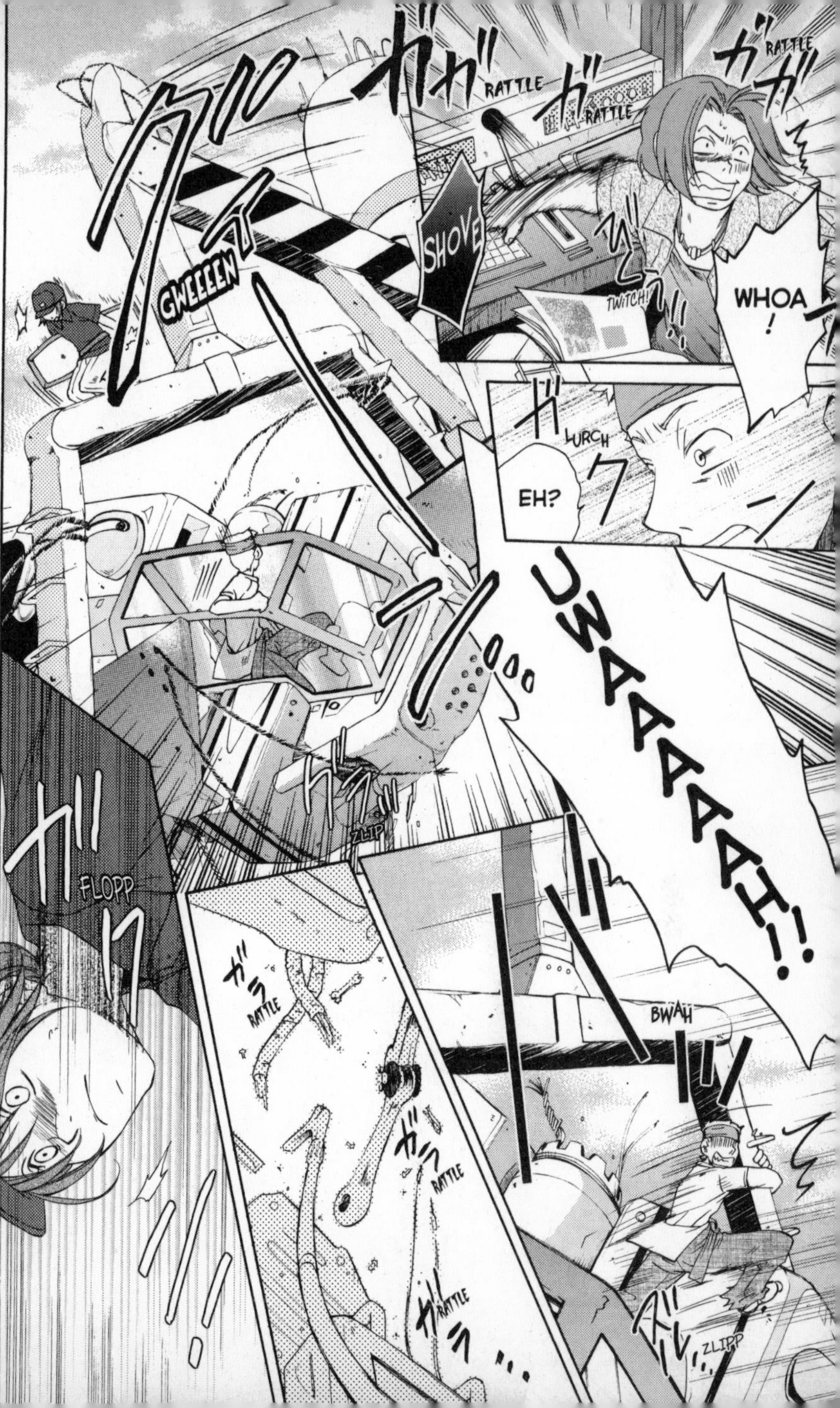
RATTLE
RATTLE
RATTLE
WHOA!
TWITCH!
SHOVE
GWEEEEN
LURCH
EH?
UWAAAAAH!!
ZLIP
FLOPP
BWAH
RATTLE
RATTLE
RATTLE
ZLIPP

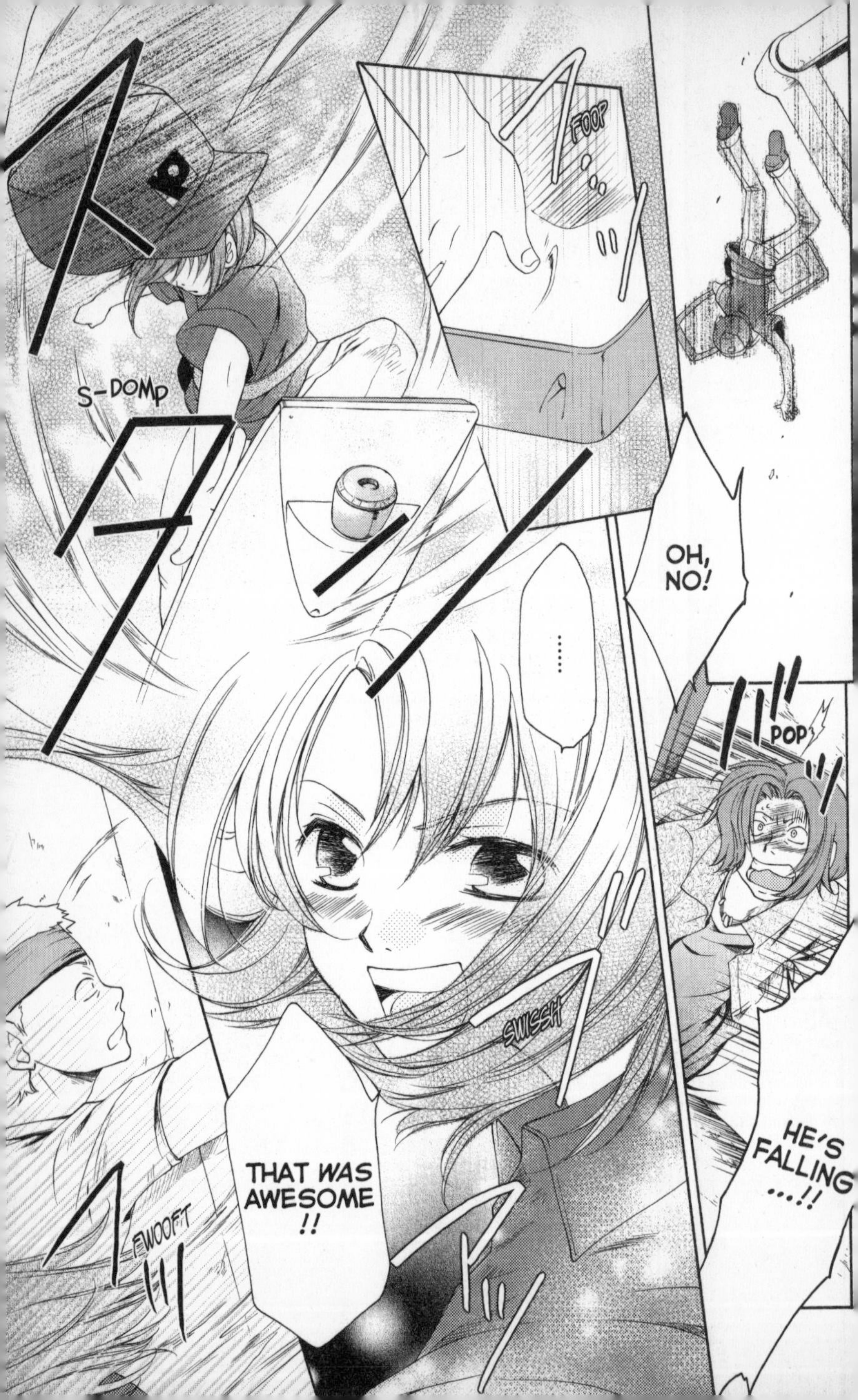
OH, NO!
POP
HE'S FALLING...!!
FOOP
......
SWISSH
THAT WAS AWESOME!!
S-DOMP
FWOOFT

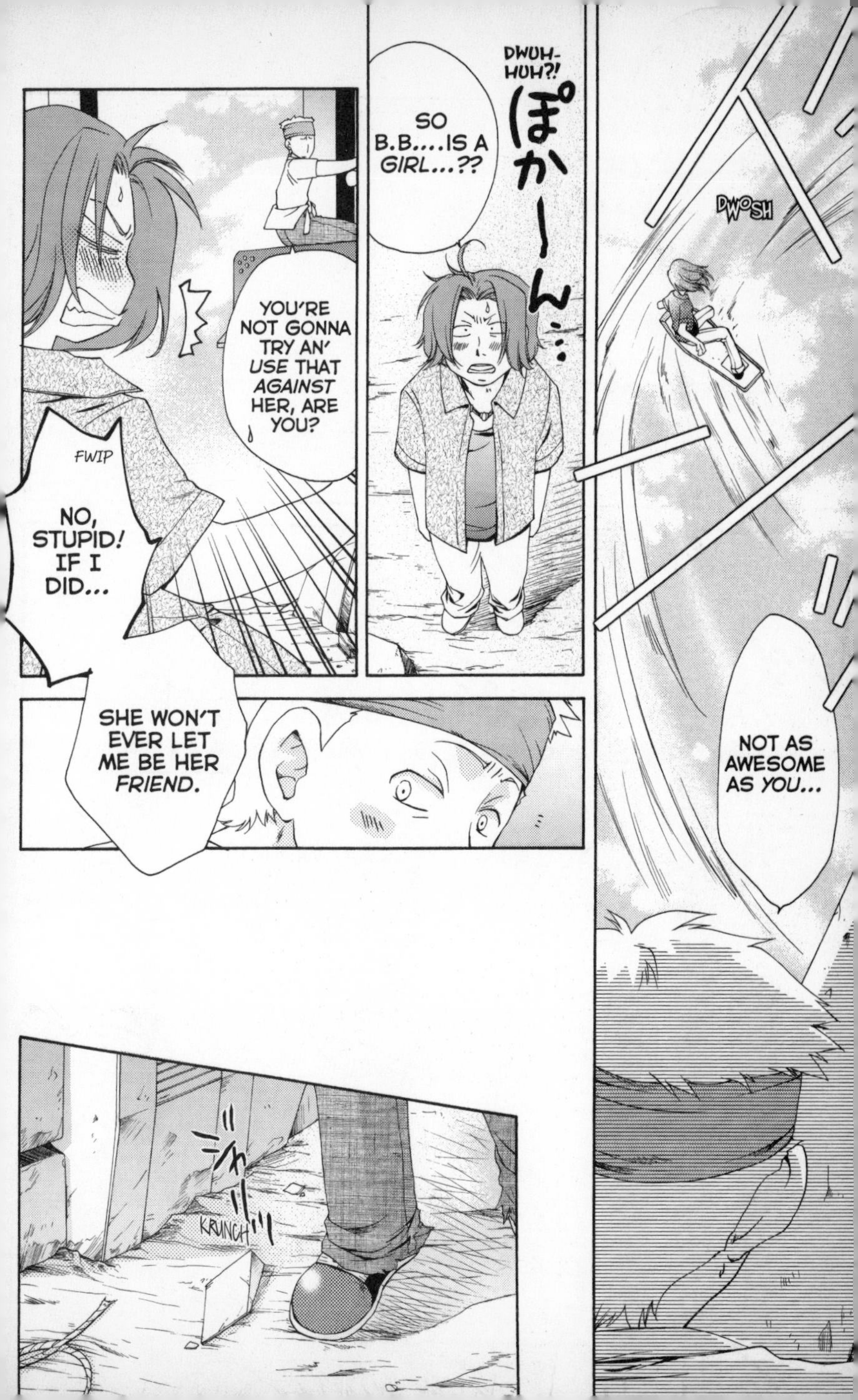
DWOSH
NOT AS AWESOME AS YOU...
DWUH-HUH?!
ぽかーん
SO B.B....IS A GIRL...??
YOU'RE NOT GONNA TRY AN' USE THAT AGAINST HER, ARE YOU?
FWIP
NO, STUPID! IF I DID...
SHE WON'T EVER LET ME BE HER FRIEND.
KRUNCH

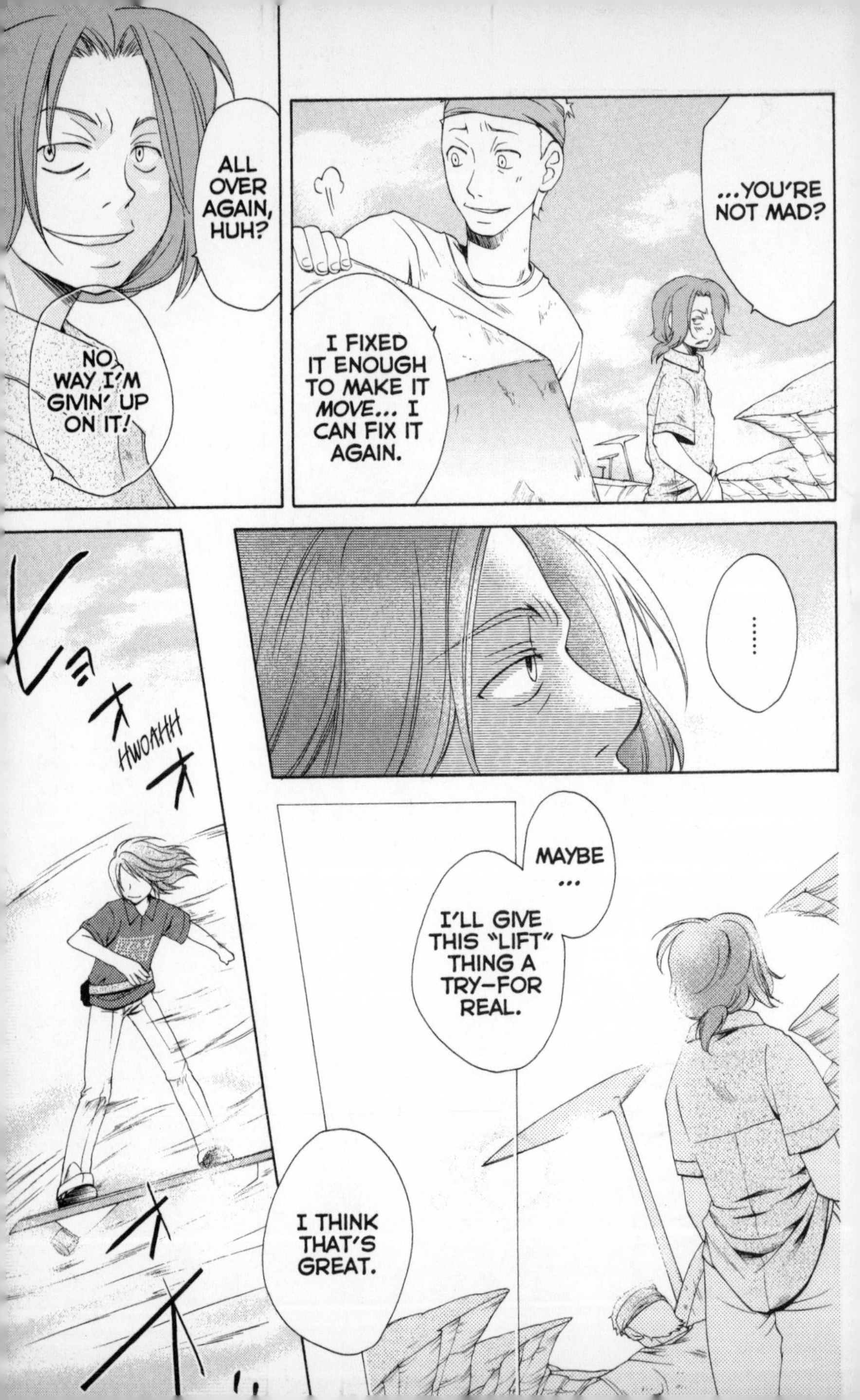
...YOU'RE NOT MAD?
I FIXED IT ENOUGH TO MAKE IT MOVE... I CAN FIX IT AGAIN.
ALL OVER AGAIN, HUH?
NO WAY I'M GIVIN' UP ON IT!
......
MAYBE... I'LL GIVE THIS "LIFT" THING A TRY—FOR REAL.
I THINK THAT'S GREAT.
HWOAHH

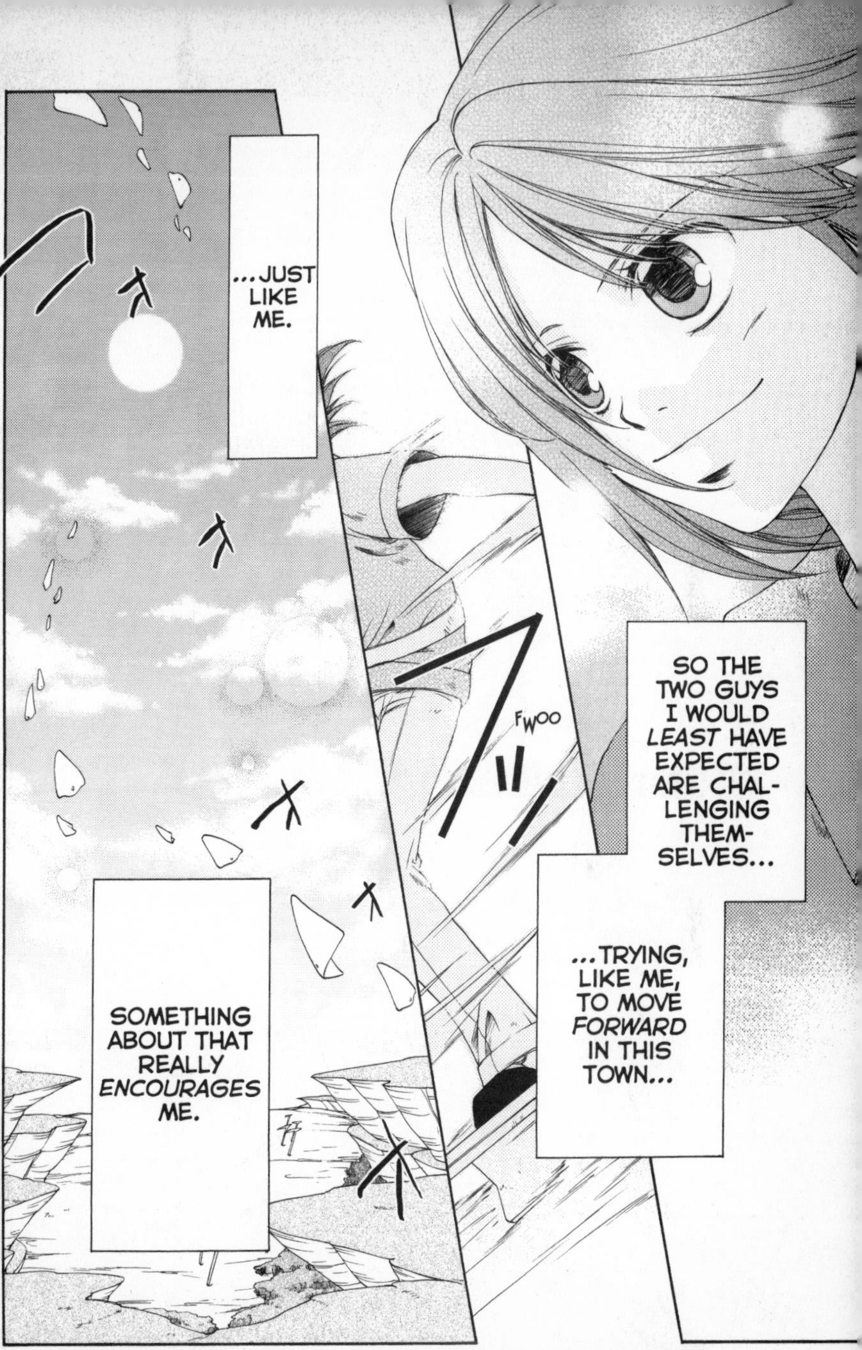
SO THE TWO GUYS I WOULD LEAST HAVE EXPECTED ARE CHAL-LENGING THEM-SELVES...
...TRYING, LIKE ME, TO MOVE FORWARD IN THIS TOWN...
FWOO
...JUST LIKE ME.
SOMETHING ABOUT THAT REALLY ENCOURAGES ME.

04 CHALLENGER END

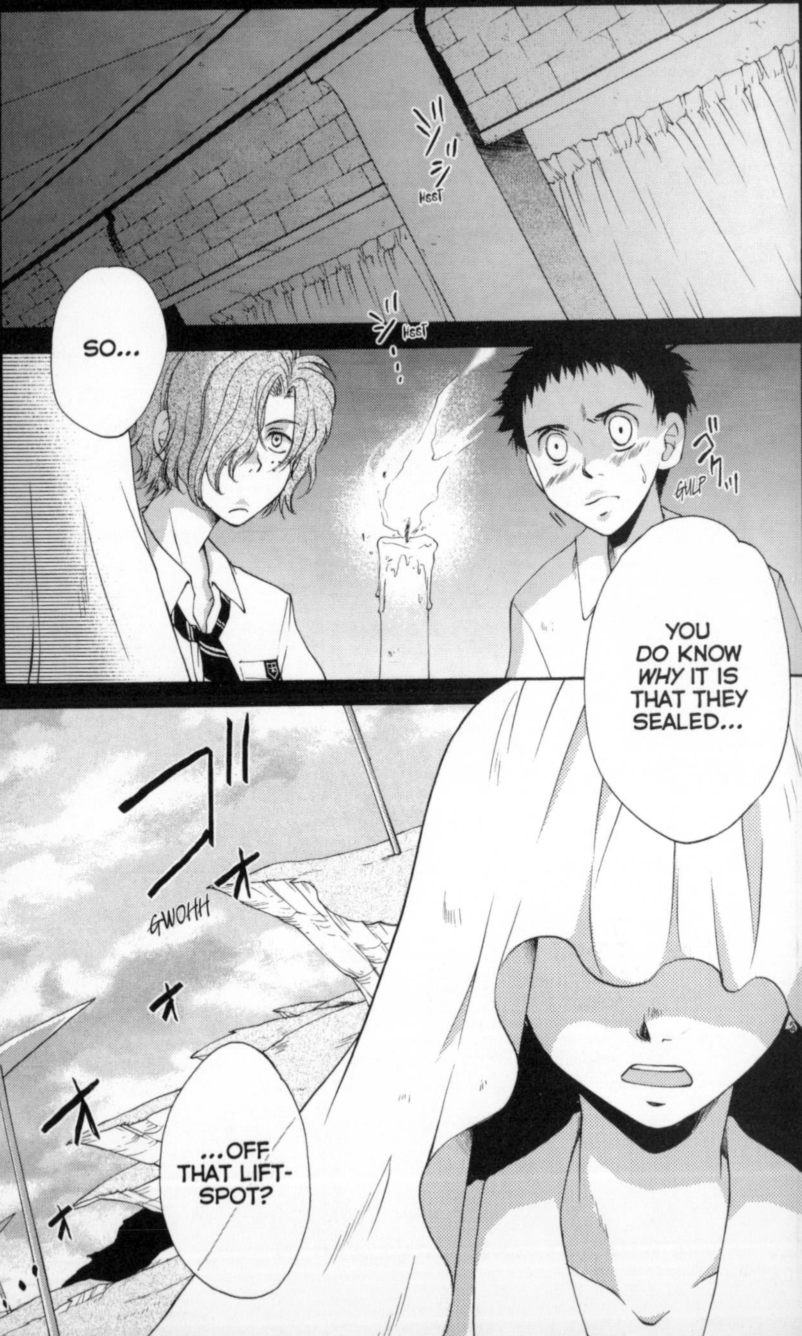
HSST
HSST
SO...
GULP
YOU DO KNOW WHY IT IS THAT THEY SEALED...
GWOHH
...OFF THAT LIFT-SPOT?

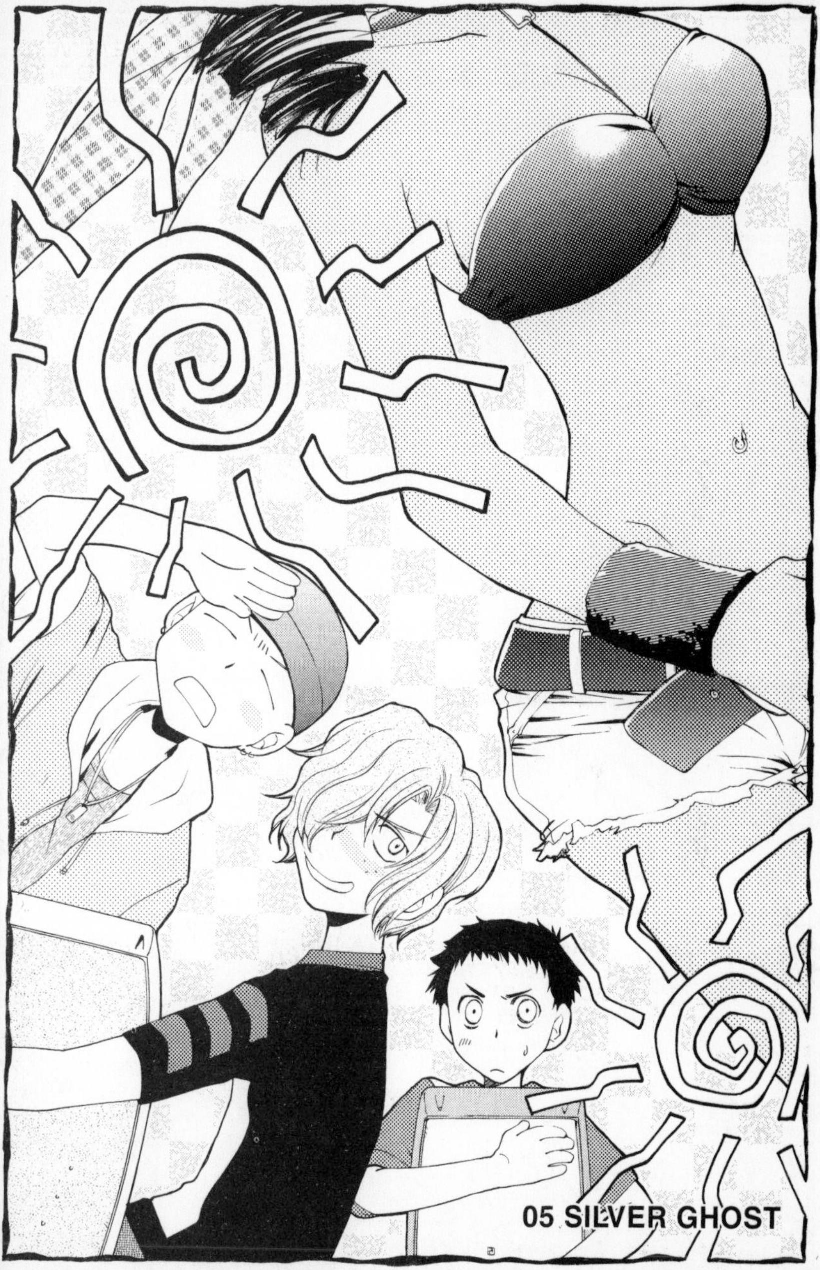
05 SILVER GHOST

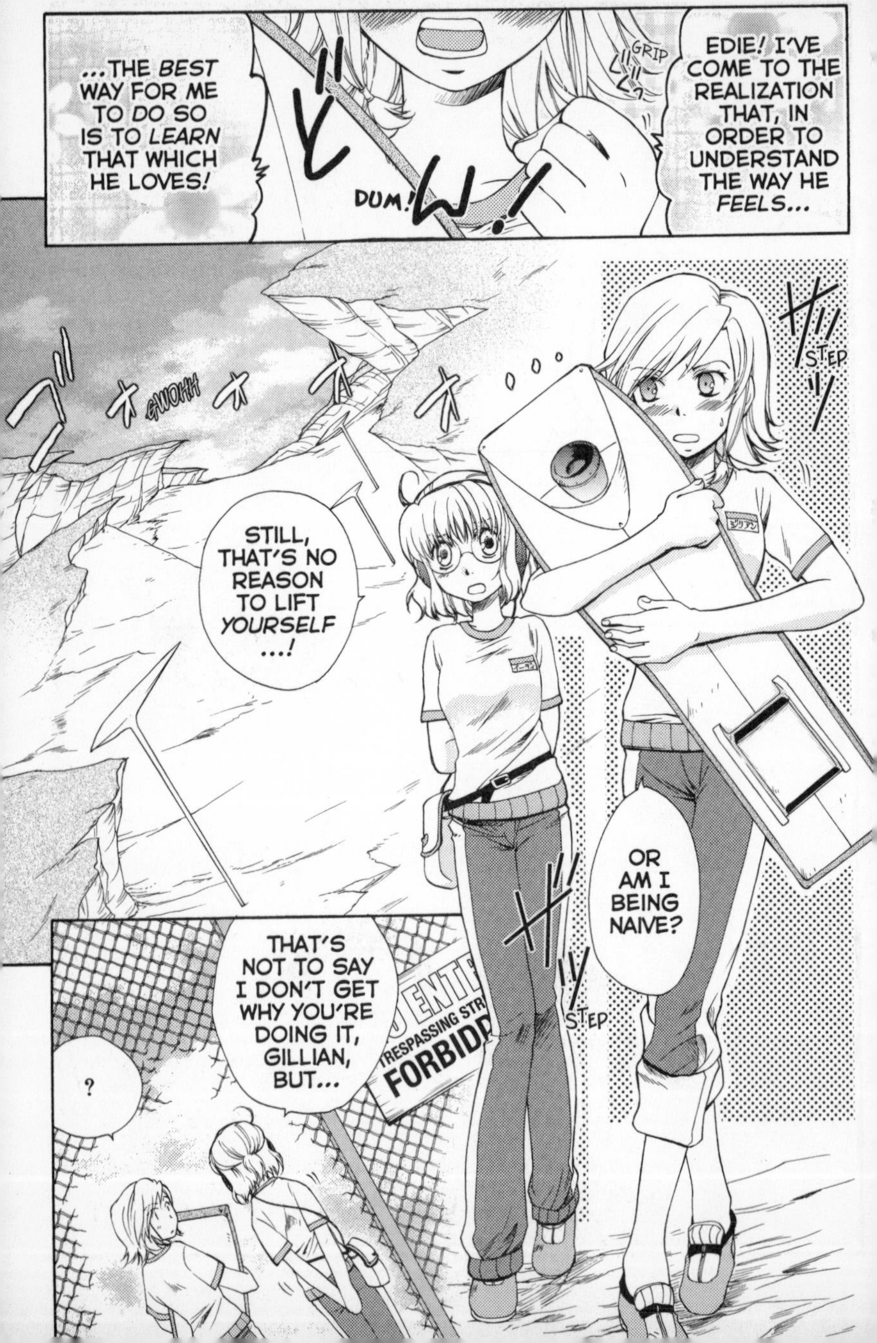
EDIE! I'VE COME TO THE REALIZATION THAT, IN ORDER TO UNDERSTAND THE WAY HE FEELS...
GRIP
DUM!
...THE BEST WAY FOR ME TO DO SO IS TO LEARN THAT WHICH HE LOVES!
STEP
GWOHH
STILL, THAT'S NO REASON TO LIFT YOURSELF ...!
OR AM I BEING NAIVE?
STEP
THAT'S NOT TO SAY I DON'T GET WHY YOU'RE DOING IT, GILLIAN, BUT...
?

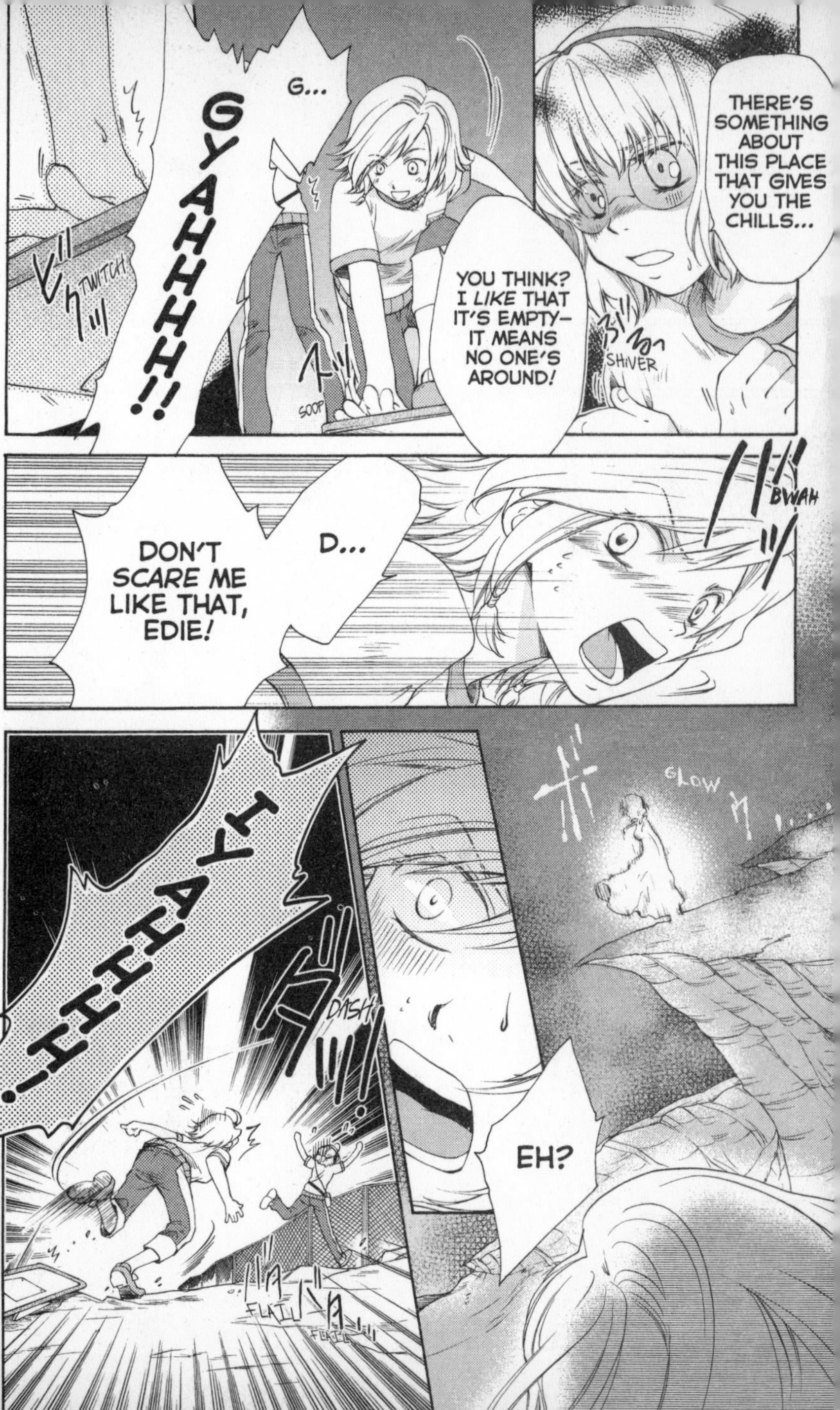
THERE'S SOMETHING ABOUT THIS PLACE THAT GIVES YOU THE CHILLS...
SHIVER
YOU THINK? I *LIKE* THAT IT'S EMPTY— IT MEANS NO ONE'S AROUND!
SOOP
G...
GYAHHHHH!!
TWITCH
BWAH
D...
DON'T *SCARE* ME LIKE THAT, EDIE!
GLOW
EH?
DASH
IYAHHHH!
FLAIL
FLAIL

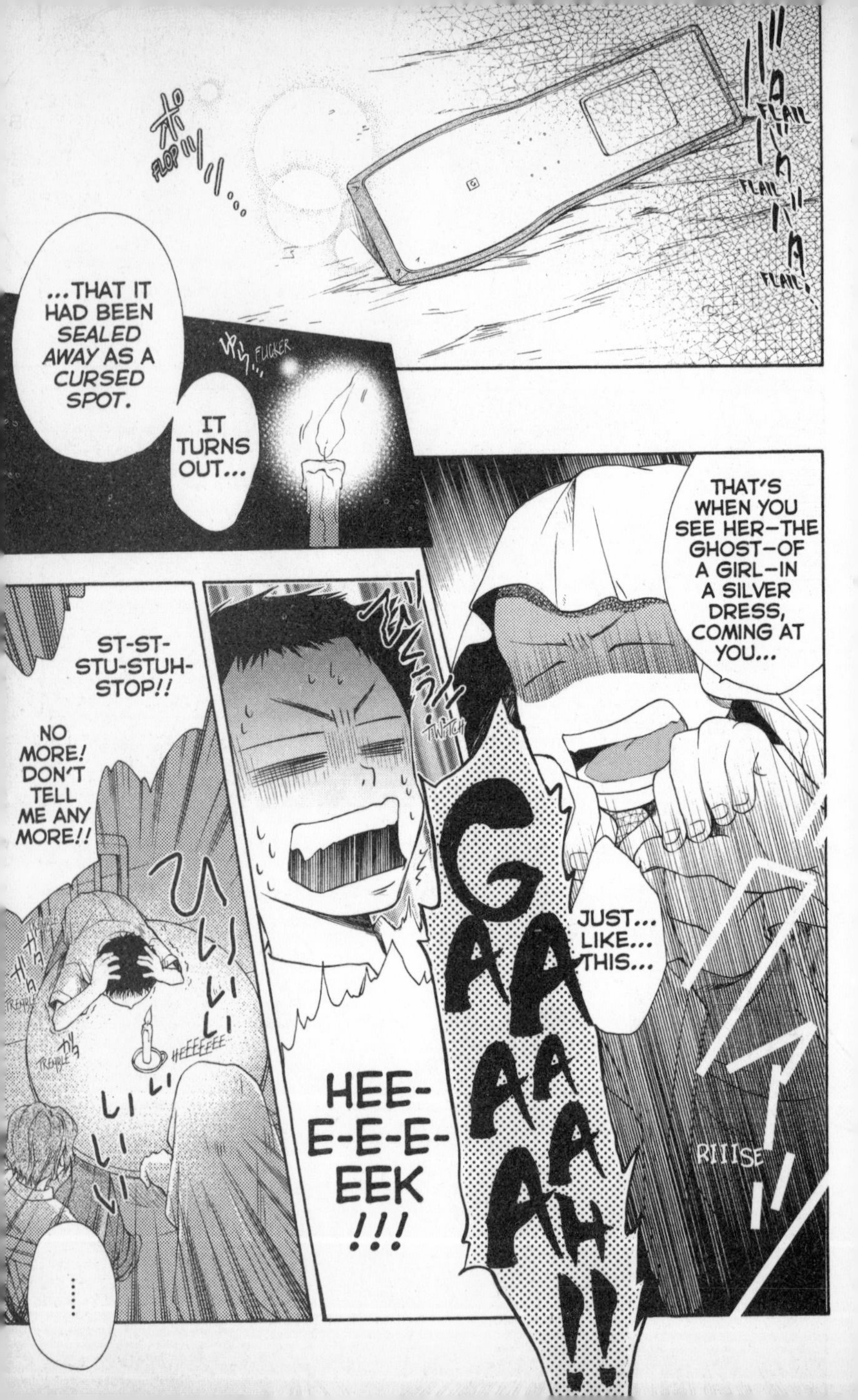
FLAIL FLAIL FLAIL
FLOP
...THAT IT HAD BEEN SEALED AWAY AS A CURSED SPOT.
FLICKER
IT TURNS OUT...
THAT'S WHEN YOU SEE HER—THE GHOST—OF A GIRL—IN A SILVER DRESS, COMING AT YOU...
JUST... LIKE... THIS...
RIIISE
GAAAAAAH!!
TWITCH
HEE-E-E-E-EEK!!!
ST-ST-STU-STUH-STOP!!
NO MORE! DON'T TELL ME ANY MORE!!
TREMBLE
HEEEEEEE
TREMBLE
TREMBLE
......

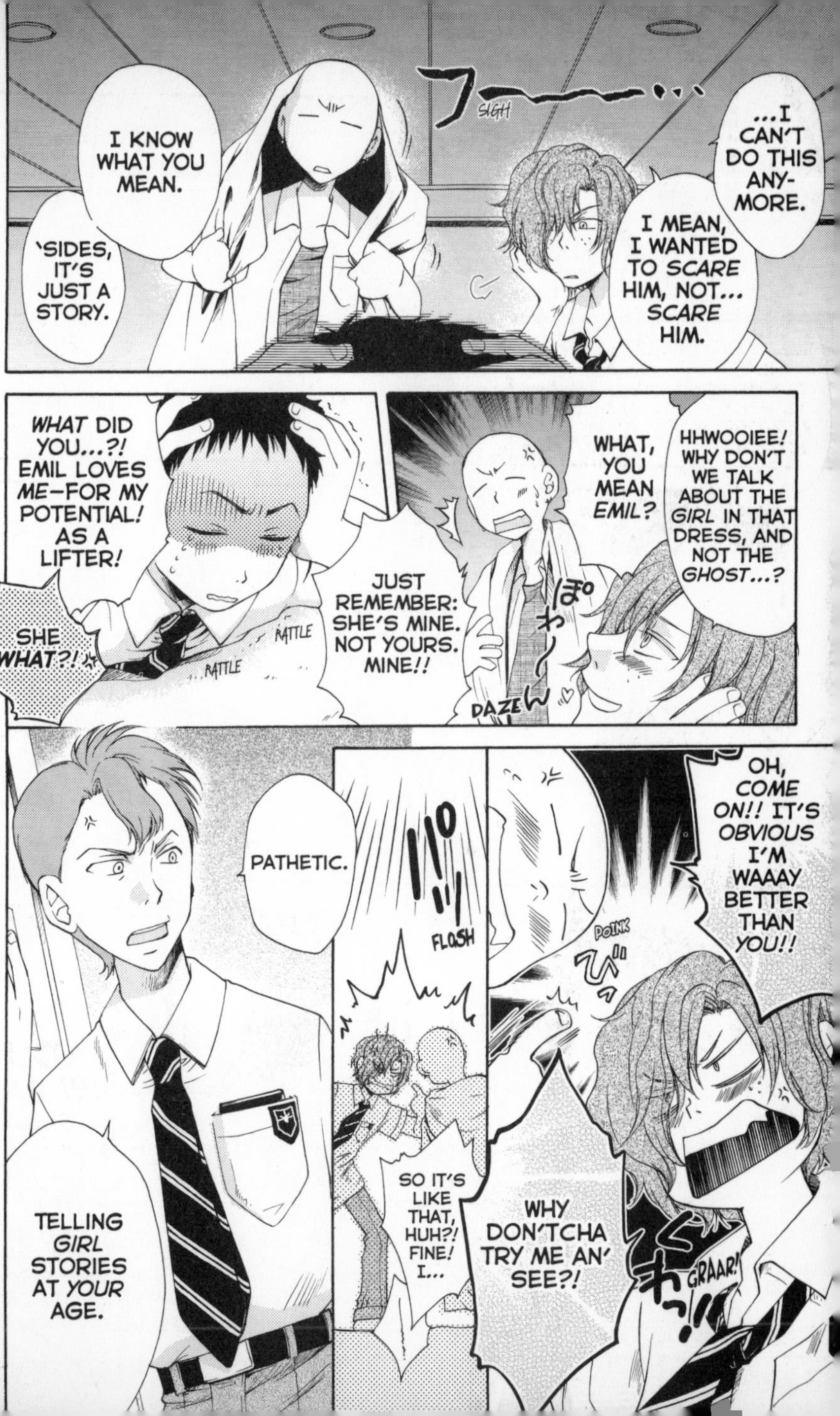
...I CAN'T DO THIS ANYMORE.
I MEAN, I WANTED TO SCARE HIM, NOT... SCARE HIM.
SIGH
I KNOW WHAT YOU MEAN.
'SIDES, IT'S JUST A STORY.
HHWOOIEE! WHY DON'T WE TALK ABOUT THE GIRL IN THAT DRESS, AND NOT THE GHOST...?
WHAT, YOU MEAN EMIL?
DAZE
JUST REMEMBER: SHE'S MINE. NOT YOURS. MINE!!
WHAT DID YOU...?! EMIL LOVES ME—FOR MY POTENTIAL! AS A LIFTER!
RATTLE
RATTLE
SHE WHAT?!
OH, COME ON!! IT'S OBVIOUS I'M WAAAY BETTER THAN YOU!!
POINK
GRAAR!
WHY DON'TCHA TRY ME AN' SEE?!
FLOSH
SO IT'S LIKE THAT, HUH?! FINE! I...
PATHETIC.
TELLING GIRL STORIES AT YOUR AGE.

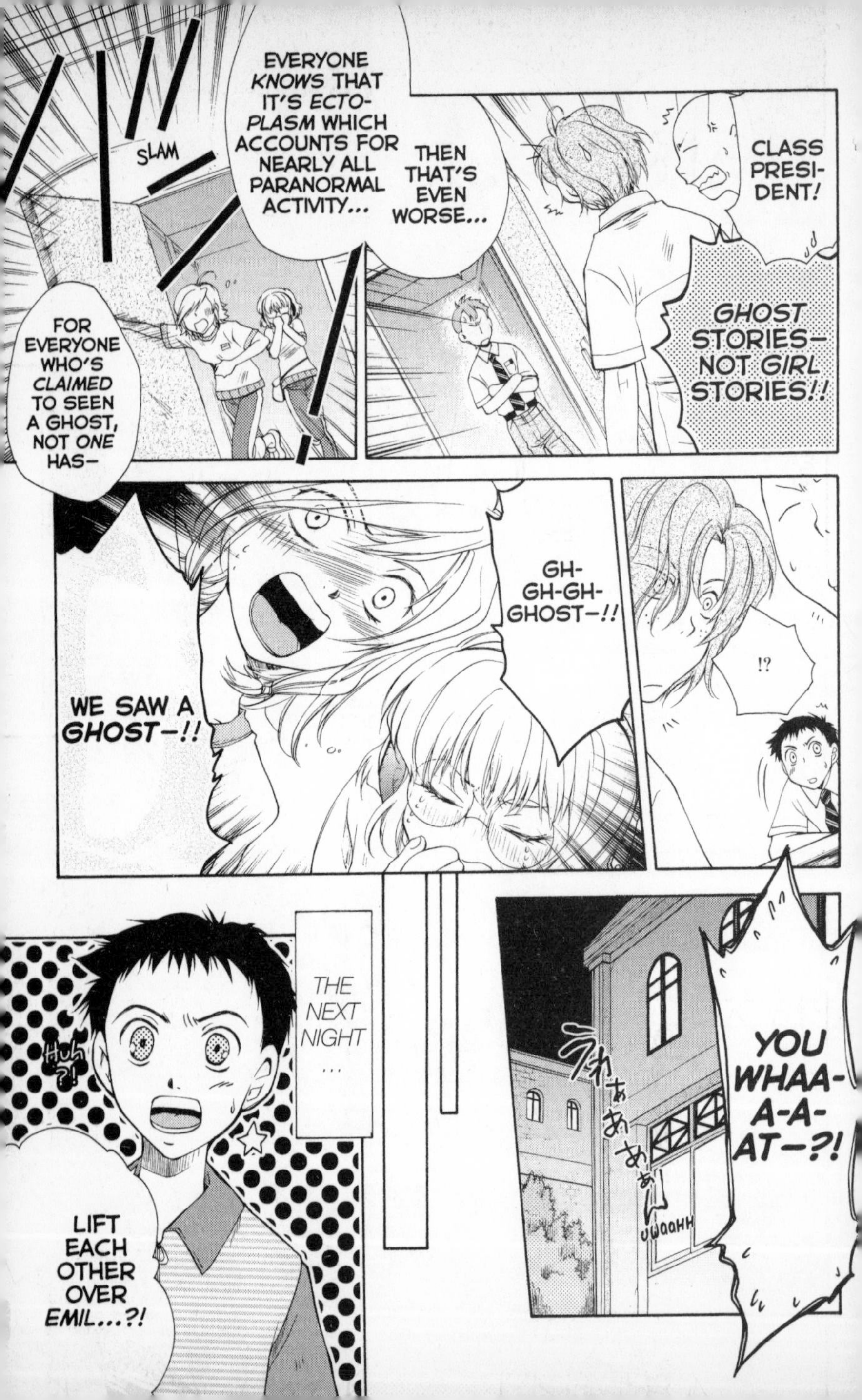
CLASS PRESIDENT!
GHOST STORIES—NOT GIRL STORIES!!
THEN THAT'S EVEN WORSE...
EVERYONE KNOWS THAT IT'S ECTO-PLASM WHICH ACCOUNTS FOR NEARLY ALL PARANORMAL ACTIVITY...
SLAM
FOR EVERYONE WHO'S CLAIMED TO SEEN A GHOST, NOT ONE HAS—
!?
GH-GH-GH-GHOST—!!
WE SAW A GHOST—!!
YOU WHAA-A-A-AT—?!
うわあああああ
UWAAHH
THE NEXT NIGHT ...
Huh?!
LIFT EACH OTHER OVER EMIL...?!

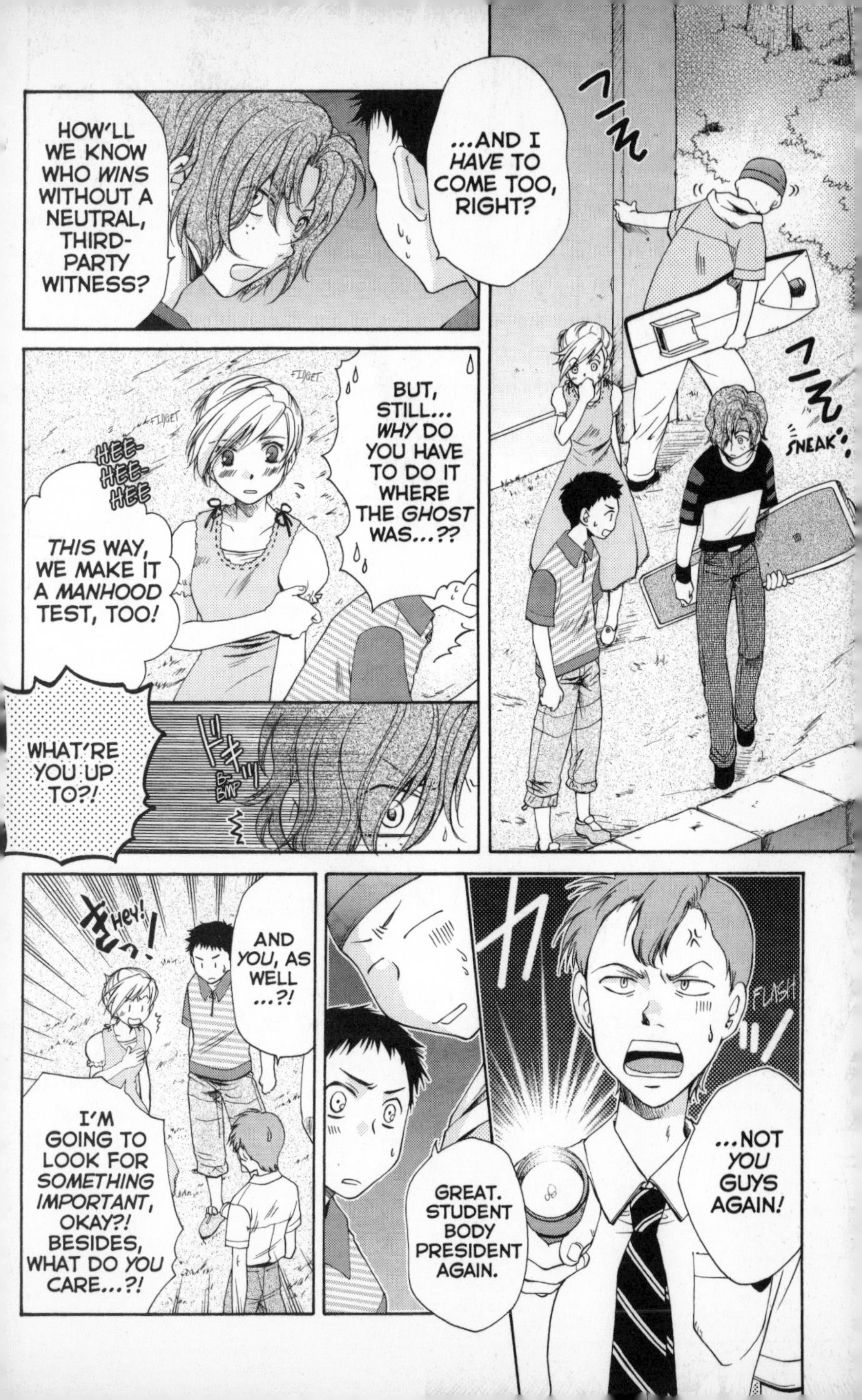
SNEAK
...AND I HAVE TO COME TOO, RIGHT?
HOW'LL WE KNOW WHO WINS WITHOUT A NEUTRAL, THIRD-PARTY WITNESS?
BUT, STILL... WHY DO YOU HAVE TO DO IT WHERE THE GHOST WAS...??
FIDGET
FIDGET
HEE-HEE-HEE
THIS WAY, WE MAKE IT A MANHOOD TEST, TOO!
B-BMP
WHAT'RE YOU UP TO?!
...NOT YOU GUYS AGAIN!
FLASH
GREAT. STUDENT BODY PRESIDENT AGAIN.
AND YOU, AS WELL...?!
HEY!
I'M GOING TO LOOK FOR SOMETHING IMPORTANT, OKAY?! BESIDES, WHAT DO YOU CARE...?!

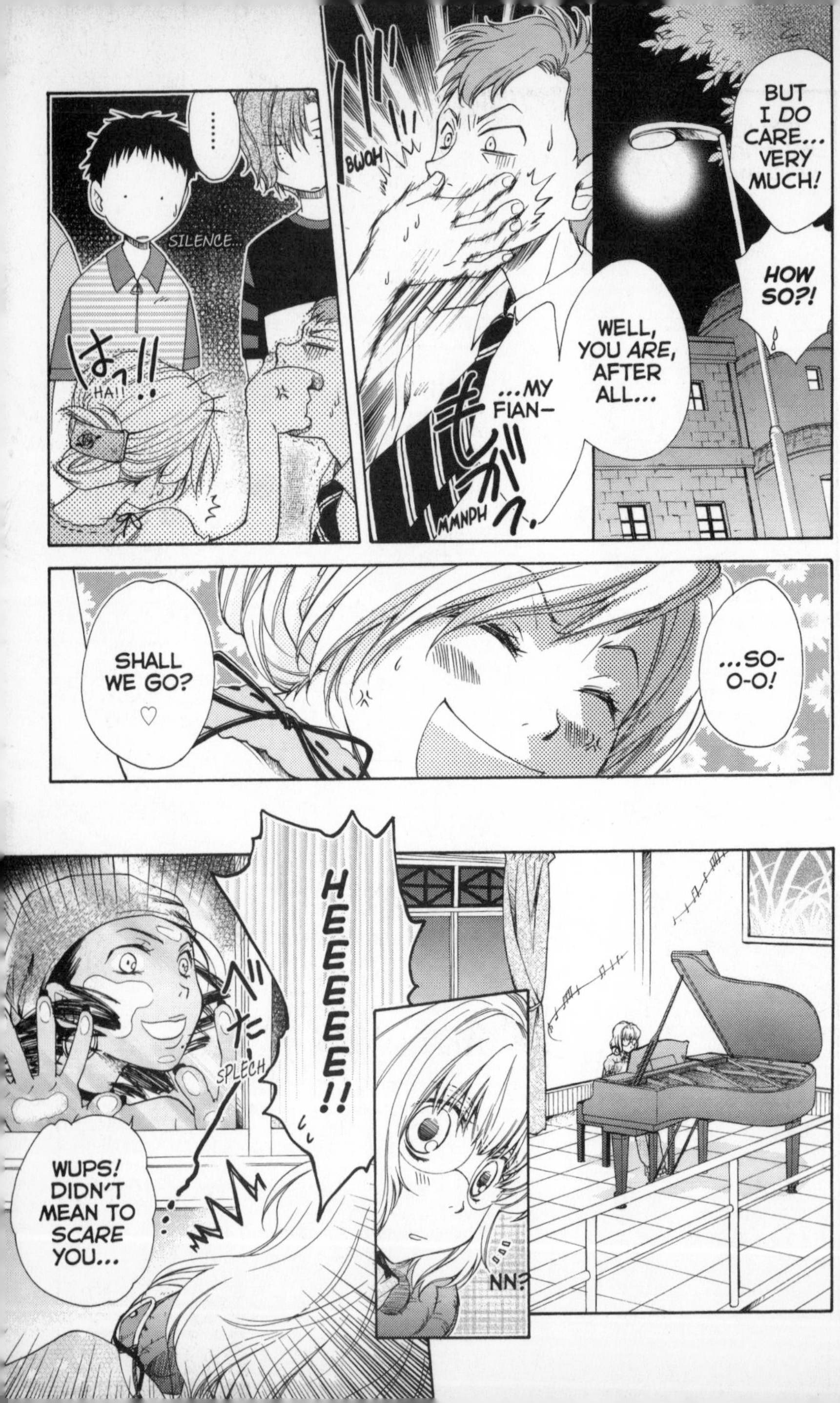
BUT I *DO* CARE... VERY MUCH!
HOW SO?!
WELL, YOU *ARE*, AFTER ALL...
...MY FIAN—
BWOH
MMNPH
......
SILENCE...
はっ!!
HA!!
...SO-O-O!
SHALL WE GO? ♡
NN?
HEEEEEE!!
SPLECH
WUPS! DIDN'T MEAN TO SCARE YOU...

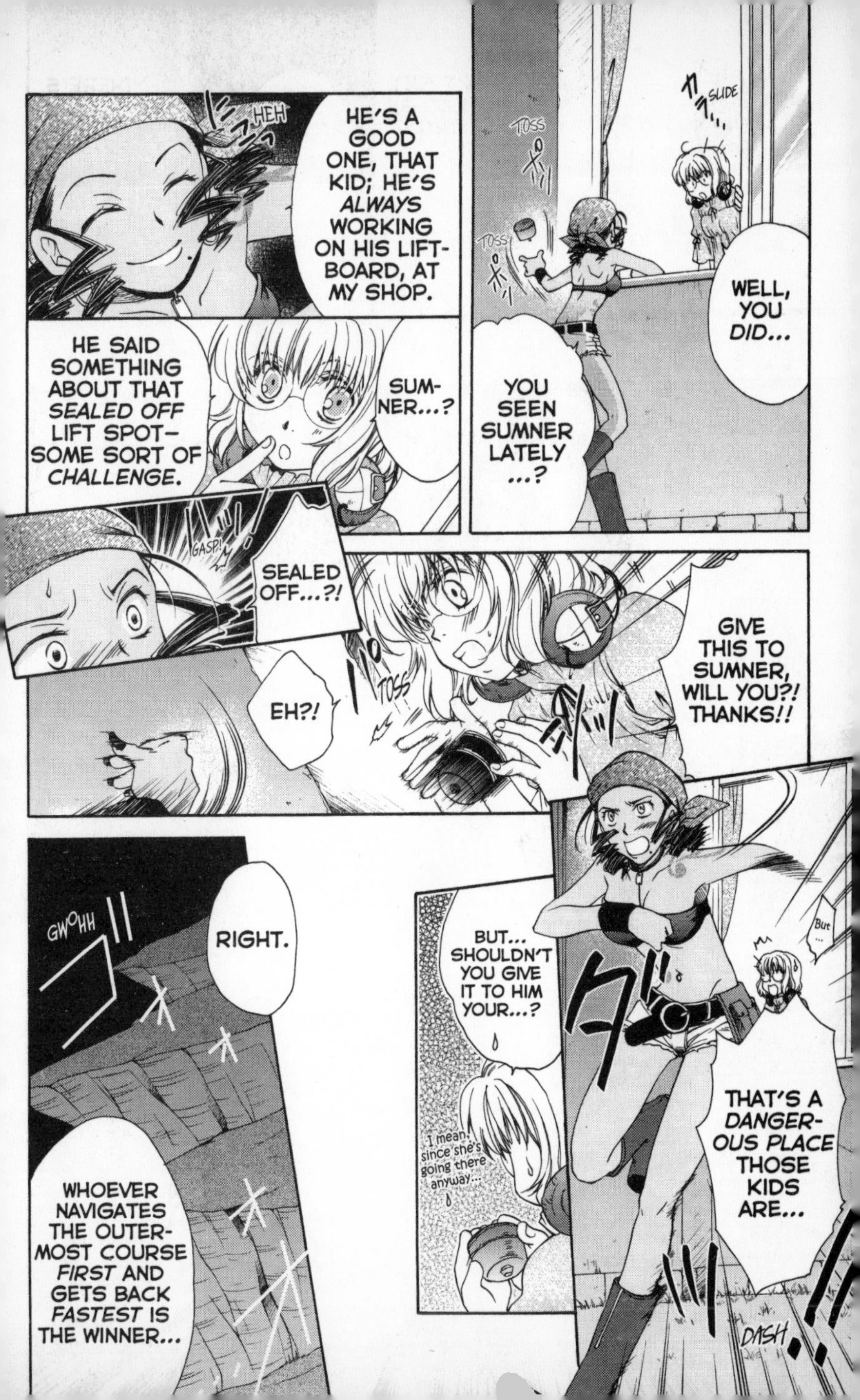
SLIDE
WELL, YOU DID...
TOSS
TOSS
YOU SEEN SUMNER LATELY...?
HEH
HE'S A GOOD ONE, THAT KID; HE'S *ALWAYS* WORKING ON HIS LIFT-BOARD, AT MY SHOP.
SUMNER...?
HE SAID SOMETHING ABOUT THAT *SEALED OFF* LIFT SPOT—SOME SORT OF *CHALLENGE*.
GIVE THIS TO SUMNER, WILL YOU?! THANKS!!
TOSS
EH?!
GASP!
SEALED OFF...?!
But...
THAT'S A *DANGER-OUS PLACE* THOSE KIDS ARE...
DASH
BUT... SHOULDN'T YOU GIVE IT TO HIM YOUR...?
I mean, since she's going there anyway...
RIGHT.
GWOHH
WHOEVER NAVIGATES THE OUTER-MOST COURSE *FIRST* AND GETS BACK *FASTEST* IS THE WINNER...

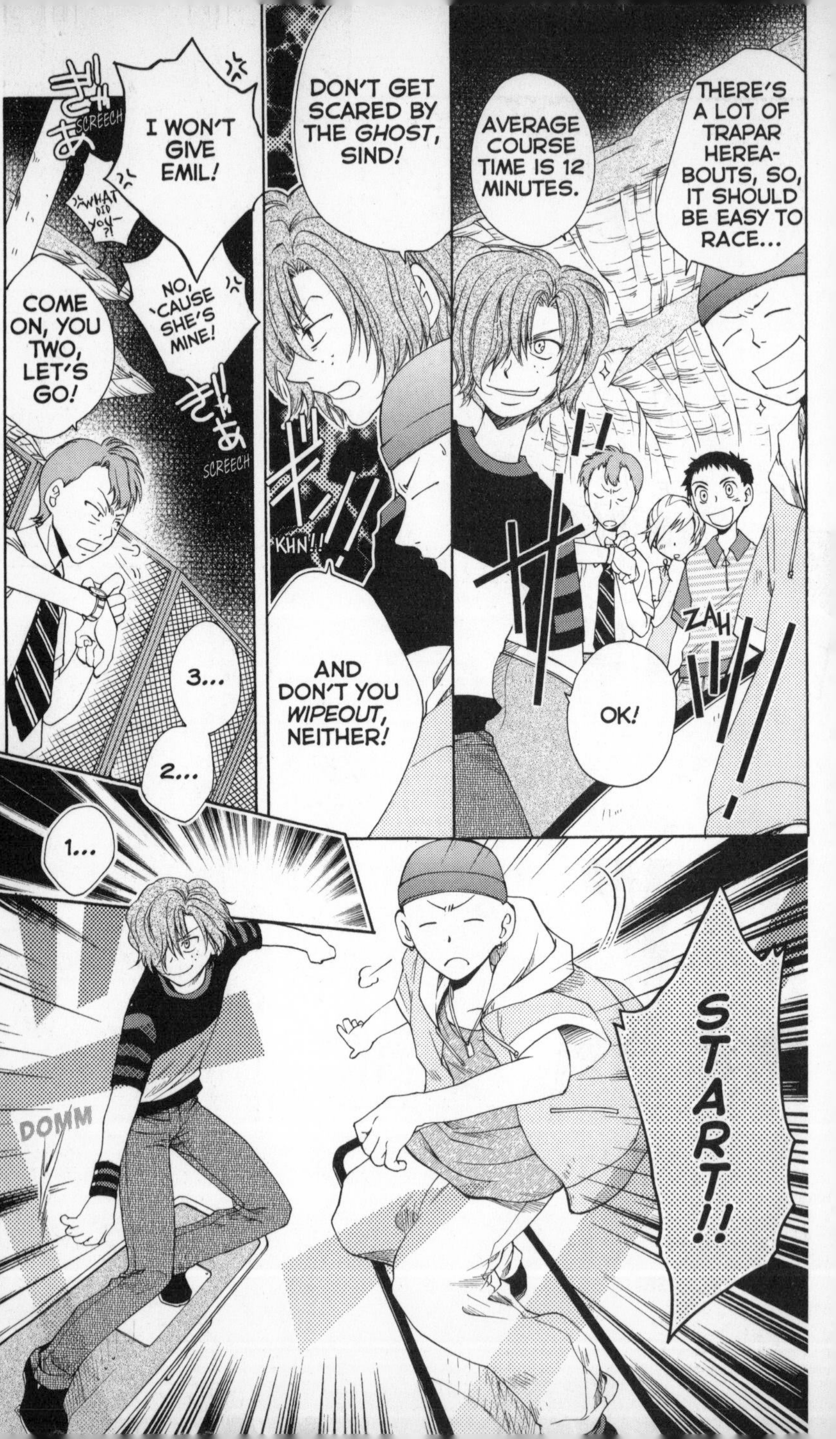
THERE'S A LOT OF TRAPAR HEREA-BOUTS, SO, IT SHOULD BE EASY TO RACE...
AVERAGE COURSE TIME IS 12 MINUTES.
ZAH
OK!
DON'T GET SCARED BY THE *GHOST*, SIND!
KHN!!
AND DON'T YOU *WIPEOUT*, NEITHER!
I WON'T GIVE EMIL!
SCREECH
WHAT DID YOU—?!
NO, 'CAUSE SHE'S MINE!
SCREECH
COME ON, YOU TWO, LET'S GO!
3...
2...
1...
START!!
DOMM

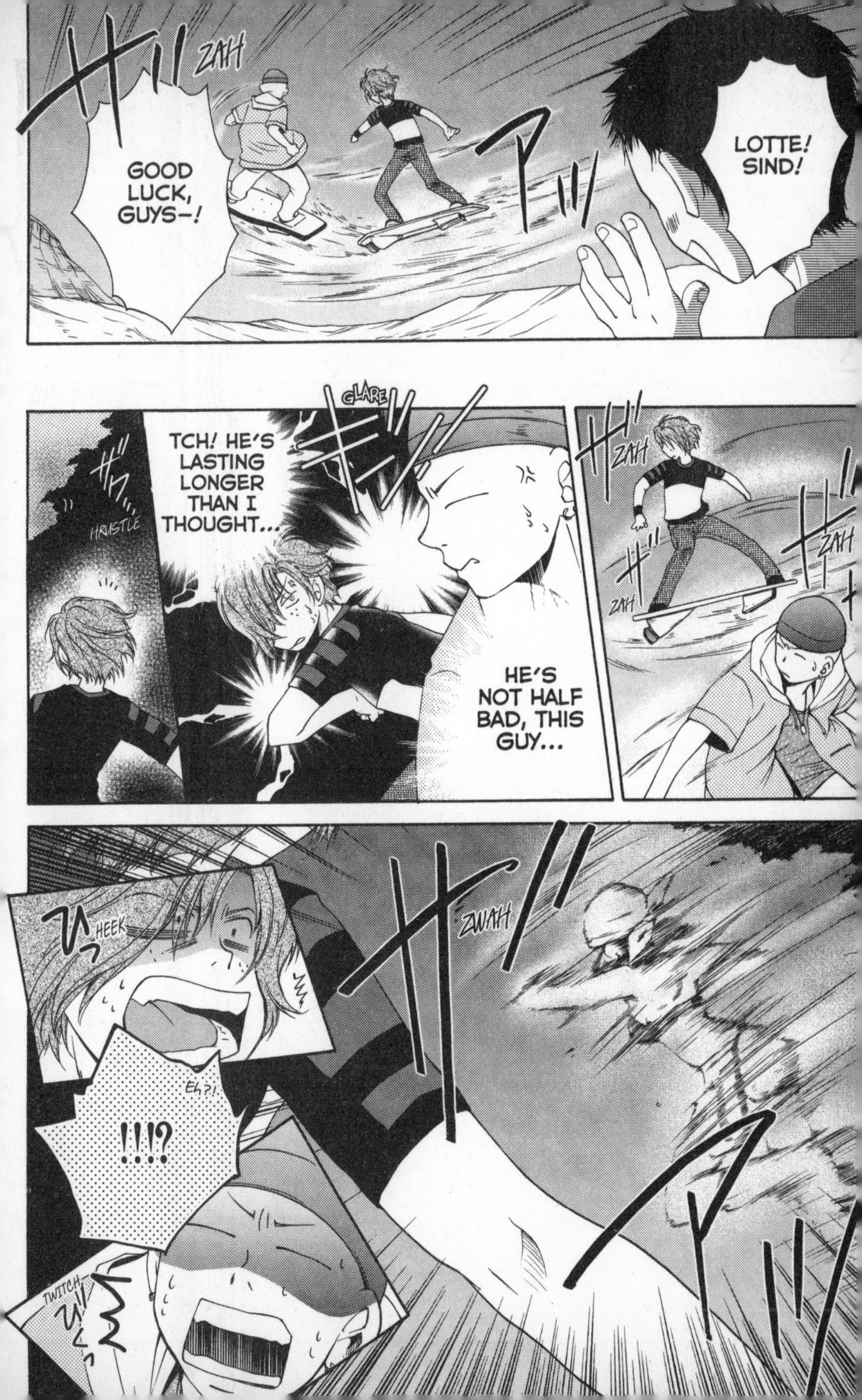
LOTTE! SIND!
ZAH
GOOD LUCK, GUYS—!
ZAH
ZAH
ZAH
GLARE
TCH! HE'S LASTING LONGER THAN I THOUGHT...
HE'S NOT HALF BAD, THIS GUY...
HRUSTLE
ZWAAH
HEEK
Eh?!
!!!?
TWITCH

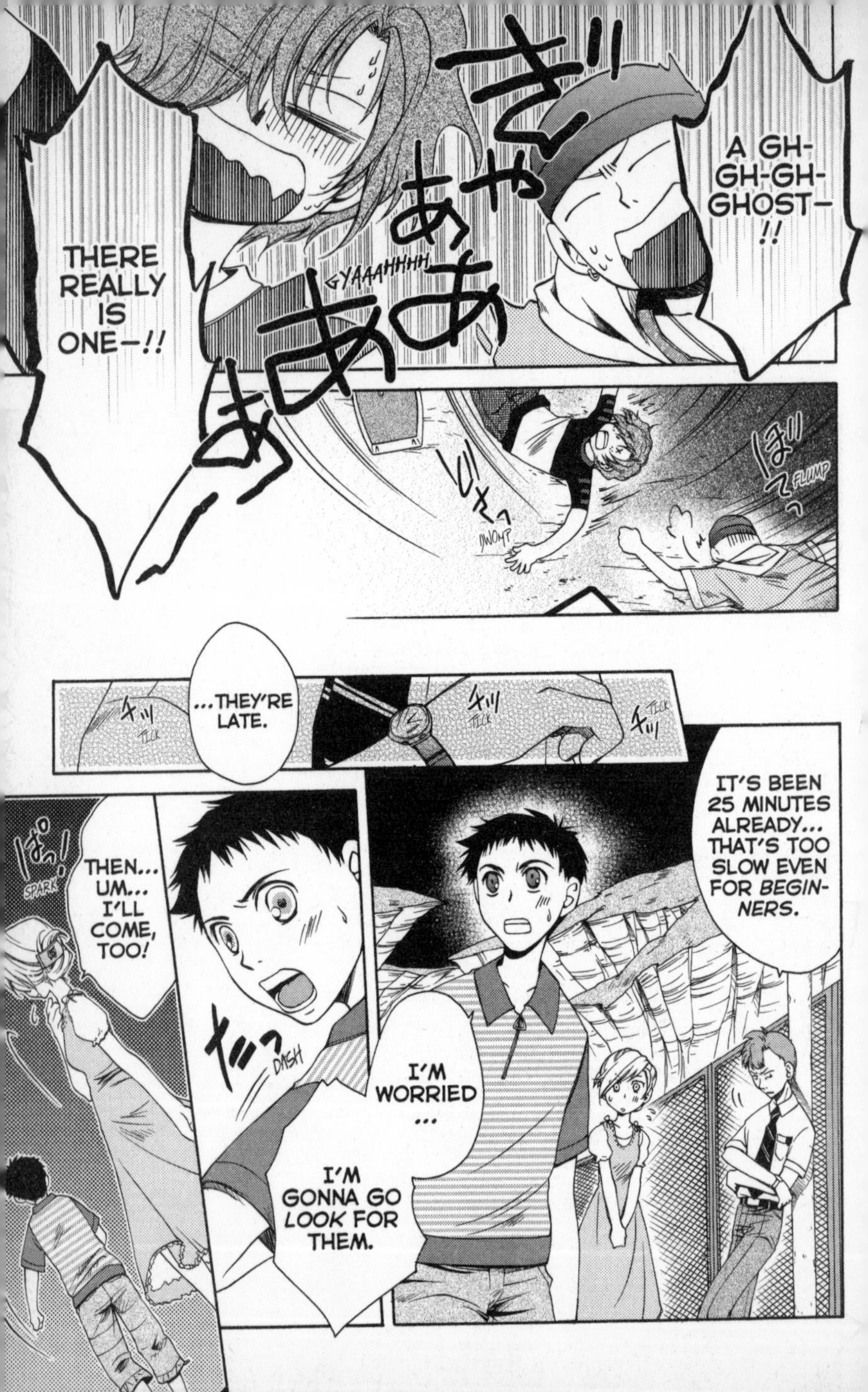
A GH-GH-GH-GHOST-!!
GYAAAHHHH
THERE REALLY IS ONE-!!
FLUMP
DWOMP
TICK
TICK
...THEY'RE LATE.
TICK
IT'S BEEN 25 MINUTES ALREADY... THAT'S TOO SLOW EVEN FOR *BEGINNERS*.
I'M WORRIED...
I'M GONNA GO *LOOK* FOR THEM.
DASH
THEN... UM... I'LL COME, TOO!
SPARK

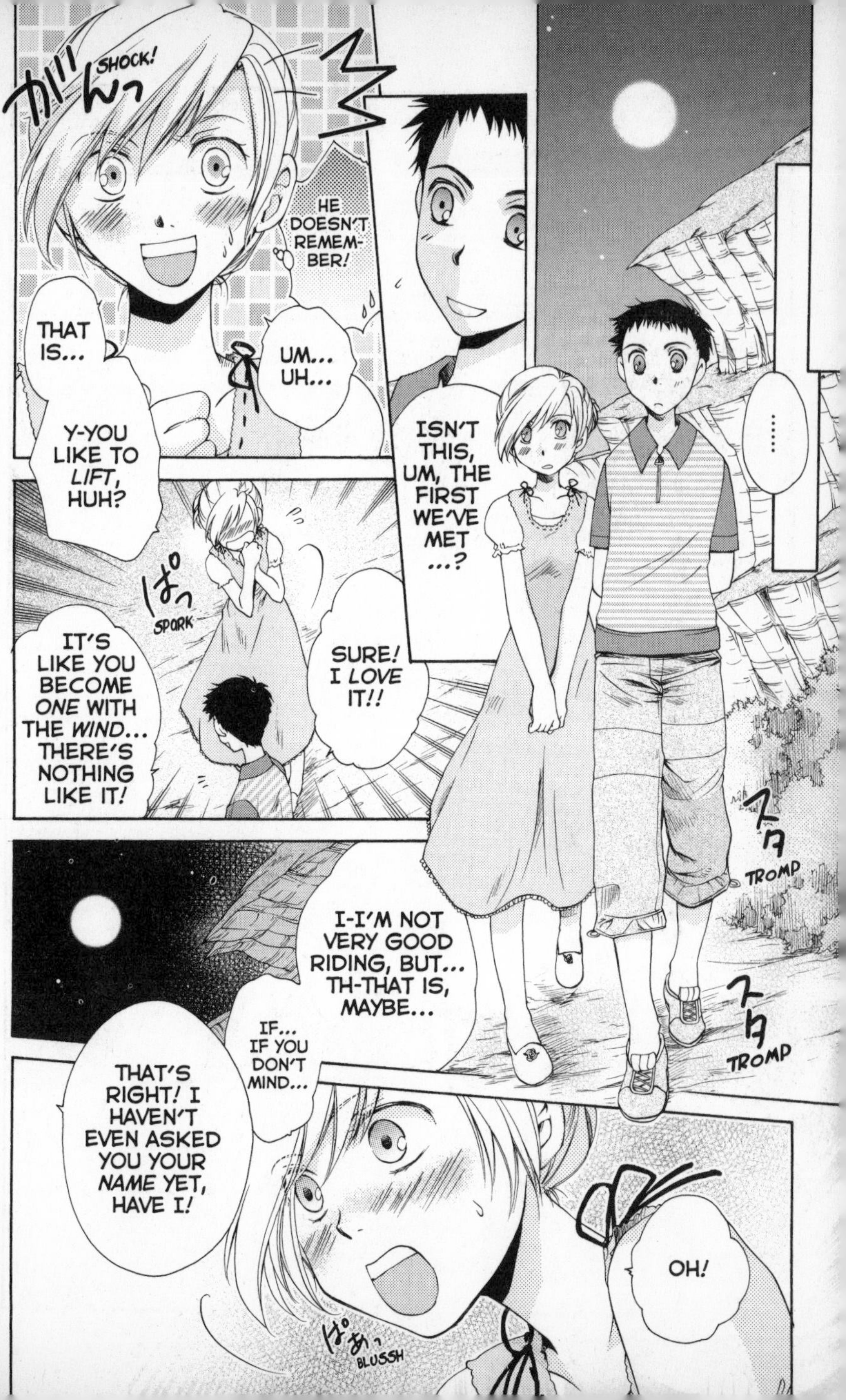
ISN'T THIS, UM, THE FIRST WE'VE MET ...?
......
スタ TROMP
スタ TROMP
カーんっ SHOCK!
HE DOESN'T REMEMBER!
UM... UH...
THAT IS...
Y-YOU LIKE TO LIFT, HUH?
SURE! I LOVE IT!!
ぱっ SPORK
IT'S LIKE YOU BECOME ONE WITH THE WIND... THERE'S NOTHING LIKE IT!
I-I'M NOT VERY GOOD RIDING, BUT... TH-THAT IS, MAYBE...
IF... IF YOU DON'T MIND...
OH!
THAT'S RIGHT! I HAVEN'T EVEN ASKED YOU YOUR NAME YET, HAVE I!
ぱあっ BLUSSH

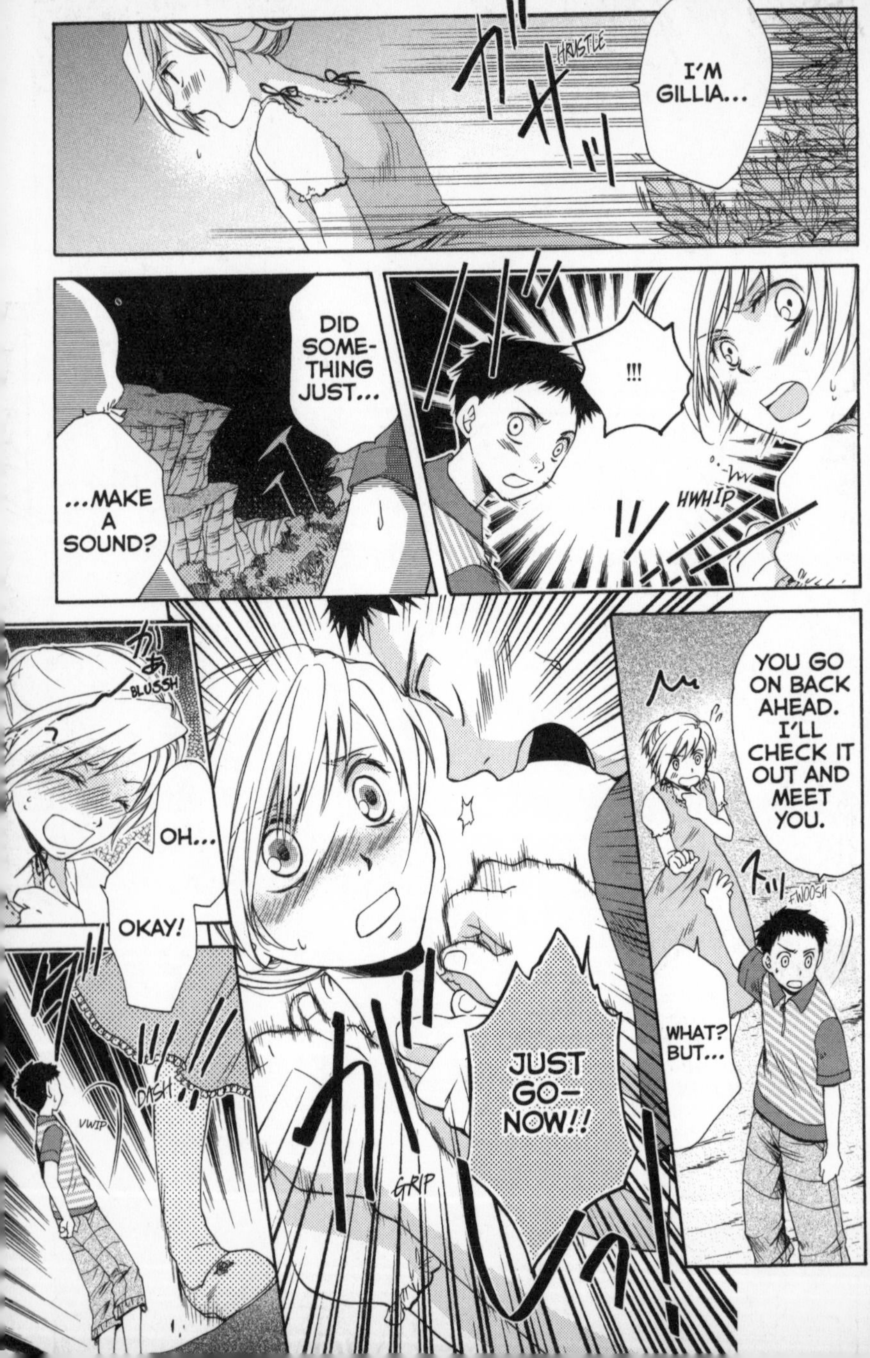
I'M GILLIA...
HRUSTLE
!!!
HWHIP
DID SOMETHING JUST...
...MAKE A SOUND?
YOU GO ON BACK AHEAD. I'LL CHECK IT OUT AND MEET YOU.
FWOOSH
WHAT? BUT...
JUST GO—NOW!!
GRIP
BLUSSH
OH...
OKAY!
DASH
VWIP

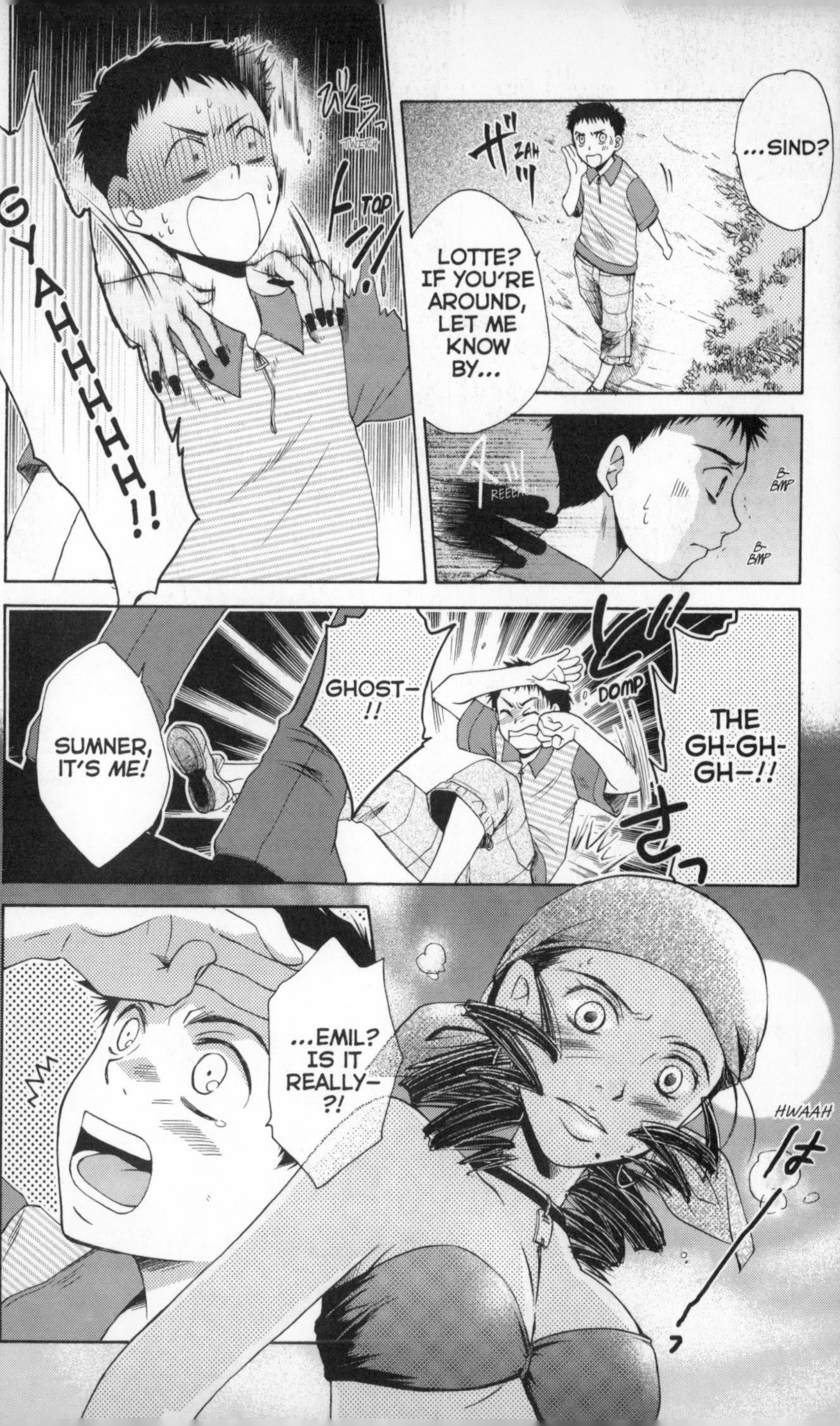
...SIND?
ZAH
LOTTE? IF YOU'RE AROUND, LET ME KNOW BY...
REEEACH
B-BMP
B-BMP
TWITCH
TAP
GYAHHHHHH!!
THE GH-GH-GH-!!
DOMP
GHOST-!!
SUMNER, IT'S ME!
HWAAH
...EMIL? IS IT REALLY-?!

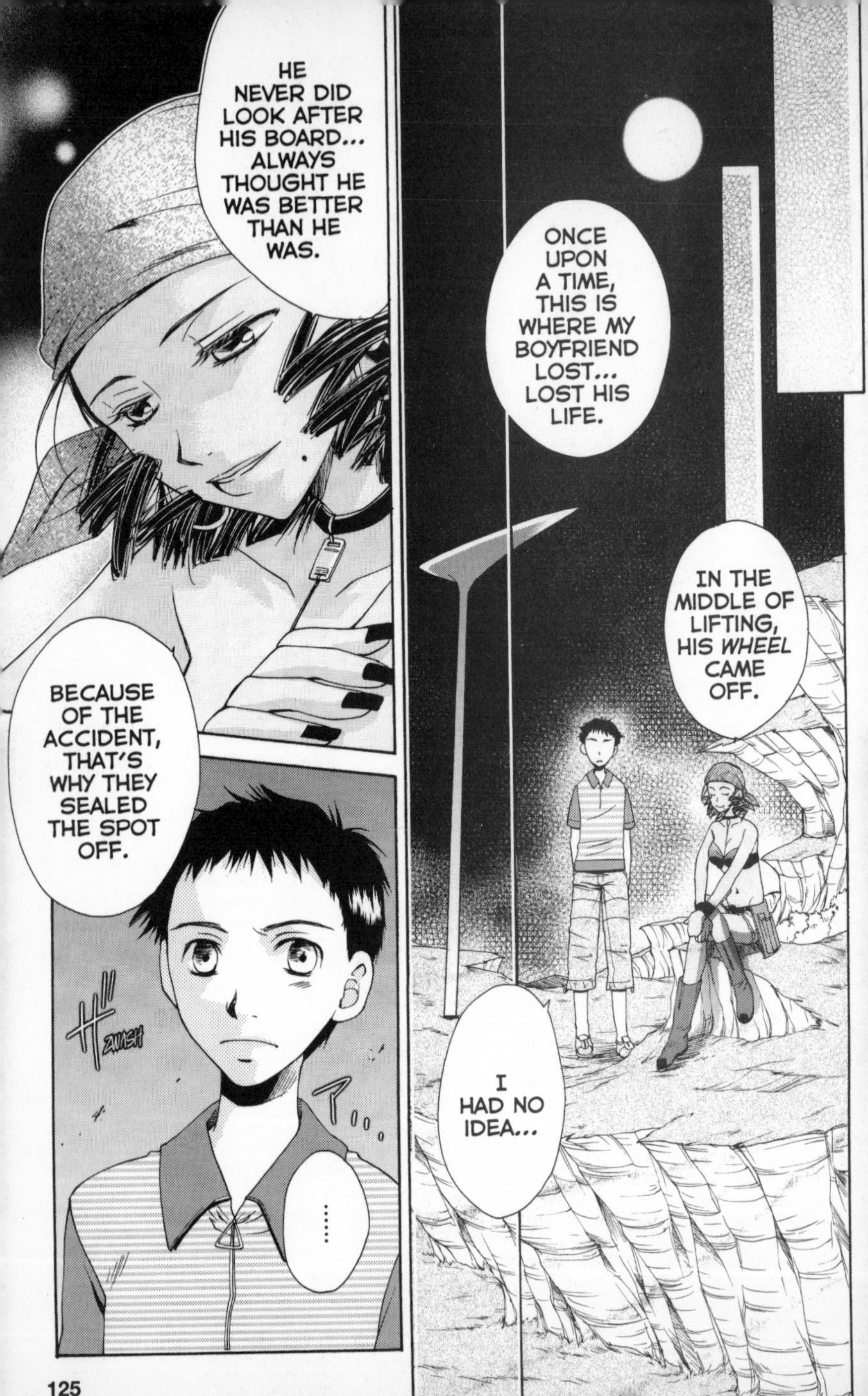
ONCE UPON A TIME, THIS IS WHERE MY BOYFRIEND LOST... LOST HIS LIFE.
IN THE MIDDLE OF LIFTING, HIS *WHEEL* CAME OFF.
I HAD NO IDEA...
HE NEVER DID LOOK AFTER HIS BOARD... ALWAYS THOUGHT HE WAS BETTER THAN HE WAS.
BECAUSE OF THE ACCIDENT, THAT'S WHY THEY SEALED THE SPOT OFF.
ZWASH
......

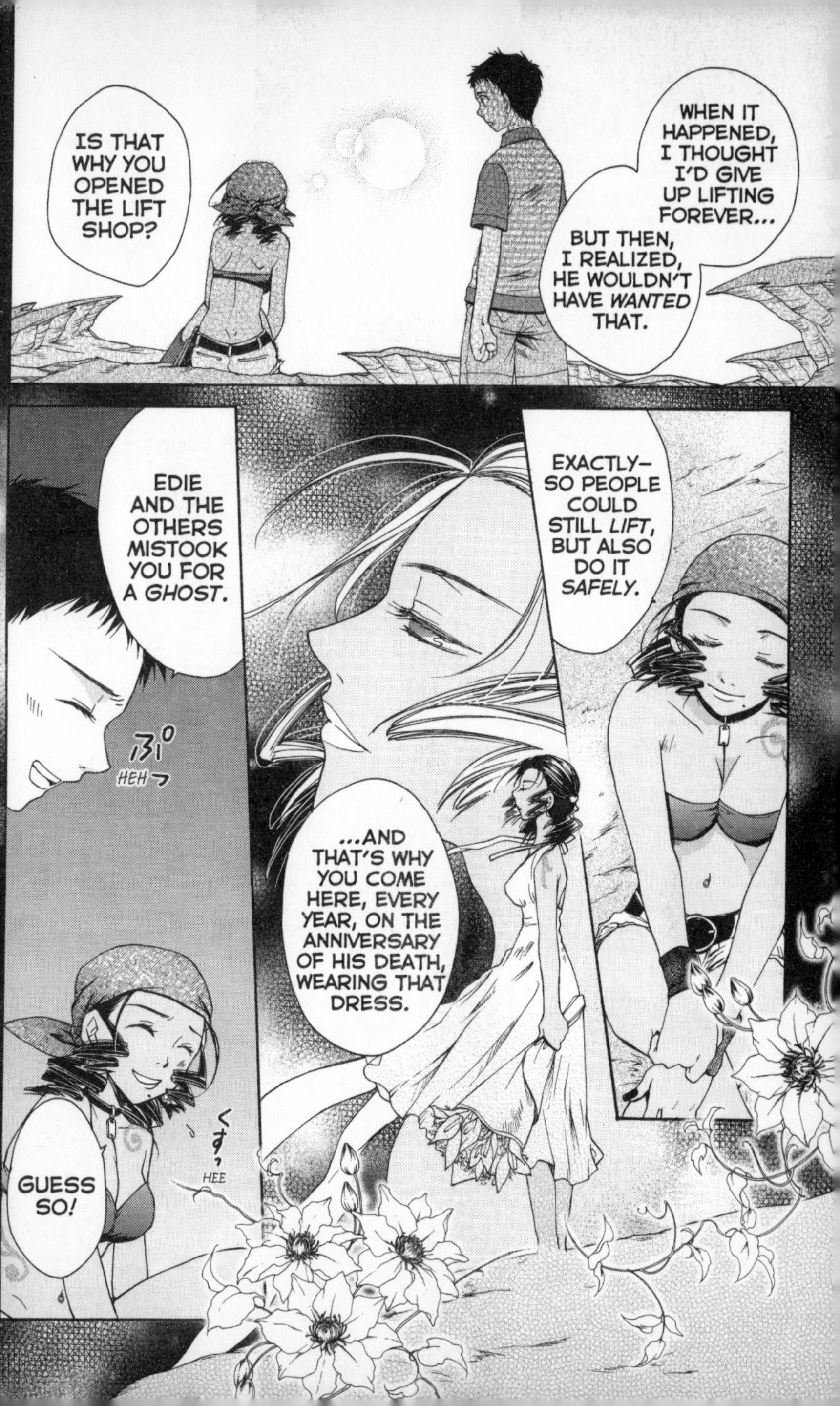
WHEN IT HAPPENED, I THOUGHT I'D GIVE UP LIFTING FOREVER...
BUT THEN, I REALIZED, HE WOULDN'T HAVE *WANTED* THAT.
IS THAT WHY YOU OPENED THE LIFT SHOP?
EXACTLY—SO PEOPLE COULD STILL *LIFT*, BUT ALSO DO IT *SAFELY*.
...AND THAT'S WHY YOU COME HERE, EVERY YEAR, ON THE ANNIVERSARY OF HIS DEATH, WEARING THAT DRESS.
EDIE AND THE OTHERS MISTOOK YOU FOR A *GHOST*.
HEH
HEE
GUESS SO!

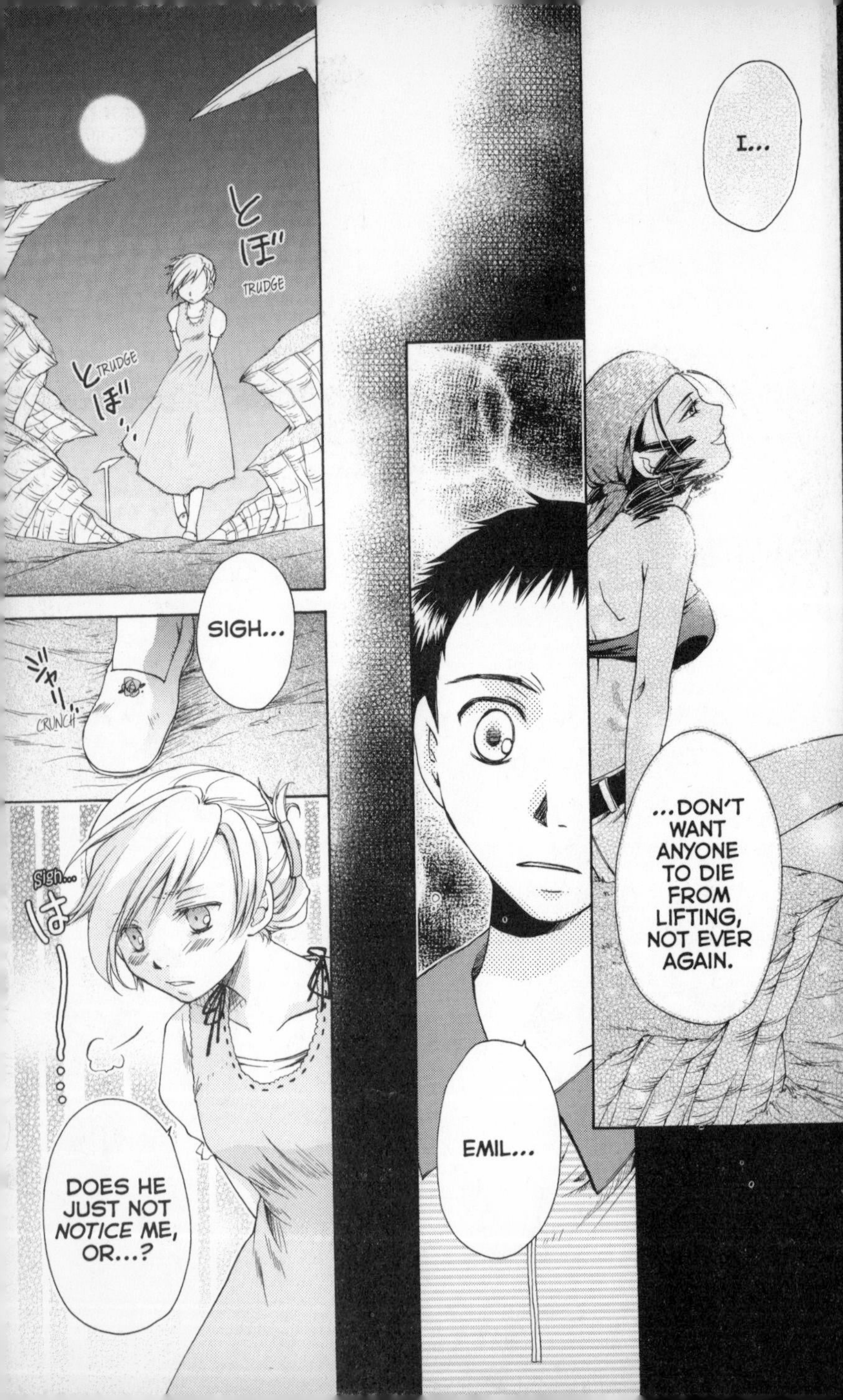
I...
...DON'T WANT ANYONE TO DIE FROM LIFTING, NOT EVER AGAIN.
EMIL...
とぼ
TRUDGE
とぼ…
TRUDGE
SIGH...
ジャリ…
CRUNCH
は———…
Sigh...
DOES HE JUST NOT *NOTICE* ME, OR...?

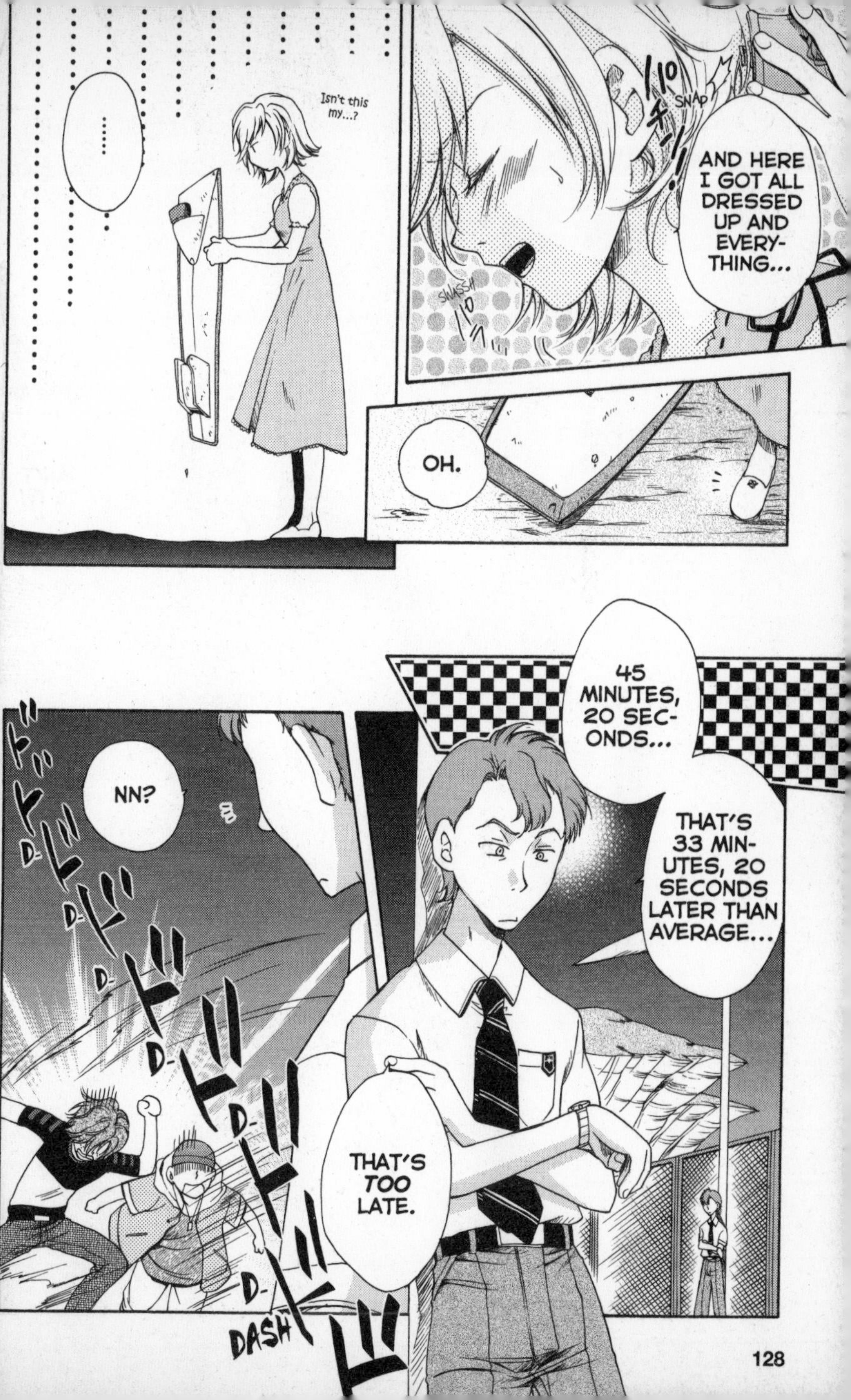
SNAP
AND HERE I GOT ALL DRESSED UP AND EVERY-THING...
SWASSH
OH.
......
Isn't this my...?
45 MINUTES, 20 SEC-ONDS...
THAT'S 33 MIN-UTES, 20 SECONDS LATER THAN AVERAGE...
THAT'S *TOO* LATE.
NN?
D-
D-
D-
D-
D-
D-
DASH

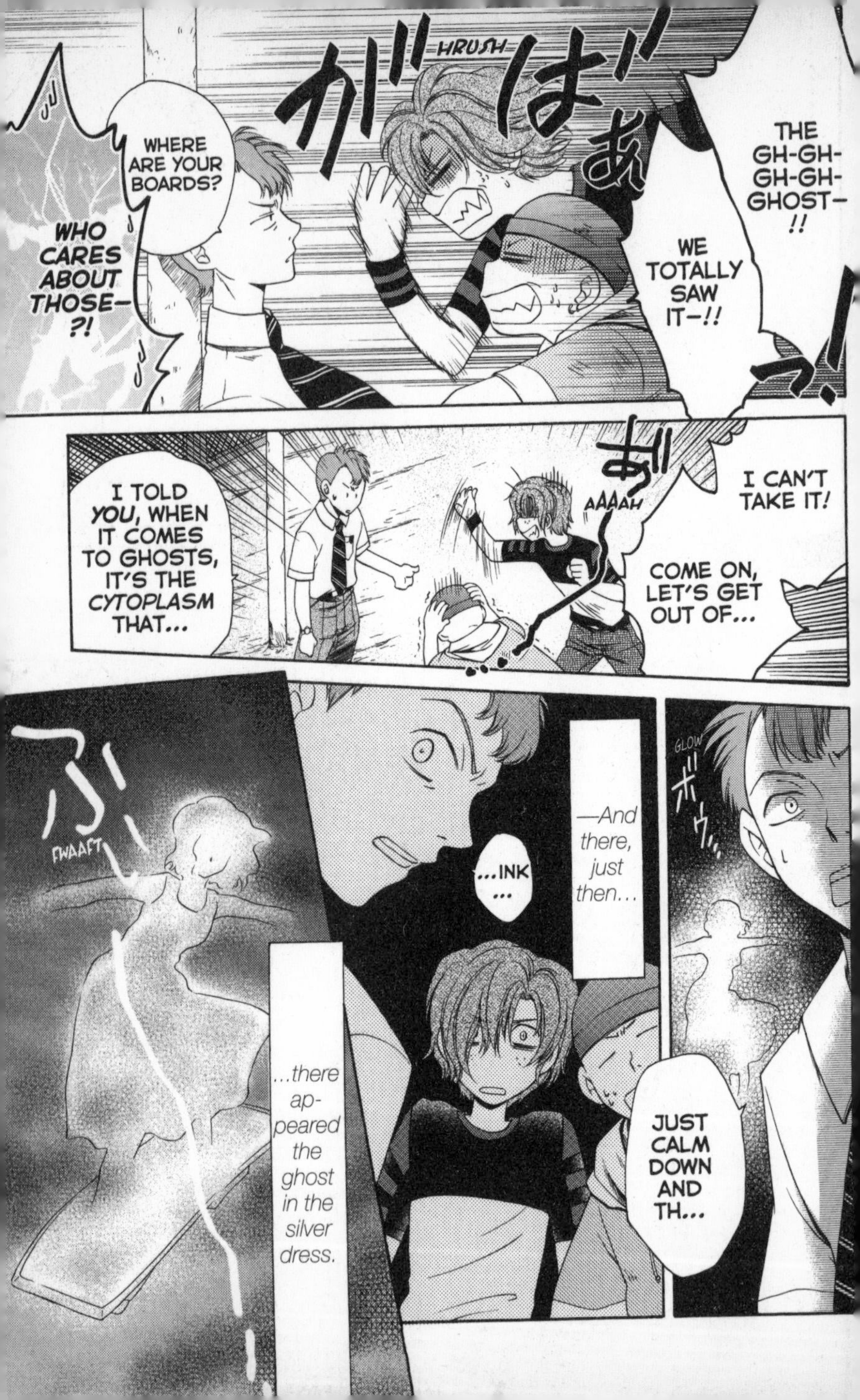
THE GH-GH-GH-GH-GHOST—!!
WE TOTALLY SAW IT—!!
がばぁっ!
HRUSH
WHERE ARE YOUR BOARDS?
WHO CARES ABOUT THOSE—?!
I CAN'T TAKE IT!
COME ON, LET'S GET OUT OF...
あ"
AAAAH
I TOLD *YOU*, WHEN IT COMES TO GHOSTS, IT'S THE *CYTOPLASM* THAT...
ボウ...
GLOW
JUST CALM DOWN AND TH...
—And there, just then...
...INK...
...there appeared the ghost in the silver dress.
ふ
FWAAFT

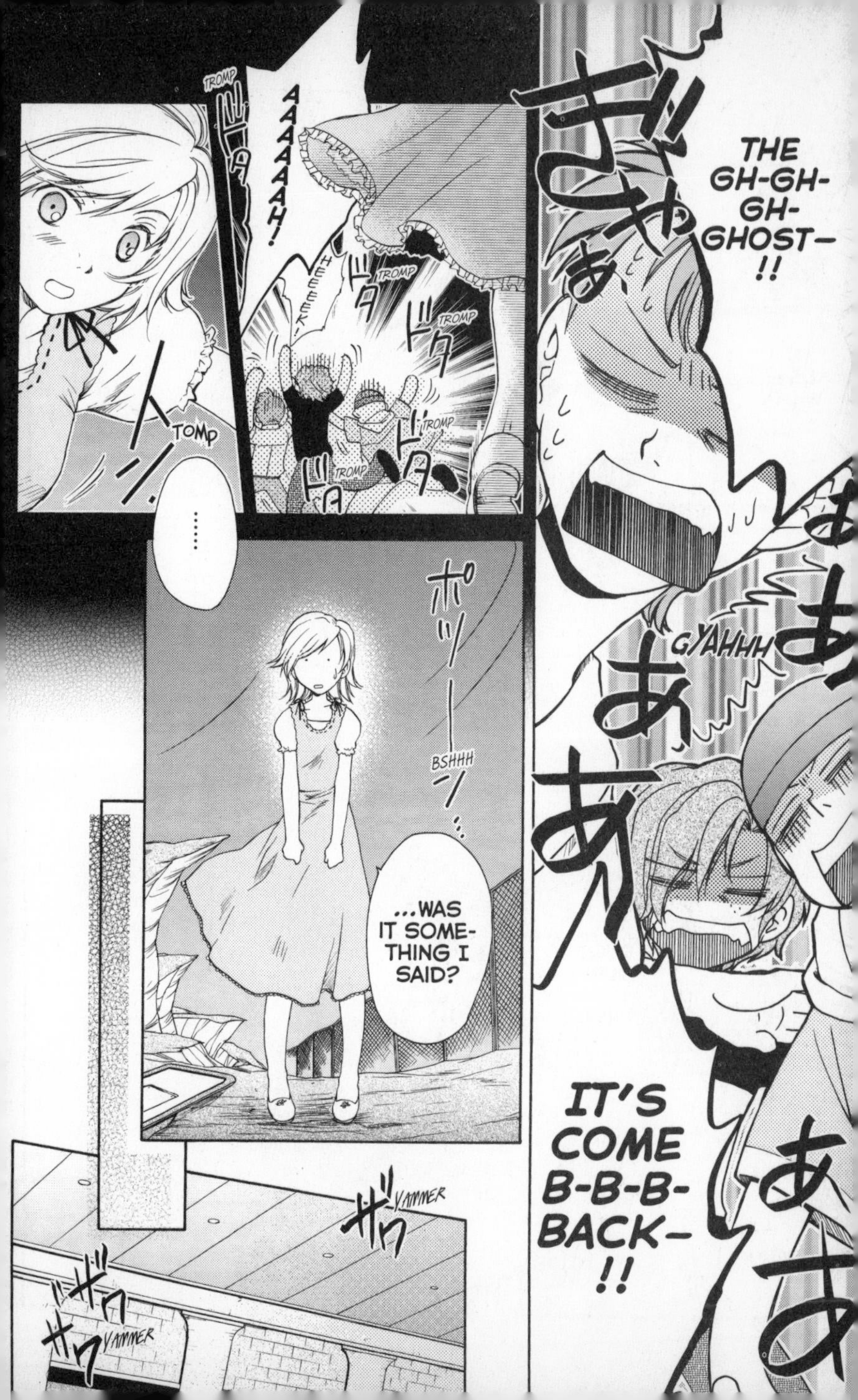

THE GH-GH-GH-GHOST—!!
GYAHHH
IT'S COME B-B-B-BACK—!!
AAAAAAH!
HEEEEK!
TROMP
TROMP
TROMP
TROMP
TROMP
TOMP
......
BSHHH
...WAS IT SOMETHING I SAID?
YAMMER
YAMMER

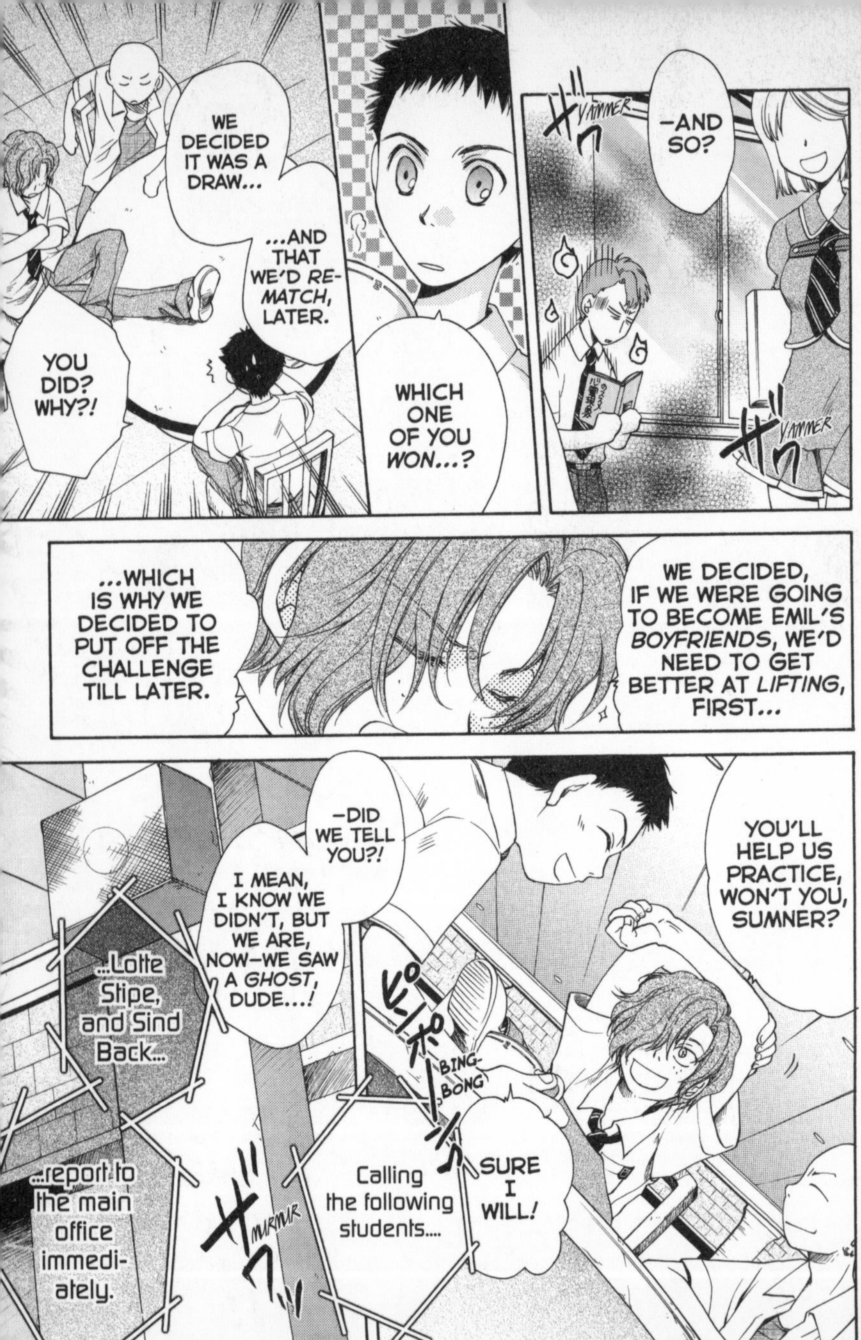
—AND SO?
YAMMER
YAMMER
WHICH ONE OF YOU WON...?
WE DECIDED IT WAS A DRAW...
...AND THAT WE'D RE-MATCH, LATER.
YOU DID? WHY?!
WE DECIDED, IF WE WERE GOING TO BECOME EMIL'S BOYFRIENDS, WE'D NEED TO GET BETTER AT LIFTING, FIRST...
...WHICH IS WHY WE DECIDED TO PUT OFF THE CHALLENGE TILL LATER.
YOU'LL HELP US PRACTICE, WON'T YOU, SUMNER?
—DID WE TELL YOU?!
I MEAN, I KNOW WE DIDN'T, BUT WE ARE, NOW—WE SAW A GHOST, DUDE...!
BING-BONG
SURE I WILL!
Calling the following students....
...Lotte Stipe, and Sind Back...
...report to the main office immediately.
MURMUR

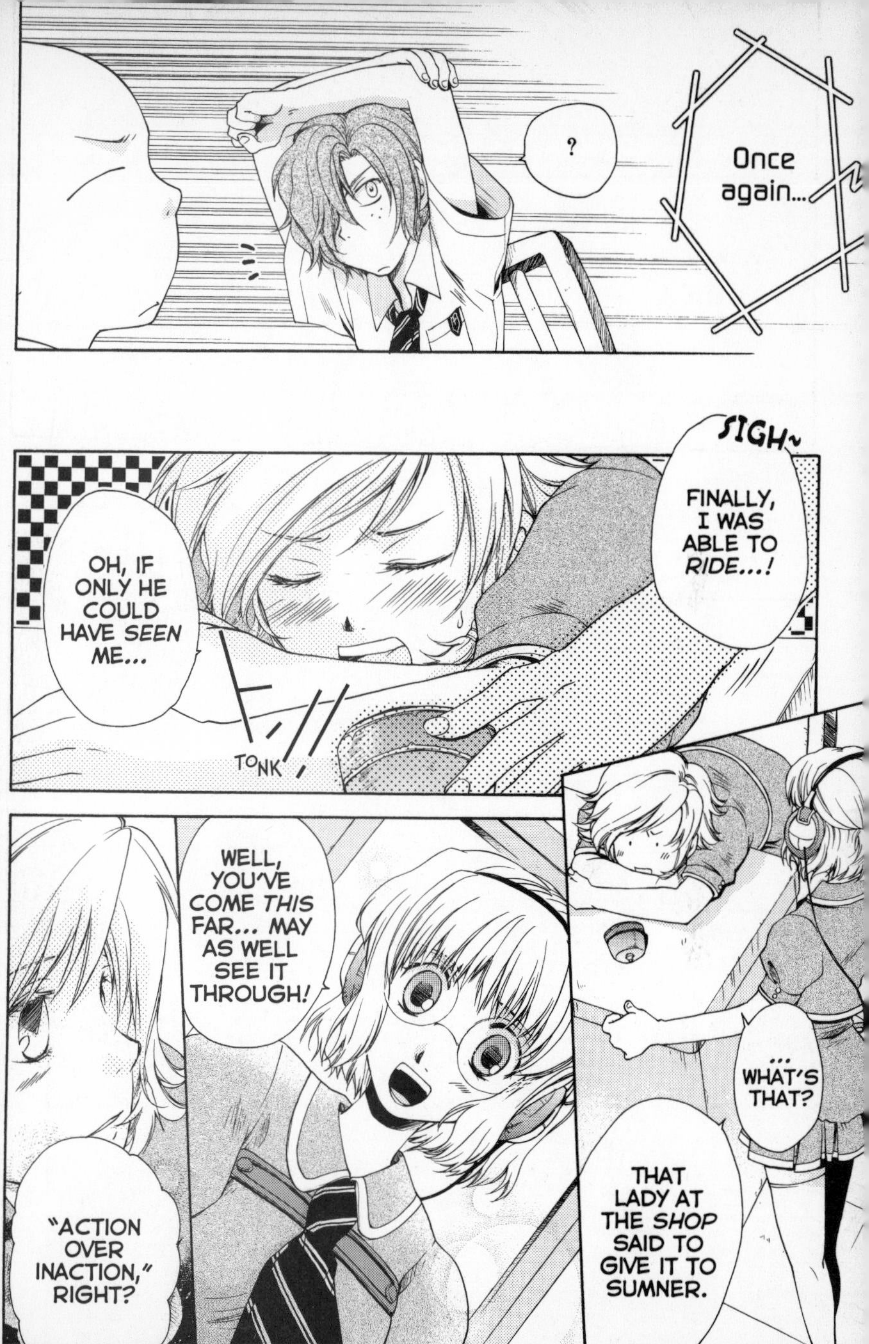
Once again...
?
SIGH~
FINALLY, I WAS ABLE TO *RIDE*...!
OH, IF ONLY HE COULD HAVE *SEEN* ME...
TONK
... WHAT'S THAT?
THAT LADY AT THE *SHOP* SAID TO GIVE IT TO SUMNER.
WELL, YOU'VE COME *THIS* FAR... MAY AS WELL SEE IT THROUGH!
"ACTION OVER INACTION," RIGHT?

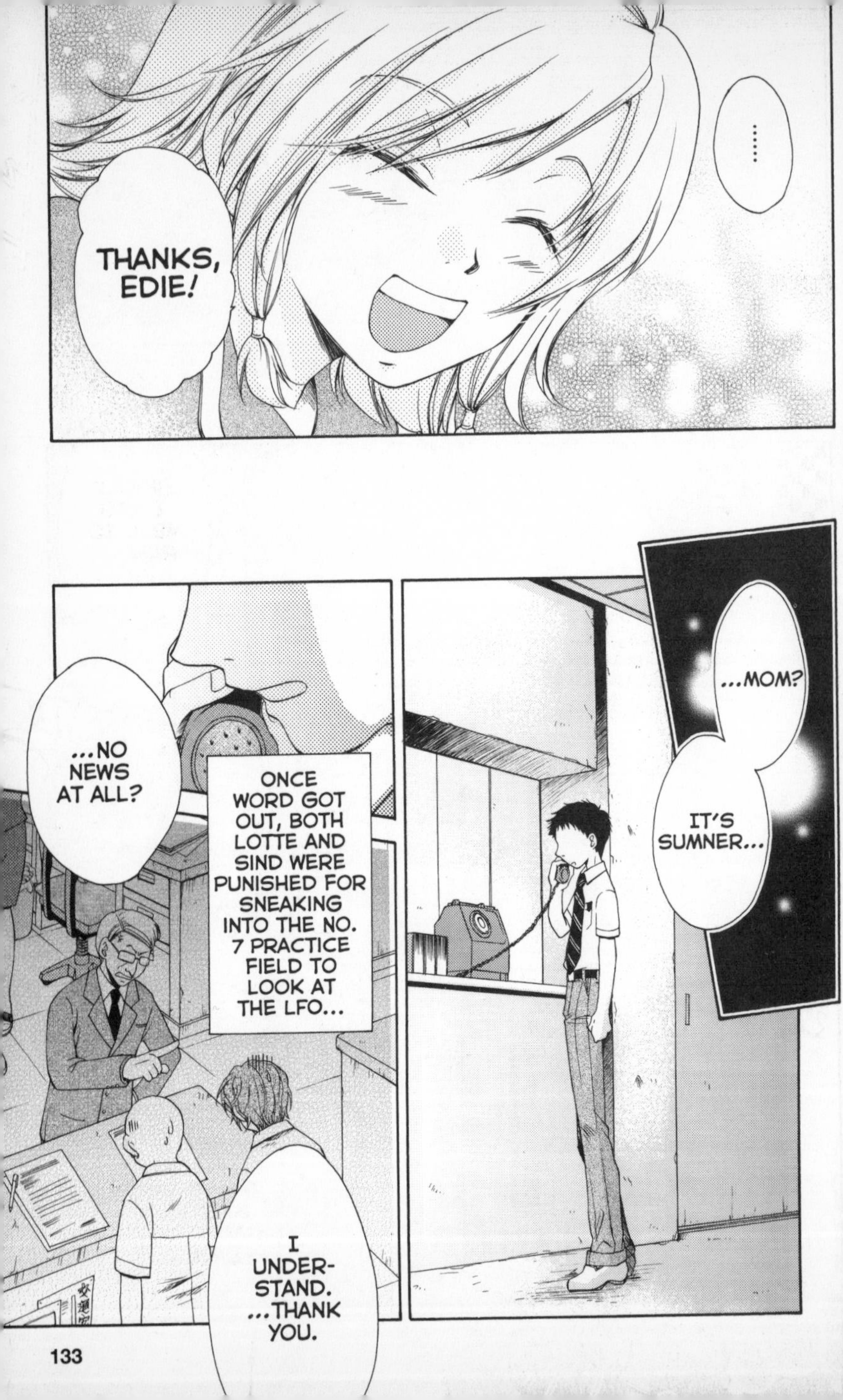
……
THANKS, EDIE!
...MOM?
IT'S SUMNER...
...NO NEWS AT ALL?
ONCE WORD GOT OUT, BOTH LOTTE AND SIND WERE PUNISHED FOR SNEAKING INTO THE NO. 7 PRACTICE FIELD TO LOOK AT THE LFO...
I UNDER-STAND. ...THANK YOU.

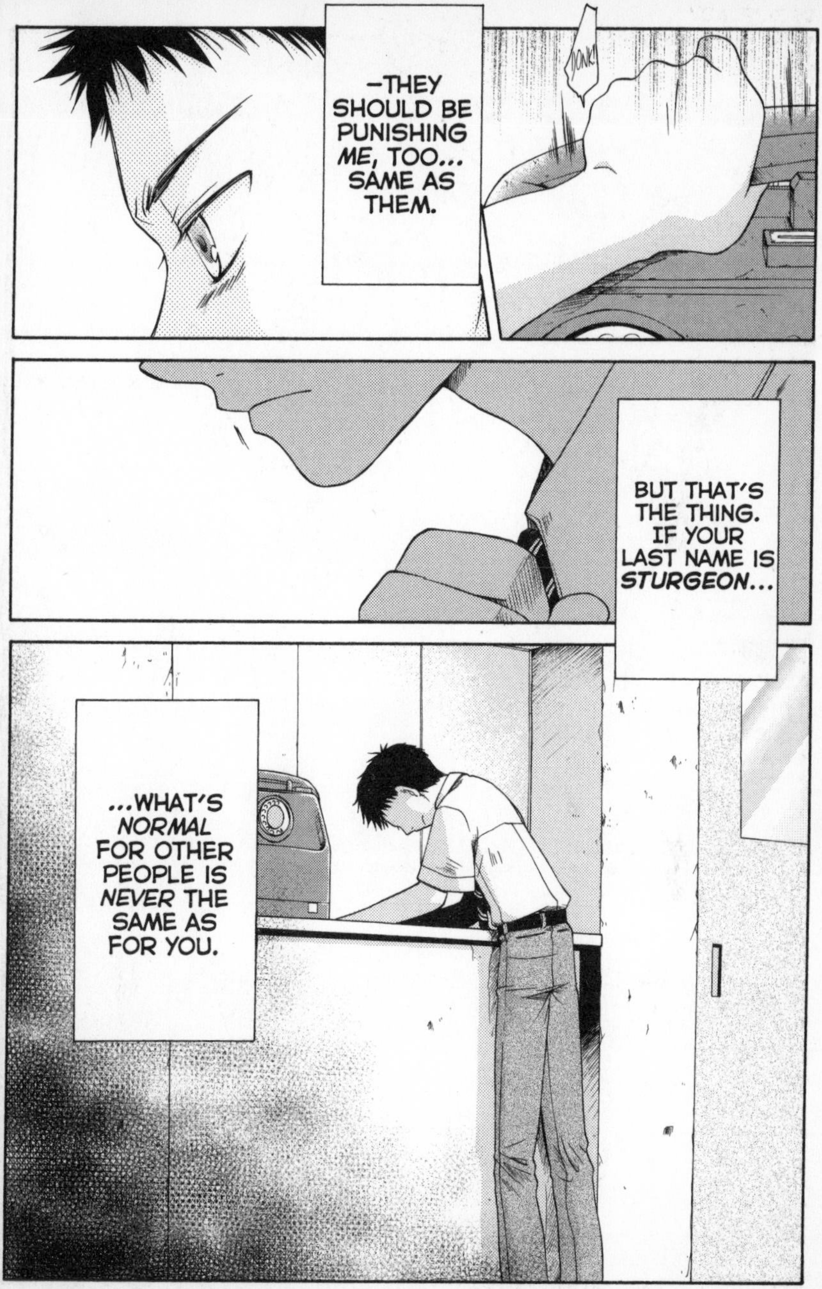
DONK!
–THEY SHOULD BE PUNISHING *ME*, TOO... SAME AS THEM.
BUT THAT'S THE THING. IF *YOUR* LAST NAME IS ***STURGEON***...
...WHAT'S *NORMAL* FOR OTHER PEOPLE IS *NEVER* THE SAME AS FOR YOU.

05 SILVER GHOST END

06 FAIRLADY

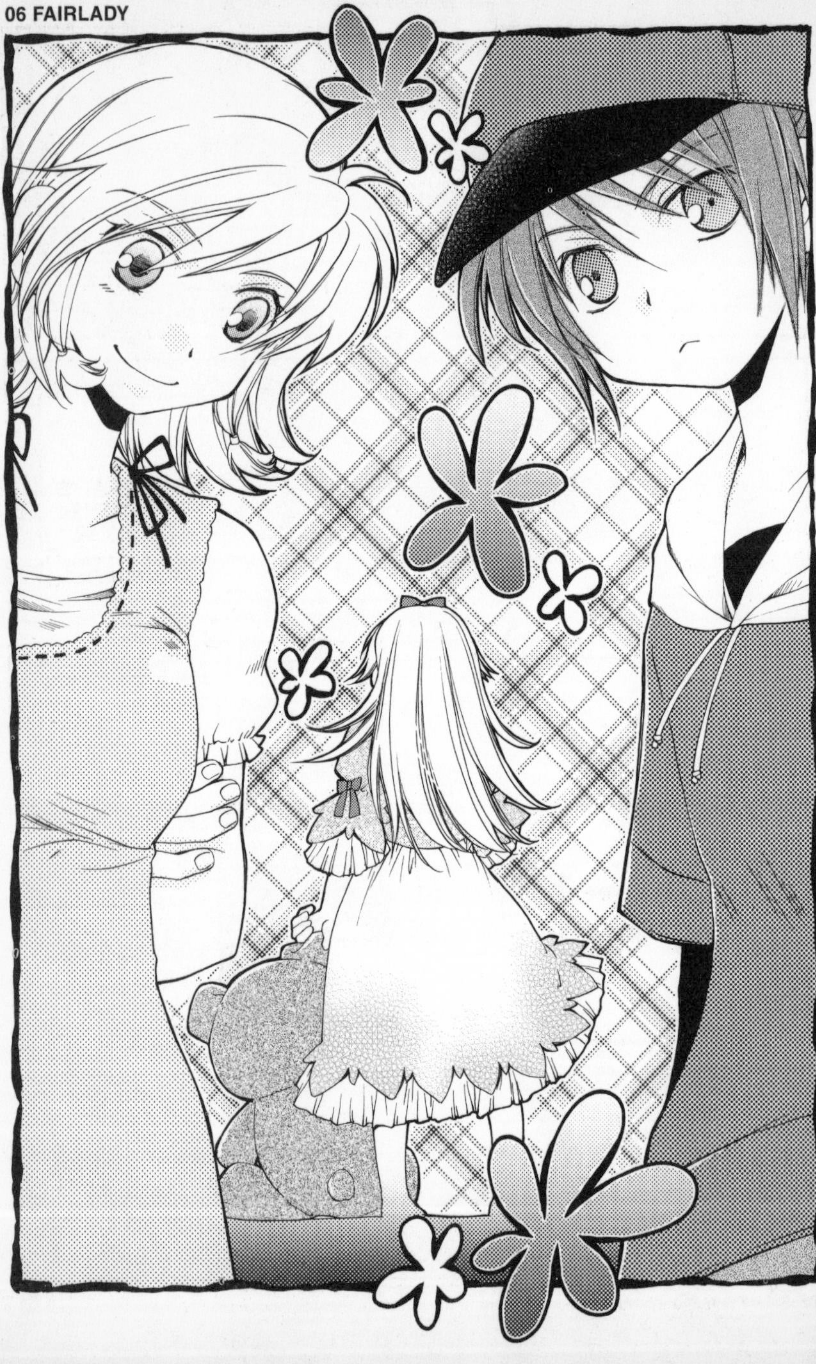

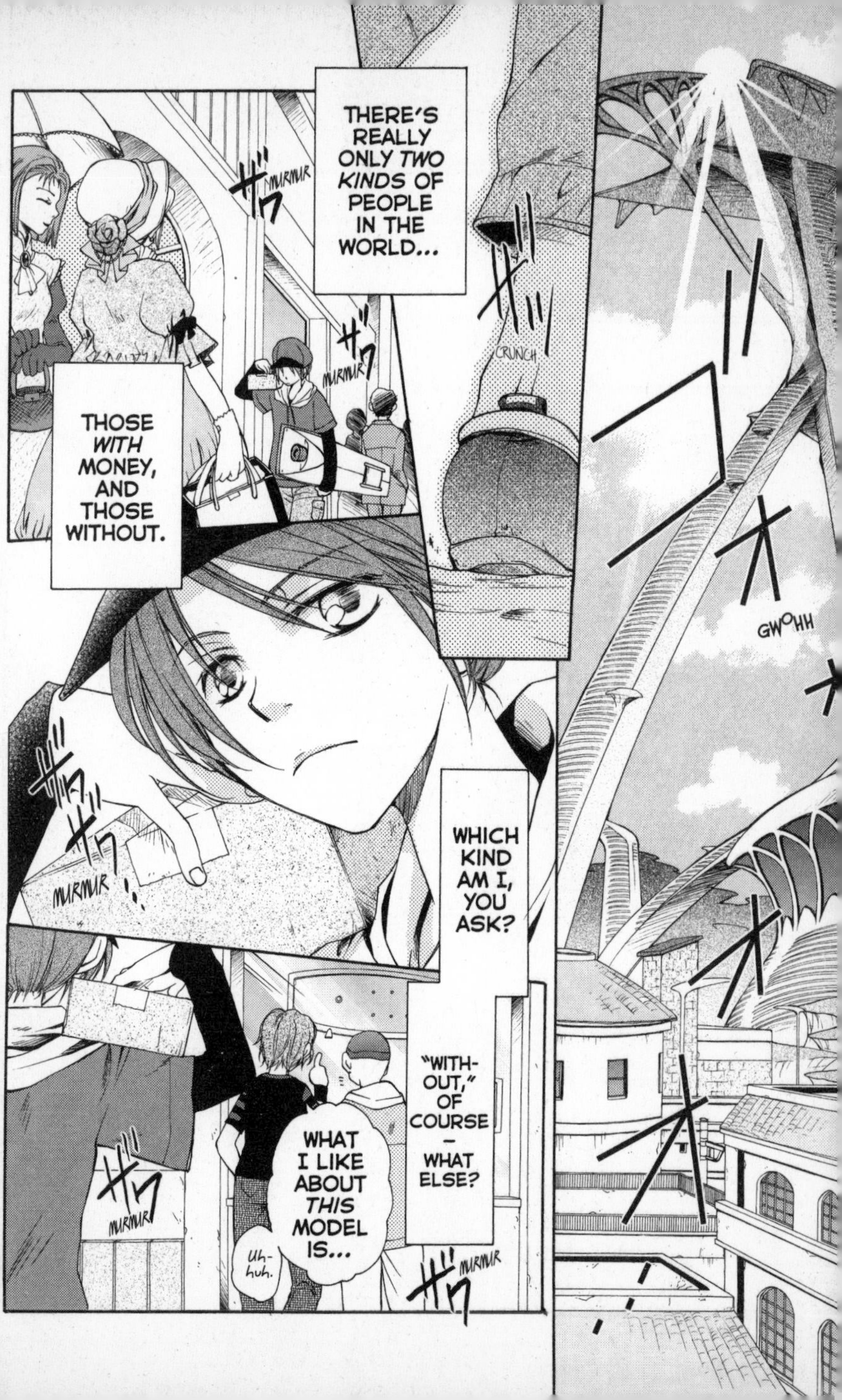
GWOHH
CRUNCH
THERE'S REALLY ONLY TWO KINDS OF PEOPLE IN THE WORLD...
MURMUR
MURMUR
THOSE WITH MONEY, AND THOSE WITHOUT.
WHICH KIND AM I, YOU ASK?
MURMUR
"WITH-OUT," OF COURSE – WHAT ELSE?
WHAT I LIKE ABOUT THIS MODEL IS...
Uh-huh.
MURMUR
MURMUR

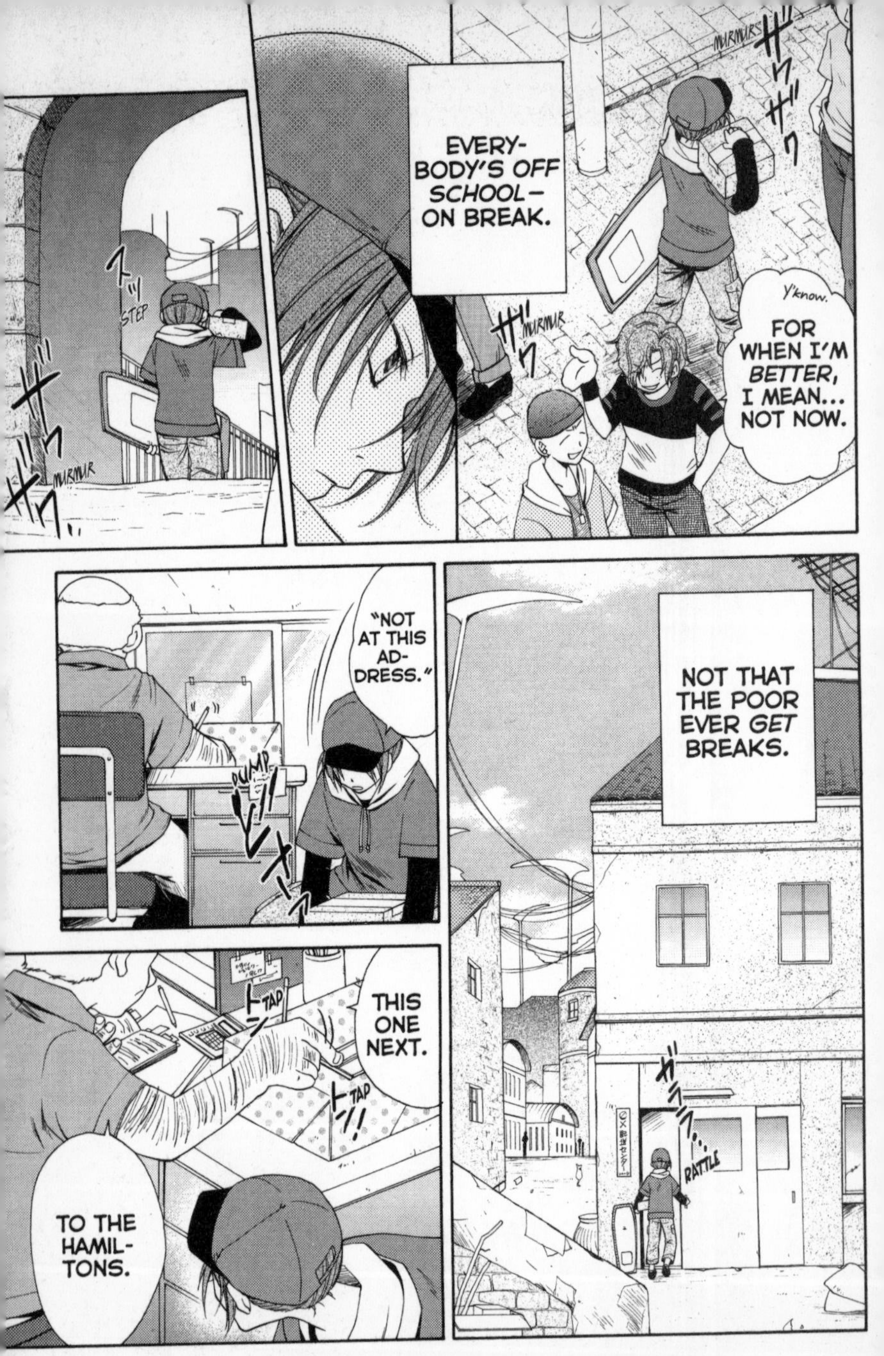
MURMURS
Y'know.
FOR WHEN I'M BETTER, I MEAN... NOT NOW.
MURMUR
EVERYBODY'S OFF SCHOOL—ON BREAK.
STEP
MURMUR
NOT THAT THE POOR EVER GET BREAKS.
RATTLE
"NOT AT THIS ADDRESS."
DUMP
THIS ONE NEXT.
TAP
TAP
TO THE HAMILTONS.

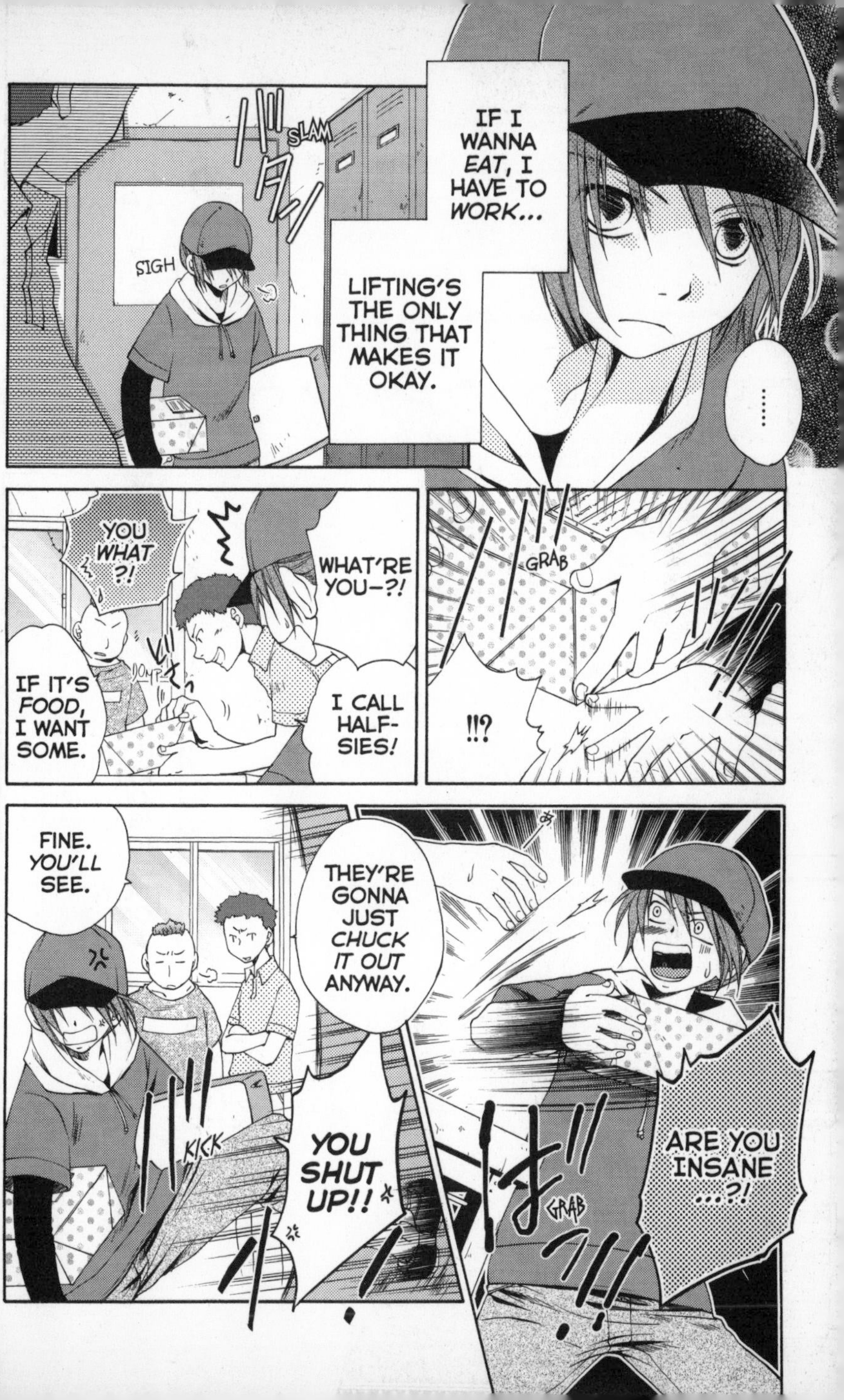
IF I WANNA EAT, I HAVE TO WORK...
LIFTING'S THE ONLY THING THAT MAKES IT OKAY.
......
SLAM
SIGH
GRAB
!!?
WHAT'RE YOU–?!
I CALL HALF-SIES!
YOU WHAT?!
IF IT'S FOOD, I WANT SOME.
GRAB
ARE YOU INSANE...?!
THEY'RE GONNA JUST CHUCK IT OUT ANYWAY.
FINE. YOU'LL SEE.
KICK
YOU SHUT UP!!

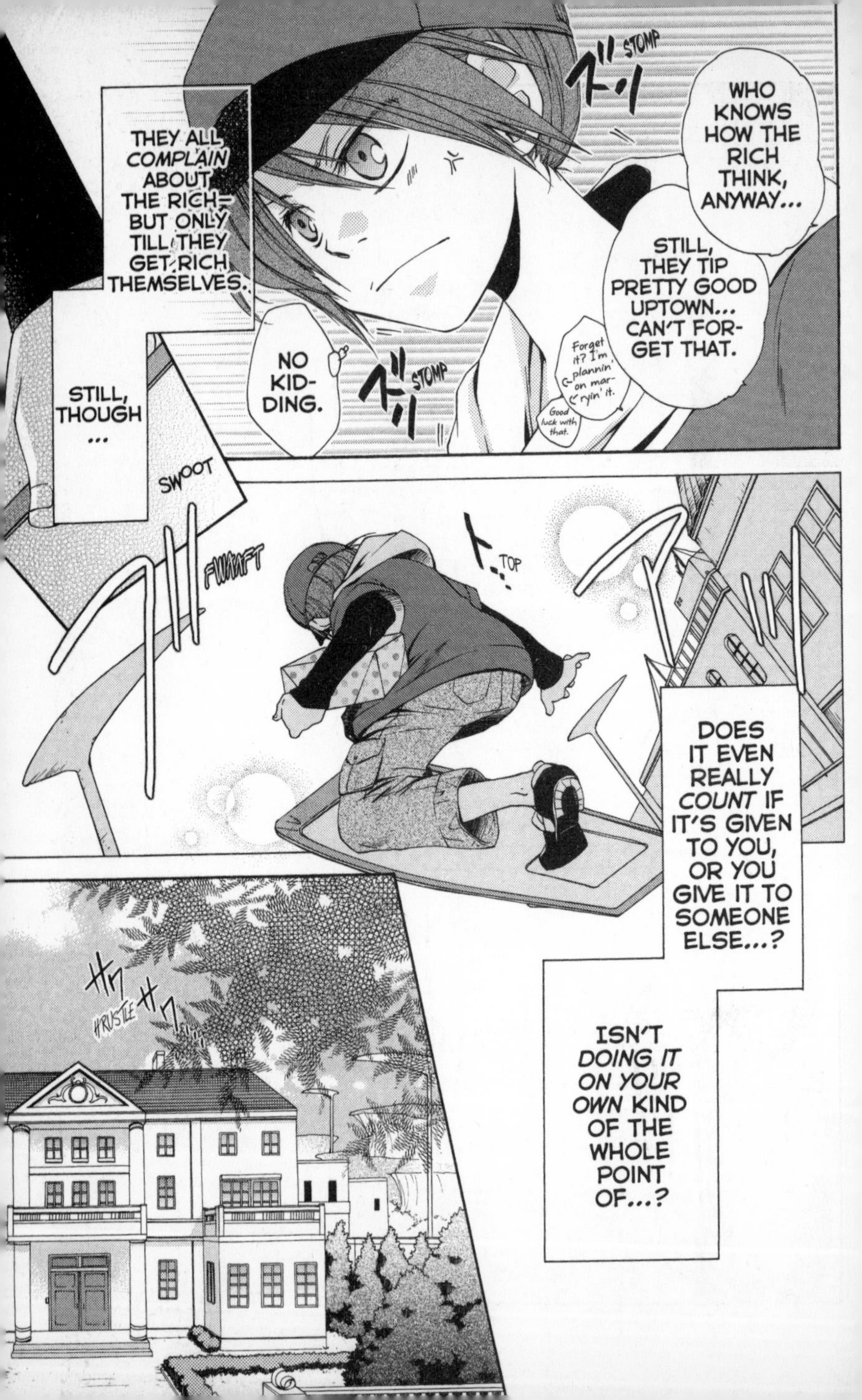
STOMP
WHO KNOWS HOW THE RICH THINK, ANYWAY...
STILL, THEY TIP PRETTY GOOD UPTOWN... CAN'T FORGET THAT.
Forget it? I'm plannin' on mar-ryin' it.
Good luck with that.
NO KID-DING.
STOMP
THEY ALL COMPLAIN ABOUT THE RICH—BUT ONLY TILL THEY GET RICH THEMSELVES.
STILL, THOUGH...
SWOOT
TOP
FWAAFT
DOES IT EVEN REALLY COUNT IF IT'S GIVEN TO YOU, OR YOU GIVE IT TO SOMEONE ELSE...?
HRUSTLE
ISN'T DOING IT ON YOUR OWN KIND OF THE WHOLE POINT OF...?

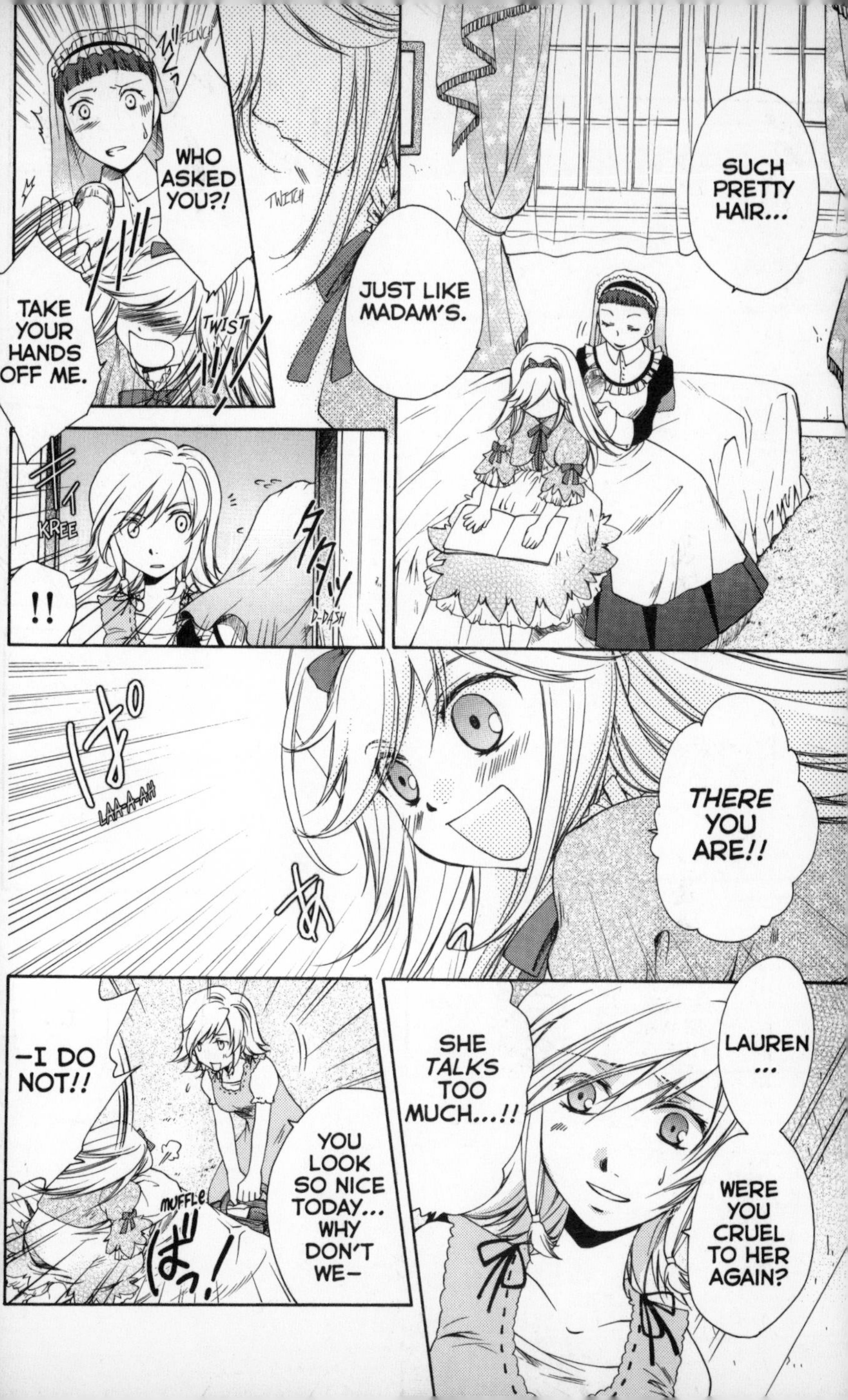
SUCH PRETTY HAIR...
JUST LIKE MADAM'S.
FLINCH
TWITCH
WHO ASKED YOU?!
TWIST
TAKE YOUR HANDS OFF ME.
D-DASH
KREE
!!
THERE YOU ARE!!
LAA-A-AH
LAUREN...
WERE YOU CRUEL TO HER AGAIN?
SHE TALKS TOO MUCH...!!
YOU LOOK SO NICE TODAY... WHY DON'T WE–
MUFFLE
–I DO NOT!!

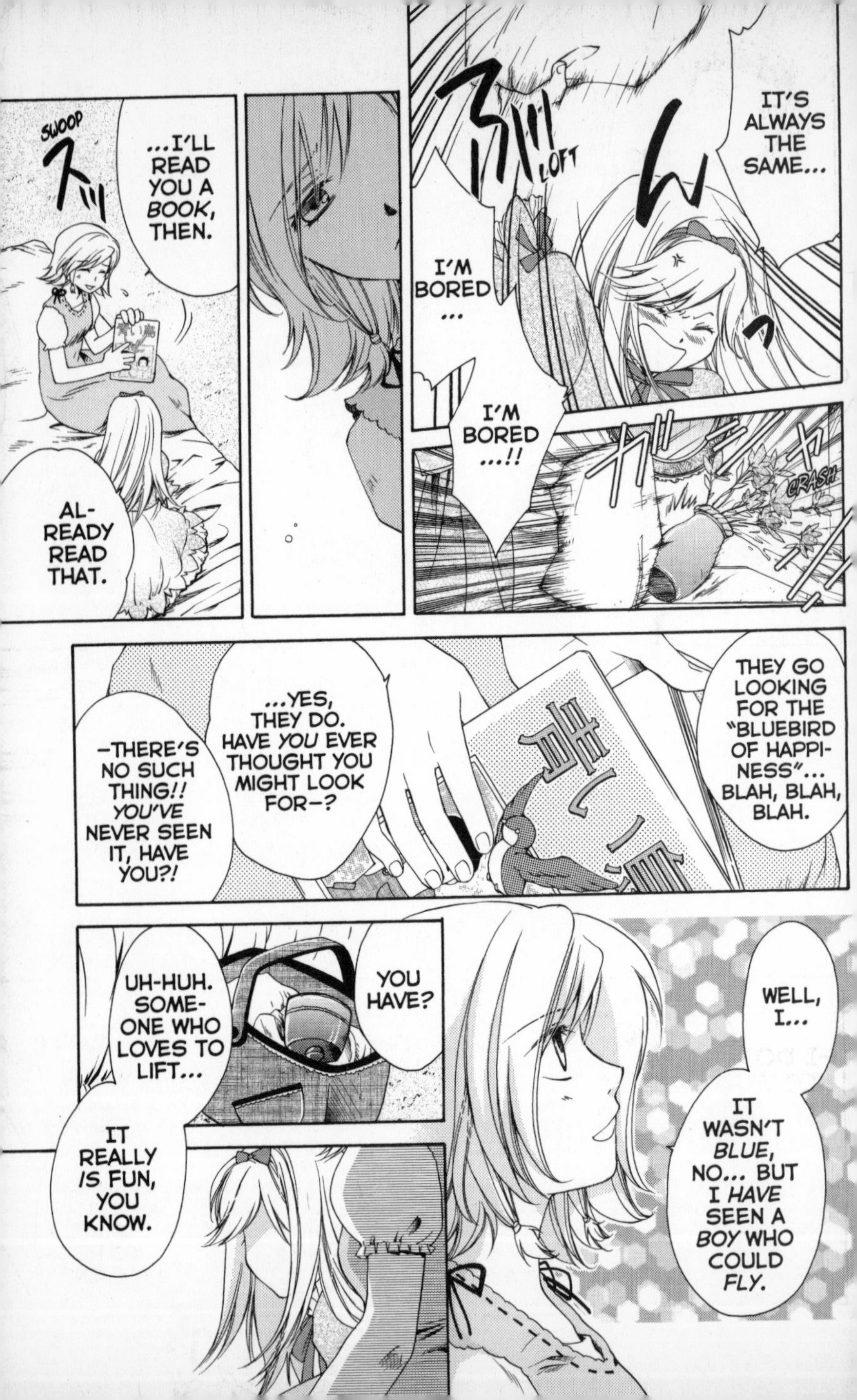

IT'S ALWAYS THE SAME...
LOFT
I'M BORED...
I'M BORED...!!
CRASH
SWOOP
...I'LL READ YOU A *BOOK*, THEN.
AL-READY READ THAT.
THEY GO LOOKING FOR THE "BLUEBIRD OF HAPPI-NESS"... BLAH, BLAH, BLAH.
...YES, THEY DO. HAVE *YOU* EVER THOUGHT YOU MIGHT LOOK FOR—?
—THERE'S NO SUCH THING!! *YOU'VE* NEVER SEEN IT, HAVE YOU?!
WELL, I...
IT WASN'T *BLUE*, NO... BUT I *HAVE* SEEN A *BOY* WHO COULD *FLY*.
YOU HAVE?
UH-HUH. SOME-ONE WHO LOVES TO LIFT...
IT REALLY *IS* FUN, YOU KNOW.

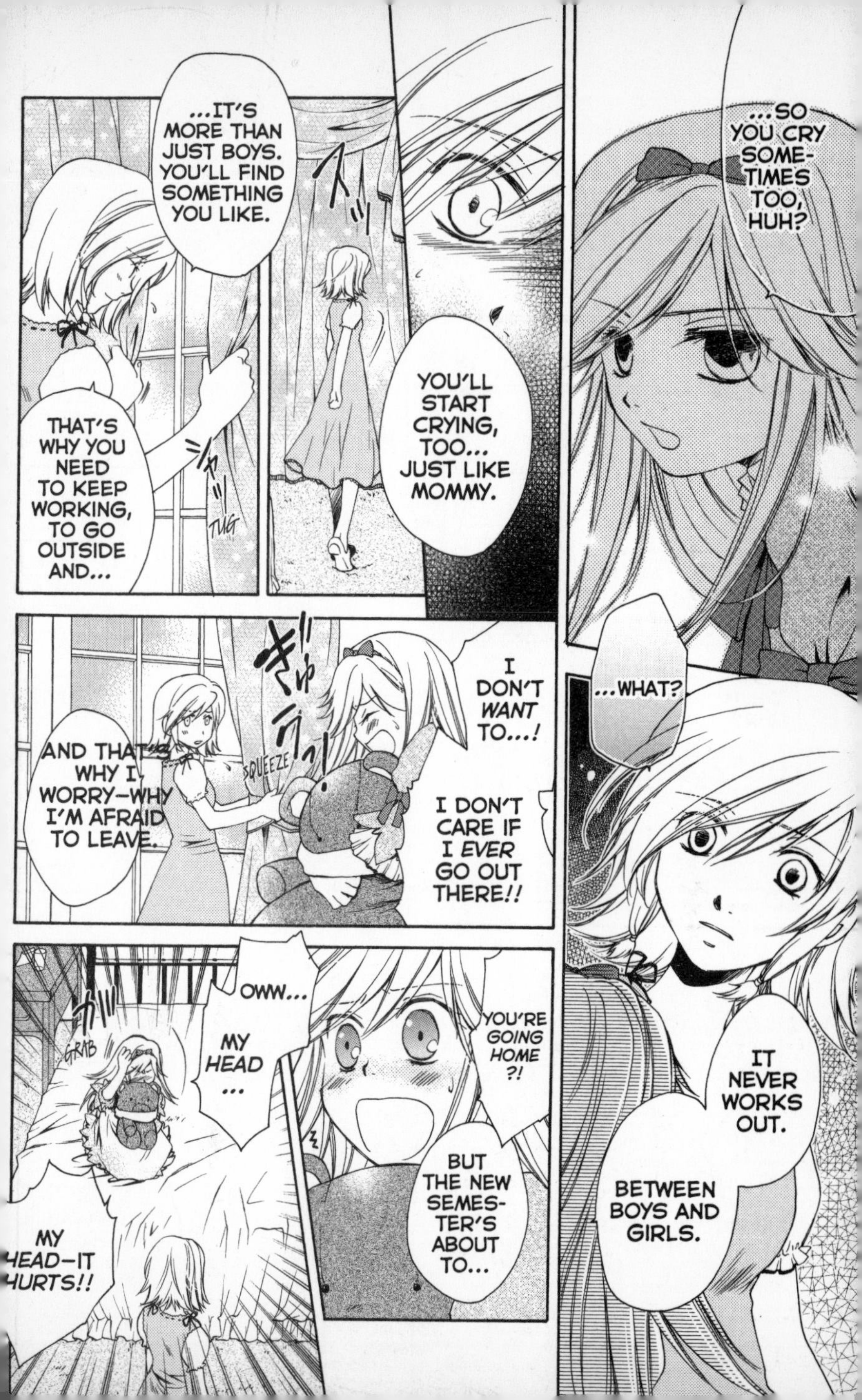

...SO YOU CRY SOMETIMES TOO, HUH?
...WHAT?
IT NEVER WORKS OUT.
BETWEEN BOYS AND GIRLS.
YOU'LL START CRYING, TOO... JUST LIKE MOMMY.
...IT'S MORE THAN JUST BOYS. YOU'LL FIND SOMETHING YOU LIKE.
THAT'S WHY YOU NEED TO KEEP WORKING, TO GO OUTSIDE AND...
TUG
I DON'T *WANT* TO...!
I DON'T CARE IF I *EVER* GO OUT THERE!!
SQUEEZE
AND THAT'S WHY I WORRY—WHY I'M AFRAID TO LEAVE.
YOU'RE *GOING HOME* ?!
BUT THE NEW SEMESTER'S ABOUT TO...
OWW...
MY *HEAD* ...
GRAB
MY HEAD—IT HURTS!!

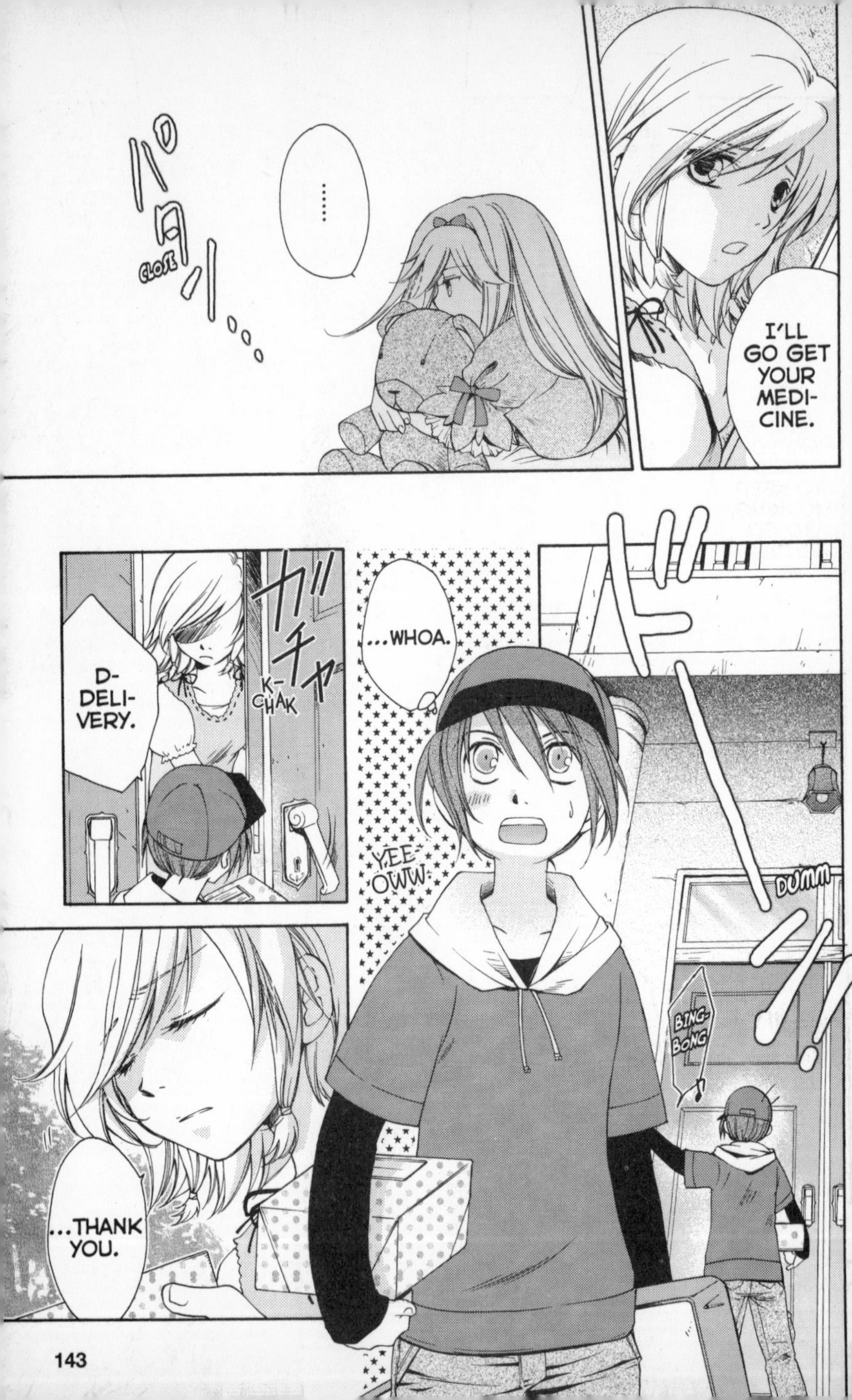
I'LL GO GET YOUR MEDI-CINE.
......
CLOSE
DUMM
BING-BONG
...WHOA.
YEE-OWW
K-CHAK
D-DELI-VERY.
...THANK YOU.

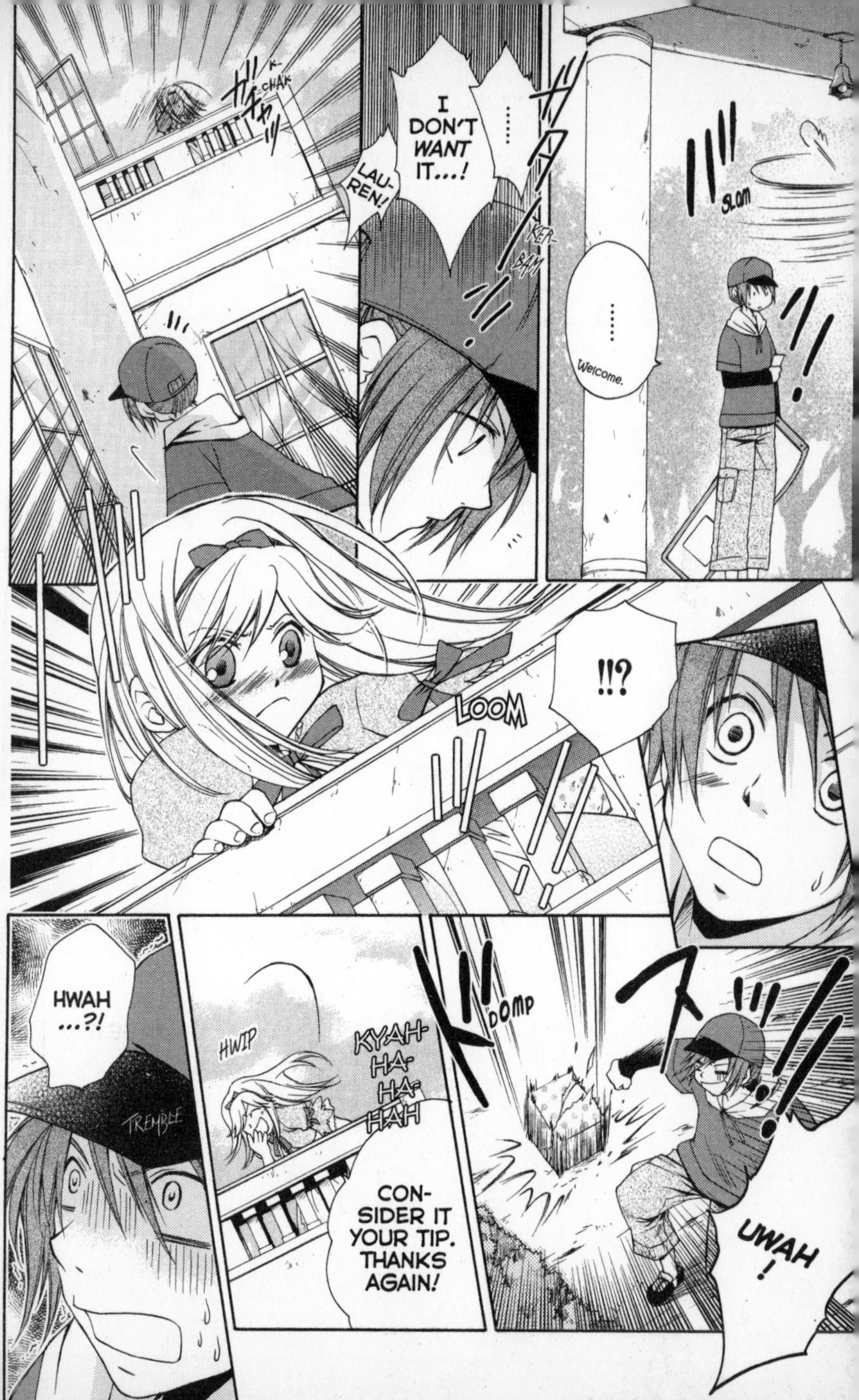
SLAM
......
Welcome.
......
I DON'T WANT IT...!
LAUREN!
KER-BAM
K-CHAK
!!?
LOOM
UWAH!
DOMP
KYAH-HA-HA-HAH
HWIP
CON-SIDER IT YOUR TIP. THANKS AGAIN!
HWAH ...?!
TREMBLE

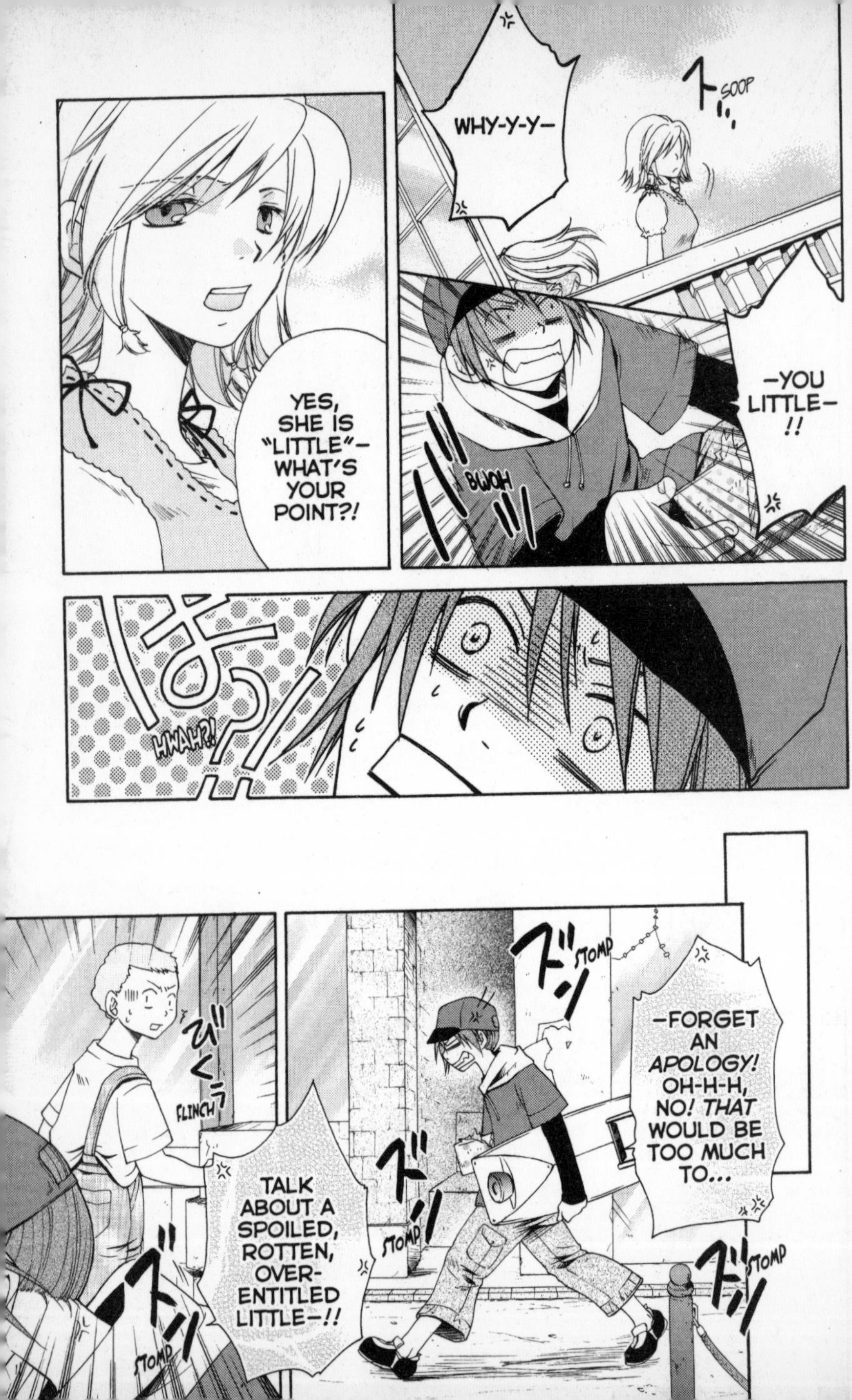
WHY-Y-Y—
SOOP
—YOU LITTLE—!!
BWOH
YES, SHE IS "LITTLE"— WHAT'S YOUR POINT?!
HWAH?!
STOMP
—FORGET AN APOLOGY! OH-H-H, NO! THAT WOULD BE TOO MUCH TO...
STOMP
STOMP
FLINCH
TALK ABOUT A SPOILED, ROTTEN, OVER-ENTITLED LITTLE—!!
STOMP

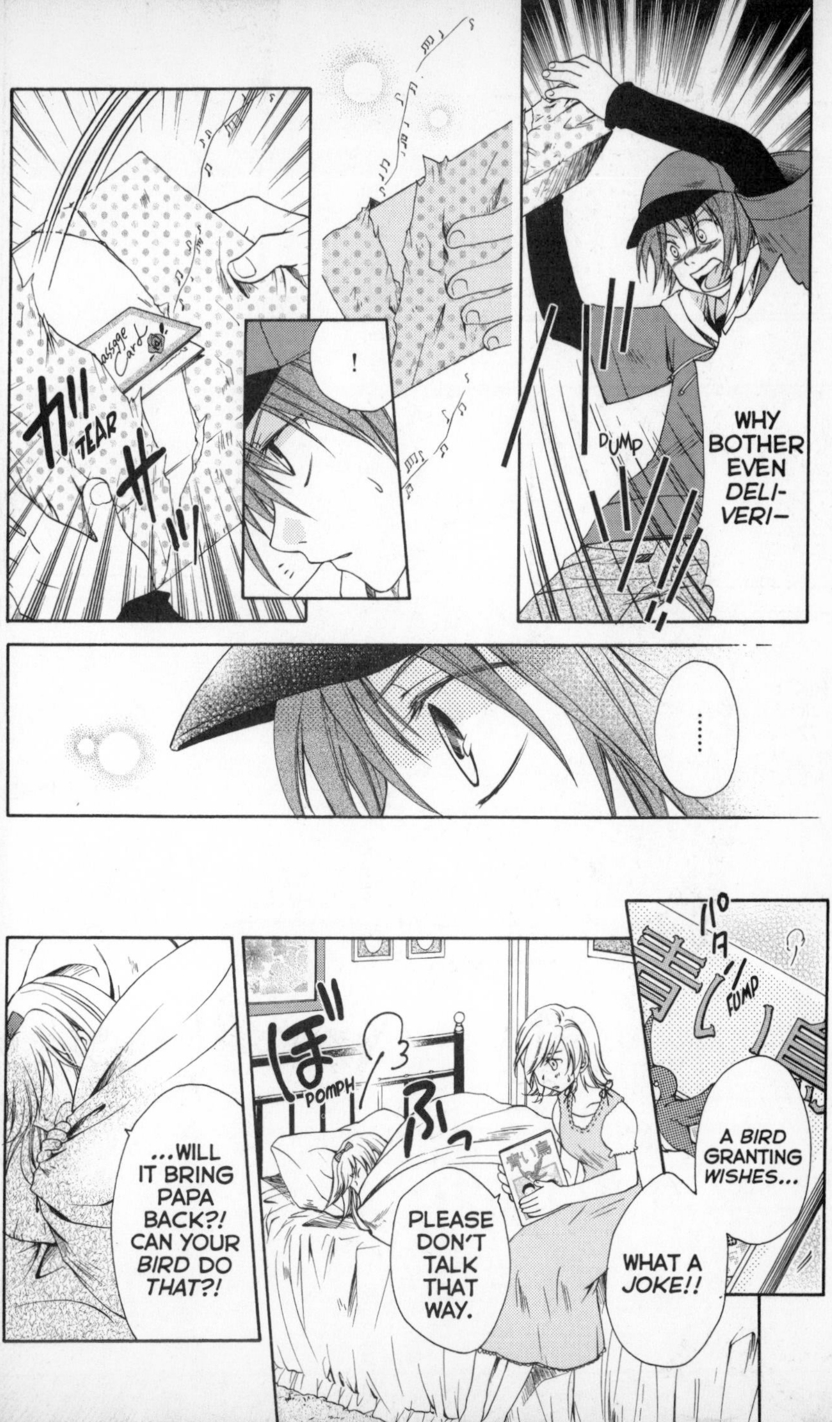
WHY BOTHER EVEN DELI-VERI—
DUMP
!
カリ TEAR
......
パタ FUMP
A BIRD GRANTING WISHES...
WHAT A JOKE!!
ぼふっ POMPH
PLEASE DON'T TALK THAT WAY.
...WILL IT BRING PAPA BACK?! CAN YOUR BIRD DO THAT?!

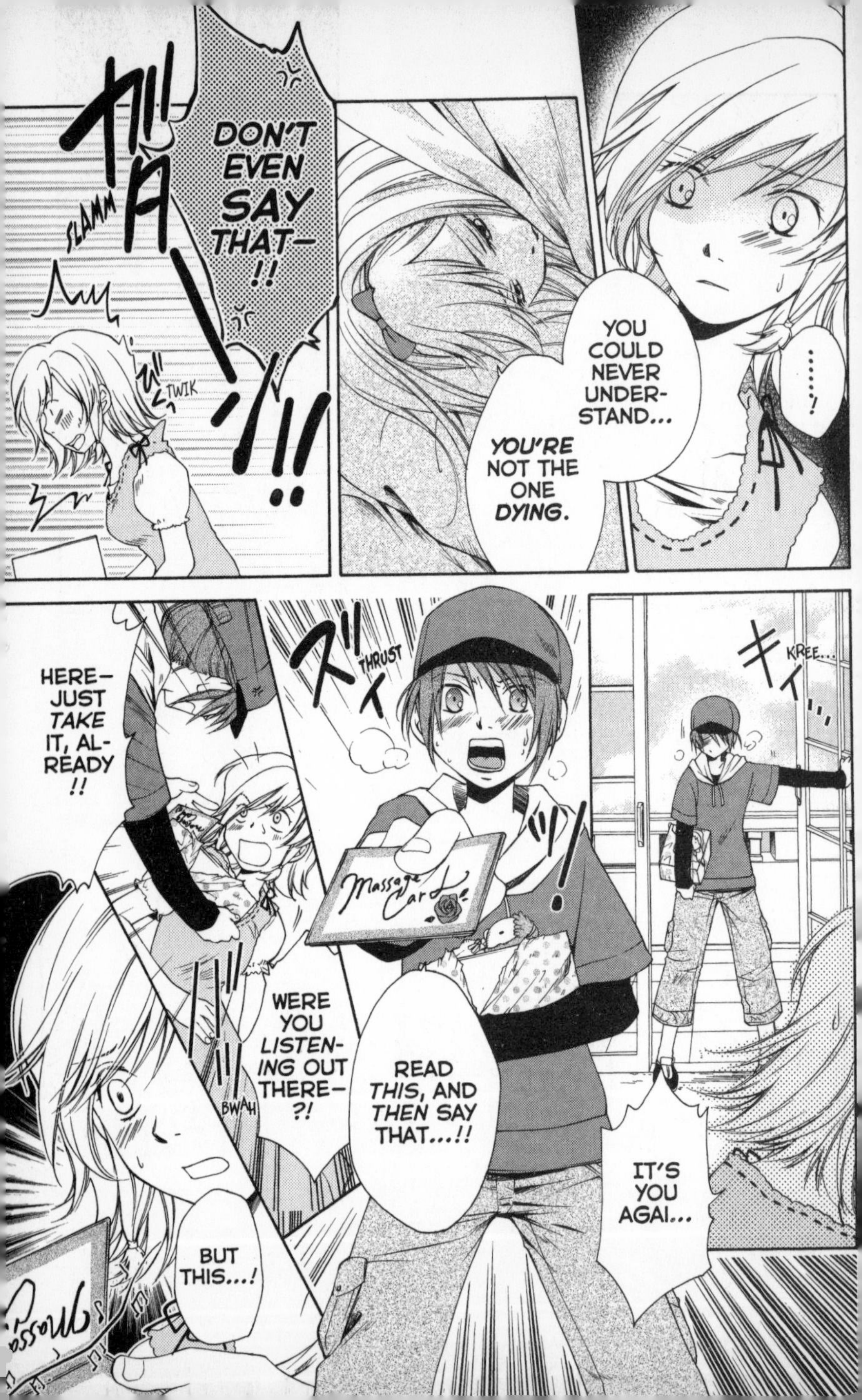
……!
YOU COULD NEVER UNDERSTAND...
YOU'RE NOT THE ONE DYING.
SLAMM
DON'T EVEN SAY THAT—!!
TWIK
KREE...
IT'S YOU AGAI...
THRUST
Massage Card
READ THIS, AND THEN SAY THAT...!!
WERE YOU LISTENING OUT THERE—?!
BWAH
HERE—JUST TAKE IT, ALREADY!!
BUT THIS...!

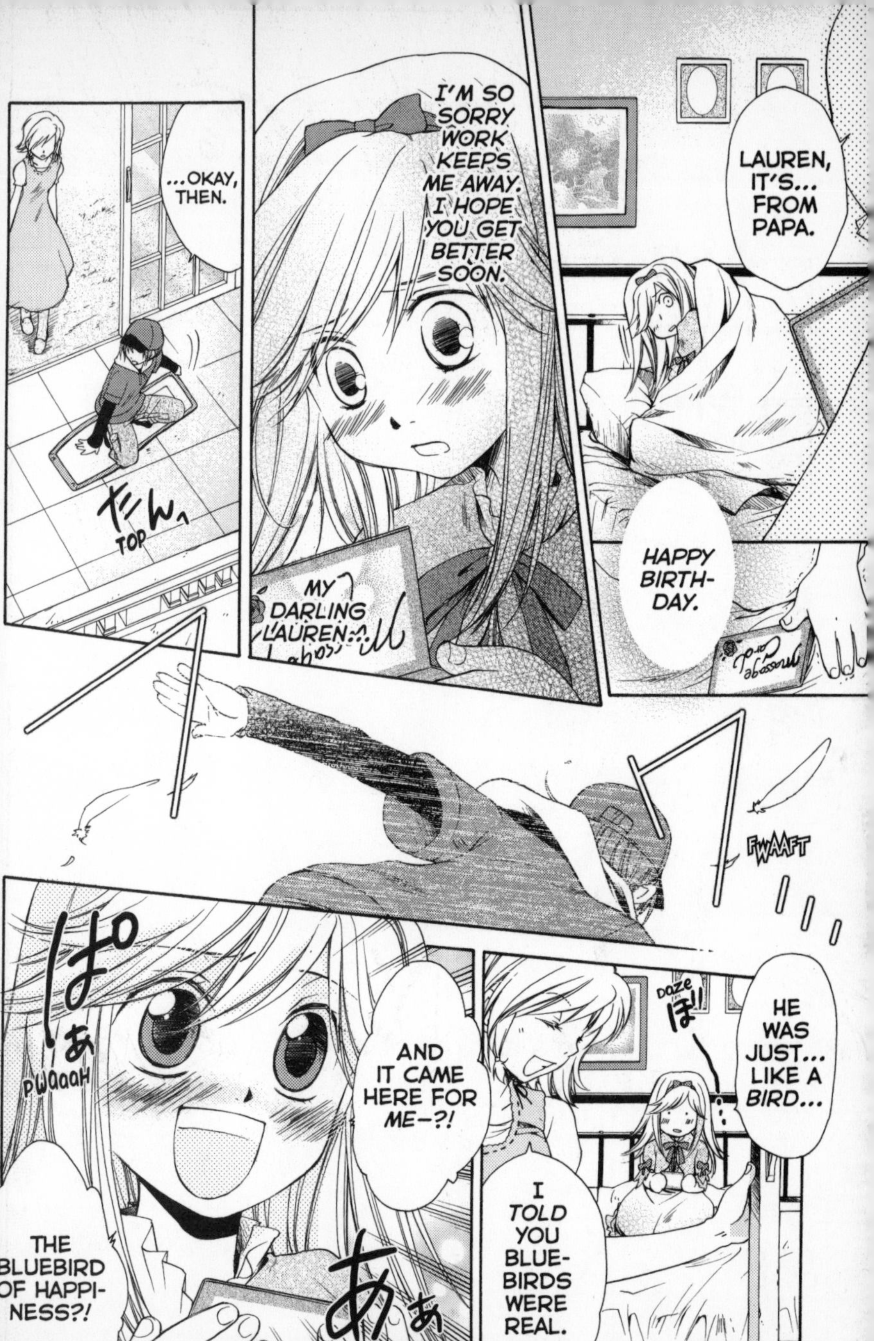

LAUREN, IT'S... FROM PAPA.
HAPPY BIRTH-DAY.
I'M SO SORRY WORK KEEPS ME AWAY. I HOPE YOU GET BETTER SOON.
MY DARLING LAUREN
...OKAY, THEN.
TOP
FWAAFT
DAZE
HE WAS JUST... LIKE A BIRD...
I TOLD YOU BLUE-BIRDS WERE REAL.
AND IT CAME HERE FOR ME-?!
PWAAAH
THE BLUEBIRD OF HAPPI-NESS?!

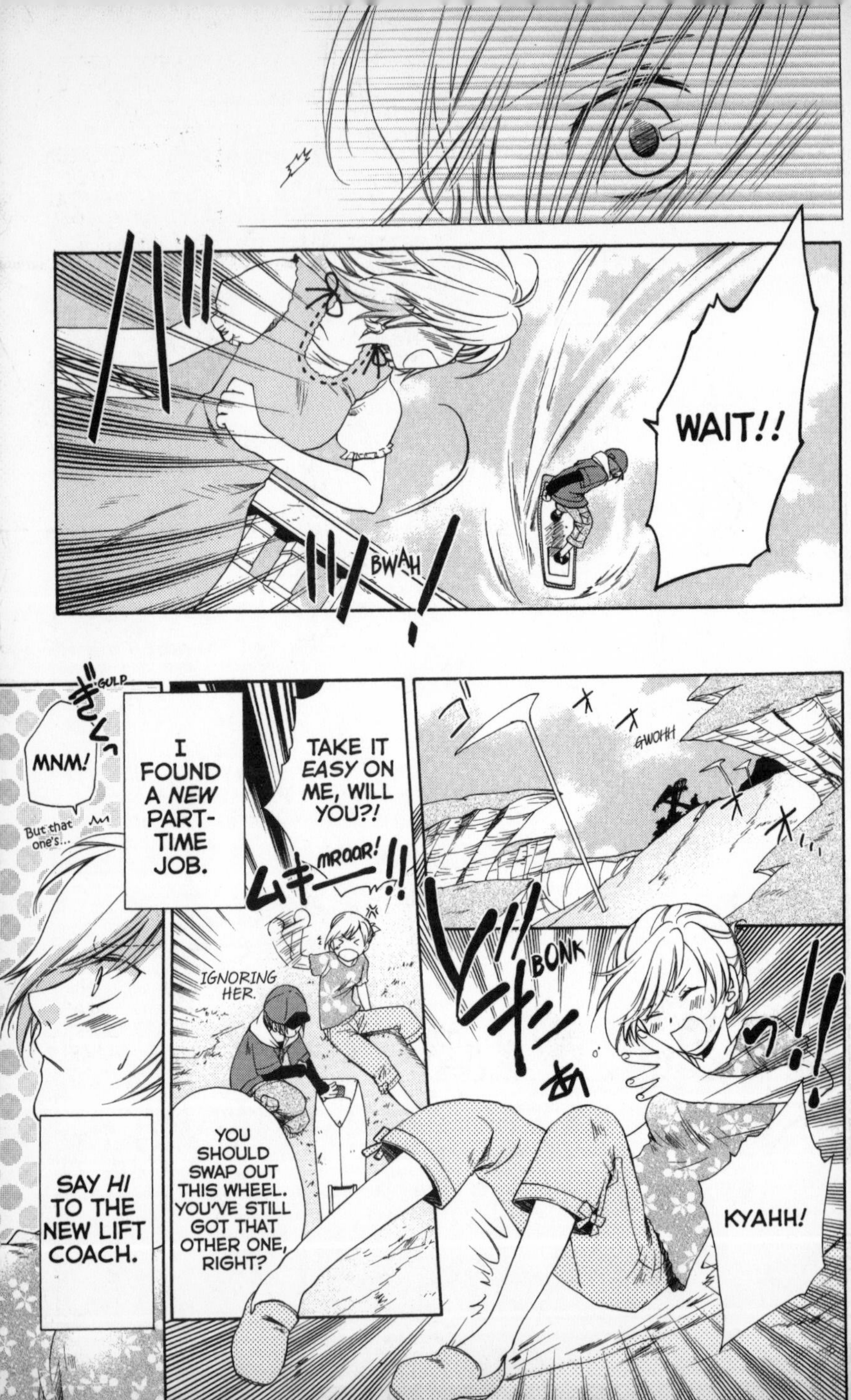

WAIT!!
BWAH
GWOHH
BONK
KYAHH!
TAKE IT EASY ON ME, WILL YOU?!
ムキー!!
MRAAR!
IGNORING HER.
YOU SHOULD SWAP OUT THIS WHEEL. YOU'VE STILL GOT THAT OTHER ONE, RIGHT?
GULP
MNM!
But that one's...
I FOUND A NEW PART-TIME JOB.
SAY HI TO THE NEW LIFT COACH.

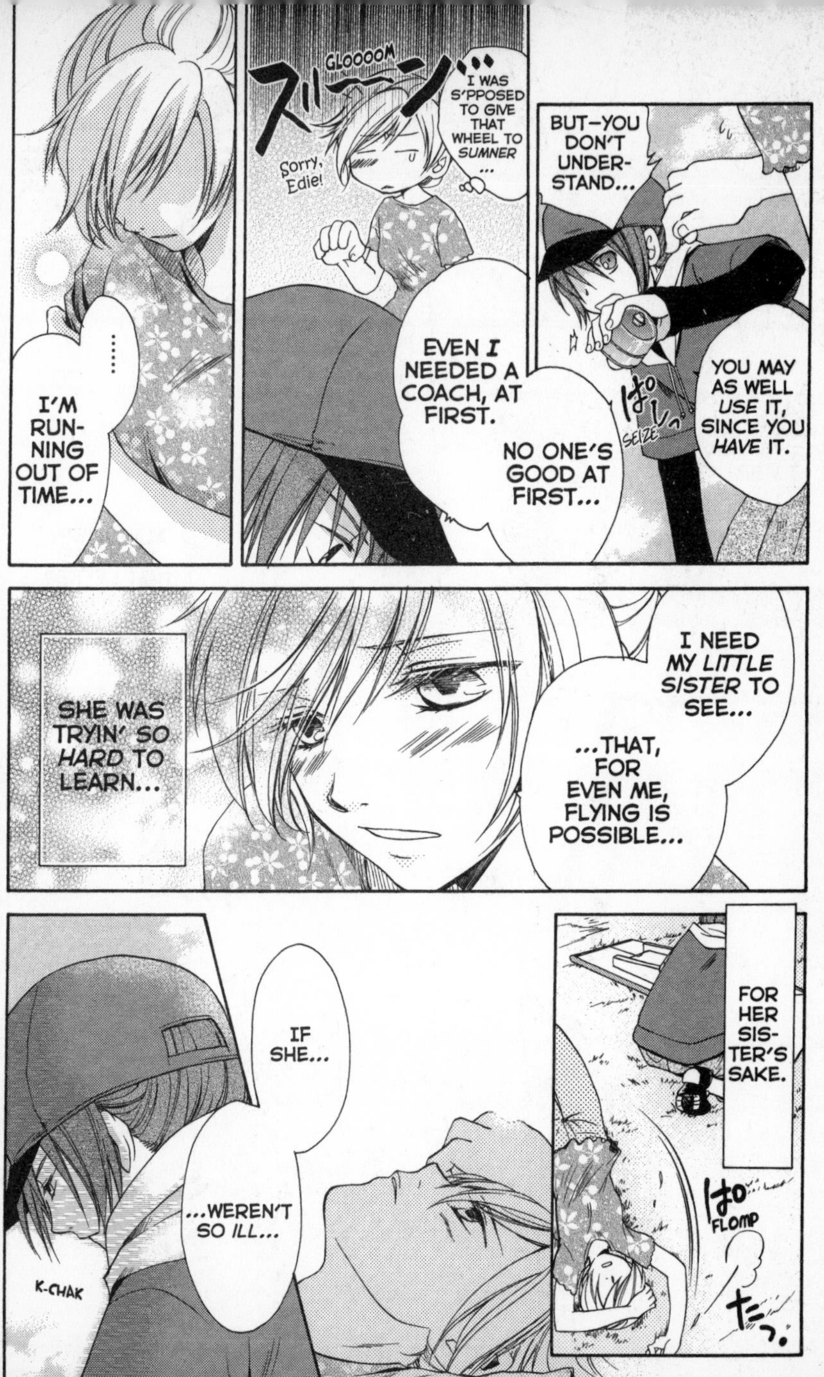
BUT—YOU DON'T UNDERSTAND...
SEIZE
YOU MAY AS WELL USE IT, SINCE YOU HAVE IT.
GLOOOOM
I WAS S'PPOSED TO GIVE THAT WHEEL TO SUMNER ...
Sorry, Edie!
EVEN I NEEDED A COACH, AT FIRST.
NO ONE'S GOOD AT FIRST...
......
I'M RUNNING OUT OF TIME...
I NEED MY LITTLE SISTER TO SEE...
...THAT, FOR EVEN ME, FLYING IS POSSIBLE...
SHE WAS TRYIN' SO HARD TO LEARN...
FOR HER SISTER'S SAKE.
FLOMP
IF SHE...
...WEREN'T SO ILL...
K-CHAK

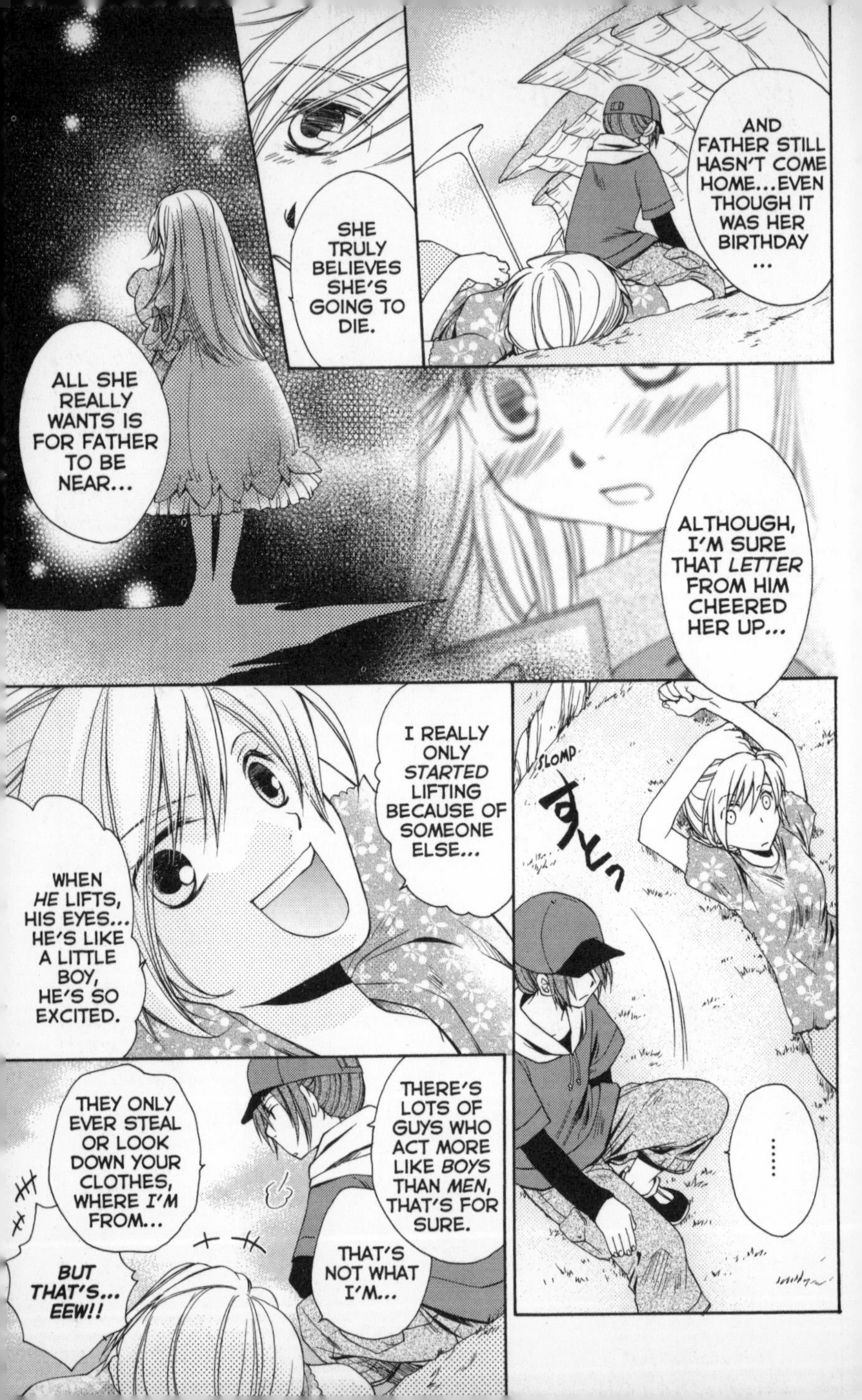
AND FATHER STILL HASN'T COME HOME...EVEN THOUGH IT WAS HER BIRTHDAY ...
SHE TRULY BELIEVES SHE'S GOING TO DIE.
ALL SHE REALLY WANTS IS FOR FATHER TO BE NEAR...
ALTHOUGH, I'M SURE THAT *LETTER* FROM HIM CHEERED HER UP...
SLOMP
......
I REALLY ONLY *STARTED* LIFTING BECAUSE OF SOMEONE ELSE...
WHEN *HE* LIFTS, HIS EYES... HE'S LIKE A LITTLE BOY, HE'S SO EXCITED.
THERE'S LOTS OF GUYS WHO ACT MORE LIKE *BOYS* THAN *MEN*, THAT'S FOR SURE.
THEY ONLY EVER STEAL OR LOOK DOWN YOUR CLOTHES, WHERE *I'M* FROM...
THAT'S NOT WHAT I'M...
BUT THAT'S... EEW!!

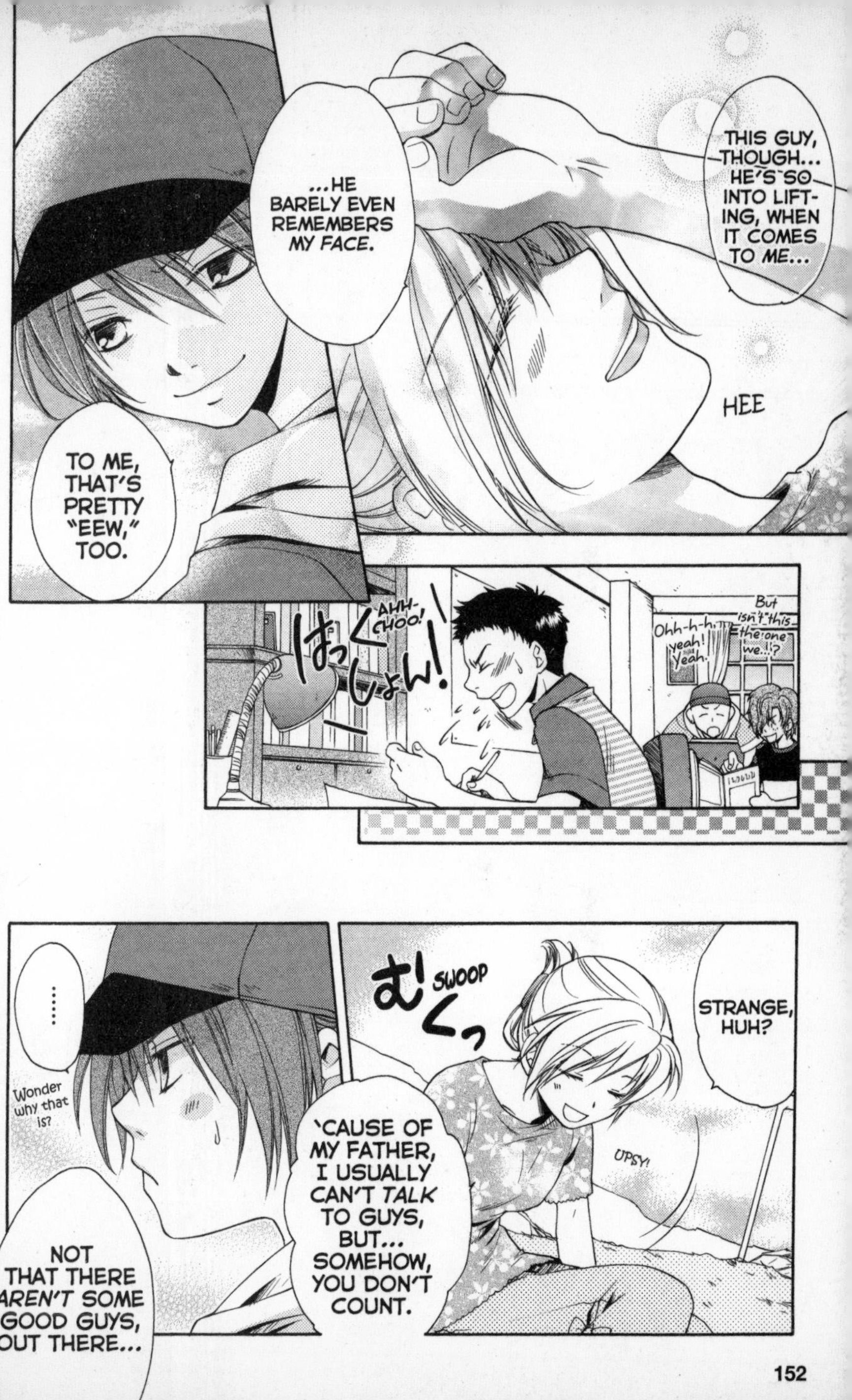
THIS GUY, THOUGH... HE'S SO INTO LIFTING, WHEN IT COMES TO ME...
HEE
...HE BARELY EVEN REMEMBERS MY *FACE.*
TO ME, THAT'S PRETTY "EEW," TOO.
But isn't this the one we...!?
Ohh-h-h, yeah! Yeah.
AHH-CHOO!
STRANGE, HUH?
SWOOP
UPSY!
'CAUSE OF MY FATHER, I USUALLY CAN'T *TALK* TO GUYS, BUT... SOMEHOW, YOU DON'T COUNT.
......
Wonder why that is?
NOT THAT THERE *AREN'T* SOME GOOD GUYS, OUT THERE...

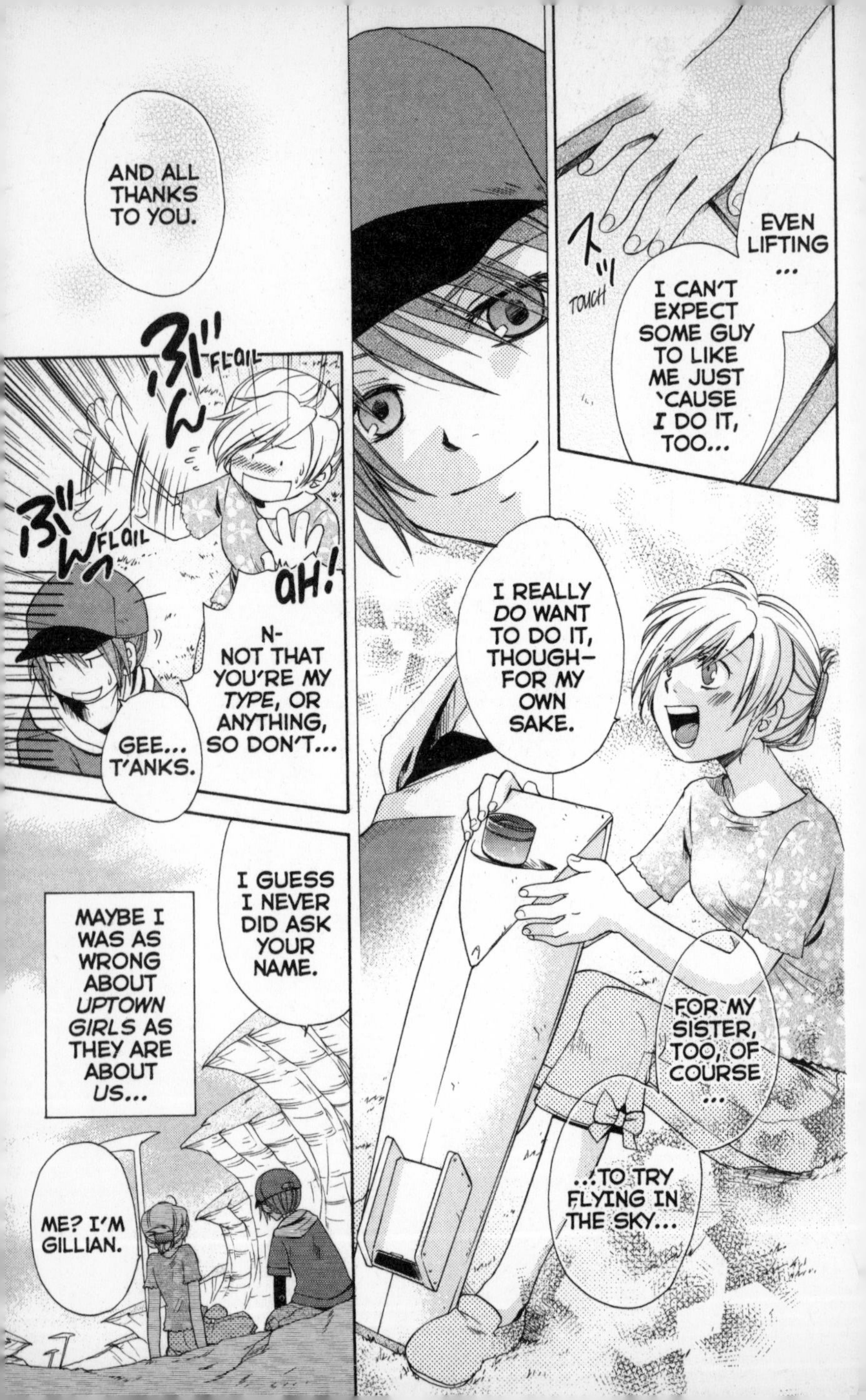
EVEN LIFTING...
スッ
TOUCH
I CAN'T EXPECT SOME GUY TO LIKE ME JUST 'CAUSE *I* DO IT, TOO...
I REALLY *DO* WANT TO DO IT, THOUGH— FOR MY OWN SAKE.
FOR MY SISTER, TOO, OF COURSE...
...TO TRY FLYING IN THE SKY...
AND ALL THANKS TO YOU.
ぶん
FLAIL
ぶん
FLAIL
AH!
N- NOT THAT YOU'RE MY *TYPE*, OR ANYTHING, SO DON'T...
GEE... T'ANKS.
I GUESS I NEVER DID ASK YOUR NAME.
MAYBE I WAS AS WRONG ABOUT *UPTOWN GIRLS* AS THEY ARE ABOUT *US*...
ME? I'M GILLIAN.

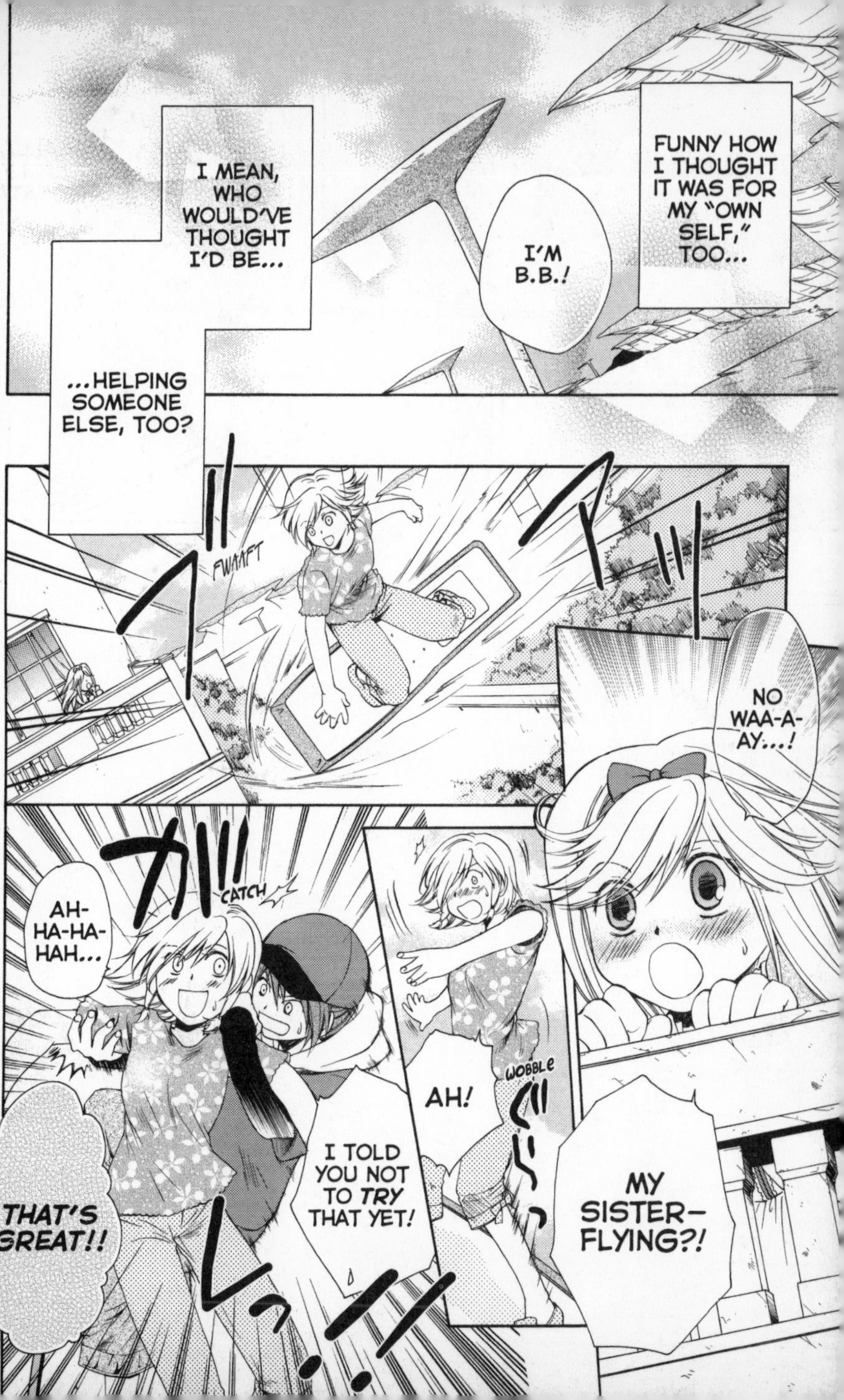
FUNNY HOW I THOUGHT IT WAS FOR MY "OWN SELF," TOO...
I'M B.B.!
I MEAN, WHO WOULD'VE THOUGHT I'D BE...
...HELPING SOMEONE ELSE, TOO?
FWAAFT
NO WAA-A-AY...!
MY SISTER—FLYING?!
WOBBLE
AH!
CATCH
I TOLD YOU NOT TO *TRY* THAT YET!
AH-HA-HA-HAH...
THAT'S GREAT!!

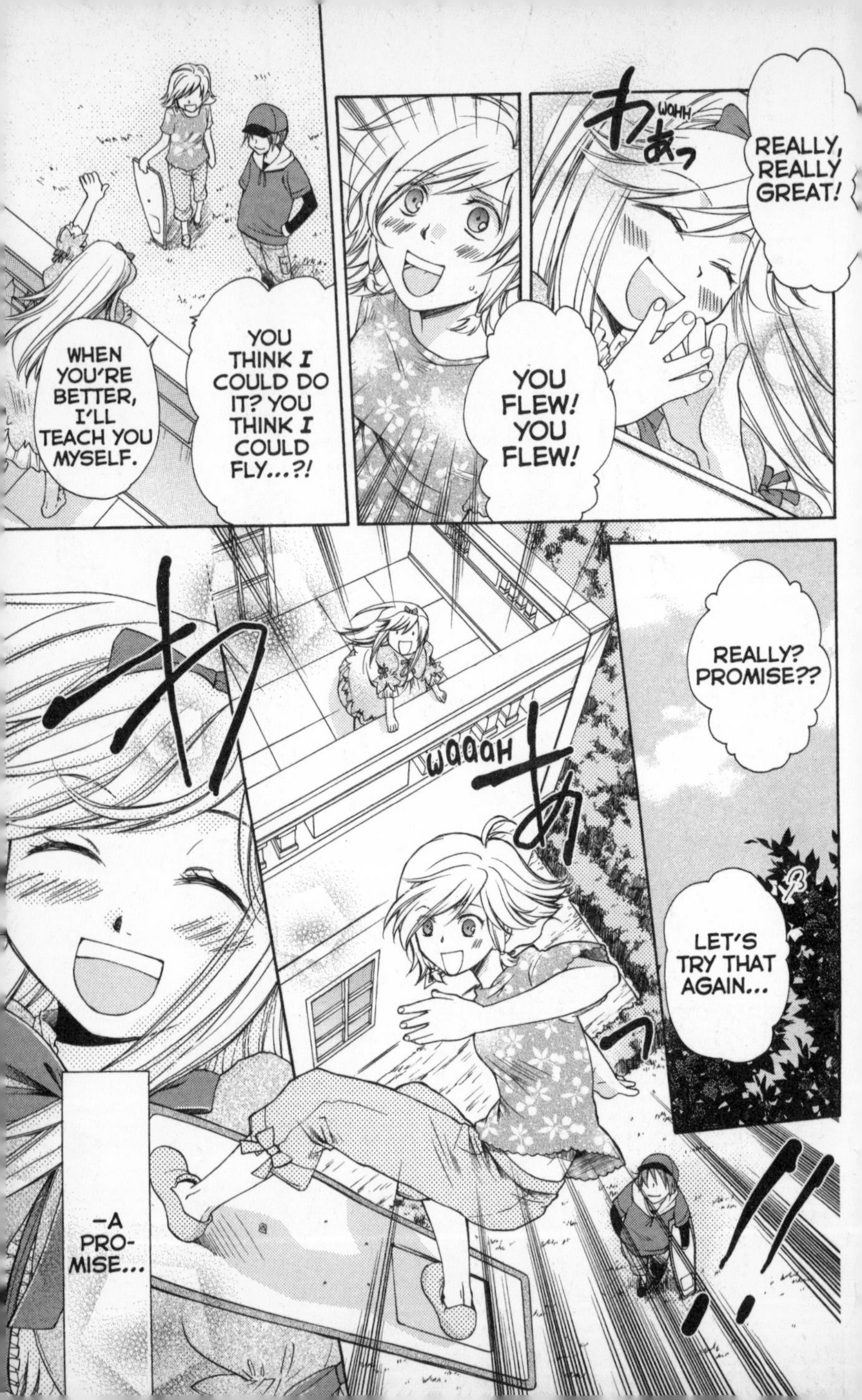
REALLY, REALLY GREAT!
わあっ WOHH
YOU FLEW! YOU FLEW!
YOU THINK *I* COULD DO IT? YOU THINK *I* COULD FLY...?!
WHEN YOU'RE BETTER, I'LL TEACH YOU MYSELF.
REALLY? PROMISE??
LET'S TRY THAT AGAIN...
わあっ WAAAH
—A PROMISE...

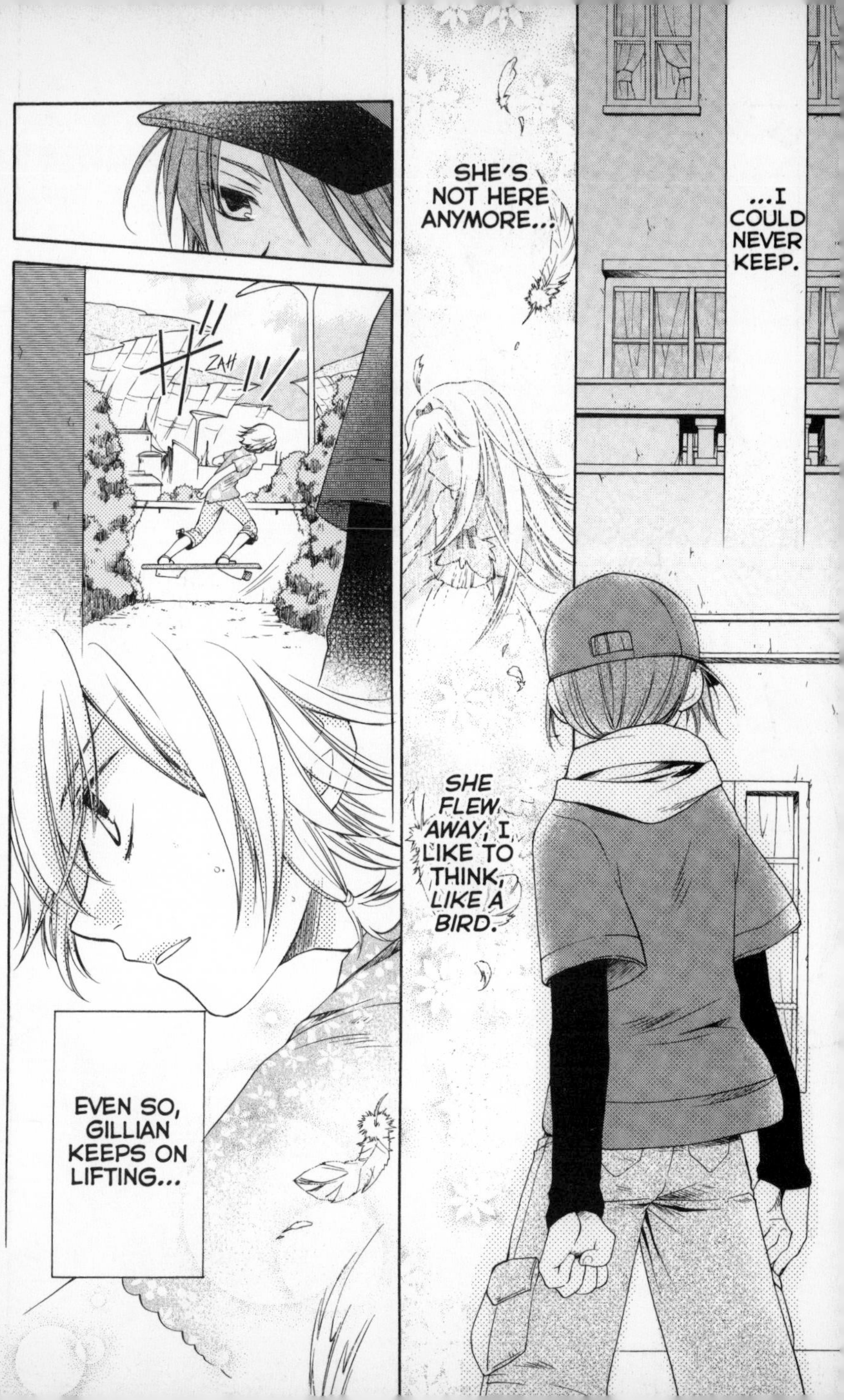
...I COULD NEVER KEEP.
SHE'S NOT HERE ANYMORE...
SHE FLEW AWAY, I LIKE TO THINK, LIKE A BIRD.
ZAH
EVEN SO, GILLIAN KEEPS ON LIFTING...

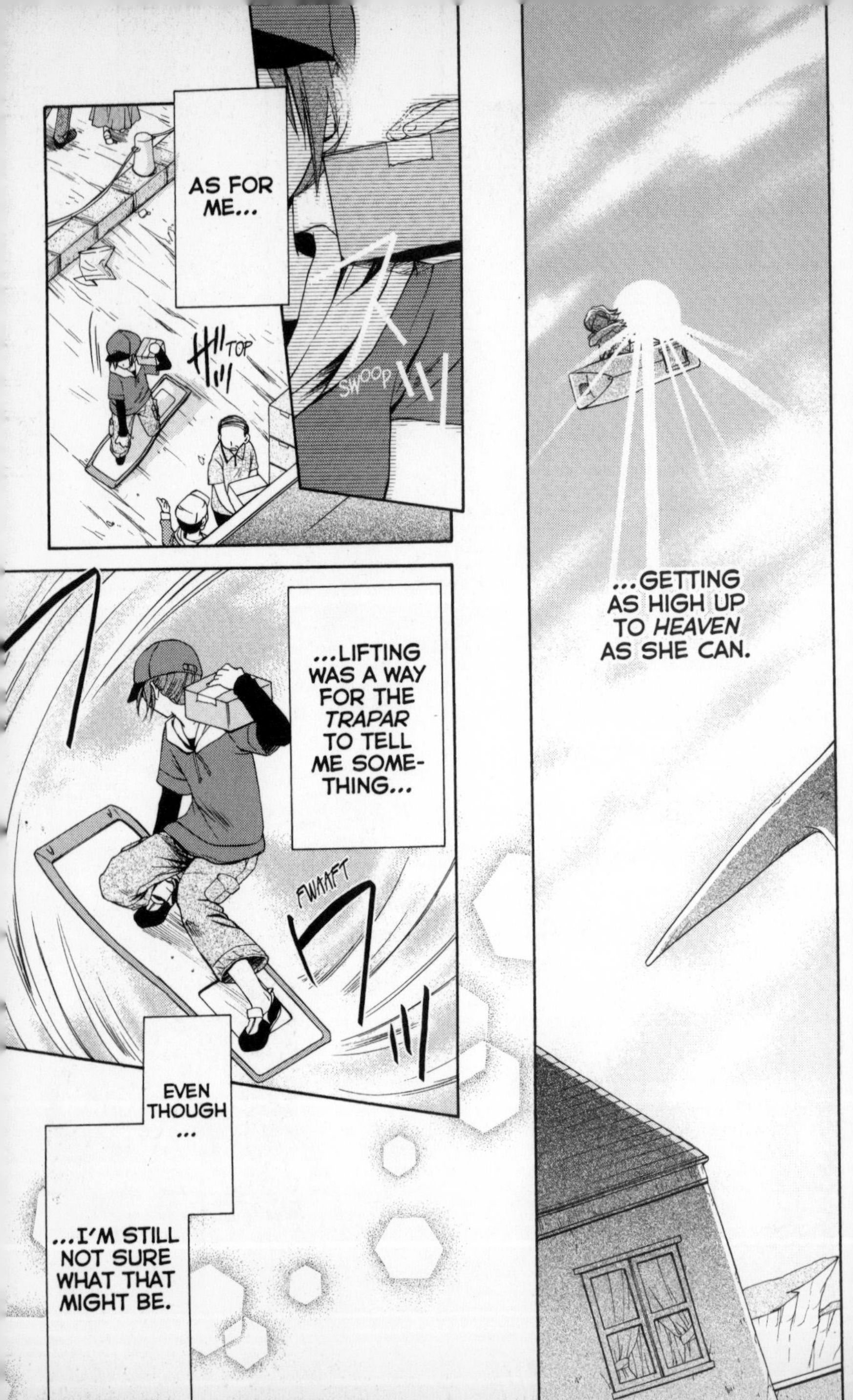
...GETTING AS HIGH UP TO *HEAVEN* AS SHE CAN.
AS FOR ME...
TOP
SWOOP
...LIFTING WAS A WAY FOR THE *TRAPAR* TO TELL ME SOME-THING...
FWAAFT
EVEN THOUGH...
...I'M STILL NOT SURE WHAT THAT MIGHT BE.

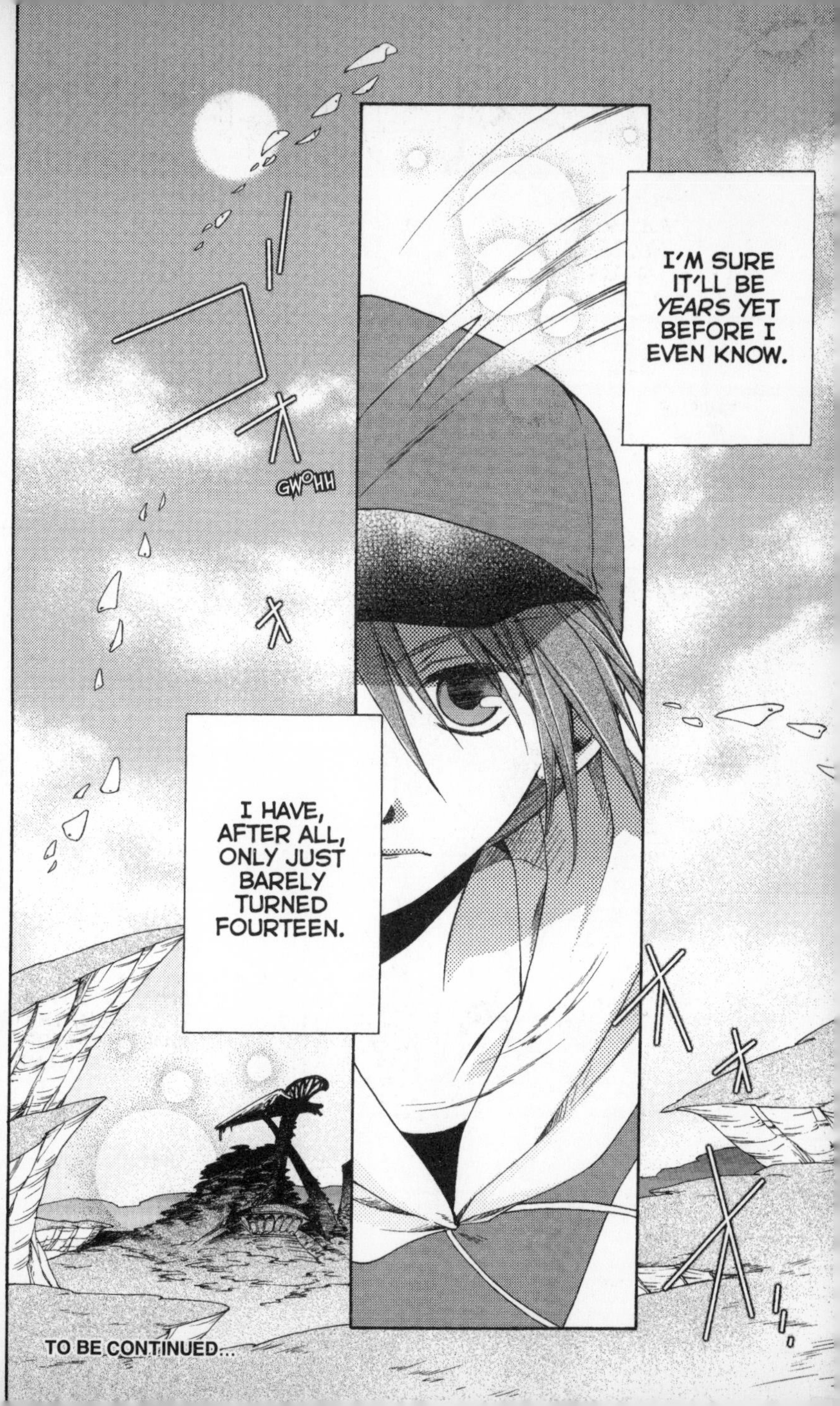
I'M SURE IT'LL BE *YEARS* YET BEFORE I EVEN KNOW.
GWOHH
I HAVE, AFTER ALL, ONLY JUST BARELY TURNED FOURTEEN.
TO BE CONTINUED...

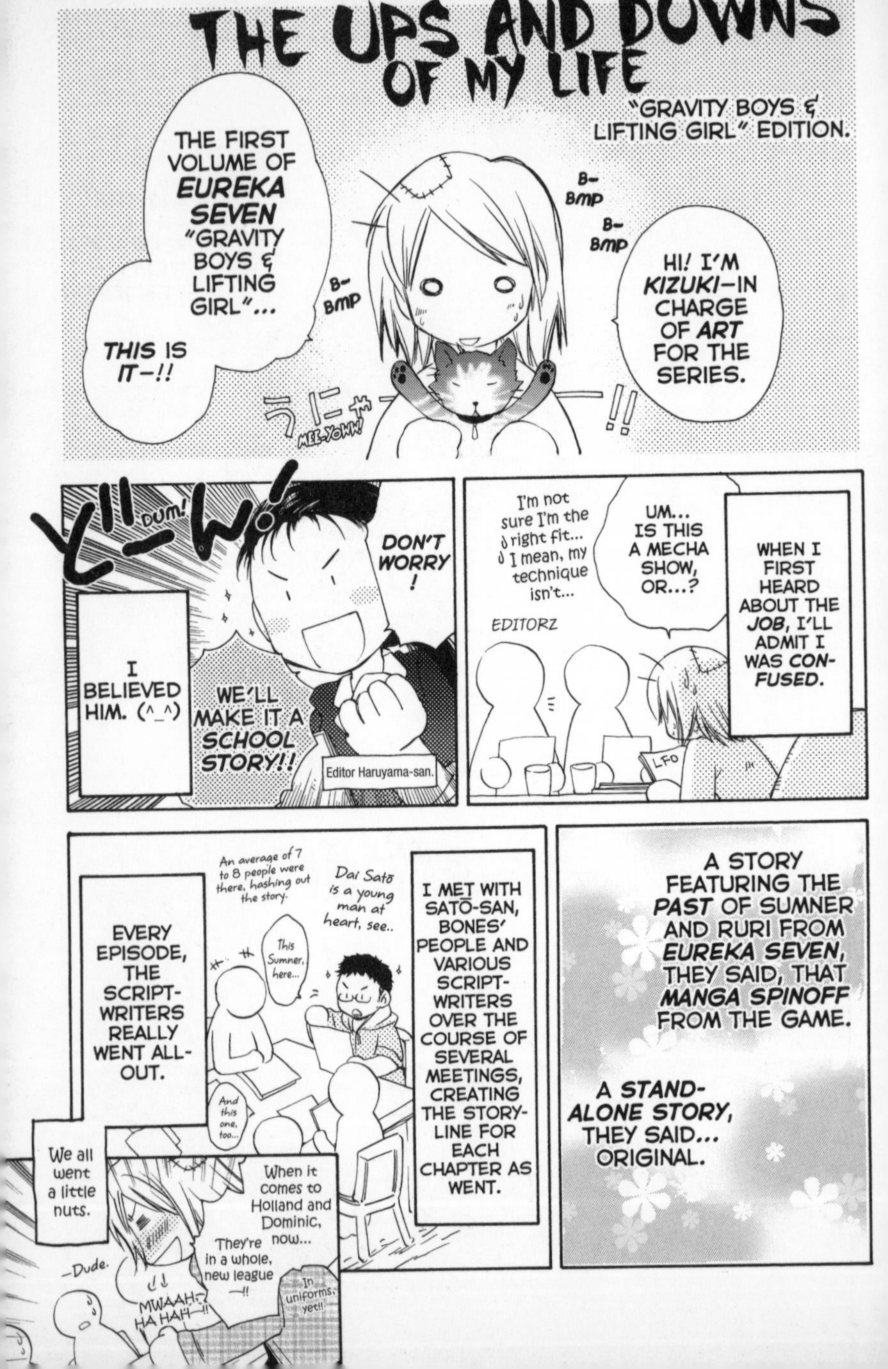
THE UPS AND DOWNS OF MY LIFE
"GRAVITY BOYS & LIFTING GIRL" EDITION.
HI! I'M KIZUKI—IN CHARGE OF ART FOR THE SERIES.
B-BMP
B-BMP
THE FIRST VOLUME OF EUREKA SEVEN "GRAVITY BOYS & LIFTING GIRL"...
B-BMP
THIS IS IT-!!
うにゃー!!
MEE-YOWN!
WHEN I FIRST HEARD ABOUT THE JOB, I'LL ADMIT I WAS CONFUSED.
UM... IS THIS A MECHA SHOW, OR...?
I'm not sure I'm the right fit... I mean, my technique isn't...
EDITORZ
LFO
DON'T WORRY!
DUM!
WE'LL MAKE IT A SCHOOL STORY!!
Editor Haruyama-san.
I BELIEVED HIM. (^_^)
A STORY FEATURING THE PAST OF SUMNER AND RURI FROM EUREKA SEVEN, THEY SAID, THAT MANGA SPINOFF FROM THE GAME.
A STAND-ALONE STORY, THEY SAID... ORIGINAL.
I MET WITH SATŌ-SAN, BONES' PEOPLE AND VARIOUS SCRIPT-WRITERS OVER THE COURSE OF SEVERAL MEETINGS, CREATING THE STORY-LINE FOR EACH CHAPTER AS WENT.
Dai Satō is a young man at heart, see..
An average of 7 to 8 people were there, hashing out the story.
This Sumner, here...
EVERY EPISODE, THE SCRIPT-WRITERS REALLY WENT ALL-OUT.
And this one, too...
When it comes to Holland and Dominic, now...
They're in a whole, new league—!!
In uniforms, yet!!
We all went a little nuts.
MWAAH HA HAH—!!
—Dude.

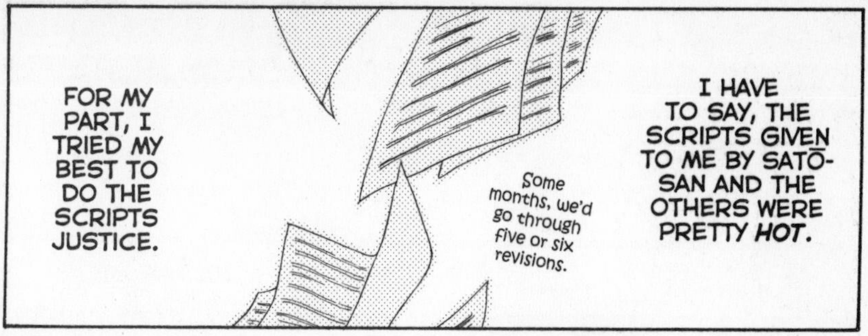
I HAVE TO SAY, THE SCRIPTS GIVEN TO ME BY SATŌ-SAN AND THE OTHERS WERE PRETTY *HOT*.
Some months, we'd go through five or six revisions.
FOR MY PART, I TRIED MY BEST TO DO THE SCRIPTS JUSTICE.

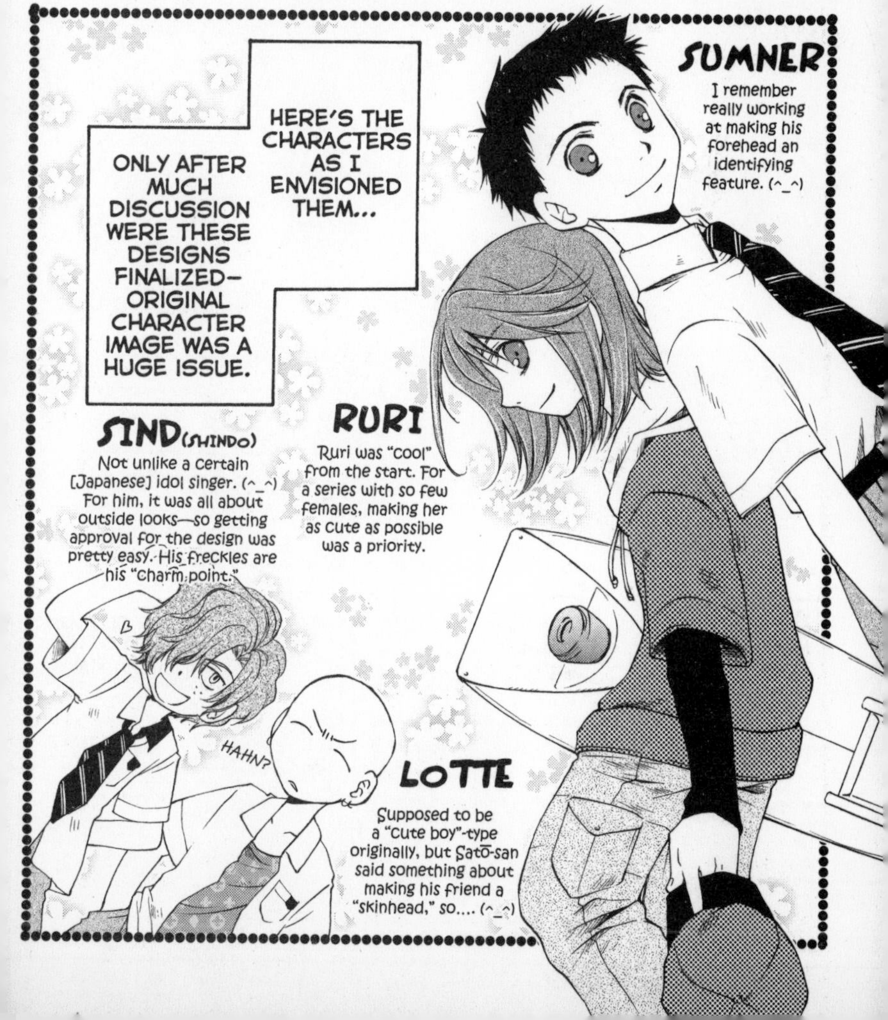
SUMNER
I remember really working at making his forehead an identifying feature. (^_^)
HERE'S THE CHARACTERS AS I ENVISIONED THEM...
ONLY AFTER MUCH DISCUSSION WERE THESE DESIGNS FINALIZED—ORIGINAL CHARACTER IMAGE WAS A HUGE ISSUE.
RURI
Ruri was "cool" from the start. For a series with so few females, making her as cute as possible was a priority.
SIND(SHINDO)
Not unlike a certain [Japanese] idol singer. (^_^) For him, it was all about outside looks—so getting approval for the design was pretty easy. His freckles are his "charm point."
HAHN?
LOTTE
Supposed to be a "cute boy"-type originally, but Satō-san said something about making his friend a "skinhead," so.... (^_^)

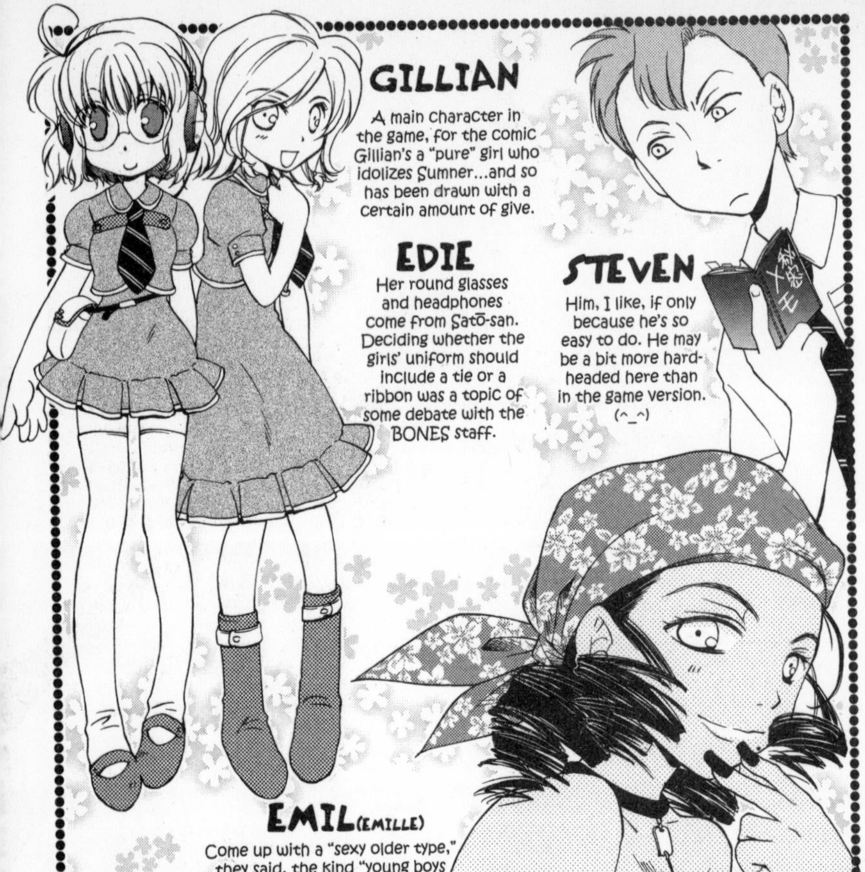
GILLIAN
A main character in the game, for the comic Gillian's a "pure" girl who idolizes Sumner...and so has been drawn with a certain amount of give.
STEVEN
Him, I like, if only because he's so easy to do. He may be a bit more hard-headed here than in the game version. (^_^)
EDIE
Her round glasses and headphones come from Satō-san. Deciding whether the girls' uniform should include a tie or a ribbon was a topic of some debate with the BONES staff.
EMIL(EMILLE)
Come up with a "sexy older type," they said, the kind "young boys really go for." So, here she is.

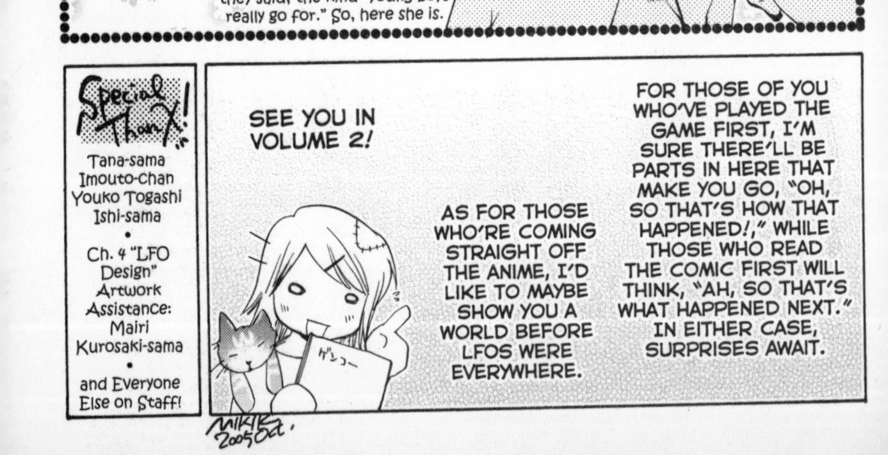
FOR THOSE OF YOU WHO'VE PLAYED THE GAME FIRST, I'M SURE THERE'LL BE PARTS IN HERE THAT MAKE YOU GO, "OH, SO THAT'S HOW THAT HAPPENED!," WHILE THOSE WHO READ THE COMIC FIRST WILL THINK, "AH, SO THAT'S WHAT HAPPENED NEXT." IN EITHER CASE, SURPRISES AWAIT.
AS FOR THOSE WHO'RE COMING STRAIGHT OFF THE ANIME, I'D LIKE TO MAYBE SHOW YOU A WORLD BEFORE LFOS WERE EVERYWHERE.
SEE YOU IN VOLUME 2!
Special ThanX!
Tana-sama
Imouto-chan
Youko Togashi
Ishi-sama
•
Ch. 4 "LFO Design" Artwork Assistance: Mairi Kurosaki-sama
•
and Everyone Else on Staff!
MIKI 2005 Oct.

SPORTS-FREE YOUTH-MANGA VERSION • EUREKA SEVEN
DAI SATŌ (Series Creator)

I had a hard time deciding on the setting for the game-version manga of "Eureka Seven." The series happens before both the anime and the game and I didn't want to give anything away, so, I had to keep a certain distance. Storylines couldn't be linked, for example, and release dates couldn't be too close together. That's how we decided to go even further back into the past, in fact—back to when Sumner was the same age as Renton (14). Of course, Renton ends up running **away** from school, so setting the whole thing **within** the academy kind of forced this into becoming an "early days" story…and thus, the "Sports-Free Youth Manga" version of the story you see before you. TO BE CONTINUED!

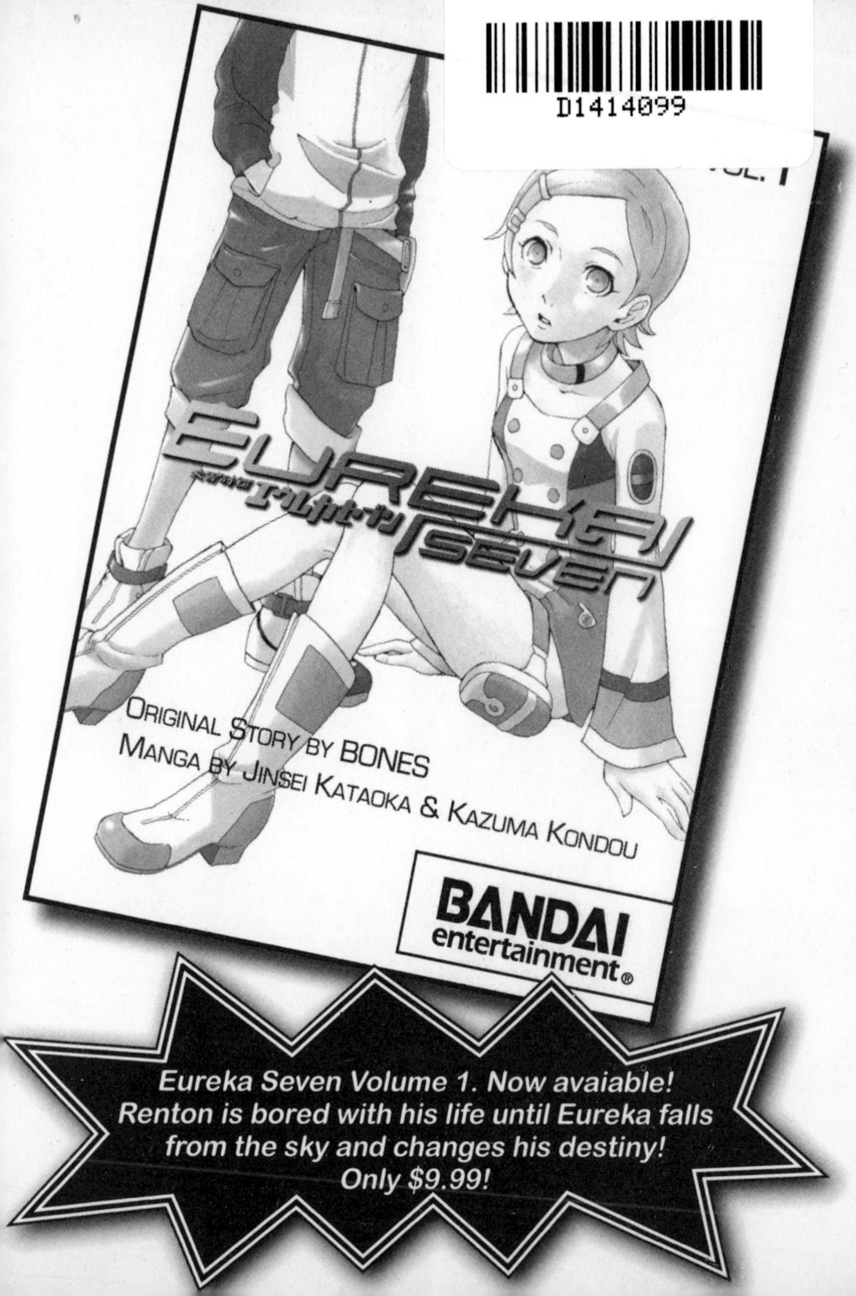
EUREKA SEVEN
ORIGINAL STORY BY BONES
MANGA BY JINSEI KATAOKA & KAZUMA KONDOU
BANDAI
entertainment®